AT THE COURT OF NAPOLEON

Also by Olivier Bernier

SECRETS OF MARIE ANTOINETTE

LOUIS THE BELOVED: THE LIFE OF LOUIS XV

LAFAYETTE: HERO OF TWO WORLDS

ART AND CRAFT

THE EIGHTEENTH–CENTURY WOMAN

PLEASURE AND PRIVILEGE: LIFE IN FRANCE, NAPLES, AND AMERICA,
1770–1790

LOUIS XIV: A ROYAL LIFE

AT THE COURT OF
NAPOLEON

Memoirs of the
Duchesse d'Abrantès

INTRODUCTION BY
Olivier Bernier

FOREWORD BY
Katell le Bourhis

DOUBLEDAY
New York London Toronto Sydney Auckland

With appreciation to Bernard d'Anglejan-Chatillon.
—Editor

PUBLISHED BY DOUBLEDAY

a division of Bantam Doubleday Dell Publishing Group, Inc.
666 Fifth Avenue, New York, New York 10103

DOUBLEDAY and the portrayal of an anchor with a dolphin are
trademarks of Doubleday, a division of
Bantam Doubleday Dell Publishing Group, Inc.

Designed by Richard Oriolo

Library of Congress Cataloging-in-Publication Data

Abrantès, Laure Junot, duchesse d', 1784–1838.
    [Mémoires. English]
At the court of Napoleon : memoirs of the Duchesse d'Abrantès /
introduction by Olivier Bernier ; foreword by
Katell le Bourhis. — 1st ed.
            p.   cm.
Translation of: Mémoires.
1. Abrantès, Laure Junot, duchesse d', 1784–1838.   2. Napoleon I,
Emperor of the French, 1769–1821.   3. France—History—Consulate
and Empire, 1799–1815.   4. France—Nobility—Biography.
I. Bernier, Olivier.   II. Title.
DC198.A3A3   1989
944.05′092—dc20
[B]   89-7850
CIP

ISBN 0-385-26639-1

Copyright © 1989 by Doubleday

The text was translated from the French and published
in Paris and Boston by The Napoleon Society, 1895.
With the exception of the portraits of Laure Junot and General Junot, all
photographs in this book are copyright © Réunion des Musées Nationaux.

All Rights Reserved
Printed in the United States of America

November 1989

First Edition

BG

FOREWORD

Katell le Bourhis

WHEN LAURE PERMON entered the world in 1785 at Montpellier in the South of France, the seemingly immutable reign of King Louis XVI and Queen Marie Antoinette was enmeshed in its last scandals at the magnificent court of Versailles. This world came to a brutal end with the storming of the Bastille in Paris on July 14, 1789. The downfall of the nearly 800-year-old royal dynasty of the Capetians had begun. And then, in January 1793, the blade of the guillotine came down on the neck of Louis XVI. With cries of freedom, equality, and fraternity for all, the Revolutionaries caused an upheaval of French society, culminating in the bloodbath of the Terror as all of monarchist Europe watched with horror. Yet the very young Laure Permon, who was born into a rich bourgeois family from the Mediterranean island of Corsica, was sheltered from the storm and prepared for a life of even greater distinction amid the new political ideas and the new leaders: she belonged to the frustrated middle class whose ambitions had been hopelessly restricted by the royal power and by the nobility and which therefore had the most to gain from the drastic political changes. Moreover, her mother was a friend of Letizia Bonaparte, mother of the soon-to-be-famous Napoleon. Young Laure's Corsican origin was enchanced by the lineage of her mother who was born a Stephanopoli-Comnène and claimed descent from the illustrious Byzantine family of the Comnènes who provided the Near East with Kings and Emperors during the time of the Crusades and in Asia Minor at an even later time.

After the fall of Robespierre, the leader of the Jacobins, the well-off Permon family lived in Paris during the formation of the Directoire regime and was visited frequently by the penniless young officer Bonaparte. He was a friend of their son, Albert, and met often with the Permons, other Corsicans, and friends who had been spared emigration or the guillotine. Still a child, Laure was fascinated by Bonaparte. His blunt manners, his way of mixing Corsican and French when speaking, his fearless energy, and exotic looks captivated the young girl's imagination.

On October 5, 1795 (the 13th Vendémiaire), Laure's father died and General Bonaparte became a hero by crushing a monarchist insurrection. Laure and the Permon family remained close to the young general, now Commander of the Army of the Interior, and they entertained this rising star who had become a member of the entourage of Director Barras. Bonaparte, the military wizard, had quickly emerged as a political power within the "Nouvelle Societé" born of the Revolution. Opposed to the *ancien régime's* claim to entitlement by birth, this post-1789 French society, based on equality, enabled new people to gain power either through political or military achievement, or by quick wealth made through economic speculation. Remembered as the epoch of the *parvenus,* it was the beginning of modern French society. In search of social models, the leaders risen from the Revolution had as example only the society they had just destroyed, the domineering, aristocratic court of Versailles. Suddenly rich and powerful, the *parvenus* wished to forget the bloody Terror and secure their new position in society. With the famous fêtes of Versailles in mind, the new social leaders felt entitled to indulge in equally high-spirited celebrations. Since the storming of the Bastille, Paris had become the center of political action and *parvenu* Parisian society germinated in the city, while Versailles lay deserted. The city with its salons, fêtes, and celebrations now replaced the court. In this new urban social world, recently liberated from the religious and social constraints of the *ancien régime,* as well as from the puritanism of the Revolution, the fêtes were as joyful as the morals were loose. The young Laure watched Bonaparte and her brother, Albert, mingle and thrive within the Nouvelle Societé of the Directoire.

Three Parisian hostesses typified this new regime based on politics, the military, and money: Madame Tallien, mistress of Director Barras; Josephine, Vicomtesse de Beauharnais, soon to be married to General Bonaparte; and Madame Récamier, the very young wife of a powerful banker. Madame Tallien and Josephine de Beauharnais had both been imprisoned during the Terror and had escaped the guillotine after the downfall of Robespierre. As queens of society, they set the tone, and only young Madame Récamier could match their stylishly eccentric Greco-Roman way of dressing. This new period took its inspiration from classical antiquity and so did fashion; everything neo-classical was the mode. Dressed in columnar, diaphanous white muslin dresses, freed of corsets, with hair done *à l'antique,* these neo-Greek statues joyfully entertained the Nouvelle Societé of influential men and pretty women in their salons. With the Reign of Terror behind them, everyone was enraptured by the new accessibility of power. Laure Permon, in that atmosphere, blossomed into a good-looking, intelligent society girl and soon appeared at balls and social gatherings, including fêtes given by Monsieur de Talleyrand. One of the first aristocrats to rally to the new regime, Talleyrand, Foreign Minister under Director Barras, entertained many of the *parvenus* in his mansion, thus providing some of them with an opportunity to polish their manners.

Women at that time were not completely excluded from political matters. But the Revolution, based on equality and freedom, had done little to change their marital expectations. With no freedom of choice, subject to arranged marriages, the most they could anticipate from their husbands was mutual affectionate respect. Although reigning social figures, the women of *parvenu* society were actually serving as symbols to display their husbands' new wealth and promotion.

With the successive glorious campaigns and the meteoric political rise of Bonaparte, Laure found herself swept up in his ascension when she became engaged to his former aide-de-camp, General Junot. On October 30, 1800, early in the Consular regime, after the victorious

General had ousted the Directory in 1799 and become First Consul, Laure Permon married Andoche Junot, then Governor of Paris. Just sixteen, the bride was ravishing and exquisitely dressed in a lavish ceremony which took place in the presence of the entire Bonaparte family. Her Corsican blood and friendship with his family satisfied the First Consul's sense of clan. He was also especially pleased with the extravagant presents and the grand celebration. Bonaparte was a man who well understood that pomp helped to romanticize his victories in battle and to strengthen his political power and that of his military entourage. He reputedly said, "The essence of what I am seeking is grandeur; what is grand is always beautiful." Thus, the young Madame Junot, submerged in political circles since her youth, was now in a brilliant social position and she displayed her panache in the new military aristocracy of the Consulate.

The First Consul and his wife, Josephine, received the new Madame Junot at an official presentation in the former royal palace of the Tuileries, which was now their home. It is claimed that Josephine, who was of aristocratic origin, once whispered, "There is a smell of kings here that one cannot breathe with impunity." Although Madame Bonaparte did not yet have ladies-in-waiting, the First Consul insisted on etiquette, quickly sketching out the Imperial court which was soon to follow. From that time on, Laure Junot would be a true insider, in the official entourage of First Consul Bonaparte as well as the imperial court of the first French Emperor, Napoleon I. She would breakfast with Josephine, ride in her carriage, dance with Eugène de Beauharnais, befriend Caroline, Joseph, and Lucien Bonaparte, and dine at the table of every political and military leader. Laure calculatingly charmed the important and powerful men and women in her husband's entourage. Pretty and intelligent, she could be very witty, even sharptongued. On the day of the magnificently orchestrated coronation of Emperor Napoleon and Empress Josephine in 1804 at Notre Dame, she proved her fierce independence and high aspirations by wearing a black velvet dress in pique at being omitted from the entourage of ladies-in-waiting to the new Empress. When subsequently scolded by the Emperor, she firmly defended herself. From the Empress's beloved palace of Malmaison to the court of the Tuileries, to the grand mansions of Paris, she flitted with spirited wit, ambition, and caprice.

Laure Junot witnessed many of the exciting scenes which occurred during an epoch of wonder and horror and her keen eye never missed a detail. She lived amid the opulence of the imperial court which was modeled more and more on the court of Versailles. She used her position to gain access to those involved in intrigues; she befriended members of the old aristocratic world, for whose return from emigration Josephine had often interceded. As time went on, more and more of the old aristocracy entered the new Emperor's court. He favored the aristocrats who had rallied to his new empire and gave many of them court positions to help ensure the strength and durability of his regime. As Emperor, Napoleon understood that their old world manners and inbred sense of etiquette well served his grandeur. The old courts of Europe laughed nervously at the faux pas of the *parvenus,* such as General Gros who reportedly answered the Emperor with the words, "Yes, Monsieur Sire."

Laure observed each rich visual detail: the brilliance of lavish costume and the profusion of diamonds, jewelry, orders, and decorations which were now *de rigueur* at court. The new Emperor increasingly demanded splendid surroundings which symbolized his power, thereby encouraging the rebirth of the traditional French industries of luxury which had been nearly extinguished during the Revolution. As a result, hundreds of dissatisfied and angry artists and artisans were put back to work. Napoleon realized that if the rebellious workers of these industries were unemployed, they would threaten his despotic power. He grandly encouraged the decorative arts by his sumptuous ceremonies and by his imperial order to redecorate his apartments in the old royal residences in the new Empire Style.

Laure Junot lived in a Paris that was perpetually in transformation as the Emperor lavished greater attention on the city than had any previous ruler of France. From her house off the Champs-Élysées, she could see the Arc de Triomphe being built. She could stroll under the famous arcade of the newly laid rue de Rivoli and her carriage could cross the Seine on one of the four new bridges ordered by Napoleon.

Laure's sharp wit captured each personality in the imperial scenarios, from the ceremonies of state to the military reviews and the victory celebrations of the imperial army. Except for fourteen months following the Peace of Amiens in 1802, most of Europe was at war during this period. As an insider, she watched the feuds between members of the imperial family, all eager for more wealth and power. To Laure, Napoleon, the magnetic Commander-in-Chief, the despotic ruler, the mythological eagle in splendor, often seemed a true Corsican man, obsessed with family loyalty. Laure Junot saw the Emperor, "the maker of kings," bestow enormous wealth and favors on his seven brothers and sisters and place them on the thrones of Rome, Holland, Tuscany, Naples, Spain, and Westphalia. The Emperor's insatiable desire for conquest kept France at war, the French population at that time including Italians, Swiss, Germans, Belgians, Dutch, and even Catalonians. The imperial eagle was planted from Paris to Rome to Hamburg to Barcelona, from Turin to Genoa to Florence, Siena, Parma. All were French cities, as were Geneva, Brussels, Luxembourg, Amsterdam, Koblenz, Trier, Mainz, and Aachen.

By 1807, Laure Junot was finally given a title. Her husband's military success in Portugal was recognized by Napoleon who made him Duc d'Abrantès. The vivacious new Duchesse d'Abrantès, prone to gossip and occasional backbiting, grasped and remembered everything that befell her. However, her wit and sharp tongue had begun to infuriate the matriarch, Letizia Bonaparte, the formidable *Madame Mère*. There were also extramarital romantic rivalries with the beautiful Pauline Bonaparte, who had a great weakness for men. The tension culminated in 1808 with the liaison of Laure d'Abrantès and Metternich, the Austrian ambassador. The Emperor was daily informed by Fouché, the head of his zealous secret police, of Laure's politically dangerous affairs and, with his infamous wrath, he ordered her to follow her husband to Spain. In 1809, the Emperor, obsessed with his urge for a dynasty and facing both monarchist and leftist Jacobin plots, divorced the incomparable Josephine, who could not bear him a child. In 1810, he married Archduchess Marie Louise of Austria, the niece of the guillotined Queen Marie Antoinette. The insatiably curious Duchesse d'Abrantès, still in Spain, made sure that everyone present provided her with detailed accounts of the ceremony.

Laure d'Abrantès, enmeshed in Bonaparte's destiny since childhood, personally experienced the ephemeral glory of the French First Empire. In 1812, Napoleon invaded Russia, at that time an empire of 41 million people, thus starting the largest military operation of the era. The

Duc d'Abrantès died in 1814, probably by suicide, and the Russian campaign proved to be the death knell of the First Empire. The still-young Duchesse watched her splendid imperial world fall apart: the victorious Russian army entered Paris and the soldiers of Czar Alexander I bivouacked on the Champs Élysées. After signing his abdication at Fontainebleau, the invincible eagle was exiled to the island of Elba.

Though she regained hope and position during the One Hundred Days of Napoleon's return to power after his escape from Elba, the disenchanted and independent Duchesse refused to see the Emperor. But after the defeat of the French imperial army at Waterloo in 1815, the final exile of the vanquished Emperor to St. Helena, and the restoration of the monarchy in France, Laure d'Abrantès found herself destitute. She was disillusioned and melancholy, but still a woman of pleasing manners, with an original and cultural turn of mind. The novelist Honoré de Balzac conceived a lively sympathy for her. The figure of this unfortunate woman, fallen from glory and now shut up in her simple lodgings, was highly romantic and Balzac was fascinated by Laure d'Abrantès's acute memory of her illustrious past. He encouraged her, if not helped her, to write her memoirs. Published in 1831 to 1835 in eighteen successive volumes, her *Mémoires Historiques* were immediately popular and profitable and helped her to regain her position, this time in the literary circles. Encouraged by loyal Bonapartists, she tirelessly wrote articles and books, until she died in 1838, exhausted and famous once again.

Some years later, in 1846, the poet Victor Hugo, an ardent admirer of Napoleon, wrote a song of expiation to the memory of the Duchesse d'Abrantès to whom burial in the Cemetery of Père La Chaise, built by order of the Emperor, had been denied by King Louis Philippe. "I guard the treasures of the Empire's glories . . . I say for the Emperor: give him back his column and for thee give her back her tomb." The memoirs of the Duchesse d'Abrantès are one of the liveliest accounts of the Napoleonic period. Her style is intimate and her only aim was to relate what she observed, whom she observed, and what she had been told. With her gift for description and precise detail, she became an essential documentary source of the Napoleonic age. Her racy, enticing portraits of the grandees of Emperor Napoleon's entourage are not only authentic but often spicy. The captivating Duchesse d'Abrantès, with her vivid anecdotes occasionally produced some historic inaccuracies for which we should forgive her, considering her patriotic fidelity to the friend of her youth and to his legend. Sometimes she gets a bit carried away, but her narrative always flows naturally and her strong personality transcends throughout.

Laure Junot, Duchesse d'Abrantès, was an exciting character, a child of the Revolution, and a sparkling insider during the Napoleonic era. The Emperor Napoleon seems a hero of modern mythology through her words, and her literary success throughout the nineteenth century has helped to propagate the glorious legend of this despotic ruler, larger than life and yet still human. Emperor Napoleon did not take kindly to opposition from foreign rulers, from his family or entourage; he is remembered as saying: "A woman ceases to charm whenever she makes herself feared." He had known the dynamic and fearless Duchesse d'Abrantès since she was a spoiled child, and he immortalized her simply as "La Petite Peste."

AT THE COURT OF NAPOLEON

INTRODUCTION TO
MME JUNOT'S MEMOIRS

Olivier Bernier

SHE WAS YOUNG, bright, pretty; she knew everyone in Paris society; then, at the age of sixteen, she made a brilliant marriage which brought her into close contact with France's dazzling new ruler: it is no wonder that Laure Permon, who became General Junot's wife in 1801, felt and behaved like someone who mattered. Indeed, there seemed to be an appealing parallel between the extraordinary rise of France under General Bonaparte and her own early happiness. As the country was restored to prosperity, as the French armies won countless victories, so the new Mme Junot moved into a grand house, became one of the foremost hostesses in Paris, and played a major role in the fledgling court surrounding Napoleon and Josephine.

For Laure, and for many of her friends, those were golden times: the new government was immensely popular, and, through her husband, she was a part of it. Social life, so rudely interrupted by the Revolution, flourished again, giving her a chance to dazzle at ball after ball. Her dresses come from Leroy, the new, wildly fashionable couturier, and she describes them lovingly: except for her husband's occasional bursts of rage, Mme Junot could look forward to the most agreeable life. And even when, within a few years, she discovered that Junot was being unfaithful, she retaliated by taking Metternich, one of the century's most famous statesmen, as one of a substantial series of lovers.

If nothing more had happened to Laure Junot, she would almost certainly not have written her Memoirs; but then, in 1813, her life changed abruptly. First, her husband went mad and committed suicide; then, the next year, the empire fell and most of her income ended with it. Undaunted, she demanded help from half the crowned heads in Europe, made friends with some of France's greatest writers and, finally, became a prolific and successful writer, a move that required courage and determination.

Still, then as now, most authors found it difficult to earn a living; luckily, Mme Junot had two major assets. First, she was a duchess: her husband had been created duc d'Abrantès by Napoleon in 1809, and even imperial titles (as opposed to those belonging to the old aristocracy) had a good deal of prestige. Gossip and social climbing—these two mainstays of American social life at the end of the twentieth century—were already rife in the France of the 1820s, and the duchess traded heavily on both her title and her social connections. Then, more important still, she was well known to have been close to Napoleon and the Bonapartes. Although, immediately after 1815, there was a strong reaction against the Emperor, his death in 1821 changed all that. Suddenly, the empire began to appear as the fount of all glamor. Seen through the golden mist of selective memory, the great man and his splendid court became a topic of consuming interest.

It all started with the *Memorial de Sainte Helène,* a memoir written by one of Napoleon's companions in exile; and that book's immense success opened the gates: from then on, the fashion for tales of the *ancien régime* was replaced by a craze of imperial souvenirs. Naturally, Mme d'Abrantès took advantage of it; and since writers were then paid according to the number of lines they wrote, she promptly produced seven volumes of reminiscences.

Naturally, that took quite a bit of filling in. Uncut, the Memoirs contain much tedious, repetitive, or unnecessary material, but time has passed and length is no longer a requirement; edited down to one volume, Mme Junot's book is fresh, informative, and amusing. Indeed, as we read it, it is hard not to feel that Napoleon's main function was to provide the writer and her friends with an ever-abundant source of hot gossip.

Oddly enough, that was a viewpoint at least partially shared by the Emperor himself: few rulers have been more strongly affected by the reactions of society, few have tried harder to co-opt it. Although Napoleon reordered the map of Europe to make it fit his convenience, dethroning dynasties and creating new ones, he never stopped caring about what the old French aristocracy—the Faubourg Saint-Germain* —thought about him. Early on, he tried to attract its young men into his army; eventually, he staffed his court with them; and always, he read the reports written by the spies sent out to hear what people said.

Indeed, the First Consul paid a great deal of attention to the way he and his family looked, and he tried to rally those members of the old aristocracy to whom he had access. At the same time, because power always deserves attention, his doings, those of his wife and siblings, became topics of universal concern. We always want to know what great men are like in private, and it was just that information Laure Junot was able to supply. As a result, her Memoirs were immensely successful: it was more fun to read about the intimacies of the imperial family than to plow through the souvenirs of self-serving statesmen and generals. One might almost say, in fact, that the coup d'état of November 1799, in which General Bonaparte seized power, was made for those who like gossip; now, at last, as in the old days before 1789, there was someone interesting to talk about. It is that atmosphere which the Memoirs of Mme Junot bring back to vivid life.

Paris, in 1799, was a city of contrasts. The violent part of the Revolution had ended five years earlier but the city itself was still visibly suffering from its effects: empty houses, filthy streets, shabbiness everywhere were made even more shocking by the extreme, flashy luxury of the new elite. With the old aristocracy dead, ruined or in exile, the new Paris society consisted of people whose sudden and enormous fortunes came from cheating the government. Bankers, who took advantage of the state's financial distress, army suppliers who turned in vastly inflated bills for below-par bread, uniforms, and guns,

* So-called after the area of Paris where the old noble families had their houses.

speculators of all kinds came together with the immediate friends of the five Directors who ruled the Republic.

Lodged, in great luxury, in the Palace of Luxembourg, and virtually all-powerful, the Directors were, nevertheless, at their wits' end. The Constitution written after the end of the Terror by the remnants of the Convention had a double object: to ensure the survival of the Republic and of those whose lives were closely linked to it; and to prevent a small, fanatical group from dominating an all-powerful Assembly. In a word, the new regime would have no king and no Robespierre.

The Executive was thus entrusted, not to one, but to five men, entitled Directors, whose decisions must be made by majority rule. The Legislature consisted of a lower house, the Conseil des Cinq Cent (Council of Five hundred) and an upper house, the Conseil des Anciens (Council of Elders). It was the Anciens who elected the Directors from a list forwarded by the Cinq Cent. Once elected, the Directors could not be voted out of office, but then, they could not dissolve the Legislature either. Thus, in case of conflict between the Executive and the Legislature, there was no possible solution. What happened, in fact, was that, because they controlled the army, the Directors arranged several successive coups, against the Right and against the Left, whenever they felt threatened. As a result, by 1799, they had thoroughly alienated the entire political spectrum.

At the same time, while their powers were, in theory, enormous, the Directors seemed unable to govern. The finances were in utter disorder, the paper currency almost worthless, unemployment rife. Even worse, after General Bonaparte's departure for Egypt, the French armies suffered a series of defeats. Under these conditions, it was clear to all informed people that the regime could not last, and that it would end in a military coup. Indeed, Barras, the one Director who had been in office since 1795, was busy looking for a compliant general. Whether he intended to set up his own dictatorship, or whether he meant to accept the huge bribes offered by the Pretender, the future Louis XVIII, and restore the monarchy, remains uncertain; but not even he thought that the Directoire could go on as it was.

It was to this fevered atmosphere that Bonaparte returned suddenly and unexpectedly, thus upsetting many people among whom his wife was first and foremost. Another legacy of the Directoire, Josephine, after losing her first husband to the guillotine, had become one of the loose-living beauties of the regime. Spendthrift and penniless, she was Barras's mistress when she caught the eye of a rising but still uncouth general, the young Napoleon Bonaparte. Barras, who was getting tired of her, saw his chance. Bonaparte, having fallen genuinely in love, was encouraged to marry Josephine and was rewarded with the command of the French army in Italy.

It was an ambiguous promotion since the army in question lacked just about everything; but, to everyone's surprise, General Bonaparte, having electrified his men, and looted with a will, went on to win a series of spectacular victories, eventually forcing Austria to sue for peace. That, of course, made him a dangerous man; not unnaturally, the Directors, who were most anxious to get rid of him, were delighted when he asked for an army with which to go and conquer Egypt. It was widely assumed that he would come back too late to make a difference; and Josephine, who was not given to chastity in retirement, embarked on a spectacular affair with a handsome young man.

So it was that her husband's landing at Saint Raphael, near Marseille, on October 9, 1799, proved most inconvenient. Like the rest of Paris, she understood that her husband was likely to play a major political role as soon as he reached the capital: it was not the moment for a messy divorce. As it was, she felt reasonably sure that Napoleon was still in love with her, but she also knew that his family detested her, and that they would be eager to paint her little indiscretions in the most lurid colors. Under the circumstances, there was only one thing to do: she set off for the South, expecting to meet her husband somewhere along the way; after a night or two of passionate lovemaking, she would have nothing to worry about.

Unfortunately, there were two possible ways to go between Paris and Marseille, and she set off on the first even as Bonaparte was traveling on the second. Thus, by mid-October, it was hard to tell who was more upset: Josephine, who returned in haste to find her husband's door locked against her, or Barras who realized that his plans had to be recast to take the new arrival into account.

As it turned out, although intelligence was not her chief characteristic, it was Josephine who came out best of the imbroglio. Just how she managed to soften Bonaparte's anger Mme Junot tells us in detail. As for Barras, betrayed among others by Sieyès, one of his fellow Directors, and by Talleyrand, until just lately his Foreign Minister, he woke up, on the morning of November 9 to find the Luxembourg ringed by armed soldiers, and a letter of resignation ready for his signature.

That the country as a whole approved the coup is certain: the Directoire was wildly unpopular, Bonaparte was the idol of the people; even so, as Mme Junot delicately hints, it almost came out wrong. Bonaparte started by asking the Cinq Cent to suspend the Constitution, expecting immediate compliance; instead, he found himself faced with an enraged Assembly who was about to outlaw him when Lucien Bonaparte, Napoleon's brother and the President of the Cinq Cent, suspended the sitting. Shocked, he retreated, but his troops, led by Joachim Murat, did what was necessary by chasing the Assembly out of its hall. After that, all was easy. A carefully picked commission of compliant members of the two houses voted to install Bonaparte as First Consul, with two other subsidiary Consuls; a new Constitution was promulgated on December 15, and the reign of Napoleon was under way.

Never, perhaps, in the entire history of France has a ruler been so widely popular. From the very first, the Consul seemed to know instinctively what was needed, what could be done, and how to do it so as to please the greatest possible number of people. The new Constitution itself—"It must be short and obscure," the Consul told its authors —was a nicely judged compromise: it retained a Parliament, that first conquest of the Revolution, while giving the three Consuls all the power they needed. And because Bonaparte was as adept at choosing the right public servants as he was at beating the enemy, the reforms which were decreed in great numbers proved popular, effective, and lasting. Within less than a year, the country could rejoice in having passed from one of the most ineffective governments in its history to one of the most successful.

The corruption, which had been endemic under the Directoire was ended at once. Suddenly, civil servants found that they were expected to be not just honest but hardworking as well—and, amazingly, they obliged. The paper currency was discontinued; the general confidence in the new regime allowed a return to gold, and that, in turn, spurred trade and industry, so that real prosperity returned unexpectedly fast.

The tax system was reformed as well, so that taxation became lighter, but collection more effective. A new code of laws, civil and criminal (much of which is still in effect today), a new system of state-sponsored education, a more efficient administration all came into being within the first three years of the Consulate; and at the same time, of course, the First Consul resumed his old habit of beating the enemy's armies wherever he encountered them. That, in turn, ended the war. By 1801, for the first time in ten years, France was prosperous, at peace, and as free as it wanted to be.

As if that were not enough, the very personality of the First Consul seemed immensely appealing: he was young, prodigiously talented and, withal, quite simple. Although very touchy about the respect due his office, he lived without any ostentation; where Barras had indulged in spectacular orgies and surrounded himself with a bevy of mistresses, Bonaparte saw chiefly his ministers and aides-de-camp, as well as those men whose achievements in a variety of fields had brought them eminence, and his amusements, as Mme Junot tells us, were thoroughly virtuous. Even those whom the Consul's brusqueness shocked were invariably seduced by Josephine's famous charm. That Bonaparte worked very hard was also well known; and if he also favored the reappearance of a free-spending upper class, that was only another point in his favor. The once-famous French luxury trades revived: Lyon silks and velvets, Paris fashions, furniture, silver were once again exported to the rest of Europe while France set the tone as it had before the Revolution.

As France prospered, so did the newly married Laure Junot. Her mother, who was nothing if not a snob, had long been a friend of the Bonaparte family; but she had also climbed hard in Paris before 1789, and proceeded to do so again almost as soon as the Terror was over. Indeed, Mme Permon had pretensions to the highest of positions: she claimed to be the direct descendant of the Comnènos Emperors of Byzantium, and was as such virtually royal herself. Unfortunately the last emperor of the line, Andronicus, died in 1153, leaving no sons, so that Mme Permon's pretensions caused many a snicker, especially since her husband had belonged to the prosperous middle class. Indeed, she soon added the aristocratic "de" to her name in an effort to glamorize herself. In fact, it was hardly necessary; Paris society, in the late 1790s, was still an ad hoc affair, and Mme Permon's salon was well attended.

Still, Laure's marriage proved highly advantageous. General Andoche Junot was Governor of Paris, which made him one of the key men of the new regime and provided him with a splendid establishment; even better, he was, he had always been, very close to Bonaparte. Thus, at one blow, Laure found herself ensconced at the very heart of the new regime. A regular member of the fledgling consular court, she was also a frequent guest at Malmaison, the Consul's house in the country. The ball to celebrate her marriage was attended by every Bonaparte in Paris; and, because her husband enjoyed a huge salary, she found herself able to live in luxury, dress in the latest fashions, and give some of the best parties in Paris. She also witnessed (and eventually told) a great deal about Napoleon, Josephine, their families, and their entourage.

That she enjoyed herself enormously is plain. France, reborn, was once again the first nation in Europe. The government was popular, stable, effective; it seemed as if the promise of a new dawn was steadily being converted into the full glory of a cloudless day.

Even better, it was soon noticed that, once again, there was a court; and Laure was very much a part of it. When the new Constitution went into effect, the First Consul moved from the Luxembourg, where the Directors had lived, to the Palace of the Tuileries. Unfortunately, the procession looked less than impressive: Laure describes for us the shabby hackney coaches in which the ministers rode; but that soon changed. The Tuileries themselves were a former royal residence which had been decorated by Louis XIV, then rearranged for Louis XVI and Marie Antoinette when they were forced to leave Versailles in October 1789. Although largely disused during the Revolution, the palace soon looked as grand as it had under the monarchy.

In this splendid setting, the First Consul naturally expected people to behave with a certain amount of ceremony. Slowly, something very like a court etiquette developed, so that by 1802, ladies were curtseying both to the Consul and to Mme Bonaparte. There were no official ladies-in-waiting, yet the wives of certain officials behaved very much as if they were filling that office. Naturally, invitations to the Tuileries and the right to attend the consular couple regularly were much coveted. This was a right that Laure naturally enjoyed. As a result, we hear a good deal about the manners and the conversation there, and may perhaps note, as impartial observers, that while a proximity to power is always thrilling, the intellectual level of conversation at the palace hardly did honor to French culture. Although Laure was far too careful to say, and even to think, that there was a parvenu flavor about the Bonapartes and their entourage, that fact nonetheless becomes clear as we read her stories.

Bonaparte's brusqueness—to use a tactful word—is vividly depicted in Mme Junot's Memoirs, and so are his mannerisms: his habit of pinching the ear of people of whom he approved, for instance, and the contempt he not infrequently displayed toward his wife. We see Josephine charming everyone in sight, running up huge bills, and managing Napoleon far more cleverly than he ever realized. And around them, their whole immediate circle comes back to life.

There are Josephine's two children by her first marriage: the suave, handsome Eugène, who knew how to please his stepfather while leading the life of what Napoleon disapprovingly called a dandy, and seducing every woman in sight. We meet his sister, the ravishing Hortense, whom Napoleon married to his brother Louis. Clearly, Mme Junot liked her; she barely hints at the fact that Hortense, to make up for her dislike of Louis, launched herself into a long series of less than discreet affairs and eventually left her husband, while still giving birth with some regularity.

Indeed, although Laure never says so outright (but we can read between the lines), the sex life of the consular family was little short of spectacular. The chastened Josephine, it is true, was now a faithful wife; but Napoleon himself was involved with many other women: around 1803, for instance, everyone knew that he was the lover of Mlle Georges, a majestic beauty and France's foremost dramatic actress, while a long series of mistresses for one night only were led up to a special room at the Tuileries.

Then there were the Bonaparte siblings, all of whom seemed to feel that the world (and the opposite sex) had been created solely for their pleasure. Mme Junot does not hesitate to make fun of Pauline, much of whose life was spent in the admiration of her own beauty; it is true that intelligence was not her main characteristic. We can, however, allow her a certain generosity. Her two (successive) husbands notwith-standing, she happily shared that perfect body with a succession of attractive young men. Just how lucky they were is shown by Canova's famous marble of Pauline in the nude.

Of Napoleon's two other sisters, only one, Caroline was almost as beautiful: Mme Junot describes her fairly, perhaps to hide the fact that she had good reason to hate her. Caroline, who married the dashing Murat, was immeasurably ambitious. She saw to it, by a combination of scenes and services*, that Napoleon made Murat, first Grand Duke of Berg, then King of Naples, so that she got to be Queen after all; and when Napoleon fell in 1814, she promptly switched her allegiance (and the Neapolitan army) to his enemies so as to keep her throne. Before that, however, she slept with any man who was likely to advance her ambitions. That, of course, was one reason why she stole Count Clem-ens Metternich from Laure and embarked on a public affair with him; as the Austrian ambassador in Paris, he was in a position to give her much useful information.

Naturally, Laure was greatly upset; but not as much as by Caroline's earlier maneuver. Having decided to take over Metternich, she simply, and effectively, told Junot about his wife's affair. Junot's fiery temper was well known to Caroline, since she was currently his mistress (he was after all Governor of Paris); she could, therefore accurately predict the appalling scenes which ensued.

At least from the point of view of posterity, Laure's affair with Metternich yielded a substantial benefit: a text in which the future Chancellor describes his mistress under the name of Adèle: "Adèle is young," he wrote, "she is pretty and generally pleases those who know her. Her face does not have classical features and I could not quite say what causes the enchanting charm of her physiognomy. I think it may be due mostly to the perfect accord between her smile and her glance, the former being both lively and tender while the latter is equally sweet and intelligent.

"Adèle is witty, and intelligent to a degree uncommon among women, but her wit is too biting. I have seldom seen her resist the pleasure of saying something sharp, even when it was about a friend of

* She acted as procuress for her brother and sheltered his amours in a discreet apartment.

whom she was really fond." It is no wonder Laure's salon was so popular; the combination of attractiveness and a sharp wit must have made for many an amusing evening.

Remarkably, Mme Junot knew when to stop; she could, no doubt, have taken her revenge on Caroline by seducing her husband, the tall, dark, and handsome Joachim Murat, who thought himself even better looking than he actually was and decked himself out in the most flamboyant costumes imaginable. A brave but incompetent general, he was endlessly unfaithful to Caroline. The couple was thoroughly united in its ambition, though, and worked very hard to convince Napoleon that they deserved to be given a kingdom.

Elisa, Napoleon's third sister, makes only the briefest of appearances in Mme Junot's Memoirs, and it is no wonder: she was unattractive, unpleasant, and stupefyingly dull. A relentless bluestocking, and quite charmless, she had lovers nonetheless; she could, after all, help further a man's career.

None of these ladies, obviously, could pose as models of virtue. Amazingly, the usually well-informed Napoleon failed to hear about most of his sisters' peccadilloes; only when the scandal became too public—as in the case of Caroline's affair with Junot—did the Emperor intervene, and even then, he could be quickly mollified.

It was in this less than virtuous atmosphere that Mme Junot moved, and she behaved no better than the imperial family. Beside Metternich, she had affairs with a dashing horseman, Fournier-Sarlovèze, an elegant (and still young) survivor of the *ancien régime,* Alexandre de Girardin and, more usefully perhaps, with Duroc, Napoleon's faithful Grand Marshal of the Palace. Since most of the characters involved were still alive when she wrote her Memoirs, and since, as a Bonapartist herself, she wanted to present the imperial family in the best light possible, she tends to be relatively discreet about it all; once again, though, we can read between the lines. And just how dull she found a more settled way of life is revealed by a startling omission: she was lady-in-waiting to Madame Mère (always referred to as plain Madame), Napoleon's austere mother, but scarcely ever mentions her. Perhaps Madame's *leitmotif,* "pourvu que ça dure" (if only it all lasts) rankled after all.

Nor do we hear much about Mme Junot's chief problem. While her husband, especially before 1808, was certainly successful, while he gave her access to Napoleon and his circle, he was frequently impossible to live with. A brave soldier, a reasonably competent general, and a devoted follower of Napoleon, Junot was unfortunately not very bright, a fact that Bonaparte quickly saw. As a result, Junot lagged behind his friends when it came time to be promoted: unlike some of the others, he never became a Marshal of France; he was never given a great command; and he could see well enough that, as time passed, Napoleon's opinion of him declined steadily. This, obviously, did not make him happy. Unable to acknowledge his own stupidity, he found his relative lack of success bewildering and unjustified. In consequence, he began to resent not only Napoleon but anyone against whom he could conveniently turn; and the person closest at hand was his wife. That, alone, would have been bad enough; but he was also given to frequent, violent rages; indeed, his dreadful temper was well-known in the army. Thus, Laure never knew when to expect an explosion. On occasion, he went beyond mere shouts and actually beat her quite badly. These ghastly scenes alternated, as is so often the case, with protestations of love and the giving of lavish presents; still, it made for a good deal of tension. At the same time, the couple was united in its ambition: in spite of the storms, both wanted more money and more titles, and they worked together quite effectively.

These shortcomings of Junot's were all the more unfortunate, from Laure's point of view, in that they limited her own social success. When the Empire was created, and a proper court organized, she could have expected to be given an important position. Instead, she was relegated to attending on Napoleon's notoriously dull and dour mother. That gave her entrée at the Palace, of course; she was still invited to, and gave, glamorous parties; her salon was brilliant and eagerly attended; but she had naturally hoped for more.

In some ways, Napoleon had never really approved of Laure—not because she refused to become his mistress, an episode she describes at length, but because she belonged to a section of society he resented. Mme Permon, as ill luck would have it, had failed to adjust her social climbing to changed circumstances. Under the illusion (partly shared by Napoleon) that the Faubourg Saint-Germain still mattered, she tended to see mostly people who scoffed at the new regime. Nothing could have annoyed the First Consul more, and he visited on the daughter some of the displeasure caused by the mother. That, together with his growing awareness of Junot's inadequacy, led him to remove Laure from his inner circle. She was not alone in this, however. As the years passed, Bonaparte changed, not always for the better; the easy, informal atmosphere of the early days was gradually replaced by an increasingly stiff etiquette; and new people—some belonging to government circles, others from the Faubourg Saint-Germain—were brought into the court.

The First Consul required other transformations as well. He soon came to feel that a mere ten years in office—the term set by the Constitution—was not enough. In 1802, he saw to it that the Senate offered him, first a second ten-year term, then life tenure; and the people to whom the question had been put in a referendum, overwhelmingly voted to approve the change. That change having been successfully managed, however, it occurred to the "Citizen First Consul" (as he was still called) that he really deserved to be king—under a different title. Thus it was that in 1804, the Senate, and the people who were again consulted, voted to make Napoleon Bonaparte hereditary Emperor of the French.

That meant, in turn, that there would be an imperial family: the new Emperor's sisters became Princesses, his brothers Princes, and all were created Imperial Highnesses. Each had to have a proper household, complete with chamberlains, equerries, and ladies-in-waiting. Napoleon himself was crowned by the Pope and, somewhat to its surprise, France found itself a monarchy once more. Of course, Mme Junot was invited to the coronation but, as she herself pointed out to Napoleon, merely as a spectator: there was no place for her in the newly created court.

Perhaps it was just as well. In spite of her undoubted devotion to the new regime, Laure was not naturally subservient. Although she may not have confronted the Emperor quite as forthrightly as she tells us, she hardly seems fitted for a kind of life where formality and boredom were mixed in equal parts. Napoleon himself commented that, at their last meeting in 1813, she treated him as if he had been a bad little boy. By 1805, in fact, there was nothing left of the easy quality of the consular court. At the Tuileries and in the other imperial palaces— Saint Cloud, Fontainebleau, Compiègne—the most stifling etiquette prevailed. Not even Josephine's famous charm could do much to dispel the heavy boredom that weighed on the court; and, of course, it all became a thousand times worse after the divorce. Marie Louise, the new Empress, had neither intelligence nor charisma. Staring bovinely ahead, unable to think of anything to say ("and how many children do you have, Madame?" was her standard contribution), she had little to add to an already dull atmosphere. Worse, from Mme Junot's point of view, she failed to acknowledge her husband's old friends, so that, after 1809, Laure was less important than ever.

Indeed, although Junot was duly created duc d'Abrantès in the first batch of Napoleon's new nobility, his duchesse was no longer grand enough to please Napoleon. Already after the coronation, and even more with the arrival of Marie Louise, the court filled with members of France's most aristocratic families. Next to them the Permons (and, even more, the Junots) looked very middle class. Mme d'Abrantès still attended the court on occasion, of course; she was still lady-in-waiting to Madame Mère, but she no longer really belonged.

Luckily for us, however, she traveled instead. First, Junot was appointed Ambassador to the court of Lisbon, and his wife went along; then he was given an army and told to conquer Portugal, an easy enough task; and finally, he was employed in the Spanish war. To a *parisienne* like Laure, foreign courts and foreign manners seemed as fascinating as they were comical. Safe in the knowledge that France was the center of the world, and that anything which diverged from French manners and French customs must be grotesque (a point of view which is by no means extinct today), she proceeded to enjoy herself as she saw it all. Thus, we have lively sketches of the courts of Madrid and Lisbon in the years before the French conquests; we can laugh along with the Ambassadress as she resolved the great hooped-skirt crisis, wonder at the intellectual level of the Houses of Bourbon and Braganza, and recapture the flavor of a world that ended forever in 1808.

That Mme Junot should have had this particular opportunity tells us a great deal about the transformation of Napoleon and his rule during those years. As the First Consul slowly evolved into the Emperor, his very conception of what government was, of what he was himself, was radically modified. It was not only that, gradually, Napoleon became more absolute: by 1805, he had begun to think that he was irresistible.

In France itself, the liberties which had been reestablished after the end of the Terror were gradually weakened, then suppressed. By December 2, 1804, the day of the coronation, freedom of the press and of assembly was gone; the elections to the legislature were so tightly controlled as to have become a sham. The one public institution, the Tribunate, in which a modicum of free speech persisted, was disbanded. Within another two years, the Emperor felt free to arrest people in far more arbitrary a manner than any king of the *ancien régime*. Finally, as the wars continued endlessly, increasingly heavy taxes were imposed on a non-consenting people; by 1810, Napoleon, once the golden hope of France, had become an out-and-out tyrant.

This dictatorship was supported by a continuous stream of victories. Napoleon, who felt he could use the French as he chose, considered the rest of Europe to be equally at his disposal. Naturally, there were kingdoms—Holland, Naples, Spain, Westphalia—for his various relatives. Worse, even when he allowed other rulers to keep their thrones, he told them exactly what to do; and to make sure they would do so he annexed convenient bits of territory. By 1810, Hamburg, in the north of Germany, and Trieste, in southeastern Europe, had become a part of France. And when, in 1810, the Emperor married an Austrian archduchess, he felt quite sure that no one would ever be able to resist him.

Even so, he had not waited for this supreme consecration in order to take over any distant country he chose: his treatment of Spain and Portugal, in which the Junots were involved, is clear proof of that. Just as, within France, the Emperor tolerated no dissent, so he expected the rest of Europe to obey his every order. That it might not be possible for certain countries to do so was no excuse; if they did not comply willingly, then he simply used force.

Portugal, in 1805, had long been an ally of England, already a thorn in Napoleon's side. Far worse, the two countries were trading partners;

indeed, the prosperity of Portugal depended on this commerce. Not unnaturally, when Napoleon sent Junot to Lisbon with the peremptory order that henceforth all British-Portuguese trade must cease, he was not obeyed nor could he be. Not only would compliance have meant immediate ruin, the government was far too weak to enforce so destructive a policy. The Queen Regnant was mad; her son, Dom João, ran the country as Regent, but with only partial authority; thus, much as Junot blustered, Dom João simply could not accede to his demands.

That being the case, Napoleon decided to conquer that country too. A French army was sent across Spain and attacked Portugal; and in spite of a spirited defense (notably at Abrantès, where it was crushed by Junot) the Portuguese army was in no condition to prevail. The royal family took ship for Brazil, and a French governor—Junot, naturally —was appointed. For Laure—who prudently skips over this episode in her Memoirs—it was rather fun; she was after all treated as if she were Queen of Portugal. For the Portuguese, on the other hand, this episode was considerably less pleasant (hence Laure's discretion), especially because the Junots helped themselves freely to the nation's treasures.

If the conquest of Portugal proved easy, it was also because Spain was the ally of France, and so weak as to allow a French army to advance right across its territory. Having agreed to this in haste, the Spaniards repented at leisure when the army in question, far from moving back to France, was eventually reinforced and, in 1808, succeeded in toppling their ruling dynasty.

What the Spanish royal family was like, Mme Junot tells us with glee; and her description is accurate enough; the imbecilic King Charles IV, his domineering wife, their sulky and silent heir, the future Ferdinand VII, whom his mother openly loathed, were hardly an appealing bunch. As for the government, it had sunk into a deep lethargy, in part due to the incompetence of Manuel Godoy, the Prime Minister.

A strapping handsome cavalry man who had caught the Queen's eye, Manuel Godoy became first her lover, then, eventually the principal minister. Given the way the Queen looks in Goya's portraits of her, we may perhaps feel that Godoy paid a high price for his elevation; what is at any rate certain is that Spain paid a high price as well. Incapable of governing, or indeed of preventing the utter dissolution of state and army, Godoy made it his invariable policy always to give in. Thus, he was responsible for the humiliating peace with France in 1800*, and was created Prince of the Peace into the bargain; and of course, he promptly assented when Napoleon demanded free passage for the French army on its way to Portugal.

Given this complete and unvarying compliance, there was really no reason for Napoleon to take over Spain as well. Of course, he was irritated at the inefficiency of its government, especially since he felt he could do so much better. Then, too, Spain had once been a maritime power, perhaps it could be made into one again. Finally, weak though it might be, an aura of glamor still clung to the Spanish monarchy; it seemed like the perfect spot for one of the Bonapartes. So it was that Napoleon called the royal family to Biarritz, under the pretext of resolving the conflict between the Queen and her son.

Once there, the Spanish Bourbons found not a conference but a jail. A carefully selected junta, also called to Biarritz, declared the throne vacant and asked Napoleon to give them a new King, and the Emperor obliged as planned; his brother Joseph, whom he had made King of Naples just two years before, was promoted to the Spanish throne. As it turned out—and as Napoleon should have realized—Joseph, who was a rather amiable fellow, was also absolutely incompetent; he made an even worse king than the hopeless Charles IV.

He also, to be fair, had graver problems; much to the Emperor's surprise, the Spaniards refused to accept their new ruler and showed the strongest attachment to the Bourbons. Worse, they loathed all the enlightened reforms decreed by the new King: they liked the Inquisition, and the feudal regime, and censorship and resisted change all the more ardently in that it was enforced on them by their invaders.

That, as Napoleon kept pointing out, was highly unreasonable. Unfortunately for him, though, the Spanish persisted in their antiquated attitudes. Far from being the walkover he had expected, the occupation of Spain required a large army which found itself confronted with something entirely new and extremely unpleasant: what we now know as guerrilla warfare. Whereas the Dutch, or the Prussians, or the Neapolitans, or even the Portuguese had known when they were beaten and behaved in consequence, the Spanish refused to acknowl-

---

* As a result of which Louisiana became French, and was then sold by Napoleon to the United States.

edge their defeat; and this proved enormously costly in men and money.

It was costly for General Junot as well. As ambassador to Portugal, Junot had been adequate: he simply had to deliver an ultimatum, after all. As commander of the army invading that country, he had performed honorably and earned his ducal title. As Governor, he had done considerably less well. He was no administrator, and showed it; and he proved even greedier and more unscrupulous than most commanders of an occupation force. It was, in fact, at this period that the Emperor began to show great dissatisfaction with the new duc d'Abrantès; instead of allowing him to return to Paris, or to serve in the main French army, Napoleon transferred him to Spain, a country already famous for ruining the careers of formerly successful generals. There, indeed, after a moment of success when he stormed Zaragoza, Junot proceeded to make a mess of his command, earning a whole series of imperial rebukes.

Nor was the new duc's disfavor improved by the Metternich scandal. The Junots were allowed back to Paris for the Emperor's wedding with Marie Louise; and while Napoleon did not approve of Laure's affair, what he really minded was the scandal caused by Junot's brutal treatment of his wife. As a punishment, therefore, the couple was sent straight back to Spain, where they were made to stay for a year. It was under these unsettled circumstances that Laure gave birth to her second son.

Partly because of this—Napoleon approved of women giving birth —the Junots were allowed to leave Spain. Laure settled back in her splendid Paris house while Junot was sent off to Italy to recruit men for the forthcoming Russian campaign. And just as things seemed to be going well, Laure proceeded to annoy the Emperor all over again. It must in all fairness be said, though, that it was only as the accidental result of her own sufferings.

What happened, simply, is that she fell passionately in love with the handsome Maurice de Balincourt. To a degree, her feelings were reciprocated; still, Balincourt could not see why he should give up his previous mistress. Enraged, Laure demanded that he do so and went so far as to confront the two of them, only to be told firmly that things were fine as they were. That was when, in a fit of amorous despair, Laure attempted suicide by downing a full bottle of laudanum.*

Luckily, she survived, but, once again, there was a major scandal. She was called to the Tuileries, where the Emperor, about to leave for Russia, scolded her and ordered her to go live outside Paris, an order which she never obeyed and he never enforced.

What Junot thought of it all, we do not know; but he can hardly have been pleased. In any event, he was proving to be a problem himself. Although he had been given a command in the Grand Army as it marched against Russia, his alternations of deep depression and manic exultation so worried Napoleon that he was sent off to the rear guard, where his military role was negligible, while, as a punishment, a decree of January 3, 1813, abolished the position of Governor of Paris.

By the end of the disastrous Russian campaign, it was quite clear that Junot could no longer be entrusted with any part of an army. At the same time, Napoleon felt a remnant of fondness for the companion of his early success; so, allowing Laure to remain in Paris, he sent Junot off to be Governor of Venice, a post which required no action whatever. That did not help, however; even as Laure began to receive despatches from her husband's secretary describing endless moments of the most peculiar behavior, Junot himself went mad, albeit in rather an amusing manner. At a ball he was giving in Ragusa, a small city near Venice, he appeared stark naked except for his epaulets, his orders, his gloves, and his dancing shoes. This rather unusual version of formal dress ended his career. At Laure's request he was sent back to France.

She herself, however, coolly stayed away from the problem. Instead of having him brought home to Paris, she had him taken to his father's house at Montbard, in Burgundy, and carefully refrained from going to visit him. It was there, in mid-1813 that the wretched Junot, announcing he was a bird, tried to fly out of a second-story window. Of course, he fell; his wounds became gangrenous, and he died within a few days.

That Laure should have chosen to distance herself from her mad husband can perhaps be understood; what is less palatable is that she

---

* A tincture of opium used as a sleeping potion and a pain killer, laudanum was also much used by the romantically desperate.

spent the rest of her life pretending that hers had been an ideal marriage and that she had been a perfect wife. In any event, while Junot's death was no doubt a relief, its consequences were less pleasant; he left no capital beside their splendidly furnished town house on the Champs Elysèes, and owed over a million francs, the equivalent of some seven or eight million of our dollars.

Once again, there seemed to be a curious parallel between Mme Junot's life and Napoleon's fate. Just as she had embarked on a dazzling social career in the golden days of the Consulate, so now she found herself a widow, and what was much worse, quite badly off. Although Junot had looted with the best of them, and had occasionally received large bonuses, he owed the bulk of his income to his salary and pensions, and both he and Laure had spent it all on a vast scale. With his death, most of his income automatically stopped. Of course, Napoleon could have continued it had he chosen to do so; but he had long been displeased with Junot; he had never really trusted Laure; and 1813 was not the right time for largesse. As it was, the widowed duchesse d'Abrantès, who is discreetly silent on the subject, found she had a choice between settling the estate, which would have left her with a modest income, or continuing her luxurious, expensive life while hoping that something would turn up some day. That, characteristically, is what she did, although her brilliant social successes must have palled, now and again, before the determined onslaught of her creditors.

In a very different way, Napoleon found that he, too, was facing trouble. Far from ending rapidly, as he thought it must, the war in Spain continued and even worsened. It was no longer just a question of dealing with bands of guerrilleros: now a proper Anglo-Portuguese-Spanish army was fighting the French. A Junta, governing in the name of Ferdinand VII was functioning in Cadiz; and worst of all, the enemy commander, the future Duke of Wellington, was proving singularly talented.

Still, Napoleon was so used to winning, so convinced that he could not lose, that he decided to ignore this running sore and embarked on a major war with the only Continental power whose very size meant it had almost endless resources. In many ways, the relationship between Napoleon and Alexander I of Russia was one of reluctant and disappointed love. There is no doubt the young Russian Tsar was deeply impressed by the strength and genius of his French counterpart; this much was evident when the two Emperors met. As for Napoleon, he was unquestionably fascinated by Alexander. Even more important, it seemed clear that the two monarchs, together, could rule Europe, and that they had agreed to do exactly that. Perhaps they both genuinely meant their accord to last; but statesmen depend, not just on their good intentions, but on the needs of their realms. From 1809 on, whether Alexander and Napoleon liked it or not, France and Russia were on a collision course.

It was not just because, amazingly, they had a common border: one of Napoleon's many conquests was the Grand Duchy of Warsaw, the central part of Poland, which he ruled directly. Far more important, Russia, like Portugal, was dependent on trade with England; and the first condition of the Tsar's alliance with France had been that Russia join in the blockade of the Continental System, which was meant to prevent English goods from reaching any part of the Continent. From the moment Alexander chose to ignore the frequent violations of the system which took place along his coasts, he and Napoleon could no longer be friends; and Alexander really had no choice. Russia, Voltaire said, was a tyranny tempered by assassination: both Alexander's father, the Emperor Paul, and his (putative) grandfather, Peter III, had been murdered. He knew very well that there were limits beyond which he dared not go.

As if to make this still worse, Napoleon proceeded to behave in the most irritating way possible. Not only did he complain loud and often about the violations of the system, he also kept mentioning the possible creation of an independent Kingdom of Poland, when a third of that country was in Russian hands; and he annexed the Duchy of Olden-burg because its coastline, in North Germany, was a haven for smug-glers. Unfortunately, the sovereign of this tiny state was the husband of Alexander's sister, the Grand Duchess Catherine; so the annexation looked like a deliberate insult.

In the end, however, it was Napoleon, not Alexander, who started the war: the half a million men of the Grand Army crossed the Niemen River, and started on its way to Moscow. The result was the greatest disaster ever sustained by the Emperor, a disaster so irretrievable, in fact, that, within eighteen months, it led to the occupation of Paris and the fall of the Bonapartes.

That should have been a catastrophe for the duchesse d'Abrantès as well; to a degree, it actually was, since she lost all the pensions which she had been receiving from the Imperial Treasury. Mere lack of money did not stop her, however; trading on her affair with Metternich, she was soon receiving the allied sovereigns and their ministers. Her title, like all those given by Napoleon, was confirmed by the restored Louis XVIII; and, far from so disinclined, Laure—she was, after all, a duchess—attended the court as if nothing had changed.

Unfortunately, her creditors were not so lighthearted. In spite of pleas directed at several kings and ministers, Laure, who was still living as if she had endless resources, found that her debts were getting to be unmanageable. For a while she sent in secret reports to one of the new King's ministers and was well paid for them. She managed to sell a rare Portuguese manuscript for the then enormous sum of eighty thousand francs (nearly half a million of our dollars), a feat all the cleverer in that Junot had stolen it in the first place. She tried selling her house to the State; indeed, Louis XVIII agreed to buy it, but Napoleon's return from Elba killed that arrangement. She tried to convince Balincourt to help; and he did, but not enough; so, she sold her house, not as well as she had hoped, along with most of its contents, and embarked on a precarious and agitated existence. Constantly moving to keep a step ahead of her creditors, forced by penury to close her salon in the mid-twenties, Laure still managed to know most of the people who mattered. Although her beauty was gone, and she dressed appallingly, her wit and intelligence remained untarnished.

Becoming far more involved in the literary world than she had been in the palmier days of the Empire, she was responsible for the publication of the works of Astolphe de Custine, a critic and analyst of singular penetration. And while she was at it, she tried to marry him; Custine was rich, which was all that mattered to her. Unfortunately, he was also a homosexual, and not even Laure could convince him that he yearned for matrimony, so that scheme never succeeded.

Custine is an interesting but minor figure. Even more to her credit, Laure also became enthralled with the work of Balzac, one of the greatest novelists ever to grace the French language. The two became fast friends—unfortunately, Balzac was as improvident as Laure herself —and it was Balzac who suggested that she write her Memoirs. The result was a triumph. As soon as the first volume came out in 1831, the new author found herself greatly in demand. She wrote novels, supplements to her Memoirs, and published regular columns in the two leading Paris newspapers, *La Mode* and *Le Temps*.

Having had to close her salon, having ended her social life, Laure suddenly found herself a celebrity all over again, and much in demand. She now actually earned enough to live on, but, by 1838, she owed nearly a million and a half francs—some ten million of our dollars— and had absolutely no way to meet that enormous debt. Her health, too, deteriorated; perhaps the laudanum had a lasting effect. As, after a brief illness, she lay dying, her creditors seized her furniture. It was thus in the most extreme poverty that she ended her brilliant, agitated life.

Laure Junot, duchesse d'Abrantès, was only fifty-two when she died; but she had made the most of her time. At the center of affairs for so many years, a perennial leader of Paris society, much admired and occasionally hated, she was a major figure of the era that went from the rise of Napoleon to that of Louis Philippe. More to the point, she knew how to observe, how to remember, how, on occasion, to ridicule. It is no wonder her Memoirs were such an instant success: the intelligence, the cutting wit Metternich describes were there on the printed page, to be enjoyed by every reader. Just as important, she knew how to select the telling detail, the exemplary anecdote; it is an entire world that comes back to life under her pen.

Of course, Laure was also frivolous, impractical, a spendthrift; but, since we are not her creditors, we can enjoy retrospectively the panache with which she behaved, and admire her for her undaunted courage in the face of adversity. As most of her contemporaries, the other stars of the imperial court, sank into obscurity, she continued to dazzle Paris; and now, more than a hundred and fifty years later, she fascinates us still.

PART I

*A Brilliant Young
General*

MEMOIRS OF
MADAME JUNOT,
DUCHESSE D'ABRANTÈS.

IN 1785 WE arrived in Paris. My mother found the provinces boring, and my father was equally desirous of returning to town. He had long wished to become a fermier général* and at this very juncture M. Rougeau was disposed to sell his situation. Negotiations were immediately opened by the friends of both parties. My father resolved to manage this business personally, and that circumstance determined our hasty journey. My father wished to see a great deal of company, and, after the fashion of the time, set a day of the week apart for giving dinner-parties.

My mother possessed the qualifications of an agreeable hostess. Her good temper and frankness of manner made her a favourite with everybody: she united to beauty of person, grace, tact, and, above all, a natural intelligence. She was, however, exceedingly deficient in education. She used to say she had never read but one book ("Telemachus");

---

* A fermier général helped collect the taxes for the King, and was allowed to keep a set percentage for himself—hence the expression "rich as a fermier général."

but, in spite of that, those who had once enjoyed her conversation never could quit her society without reluctance and regret. How many poets and distinguished literary characters have I seen spell-bound by the charm, not of her person, but of her manners!

No one could tell a story with more piquant originality. Often have my brother and myself sat up until three o'clock in the morning listening to her. But what particularly marked her character was her perfection in that most difficult art of presiding in her drawing-room.

One of my mother's first cares on arriving in Paris was to inquire after Napoleon Bonaparte. He was at that time in the Military School of Paris, having quitted Brienne in the September of the preceding year. My uncle Demetrius had met him just after he alighted from the coach which brought him to town. "And truly," said my uncle, "he had the appearance of a fresh importation. I met him in the Palais Royal, where he was gaping and staring with wonder at everything he saw. He would have been an excellent subject for sharpers, if, indeed, he had had anything worth taking!"

My uncle invited him to dine at his house; for though he was a bachelor, he did not choose to dine at a coffee house. He told my mother that Napoleon was very morose. "I fear," added he, "that that young man has more self-conceit than is suitable to his condition. When he dined with me he began to declaim violently against the luxury of the young men of the Military School. After a little he turned the conversation upon Manea, and the present education of the young Maniotes, drawing a comparison between it and the ancient Spartan system of education. His observations on this head he told me he intended to embody in a memorial to be presented to the Minister of War. All this, depend upon it, will bring him under the displeasure of his comrades, and it will be lucky if he escape being run through."

A few days afterwards my mother saw Napoleon, and then his irritability was at its height. He would scarcely bear any observations, even if made in his favour, and I am convinced that it is to this uncontrollable irritability that he owed the reputation of having been ill-tempered in his boyhood and splenetic in his youth.

My father, who was acquainted with almost all the heads of the Military School, obtained leave for him sometimes to come out for recreation. On account of an accident (a sprain, if I recollect right) Napoleon once spent a whole week at our house. To this day, whenever I pass the Quai Conti, I cannot help looking up at a garret window at the left angle of the house on the third floor. That was Napoleon's chamber when he paid us a visit, and a neat little room it was. My brother used to occupy the one next to it. The two young men were nearly of the same age; my brother, perhaps, had the advantage of a year or fifteen months. My mother had recommended him to cultivate the friendship of young Bonaparte; but my brother complained how unpleasant it was to find only cold politeness where he expected affection.

This repulsiveness on the part of Napoleon was almost offensive, and must have been sensibly felt by my brother, who was not only remarkable for the mildness of his temper, and the amenity and grace of his manner, but whose society was courted in the most distinguished circles of Paris on account of his talents. He perceived in Bonaparte a kind of acerbity and bitter irony, of which he long endeavoured to discover the cause.

"I believe," said Albert one day to my mother, "that the poor young man feels keenly his dependent situation." "But," exclaimed my mother, "his situation is not dependent; and I trust you have not made him feel that he is not quite at home while he stays here."

"Albert is not wrong in this matter," said my father, who happened to be present. "Napoleon suffers on account of his pride, but it is pride not to be censured. He knows you; he knows, too, that your family and his are in Corsica equal with regard to fortune. He is the son of Letizia Bonaparte, and Albert is yours. I believe that you are even related; now he cannot easily reconcile all this with the difference in the education he receives gratis in the Military School, separated from his family, and deprived of those attentions which he sees here lavishly bestowed upon our children."

"But you are describing envy, not pride," replied my mother.

"No, there is a great difference between envy and the feelings by which this young man is disturbed. The warmth of your friendship for the mother has caused you to place the son in a continually painful situation; for painful it must be, since the reflection will recur to him: Why is not my family situated like this?"

"Absurd!" cried my mother; "to reason thus would be both foolish and wicked in him."

"He would be neither more foolish nor more wicked than the rest of the world. It is but feeling like a man. What is the reason he has been in a constant state of ill-humour since his arrival here? Why does he so loudly declaim against the *indecent luxury* (to use his own words) of all his comrades? Why? because he is every moment making a comparison between their situation and his own! He thinks it ridiculous that these young men should keep servants when he has none. He finds fault with two courses at dinner, because, when they have their *picnics,* he is unable to contribute his share. The other day I was told by Dumarsay, the father of one of his comrades, that it was in contemplation to give one of the masters a *déjeuner,* and that each scholar would be expected to contribute a sum certainly too large for such boys. Napoleon's censure is so far just. Well! I saw him this morning, and found him more than usually gloomy. I guessed the reason, and broke the ice at once by offering him the small sum he wanted for the occasion. He coloured deeply, but presently his countenance resumed its usual pale yellow hue. He refused my offer."

"That was because you did not make it with sufficient delicacy," cried my mother. "You men are always such bunglers!"

"When I saw the young man so unhappy," continued my father, without being disconcerted by my mother's warmth of manner, to which he was accustomed, "I invented an untruth, which Heaven will doubtless pardon. I told him that, before his father expired in our arms at Montpellier, he gave me a small sum to be applied to the wants of his son in cases of emergency. Napoleon looked at me steadfastly, with so scrutinizing a gaze that he almost intimidated me. 'Since this money comes from my father, sir,' said he, 'I accept it; but had it been a loan I could not have received it. My mother has already too many burthens, and I must not increase them by expenses beyond my means, particularly when they are imposed upon me by the stupid folly of my comrades.' You see then," continued my father, "if his pride is so easily wounded at the school by strangers, what must he not suffer here, whatever tenderness we may show him?"

W H E N , in 1789, the Revolution began, Napoleone Buonaparte, as he then spelled his name, had already graduated from the
Royal Military school; he began his career as a second lieutenant,
and did not really distinguish himself until the siege of Toulon in
1793 when his success was rewarded with a promotion from
captain to brigadier general. Even then, his officer's pay was his
only income; and in a time of rapid inflation it was grossly
insufficient. Whatever small resources his widowed mother still
had vanished in the great upheaval; thus it was a very poor and
hungry young man who watched the fall of the monarchy, the
emergence of Robespierre as a major power in the new Republic
and the beginnings of the Reign of Terror.

In striking contrast to his later positions, General Buonaparte
thoroughly approved of the new government; he was, if anything, rather to its left, a position which caused him considerable
difficulties when Robespierre fell in the summer of 1794; but
there is good reason to believe that his politics owed more to
opportunism than to conviction. As for the Permon family,
whose position was very much to the right of the young General's, it had a great deal to lose. The offices of the fermiers génér-
aux were abolished, banking and trade came to a virtual standstill
by 1792, while the kind of refined luxury which Mme Permon
had enjoyed was no longer possible. Thus, although not necessarily royalist, the Permons found the period between 1792 and
1796 a most difficult and unpleasant one. They survived it but
loathed its excesses.

I may say that I first knew Bonaparte when he visited us during the
Reign of Terror. Previously I had only a confused recollection of him.
When he came to see us after our return to Paris, his appearance made
an impression upon me which I shall never forget. At that period of his
life Bonaparte was decidedly ugly; he afterwards underwent a total
change. I do not speak of the illusive charm which his glory spread
around him, but I mean to say that a gradual physical change took
place in him in the space of seven years. His emaciated thinness was

converted into a fulness of face, and his complexion, which had been yellow and apparently unhealthy, became clear and comparatively fresh; his features, which were angular and sharp, became round and filled out. As to his smile, it was always agreeable.

The mode of dressing his hair, which has such a droll appearance as we see it in the prints of the passage of the bridge of Arcola, was then comparatively simple; for young men of fashion (the *muscadins*), whom he used to rail at so loudly at that time, wore their hair very long. But he was very careless of his personal appearance; and his hair, which was ill-combed and ill-powdered, gave him the look of a sloven. His small hands, too, underwent a great metamorphosis: when I first saw him they were thin, long, and dark; but he was subsequently vain of their beauty, and with good reason.

I recollect Napoleon entering the courtyard of the Hôtel de la Tranquillité in 1793, with a shabby round hat drawn over his forehead, and his ill-powdered hair hanging over the collar of his gray great-coat, without gloves, because he used to say they were a useless luxury, with boots ill-made and ill-blacked, with his thinness and his sallow complexion; and when I think what he was afterwards, I do not see the same man in the two pictures. He spoke French very badly, frequently committing the greatest mistakes, and his ignorance on certain points of ordinary education was remarkable. Yet in spite of those disadvantages every one listened to him with delight.

Bonaparte came daily to visit my mother, and he frequently entered into warm political discussions with persons whom he met at her residence. These discussions almost always led to violent language, which displeased my mother. But Bonaparte was unfortunate; she knew it, and that consideration rendered her indulgent to him.

My mother told me one day that she had learned some particulars respecting General Bonaparte which much distressed her, the more especially as she could do nothing to assist him. These particulars had been communicated to her by Mariette, her *femme-de-chambre*.

Mariette was a very pretty and good girl; Bonaparte's servant admired her and wished to marry her. She, however, did not like him; and as he was, moreover, poor, she declined his offer. I give these details because they are connected with an affair which I shall presently have to allude to. Bonaparte's servant informed Mariette that the General was often in want of money.

"But," added he, "he has an aide-de-camp who shares with him all he gets. When he is lucky at play, the largest share of his winnings is always for his General. The aide-de-camp's family sometimes sends him money, and then almost all is given to the General. The General," added the man, "loves this aide-de-camp as dearly as if he were his own brother." This aide-de-camp was no other than Junot, who was destined at a later period to be my husband!

On Bonaparte's return to Paris, after the misfortunes of which he accused Salicetti of being the cause, he was in very destitute circumstances. His family, who were banished from Corsica, found an asylum at Marseilles; and they could not now do for him what they would have done had they been in the country whence they derived their pecuniary resources. From time to time he received remittances of money, and I suspect they came from his excellent brother Joseph, who had then recently married Mademoiselle Clary; but, with all his economy, these supplies were insufficient. Bonaparte was therefore in absolute distress.

Junot often used to speak of the six months they passed together in Paris at this time. When they took an evening stroll on the Boulevard, which used to be the resort of young men, mounted on fine horses, and displaying all the luxury which they were permitted to show at that time, Bonaparte would declaim against fate, and express his contempt for the dandies with their whiskers and their *oreilles de chien,* who, as they rode past, were eulogizing in ecstasy the manner in which Madame Scio sang *paole pafumée, paole panachée.**

"And it is on such beings as these," he would say, "that Fortune confers her favours. Heavens! how contemptible is human nature!"

Junot, whose friendship for Bonaparte was of that ardent kind which is formed only in youth, shared with him all that he received from his family, who, though not rich, were in easy circumstances. He used sometimes to resort to the gaming-table, but before he did so he invariably deposited in the hands of Bonaparte three-quarters of the

---

* This affected mode of dropping the r was common among the dandies of that time, or, as they used to be called, the *incroyables.*

allowance he had received from Burgundy: the other quarter was allotted to the chances of *vingt-et-un*. Junot was often successful at play: on those occasions the two friends used to make merry, and pay off their most pressing debts.

E A R L Y in 1795, M. Permon, Laure's father, died suddenly. At the same time, the fall of Robespierre and the end of the Terror brought with them, if not yet a return to normality, at least a lessening of danger for the well-to-do. Thus it was that Laure's mother and her brother decided to move from the hotel where they had been staying to a house—small but quite luxurious—which they now bought. At the same time, the political situation remained unsettled; grave shortages continued to plague the disorganized economy; widespread unemployment, and the distress it caused, seemed not unlikely to cause further convulsions; thus, while the Permons resumed the kind of upper-class life to which they had been accustomed before the Revolution, they were careful to do so as discretely as possible.

The house to which we removed in 1795 was situated in the Chausée d'Antin; it was the small house (everybody knows that all the houses in this part of the Chaussée d'Antin were nothing more, anterior to the Revolution), of M. de Varnachan, formerly a farmer-general of taxes; it was commodious, and its small appearance was a recommendation at a time when all were striving to make as little show as possible, and to conceal their wealth.

We now learned with astonishment the good fortune which had befallen Bonaparte. My mother, absorbed by her grief at my father's death, had not a thought to bestow on any singularity which the conduct of the young General might present when compared with his own words; she even saw him again without having the inclination to remind him of it. For the rest, a great change had taken place in Bonaparte, and the change in regard to attention to his person was not the least remarkable. One of the things to which my mother had a particular dislike was the smell of wet dirty boots put to the fire to dry; to her this smell was so unpleasant that she frequently left the room, and did not return till the boots had been thoroughly dried and removed from the fire; but this was followed by another, namely, the creaking noise produced by the dry sole, to which I also have a great antipathy.

In those disastrous times, when it was a matter of luxury to ride in a hackney-coach, it may easily be conceived that those who had but sufficient to pay the price of a dinner did not take great delight in splashing others, but retained sufficient philosophy to soil their shoes or boots by walking. My mother admitted the justice of the remark, but she nevertheless held her perfumed handkerchief to her nose whenever Bonaparte placed his little feet upon the fender. He at length perceived this, and, being at that time exceedingly afraid of displeasing my mother, he would prevail upon our maid to brush his boots before he came in. These trifling details, which are nothing in themselves, become interesting when we recollect the man to whom they relate.

After the failure of the Jacobin insurrection on October 4th, which the young general put down at the government's orders, muddy boots were out of the question. Bonaparte never went out but in a handsome carriage, and he lived in a very respectable house, Rue des Capucines. In short, he had become a necessary and important personage, and all as if by magic; he came every day to see us, with the same kindness and the same familiarity; sometimes, but very rarely, he brought along with him one of his aides-de-camp, either Junot or Muiron; at other times his uncle Fesch, a man of the mildest manners and most even temper.

At this period famine prevailed in Paris in a greater degree than anywhere else: there was a real want of bread, and other kinds of provisions began no longer to find their way to the city. This was the effect of a plan of insurrection. The distress was dreadful. The discredit of the assignats* increased with the general misery. Labouring people ceased to work, and died in their garrets, or went and joined the bands of robbers and vagabonds which began to collect in the provinces. In Paris itself we were not free from them.

Bonaparte was at that time of great assistance to us. We had white bread for our own consumption; but our servants had only that of the Section, and this was unwholesome and barely eatable. Bonaparte sent

* The paper currency which had replaced gold.

us daily some army bread, which we very often ate with great pleasure. At the period in question he saved more than a hundred families from perishing.

He caused wood and bread to be distributed among them at their own homes; this his situation enabled him to do. I have been charged by him to give these bounties to more than ten unfortunate families who were starving. Most of them lived in the Rue Saint Nicolas, very near our house. That street was then inhabited only by the most indigent people: whoever has not ascended to their garrets can have no conception of real wretchedness.

My mother's mourning was deep; etiquette required absolute solitude, which preyed daily more and more upon her naturally delicate health. M. Duchannois told her one day that, in the circumstances in which she was placed, decorum might require her not to go into company, but that she ought to take some amusement. In consequence, he recommended her to hire a box at one of the theatres, and to go to it in the most profound incognito; she might listen to good music, surrounded by friends; and their attentions, and her soul wrapt in a soft lethargy, would cause her to forget her griefs for a few hours at least. My mother accordingly took a box at the Feydeau, where she passed an hour or two every evening. Bonaparte never missed coming thither. He was not fond of French music, and, to confess the truth, the notes of Madame Scio and Gaveaux-Bouche* were not calculated to give him a liking for it.

About this time Bonaparte had a strange conference with my mother, so strange, indeed, that even to this day I cannot suppress a smile whenever I think of it. One day Bonaparte told my mother that he had to propose a marriage which should unite the two families. "It is," added he, "between Paulette and Permon. Permon has some fortune." (It was not then known that we had found nothing at my father's death.) "My sister has nothing, but I am in a condition to obtain much for those belonging to me, and I can get a good place for her husband. This alliance would make me happy. You know what a pretty girl my sister is. My mother is your friend. Come, say 'Yes,' and the business shall be settled." My mother said neither yes nor no; she

* He had a very wide mouth, and was so called to distinguish him from Gavaudan.

replied that my brother was of age, that she should not influence him either one way or the other, and that all depended on his own will.

Bonaparte confessed that Permon was so remarkable a young man that, though only twenty-five, he had maturity and abilities which would qualify him for public employments. Thus far what General Bonaparte said was natural and suitable. It related to a match between a young female of sixteen and a young man of twenty-five. This young man was supposed to possess an income of ten thousand livres; he had an agreeable person; painted like Vernet, whose pupil he was; played on the harp much better than Krumpholtz, his master; spoke English, Italian, and modern Greek, as well as French; wrote verses like an angel; transacted business with a facility and intelligence which distinguished him among those who were connected with him in the Army of the South. Such was the man whom Bonaparte demanded for his sister, a beautiful creature, it is true, and a good girl, but nothing more.

To all that I have just said of my brother might be added that he was the best of sons, exemplary in his duties as a member of society, as well as in those of a friend, a brother, and a kinsman. I shall perhaps be charged with letting my heart run away with my pen, and listening too much to its suggestions. No, I am not swayed by prejudice; what I say of my brother is nothing but the strictest truth.

Such, then, was my brother when Bonaparte proposed to my mother a match between him and Mademoiselle Pauline Bonaparte, called by her family and all her friends *"Pretty Paulette."* This proposal he followed up by the plan of a second alliance between me and Louis or Jerome. "Jerome is younger than Laurette," said my mother, laughing. "Indeed, my dear Napoleon, you are acting the high priest to-day; you are marrying everybody, even in their teens."

Bonaparte laughed too, but with an air of embarrassment. He admitted that when he got up that morning a marriage-breeze had blown upon him; and, to prove it, he added, kissing my mother's hand, that he had made up his mind to ask her to commence the union of the two families by a marriage between him and herself, as soon as a regard to decency would permit.

My mother has frequently related to me this extraordinary scene, so that I am as well acquainted with it as if I had been the principal actress in it. She eyed Bonaparte for some seconds with an astonishment bordering upon stupefaction; and then burst into so hearty a laugh that we heard her in the next room, where there were three or four of us.

Bonaparte was at first much vexed at this manner of receiving a proposal which appeared to him quite natural. My mother, who perceived it, hastened to explain herself, and told him that it was she, on the contrary, who in this affair played, at least in her own eyes, a perfectly ridiculous part.

"My dear Napoleon," said she, when she had done laughing, "let us talk seriously. You fancy you are acquainted with my age. The truth is, you know nothing about it. I shall not tell it you, because it is one of my little weaknesses. I shall merely say that I am old enough to be, not only your mother, but Joseph's too. Spare me this kind of joke; it distresses me, coming from you."

Bonaparte assured her, over and over again, that he was serious; that the age of the woman whom he should marry was indifferent to him, if, like herself, she did not appear to be past thirty; that he had maturely considered the proposal which he had just made to her; and he added these very remarkable words: "I am determined to marry. They want to give me a woman who is charming, good-tempered, agreeable, and who belongs to the Faubourg St. Germain. My Paris friends are in favour of this match. My old friends dissuade me from it. For my own part, I wish to marry, and what I propose to you suits me in many respects. Think about it."

My mother broke off the conversation, telling him, laughingly, that for her own part she had no occasion to think any further; but, as to what concerned my brother, she would speak to him about it, and communicate his answer on the Tuesday following—it was then Saturday. She gave him her hand, and repeated, still laughing, that though she had some pretensions, they did not aspire so high as to conquer the heart of a man of twenty-six, and that she hoped their friendship would not be interrupted by this little affair.

"At any rate, think of it," said Bonaparte.

"Well, well, I will think of it," replied my mother, laughing as heartily as before.

I was too young to be made acquainted with this conversation at the time when it occurred. It was not till my marriage that my mother related to me the particulars here detailed. My brother made a note of this singular affair. Had Bonaparte's overtures been accepted, he would never have become what he afterwards was.

As late as 1797, still, the habits of the Revolution lingered. Private individuals were afraid of appearing wealthy by receiving company habitually, and they contented themselves with frequenting public assemblages, where, at that time, the best society was to be found. It would scarcely be believed at the present day that the most elegant women went to dance at the Thelusson* and the Richelieu** balls; but persons of all opinions, of all castes, were there intermingled, and laughed and danced together in the utmost harmony.

One day at the Thelusson ball a droll adventure befell Madame de D., who sometimes took her daughter with her.

Madame de D. had arrived very late. The great circular room was quite full, and it was impossible to find two places. Nevertheless, by dint of elbowing and entreaties, these ladies penetrated to the centre of the room. Madame de D., who was not of an absolutely timid character, looked about on all sides to see if she could at least discover one seat, when her eyes encountered a young and charming face, surrounded by a profusion of light hair, with a pair of large dark-blue eyes, and exhibiting altogether the image of the most graceful of sylphs. This young female was conducted back to her seat by M. de Trénis, which proved that she danced well; for M. de Trénis invited none to the honour of being his partners but such as deserved the character of *good dancers*.

The graceful creature, after curtsying with a blush to the Vestris of the ball-room, sat down by the side of a female who appeared to be her elder sister, and whose elegant dress excited the notice and envy of all the women at the ball. "Who are those persons?" said Madame de D. to the old Marquis d'Hautefort, who escorted her. "What! is it possible that you do not recognize the Viscountess Beauharnais? It is she and her daughter. She is now Madame Bonaparte.*** But stay, there is a

* At the Hôtel Thelusson, at the extremity of the Rue Cerutti, facing the Boulevard, there was at that time an immense arcade. Murat purchased it during the Consulate.
** Held in like manner at the Hôtel Richelieu.
*** At this period Madame Bonaparte was not much known in the world, nor had she been presented at the Court of Marie Antoinette. The real fact was, that Madame de D. did not know her.

vacant place by her; come and sit down; you may renew your acquaintance with her."

Madame de D., without making any reply, took the arm of M. d'Hautefort, and drew him, whether he would or not, into one of the little saloons which preceded the great rotunda. "Are you mad?" said she to him, when they had reached the room. "A pretty place, truly, by the side of Madame Bonaparte! Ernestine would of course have been obliged to make acquaintance with her daughter. Why, Marquis, you must have lost your wits." "No, 'faith! What harm can there be in Ernestine's making acquaintance, or even forming a close friendship, with Mademoiselle Hortense de Beauharnais? She is a charming girl, sweet-tempered, amiable." "What is all that to me! I will never connect myself with such persons. I do not like people who disgrace their misfortunes." M. d'Hautefort shrugged his shoulders and held his tongue.

"Eh! mon Dieu! who is that beautiful woman?" inquired Madame de D., pointing to a female who entered the ball-room, and on whom all eyes were instantly fixed. This lady was above the middle height, but a perfect harmony in her whole person took away all appearance of the awkwardness of too lofty a stature. It was the Venus of the Capitol, but still more beautiful than the work of Phidias; for you perceived in her the same perfection of features, the same symmetry in arms, hands, and feet, and the whole animated by a benevolent expression, a reflection of the magic mirror of the soul, which indicated all that there was in that soul, and this was kindness.

Her dress did not contribute to heighten her beauty, for it consisted of a plain robe of India muslin, with folds in the antique style, and fastened by a cameo on each shoulder; a gold belt encircled her waist, and was likewise fastened by a cameo; a broad gold bracelet confined her sleeve considerably above the elbow; her hair, of a glossy black, was short, and curled all round her head, in the fashion then called *à la Titus;* over her fair and finely-turned shoulders was thrown a superb red cashmere shawl, an article at that time very rare and in great request. She disposed it around her in a manner at once graceful and picturesque, and formed altogether a most enchanting figure.

"That is Madame Tallien,"* said M. d'Hautefort to Madame de D. "Madame Tallien!" exclaimed she. "Good God! how could you bring me to such a place, my dear friend?" "I defy you to find in all Paris a place where better company is brought together." He then muttered some of the civil things which he had at the service of those who displeased him.

At this moment a very strong scent of attar of roses suddenly pervaded the apartment. A crowd of young men, of the class then called *incroyables,* rushed towards the door to meet a young lady who had but just arrived, though it was exceedingly late. Her figure was not good, but her little feet danced to admiration. She was dark, but her black eyes sparkled with expression. Her face beamed with intelligence, and expressed at the same time all the kindness of the simplest person. She was a good friend, and the most amusing of women.

In short, she pleased; she was a toast of the day. All the remarkable men surrounded her as soon as she appeared. M. Charles Dupaty, M. de Trénis, and M. Lafitte immediately asked her to dance with them; she answered each with an expression of good-humour and intelligence, smiling in such a manner as to exhibit her ivory teeth; she continued to advance, shedding fragrance throughout the whole room.

Madame de D., who was annoyed by the perfume, and who, like all busybodies, found fault with what others liked, began to fidget about on the bench upon which she had found a seat, and at length said aloud, "Upon my word, I think that must be either Fargeon, the perfumer's wife or his daughter. 'Tis enough to make the strongest man faint." "It is Madame Hamelin,"** said M. d'Hautefort. Next day he told us that nothing had amused him more that evening than being in attendance on Madame de D., and having to name the persons who were real bugbears to her. "Madame Hamelin!" she exclaimed— "Madame Hamelin! Come, Ernestine," added she, in a voice tremulous with anger, "put on your *palatine,* and let us go." All that could be said served only to hasten her departure. "And that Marquis," repeated she, in a tone of indignation, "to assure me that I should here meet with my

* Mme Tallien, the wife of one of the men who brought about the fall of Robespierre, was one of the most fashionable women in Paris.
** A young woman of great elegance and loose morals; she was a close friend of Mmes. Bonaparte and Tallien.

former society! Yes, indeed; for this hour past I have been falling out of the frying-pan into the fire. Come, my dear, let us go."

ALTHOUGH Napoleon was unquestionably a military genius, it can well be argued that his talent for politics was even greater than his gift for winning battles. Thus, from the very beginnings of the Directoire, he courted the Directors—they were known as the five kings of the Republic—and made it very plain he was at their disposal. As a result, they called on him to put down a right-wing, royalist rising on October 5, 1795; he succeeded, using cannon to dispose of the rebels, and, immediately afterwards, became one of the best treated officers in the army. Within three weeks, he was promoted from brigadier to lieutenant general. Then, on March 9, 1796, he gave a further proof of his devotion to the regime by marrying Josephine de Beauharnais. He was, in fact, in love with that highly seductive, if no longer very young woman; but he also overlooked the fact that she had been a mistress of one of the Directors, and that the Director in question—Barras—was eager to get rid of her.

His reward followed swiftly: two days after the wedding, he was appointed commander in chief of the French army in Italy. That, however, was not as dazzling a promotion as it seemed. The army in question lacked everything, from guns to shoes. It seemed very likely, therefore, that the twenty-eight-year-old general would come a cropper—a neat way of disposing of a potential danger to the ever weaker government. Instead, he went on to win a series of brilliant victories.

The Army of Italy surprised us every day by the prodigies communicated in its bulletins. The Directory, which disliked General Bonaparte, would fain have thrown a veil over the glory of the young hero; but the country, which he had saved from Austrian invasion, the soldiers, whom he led to victory, had thousands of voices to proclaim it.

It would be very difficult to convey even a slight idea of the enthusiasm with which Bonaparte was received when he arrived at Paris. The French people are volatile, not very capable of constancy in their affections, but keenly alive to the sentiment of glory. Give them victories, and they will be more than content, they will be grateful.

The Directory, like all authorities that are too weak and impotent to produce and to direct, though it was called the *Executive Directory,* regarded with jealousy, which soon became hatred, that feeling of worship and gratitude manifested by the French people for their young hero. A single movement seemed to set in action those five men, not one of whom was capable of comprehending Bonaparte. Incapacity, corruption, and an unbounded ambition, under a Republican exterior, were the elements of the power which then ruled us, and which desired no glory but that of its immediate creatures. Bonaparte had emancipated himself since he had been sent to Italy, and his laurels and those of his army were *personal property,* as much as anything can legally be.

Had Bonaparte's vanity been ever so great, it must have been satisfied; for all classes joined, as I have said, to give him a cordial welcome on his return to his country. The populace shouted, "Long live General Bonaparte! Long live the conqueror of Italy, the pacificator of Campo-Formio!" The shopkeepers said, "May God preserve him for our glory, and deliver us from the yoke of the Directors!" The higher class, *ungagged* and *unbastilled,* ran with enthusiasm to meet a young man who in a year had advanced from the battle of Montenotte to the Treaty of Leoben, and from victory to victory. He may have committed errors, and even grave ones, since that time, but he was then a Colossus of great and pure glory.

All the authorities gave him magnificent entertainments; the Directory exhibited itself in all its burlesque pomp of mantles and hats with feathers, which rendered the meeting of the five members of the supreme power sufficiently ridiculous. But in other respects the *fêtes* were fine, and they had in particular the charm attached to things which are supposed to be lost, and which are recovered. Money circulated, and the result of all this was that everybody was pleased.

One of the most magnificent entertainments, and above all one of the most elegant, was that given by M. de Talleyrand at the Foreign Office. He always displayed admirable skill in the arrangements of the entertainments which he gave; indeed, when a man possesses good sense he shows it in everything he does. He then resided at the Hôtel Galifet, Rue du Bac, and, though the rooms were small for the company assembled there that evening, the *fête* was admirable. All the most elegant and distinguished people then in Paris were there.

My mother was absolutely bent on going. She was not quite well; but when she was dressed and had put on a little rouge, she looked enchanting; and I can affirm that I saw that night very few women who surpassed her in beauty. We were both dressed alike, in a robe of white crape trimmed with two broad silver ribbons, and on the head a garland of oak-leaves with silver acorns. My mother had diamonds, and I pearls. That was the only difference between our dresses.

In the course of the evening my mother was walking through the rooms, arm-in-arm with M. de Caulaincourt on one side, and me on the other, when we found ourselves face to face with General Bonaparte. My mother saluted him and passed on, when the General advanced a few steps and spoke to her. My mother was, in my opinion, rather too dry; her ill-humour was not yet quite dispelled, but in her excellent heart there was nothing like rancour. It was the reverse with the General. Be this as it may, he appeared to look at my mother with admiration. Indeed, that evening in particular she was truly captivating.

The General spoke in a low tone for some seconds to the Turkish Ambassador, whom he held by the arm. The Turk uttered an exclamation, and fixed upon my mother his large eyes, to which, when he chose, he could give a look of stupidity, and then made a sort of obeisance. "I told him that you are of Greek extraction," said Bonaparte to my mother, saluting her by way of adieu. Then, holding out his hand, he pressed hers in a friendly manner, and left us after a short conversation, which nevertheless attracted the attention of the company, though it lasted but a few minutes.

Late in 1797, Joseph Bonaparte, Napoleon's elder brother, was elected to the Council of Five Hundred.* He then completed the fitting-up of his pretty house in the Rue du Rocher, and prepared to receive company. He was expecting his mother and his youngest sister

* The lower house of Parliament; the upper house was the Conseil des Anciens.

Caroline. Mademoiselle Désirée Clary had just married Bernadotte.*
We were at the wedding, which took place in a very plain manner in
Joseph's house. Mademoiselle Clary was rich, and extremely pleasing in
person and manners; Bernadotte made a very good match.

Of all Bonaparte's brothers none have been so misrepresented, and
that generally, as Joseph. I have read a multitude of memoirs, and
everywhere found a caricature by which he has been judged, substi-
tuted for his real aspect. Joseph, moreover, is not the only one of the
family that I shall replace in his proper light; and this I can do with the
greater facility, because all its members are as well known to me as my
own relations, in consequence of an intimate association of many years,
and at a less exalted period of their lives.

My brother was particularly intimate with Joseph. I know not when
this friendship commenced; but I believe that it was at the time when
my brother, in order to escape the requisition, was at Marseilles and
Toulon with Salicetti.

Joseph Bonaparte is one of the most excellent men that can be met
with. He is good-natured, intelligent, a student of French and Italian
literature, and unaffectedly fond of retirement. Much has been said, but
to no purpose, relative to the weak conduct of Joseph when he ruled
over Naples and in Spain. I know not what he did, or what he could
have done at Naples; but this I know, that in Spain he could do no
better, because he went there against his inclination, and it distressed
him exceedingly to be obliged to go to that unhappy country, filled
with troubles and dissensions, where the dagger or the blunderbuss
threaten you every moment,—a country where all the good that he
did, and I am certain that he did a great deal, was accounted only as a
duty performed.

Joseph is handsome, very like the Princess Pauline. They have both
the same delicate features, the same winning smile, the same kind look.
Joseph has always been a great favourite with our family. At Montpellier, after his father had breathed his last in my mother's arms, Joseph
came to live with his uncle Fesch in the house of my parents. I mention
this because Joseph never forgot it; on the contrary, he always tendered

* The future King of Sweden.

47

me his hand to testify his gratitude for what my mother had done for him.

Madame Joseph Bonaparte is an angel of goodness. Pronounce her name, and all the indigent, all the unfortunate in Paris, Naples, and Madrid, will repeat it with blessings; yet she was never at Madrid, and knew nothing of that foreign land but from the accounts of it that were given to her. Never did she hesitate a moment to set about what she conceived to be her duty. Accordingly, Madame de Survilliers* is adored by all about her, and especially by her own household; her unalterable kindness, her active charity, gain her the love of everybody, and in the land of exile she has found a second native country.

She was fondly attached to her sister, the Queen of Sweden. The latter is an inoffensive, and in my opinion an excellent, creature; but she has one defect which her present situation renders almost a vice,— she is a mere cipher. Her character has no colour. Nay, more, she may easily be persuaded to do any person an ill turn, merely because she is not aware of the drift of the procedure. The Queen of Sweden was prodigiously fond of everything that was melancholy and *romantic.*

When she married Bernadotte, she had a face of which I shall say nothing, because we were then thought to be exceedingly like each other. She had very fine eyes, and a most pleasing smile. Lastly, she had not too much *embonpoint,* as at the time of her departure for Sweden, and she was altogether a very agreeable person. She was fond of her husband, which was natural enough; but that fondness became a down-right annoyance to the poor Bearnese, who, having nothing of a hero of romance in his composition, was sometimes extremely perplexed by the part. She was continually in tears when he had gone out because he was absent; when he was going out, more tears; and when he came home she still wept because he would have to go away again, perhaps in a week, but at any rate he would have to go.

Louis Bonaparte, Napoleon's younger brother, was engaging at eighteen, subsequently his infirmities gave him the appearance of an old man before his time; this rendered him morose in appearance, and miserable in reality. He resembled his sister Caroline when he was

---

* The name afterwards assumed by King Joseph. The Queen also used it in Germany, where she then resided.

young and in health; there was the same cast of countenance, and the same expression when Caroline's features were at rest; but as soon as they were animated by her smile or her look, all resemblance vanished.

Louis is a mild, easy, good-natured man. The Emperor, with his whim of making kings of all his brothers, could not find one who would fall in with it. His sisters, on the contrary, seconded him, for they were devoured by ambition; but on this point the men have always shown a firm and determined will. Louis told him as much when he was setting out for Holland. "I will do what I like," said the young King to his brother. "Let me act freely, or let me remain here. I will not go to govern a country where I shall be known only by disaster."

The Emperor was inflexible in his will. He sent Louis to Holland; the unfortunate young man went to experience a slow and cruel agony among its canals and marshes. The greater part of his present ailments proceed from that damp atmosphere, particularly unhealthy for a child of the South like him. He obeyed, and his wife was destined there to feel the keenest anguish—her maternal heart was wrung by the death of her first-born.*

Lucien** and his wife arrived at Paris at the same time, I believe, as did Madame Letizia and Caroline Bonaparte. The General came to Paris, and afterwards set out again for Toulon. The Egyptian expedition was in preparation. Applications from all quarters poured in from young men, who, in ignorance of its destination, but hoping that it might be for Constantinople or England, enrolled themselves in crowds.

At the period I am speaking of (that is, in 1797), Lucien might be about twenty-two years of age; he was tall, ill-shaped, having limbs like those of the field-spider, and a small head, which, with his tall stature, would have made him unlike his brothers had not his physiognomy attested their common parentage. Lucien was very near-sighted, which made him half shut his eyes and stoop his head. This defect would have given him an unpleasing air if his smile, always in harmony with his features, had not imparted something agreeable to his

* The eldest of the children of Louis and Hortense Beauharnais died of croup, at the Hague, in 1804.
** Napoleon's next younger brother.

49

countenance. Thus, though he was rather plain, he pleased generally. He had very remarkable success with women who were themselves very remarkable, and that long before his brother arrived at power. With respect to understanding and talent, Lucien always displayed abundance of both.

In early youth, when he met with a subject that he liked, he identified himself with it; he lived at that time in an ideal world. Thus, at eighteen, the perusal of Plutarch carried him into the Forum and the Piraeus. He was a Greek with Demosthenes, a Roman with Cicero; he espoused all the ancient glories, but he was intoxicated with those of our own time. Those who, because they had no conception of this enthusiasm, alleged that he was jealous of his brother, have asserted a wilful falsehood, if they have not fallen into a most egregious error. This is a truth for which I can pledge myself. But I would not with equal confidence assert the soundness of his judgment at this same period, when Bonaparte, at the age of twenty-five, laid the first stone of the temple which he dedicated to his immortality.

Not naturally disposed, by the grandeur of his genius, to view things in a fantastic light, and attaching himself solely to their reality, Bonaparte proceeded direct to the goal with a firm and steady step. He had in consequence the meanest idea of those who kept travelling on, as he expressed it, in the kingdom of fools. From this rigorous manner of judging persons of ardent imaginations, it may be supposed that Lucien was smartly reprimanded whenever he addressed to him any of the philippics or catilinaria of the young Roman. Napoleon forgot that he himself, a few years before, whilst still in Corsica, had given proof of equally violent exaltation.

Madame Lucien was tall, well-shaped, slender, and had in her figure and carriage that native grace and ease which are imparted by the air and sky of the South; her complexion was dark, and she was pitted with the smallpox; her eyes were not large, and her nose was rather broad and flat: in spite of all this she was pleasing, because her look was kind, her smile sweet, as well as her voice: she was graceful, in short, and good as an angel. Her love for her husband rendered her quick in adapting herself to her position; in a few weeks she became an elegant woman, wearing to admiration all that issued from the hands of Leroi,

Mademoiselle Despaux, and Madame Germon, then the most fashionable dressmakers in Paris.

On his first visit to Paris Lucien made but a short stay there; on his return from Germany he and his wife settled in Paris, and lived at this period in Grande Rue Verte, Faubourg Saint Honoré.

Madame Bacciochi—Napoleon's sister Elisa—resided, like Lucien, in the Rue Verte. Madame—Napoleon's sister Pauline—Leclerc, who arrived from Italy soon after the period which I have just mentioned as that of the meeting of the family, took a house in the Rue de la Ville-l'Evêque. We formed, of course, nearly the centre of the Corsican colony, in the heart of Paris; thus, not a day passed on which some of the brothers or sisters did not visit us, or we them.

Caroline Bonaparte, who changed her name from the too Italianate Annunziata, and who came with her mother from Marseilles, was then twelve years old. Handsome arms, small hands, delightful in form and whiteness, small well-turned feet, and a brilliant complexion—such were the characteristics of her beauty, with the addition of fine teeth, rosy cheeks, very fair but round shoulders, a figure rather too robust, and a manner not very elegant. Caroline was in other respects a very good girl, and we were as much together as my more intimate acquaintance with Mademoiselle de Perigord and Mademoiselle de Caseux permitted.

Caroline was placed in a boarding-school at St. Germain, with Madame Campan, not to finish her education, for it had not even been begun. Of Madame Leclerc we saw more than of any other in the family. She came every day to my mother, who was very fond of her, and petted her—that is the right word—by passing over with more indulgence than her mother the thousand and one whims which were bred, gratified, and abandoned in a day. Many people have extolled the beauty of Madame Leclerc; this is known from portraits and even statues of her; still, it is impossible to form any idea of what this lady, truly extraordinary as the perfection of beauty, then was, because she was not generally known till her return from St. Domingo, when she was already faded, nay withered, and nothing but the shadow of that exquisitely beautiful Paulette, whom we sometimes admired as we admire a fine statue of Venus or Galatea. She was still fresh on her arrival at Paris from Milan; but this freshness was of short duration; by the time she had lived a year in Paris she began to be a very different person from the Paulette of Milan.

At this period she was an excellent creature; it has been said since that she was malicious, and this report has been spread even by persons of her household; I know not whether greatness changed her disposition.

General Bonaparte, after staying but a few weeks at Paris, when on the point of leaving Europe with the chance of never returning, had been influenced by a feeling of violent irritation. My brother, who in Italy had always kept upon the best terms with the General, had called to see him at Bonaparte's request. Albert went several times, and always came back more and more certain that Napoleon was excessively mortified by the course of events. "I plainly perceive," said Albert, "that his great spirit is too much compressed in that narrow centre, within which those needy Directors wish to confine it: it is a free flight in untrammelled space that such wings demand. He will die here; he must begone. This morning," added Albert, "he said to me: 'This Paris weighs me down like a cloak of lead!' And then he paced to and fro."

"And yet," replied Albert, "never did grateful country hail more cordially one of its children. The moment you appear, the streets, the promenades, the theatres, ring with shouts of 'Vive Bonaparte!' The people love you, General."

While my brother thus spoke, Bonaparte, he said, looked steadfastly at him. He stood motionless, his hands crossed behind him, and his whole countenance expressing attention mingled with the liveliest interest: he then began walking again with a pensive look.

"What think you of the East, Permon?" he abruptly asked my brother. "You seem to have had an excellent education; for your father, I believe, originally destined you for the Diplomatic Service, did he not?" My brother replied in the affirmative. "You speak modern Greek, I believe?" Albert nodded assent. "And Arabic?" Albert answered in the negative, adding that he could easily learn to speak it in the course of a month.

"Indeed! Well, in that case, I—" Here Bonaparte paused, as if fearful that he had said too much. He nevertheless reverted to the subject a moment afterwards, and asked Albert if he had been at M. de Talleyrand's ball. "That was a delightful *fête,*" he added; "my Army of

Italy would be very proud if it knew that its Commander had received such high honours. Yes, the Directors have done things nobly. I should not have supposed that they had such skill in paying compliments: what luxury!" He walked about for a considerable time without speaking, and then resumed: "It was more magnificent than our royal entertainments of old. The Directory ought not thus to forget its republican origin. Is there not pretension in appearing in such pomp before those who, in fact, can counterbalance its power? I represent the army!" added Bonaparte; "yes, I represent the army, and the Directors know whether the army is at this moment powerful in France."

Nothing could be more true than this last insinuation of Bonaparte. At this period the army actually possessed great influence, and a distant expedition was already much talked of in public. Bonaparte asked my brother several questions relative to this subject. Albert answered that it was generally believed that the projected expedition was destined against England.

The smile that now played upon Napoleon's lips, as Albert afterwards told us, had so strange, so incomprehensible an expression, that he could not tell what to make of it.

"England!" he then rejoined. "So you think in Paris that we are going to attack it at last? The Parisians are not mistaken; it is indeed to humble that saucy nation that we are arming. England! If my voice has any influence, never shall England have an hour's truce. Yes, yes; war with England for ever, until its utter destruction! Permon, if you choose, I will take you with me; you speak fluently English, Italian, Greek. Yes; I will take you with me."

The conversation detailed here is the summary of what passed at five or six interviews. My brother heard in all quarters a variety of surmises concerning the projected expedition. The secret was long kept, but at length it was divulged; for Bonaparte, covetous of all kinds of glory, resolved to surround himself with the splendour which the arts and sciences impart to everything. He laid the Institute itself under contribution. An immense battalion accompanied the new Alexander to the banks of the Nile, whence it was destined to bring back a trophy more brilliant than any that blood can give to posterity.

As soon as my brother learned that the expedition was destined for so distant a country his resolution was taken; he arranged his affairs, and prepared for his departure. My mother, when she knew it, threw herself in a manner at his feet, entreating him not to forsake her. Albert needed no second supplication; he remained.

Among the young officers whom Bonaparte had introduced to my mother, when he was appointed to the command of the Army of the Interior, she distinguished one, as well on account of his manners, blunt without rudeness, and his open countenance, as for the extreme attachment which he manifested for his General. This attachment bordered upon passion. He evinced an enthusiasm so touching that my mother, whose elevated soul and loving heart were capable of appreciating all exalted sentiments, had immediately distinguished Colonel Junot, and from that moment she felt the sincerest friendship for him. I was then quite a girl, and never dreamt that the handsome Colonel, with light hair, elegant dress, engaging countenance, and yet serious look, would come three years afterwards and, out of love, solicit the hand of the little girl whom at that time he scarcely noticed.

Of all the officers composing Bonaparte's staff Colonel Junot had the most adventurous and the most fortunate destiny. He bore, in recent scars, the glorious marks of a valour which his bitterest enemies have not attempted to deny him. The General-in-Chief had known how to appreciate it, and with the origin of his fortune were connected several remarkable acts, not only of courage, but also of honour and generosity. It was at the siege of Toulon that the General had become acquainted with him, and in a manner which, for its singularity, deserves to be related at length.

Junot was born at Bussy-Legrand, in the department of the Côte d'Or, on the 24th September, 1771, and it may be observed, by the way, that he received for a Christian name that of the saint whose festival happened to fall on the day of his birth; hence he had the most singular name perhaps in France—it was Andoche. acquainted with Marmont, who was a pupil at the same college, and here they contracted that friendship which nothing ever diminished, though both of them pursued the same career. This friendship ended only with Junot's death in 1813.

Junot was a man of a very extraordinary character, which was not always duly appreciated by those about him, because he himself sometimes threw an obstacle in the way, in consequence of a defect which really was a drawback from his many good qualities,—I mean an extreme irritability, easily excited in him by the mere appearance of a fault. Whenever he had reason to suspect any one, more especially a person under his command, of neglect in matters connected with the service, he could not help reproving him for it, and the more harshly, as, in the like case, he would have been just as severe towards one of his own relations. On such occasions his frankness did not allow him one circumlocutory word.

Junot had lofty ideals; he was a stranger to falsehood, and was endowed with a generosity which his enemies have endeavoured to represent as a vice, but which his numerous family, who for fifteen years had no other support than him, a great number of crippled soldiers, of widows encumbered with children, who received pensions and relief from him, will never call anything but the virtue of a noble heart.

He possessed in an eminent degree the qualities of a good son, a warm friend, and an excellent father. I recollect Mr. Fox telling me one day how he was struck the preceding evening, when leaving the opera-house, on seeing Junot paying as much attention and respect to his mother as he could have done to the first peeress of England.*

Having begun life with the Revolution, Junot was absolutely one of its children. He was scarcely twenty when the first roll of the drum was heard. A war-cry rang throughout the kingdom; the most discreet panted for combat; all were tired of repose. Had not Junot been my husband, I should tell how he became all at once a young Achilles. Suddenly smitten with a passion for arms, he wholly forgot the luxurious and indolent life which till then he had led. It was then that he entered into that celebrated battalion of volunteers of the Côte-d'Or, so renowned for the number of generals and great officers of the Empire who sprang from its ranks.

After the surrender of Longwy, the battalion was ordered to Toulon

---

* Mr. Fox meant by no means to satirize France by appearing to think it admirable that a son should give his arm to his mother. It was the extraordinary care and attention that struck him, as he himself acknowledged.

to join the forces collected to retake it from the English. This was the most critical moment of the Revolution. Junot was sergeant of grenadiers, which rank had been conferred on him upon the field of battle. Often, when relating to me the circumstances of the first years of his adventurous life, did he speak of that event as the most extraordinary that had befallen him. He said, with that accent which persuades because it is true, that, in the whole course of his career, nothing ever threw him into such a delirium of joy as that which he experienced when his comrades, all of them as brave as himself, appointed him their sergeant, when their commander confirmed their appointment, and he was lifted on a tremulous platform supported by bayonets still dripping with the blood of the enemy.

During the siege of Toulon, Bonaparte asked for some one who could write a good hand. Junot stepped out of the ranks and offered his services. Bonaparte recognized in him the sergeant who had already attracted his notice. He told him to place himself somewhere to write a letter, which he would dictate. Junot chose the corner of the battery. Scarcely had he finished the letter when a bomb, fired by the English, burst at the distance of ten paces and covered him, as well as the letter, with mould and dust. "Capital!" said Junot, laughing; "we wanted some sand to dry the ink."

Bonaparte fixed his eyes on the young sergeant; he was quite calm, and had not even started. This circumstance decided his fortune. He continued with the Commandant of the artillery, and did not return to his corps. Afterwards, when the city was taken and Bonaparte appointed General, Junot asked no other reward for his good conduct during the siege but to be appointed his aide-de-camp, preferring an inferior rank to that which he might have had by remaining in the corps; but in this case he would have been obliged to leave Bonaparte, and Junot could not make up his mind to that.

Junot was soon attached to his General with a devotedness that became adoration. Without taking the full measure of the giant who was before him, his penetrating mind set him down for a great man. I subjoin an extract from a letter written in 1794, when Junot's father, alarmed at the resolution of his son, asked him for information concerning the man to whose fortunes he had attached himself. "Why have you left the Commandant Laborde? Why have you left your corps? Who is this General Bonaparte? Where has he served? Nobody knows him here."

Junot answered his father, and explained to him why he had preferred the service of the staff, especially that active service which he was likely to have with his General, to the more tardy results that would have attended his remaining with his battalion. He then added: "You ask me who is this General Bonaparte. I might answer in the words of Santeuil:

> " 'Pour savoir ce qu'il est il faut être lui-même'
> (to know what he is you have to be himself)

but this much will I tell you, that as far as I can judge he is one of those men of whom Nature is sparing, and whom she throws into the world but once in a century."

I have already observed that Junot lavished his blood for the glory of his country. I shall here mention a few instances. During the campaign in Italy, at the Battle of Lonato, he received, as we have just seen, a wound on his left temple; but the most frightful of his wounds was a gun-shot wound received in Germany when only a volunteer; it must have been terrible, to judge from the scar, which made one shudder. The pulsation of the brain might be perceived there; this scar was at least an inch long, and seven or eight lines in depth. At frequent intervals during the three or four years succeeding that campaign, this wound would break open afresh in a manner equally singular and alarming, and, the blood flowing profusely from it, Junot ran the risk every time of bleeding to death.

One day, at Milan, being at the house of Madame Bonaparte, where they were playing at vingt-et-un, Junot was sitting at a round table with his back towards the door of the cabinet of the General-in-Chief. The General opened his door without being heard; he made a sign to be silent, and, coming up softly, laid hold of the fine light head of hair which the young aide-de-camp then had, and pulled it sharply. The pain was so acute that Junot could not suppress a faint cry; he smiled, but his face turned pale as death, and then alarmingly red. The General withdrew his hand; it was covered with blood!

To a brilliant and creative imagination Junot joined an acute understanding that was most prompt in seizing any new idea the moment it presented itself to him. He learned everything with inconceivable rapidity. He was very ready at composing verses, was an excellent actor, and wrote wonderfully well. His temper was warm, sometimes passionate, but never was he coarse or brutal.

The part he occupied, formerly so eminent under the Bourbons, was infinitely more important under the Emperor. The Governor of Paris* had the command of nearly 80,000 men; he was the only Governor who ever had such great power, extending to Blois, and, I believe, even to Tours. All officers of distinction, foreign or French, who passed through Paris, were received by him. Every person of any renown who came to France was admitted to the hospitalities of the Governor of Paris; and, from the first day of his nomination, Junot strove to imitate the Duc de Brissac, if not in his two queues and his white scarf, at least in the politeness of his manners. This desire of standing well in his intercourse with the social world dates even much further back, notwithstanding Junot's fondness for the Republic, and his aversion to ancient customs.

L I K E Bonaparte, Junot was thoroughly identified with the Revolution and the new regime; but that was not at all the case for Mme Permon. Socially ambitious, and a great snob, she took advantage of the poverty of many returning members of the old aristocracy: no longer able to have their own salons, they were willing to visit people whom they would not have deigned to notice before 1789. As the wife of a fermier général, Mme Permon had belonged to the moneyed bourgeoisie, and received other people of the same milieu. Now, she could attract some of the greatest names in France; but to keep them coming, she had to pose as an aristocrat, one who loathed the republic—an attitude Bonaparte rightly found repulsive.

Among the ladies who had recently returned to France, and who were frequent visitors at my mother's house, there was one who is still

* Junot became Governor of Paris in 1800. It was one of the First Cousul's earliest appointments.

vividly present to my recollection as though I had seen her only a few days since. This was Madame de Contades, the daughter and sister of the MM. de Bouillé who distinguished themselves at the affair of Varennes.

Madame de Contades was a person whose appearance never failed to make a profound impression at first sight. She was not remarkable for beauty, but there was something very pleasing about her. There was an expression in her look and smile which I never observed in any but one woman besides herself. She was not gloomy, far from it; and yet one could scarcely venture to laugh in her presence unless she first set the example. When she turned round her goddess-like head, crowned with luxuriant black hair, and cast a glance at any one, that look was a command which exacted obedience.

Her hatred of Bonaparte was exceedingly amusing. She would not grant him the merit of deserving his military fame. "Pshaw!" she would say when my mother spoke of his victories in Italy and Egypt; "I could do as much with a look." She was no less diverting when Bonaparte's sisters came under her review. She would not acknowledge the beauty of Madame Leclerc any more than the glory of her brother. Her eccentric opinion on this subject once gave rise to a tragi-comic incident at my mother's house.

Bonaparte had just departed for Egypt; and the different members of his family, bright with the reflections of the glory he had cast upon them during his brief stay in Paris, had already commenced their noviciate of royalty. Madame Leclerc, who had a taste for absolute power, was nothing loath to unite the influence of her brother's reputation to that of her own beauty. That beauty, indeed, appeared so perfect that nobody ever thought of disputing it. As her dominion as yet consisted only of her beauty, she spared no pains to make the most of it; and in this she certainly succeeded, when she did not, as unfortunately too often happened, display the airs of an insufferable spoiled child.

One evening my mother gave a ball at her residence in the Rue Sainte Croix. She had invited, according to her custom, the most select society of the Faubourg Saint Germain. As to the other party, the only individuals belonging to it were the Bonaparte family, and a few gentlemen, who, like M. de Trenis, were fine dancers, and were for that reason regularly invited by the few families who gave parties at that time.

Madame Leclerc informed us that she had prepared for the occasion a dress which, to use her own expression, she expected would *immortalize her*. This dress was a subject of the most serious consideration with her, at least a week before she was destined to wear it, and she enjoined the strictest secrecy on Madame Germon and Charbonnier.* She requested permission to dress at our house, which she frequently did in order that she might enter the ball-room with her dress completely fresh and in all its beauty.

Only those who knew Madame Leclerc at that time can form any idea of the impression she produced on entering my mother's drawing-room. The head-dress consisted of *bandelettes* of a very soft fine kind of fur, of a tiger pattern. These *bandelettes* were surmounted by bunches of grapes in gold; but the hair was not dressed so high as it is now worn. She was a faithful copy of a Bacchante, such as are seen in antique statues or cameos; and, in truth, the form of Madame Leclerc's head, and the classic regularity of her features, emboldened her to attempt an imitation which would have been hazardous in most women.

Her robe of exquisitely fine India muslin had a deep bordering of gold; the pattern was of grapes and vine-leaves. With this she wore a tunic of the purest Greek form, with a bordering similar to her dress, which displayed her fine figure to admirable advantage. This tunic was confined on the shoulders by cameos of great value. The sleeves, which were very short, were lightly gathered on small bands which were also fastened with cameos. Her girdle, which was placed below the bosom, as is seen in the Greek statues, consisted of a gold band, the clasp of which was a superbly cut antique stone. She entered the drawing-room without her gloves, displaying her beautiful white round arms, which were adorned with gold bracelets.

It is impossible to describe the effect her appearance produced. Her entrance seemed absolutely to illumine the room. The perfect harmony in every part of the beautiful whole elicited a buzz of admiration, which was not very complimentary to the other ladies present. The gentlemen all thronged round her as she advanced towards a seat which

---

* A milliner and a hairdresser at that time much in favour.

my mother had reserved for her, for Paulette was a particular favourite of my mother's, who, indeed, regarded her almost as her own child.

The ladies were all much piqued at the beauty and the elegant dress of Mademoiselle Bonaparte, the wife of General Leclerc. They whispered to one another, but loud enough to be heard by Paulette, that such an impudent display of extravagance was exceedingly unbecoming in a woman who had been almost starved only three years before. But these expressions of female envy were speedily drowned by the admiration of the other sex.

The beauty of Madame de Contades was entirely eclipsed, and soon after Madame Leclerc's entrance she found herself abandoned by her circle of admirers; or if any of them approached her, it was only to make some provoking remark complimentary to the charms of Paulette. "Give me your arm," said she to a gentleman near her, and the next moment the Diana-like figure of Madame de Contades was seen moving across the drawing-room and advancing towards Madame Leclerc.

The latter had withdrawn to my mother's boudoir, because, she said, the heat of the drawing-room and the motion of the dancers made her ill; though, I believe, the true reason was that a long sofa in the boudoir afforded her the opportunity of displaying her graceful figure and attitudes to the best advantage. This manoeuvre, however, proved unlucky for her.

The room was small and brilliantly lighted, and as Madame Leclerc reclined upon the sofa a stream of light descended full upon her head. Madame de Contades looked at her attentively; and instead of making any of the ill-natured observations which had fallen from the other ladies, she first admired the dress, then the figure, then the face. Returning a second time to the *coiffure,* she expatiated on its taste and elegance; then suddenly turning to the gentleman on whose arm she was leaning, she exclaimed, "Ah, mon Dieu! mon Dieu! how unfortunate that such a pretty woman should be deformed! Did you never observe it? What a pity it is!"

Had these exclamations been uttered in the drawing-room it is probable that the sound of the music and the dancing would have drowned Madame de Contades's voice, though she generally spoke in a pretty loud tone; as it was, every word resounded through the little boudoir, and the scarlet which suffused the face of Madame Leclerc was much too deep to improve her beauty.

Madame de Contades fixed her eyes of fire on Paulette, as if she would look her through, and the tone of compassion in which she uttered the words, "What a pity!" sufficiently informed Paulette that her triumph was at an end. All this (which perhaps I have described with rather too much prolixity) took place in the space of little more than a minute; but these details are necessary to show the mode in which the attack was managed, and the success with which a woman of ingenuity may avenge her wounded vanity.

"What is the matter?" inquired some one who stood near Madame de Contades. "The matter!" said she, "do you not see the two enormous ears which disfigure either side of her head? I declare if I had such a pair of ears I would have them cut off, and I will advise Madame Leclerc to do so. There can be no harm in advising a woman to have her ears cut off."

All eyes were now turned towards Madame Leclerc's head, not, as before, to admire it, but to wonder at the deformity with which its beauty was disfigured. The truth is, that Nature must have been in one of her most capricious moods when she placed two such ears on the right and left of a charming face. They were merely pieces of thin white cartilage, almost without any curling; but this cartilage was not enormous, as Madame de Contades said; it was merely ugly, by contrast with the beautiful features which accompanied it.

A young woman but little accustomed to society is easily embarrassed; this was the case with Madame Leclerc when she read in the faces of her surrounding admirers the effect produced by the remarks of Madame de Contades. The result of this scene was that Paulette burst into tears, and on the plea of indisposition retired before midnight.

Paulette's mother, Madame Letizia Bonaparte* was one of the handsomest women in Corsica, though her fine face was wrinkled by many

* Napoleon's mother.

cares. The first time I saw her she was dressed in an absurd way; yet, nevertheless, she made a strong impression upon me.

Madame Bonaparte was a lofty and elevated character. A widow at an early age, in a country where the head of a family is everything, the young mother found it necessary to develop all the energy of her character. She was gifted with that delicacy of perception which distinguishes the Corsicans, but in her this quality did not degenerate into hypocrisy, as in some of her children. Indeed, she was habitually frank. She evinced firmness in certain circumstances, but in others obstinacy. This was obvious in a number of the systematic triflings which composed a part of her life.

She was very ignorant, not only of our literature, but of that of her own country. She had, however, some knowledge of the usual forms of society, of which she had seen a little in the course of her acquaintance with M. de Marboeuf and other distinguished men, who visited much at her house at the time of the occupation of Corsica. But this slight knowledge of the world was to her rather a source of inconvenience than of advantage, inasmuch as it put her in constant dread of committing some blunder. Her haughtiness, which was not offensive, became dignity when elevated to her new situation. She was kind at heart, but of a cold exterior, possessed of much good sense, but little shrewdness or knowledge of the world; and at the period of which I speak she was very scrupulous in exacting from everybody what she considered her due.

She was a very good mother, and her children, with one exception, were good to her in their turn. They treated her with every respect, and showed her assiduous attention. Lucien and Joseph were particularly attached to her. As for Napoleon, he was not so respectful and attentive to his mother as his brothers were; and we shall presently see the cause of his remissness. Madame Bacciochi evinced no particular regard for her mother. But for whom did she ever show regard? I always thought her the most disagreeable woman I had ever met with; and it is quite astonishing to me how M. de Fontanes, a man of such superior mind, such elegant manners, the very essence of sociability, should have admired Madame Bacciochi in the way he did.

On the evening of the 9th of October my mother had a few friends with her. Madame de Caseaux, her daughter, Madame de Mondenard, my mother, and several gentlemen of our acquaintance were seated at a large round table playing at *loto-dauphin,* a game of which my mother was very fond. Suddenly a cabriolet drove up to the door, a young gentleman jumped out of it, and in a minute was at the top of the staircase. It was my brother Albert.

"Guess what news I bring you!" said he. As we were all in high spirits, and his countenance bespoke him to be so too, all sorts of absurd guesses were made, at which Albert constantly shook his head. "Nonsense!" said my mother, taking up the bag containing the little balls. "If there were a change in the government of the Republic you could not make it an affair of greater importance." "Well, mother," replied Albert, seriously, "what you say now in jest may possibly be realized. *Bonaparte is in France!*"

When my brother uttered these last words the whole party seemed struck motionless, as if by a magic wand. My mother, who had just drawn a ball out of the bag, held her little hand raised in the air, and, the bag having fallen down, the balls were rolling about the carpet in every direction without exciting the notice of anybody. Every one sat as if petrified. Albert was the only person who was conscious of the drollery of our position, and a burst of laughter, which he could not repress, brought us to ourselves.

"Bonaparte in France!" exclaimed my mother; "it cannot be possible. I saw his mother this very day at five o'clock, and she had no idea of his return." "It is, nevertheless, true," said Albert. "I was with Brunetière just now, when a messenger was sent by Gohier to fetch him. He desired me to wait till he came back from the Luxembourg; and he returned in about half an hour. He informed me that Bonaparte arrived two days ago at Fréjus. He added that he found Madame Josephine Bonaparte at Gohier's, where she had been dining, and where she received the first announcement of this important intelligence. And," added Albert, speaking in a half-whisper to my mother, "I understand she was not so well pleased as might have been expected."*

No language can convey any idea of the state of excitement occasioned throughout France by Bonaparte's arrival. Bourrienne was right in saying that it amounted to a positive frenzy. From the 9th of

* Josephine had been very visibly unfaithful to Napoleon during his absence.

October all around us was in continual agitation. On the 10th Josephine set off to meet her husband, but without knowing exactly what road he would take. She thought it likely he would come by way of Burgundy, and therefore Louis and she set off for Lyons.

Madame Bonaparte was a prey to great and well-founded uneasiness. Whether she was guilty or only imprudent, she was strongly accused by the Bonaparte family, who were desirous that Napoleon should obtain a divorce. The elder M. de Caulaincourt stated to us his apprehensions on this point; but whenever the subject was introduced, my mother changed the conversation, because, knowing as she did the sentiments of the Bonaparte family, she could not reply without either committing them or having recourse to falsehood.

She knew, moreover, the truth of many circumstances which M. de Caulaincourt seemed to doubt, and which her situation with respect to Bonaparte prevented her from communicating to him.

Madame Bonaparte committed a great fault in neglecting at this juncture to conciliate her mother-in-law, who might have protected her against those who sought her ruin and effected it nine years later; for the divorce in 1809 was brought about by the joint efforts of all the members of the Bonaparte family, aided by some of Napoleon's most confidential servants, whom Josephine, either as Madame Bonaparte or as Empress, had done nothing to make her friends.

Bonaparte, on his arrival in Paris, found his house deserted; but his mother, sisters, and sisters-in-law, and, in short, every member of his family except Louis, who had attended Madame Bonaparte to Lyons, visited him immediately. The impression made upon him by the solitude of his home and its desertion by its mistress was profound and terrible, and nine years afterwards, when the ties between him and Josephine were severed for ever, he showed that it was not effaced. From not finding her with his family he inferred that she felt herself unworthy of their presence, and feared to meet the man she had wronged. He considered her journey to Lyons as a mere pretence.

M. de Bourrienne* says that for some days after Josephine's return Bonaparte treated her with *extreme coldness*. As he was an eye-witness, why does he not state the whole truth, and say that on her return

* Napoleon's secretary and the author of copious memoirs.

Bonaparte *refused to see her, and did not see her?* It was to the earnest entreaties of her children that she owed the recovery, not of her husband's love, for that had long ceased, but of that tenderness acquired by habit, and that intimate intercourse which made her still retain the rank of consort to the greatest man of his age.

Bonaparte was at this period much attached to Eugène Beauharnais, who, to do him justice, was a charming youth. He knew less of Hortense,* but her youth and sweetness of temper, and the protection of which as his adopted daughter she besought him not to deprive her, proved powerful advocates, and overcame his resistance. In this delicate negotiation it was good policy not to bring any other persons into play, whatever might be their influence with Bonaparte, and Madame Bonaparte did not therefore have recourse either to Barras, Bourrienne, or Berthier. It was expedient that they who interceded for her should be able to say something without the possibility of a reply.

Now, Bonaparte could not, with any degree of propriety, explain to such children as Eugène or Hortense the particulars of their mother's conduct. He was therefore constrained to silence, and had no argument to combat the tears of two innocent creatures at his feet exclaiming: "Do not abandon our mother; it will break her heart! And ought injustice to take from us poor orphans the support of one whom Providence has sent to replace him of whose natural protection the scaffold has already deprived us?"

The scene, as Bonaparte has since stated, was long and painful, and the two children at length introduced their mother, and placed her in his arms. The unhappy woman had awaited his decision at the door of a small back staircase, extended at almost full length upon the stairs, suffering the acutest pangs of mental torture.

Whatever might be his wife's errors, Bonaparte appeared entirely to forget them, and the reconciliation was complete. Of all the members of the family, Madame Leclerc was most vexed at the pardon which Napoleon had granted to his wife. Bonaparte's mother was also very ill-pleased; but she said nothing.

* Eugène and Hortense de Beauharnais were Josephine's children by her first husband.

PART II

The Savior of

France

THE REVOLUTION OF the 8th of November, 1799, in which Bonaparte overthrew the Directoire, and made himself First Consul, followed all this within less than a month. It is undoubtedly the most important of the nine which we have experienced in the course of seven years:* it not only changed the destiny of France, but exercised a powerful influence upon that of Europe and the world. Nevertheless, none of the events which had preceded it had passed with so much apparent calm. France was so tired of the Directoire that anything which should replace it would have been well received, and was happy in obeying an authority that offered some guarantee; the past answered for the future which General Bonaparte announced.

He only was seen in this Consular Triumvirate; Sieyès and Roger-Ducos** stood unobserved in the shade; and the young General served

---

* First, the 31st of May, the fall of the Girondins. 2. The 5th of April, the fall of the priestly party. 3. The 27th of July. 4. The 2nd of April, the defeat of Barrère, Collot d'Herbois, and Billaud-Varennes. 5. The 20th of May, execution of Romme, Soubrani, etc., and defeat of the Jacobins. 6. The 5th of October, the Directorial Government. 7. The 5th of September, the second Emigration. 8. The 19th of June, fight of the Directors among themselves; Sieyès and Barras conquer Merlin of Douai, Treilhard, etc. 9. The days of November, and the establishment of the Consular Government.
** Respectively Second and Third consul.

as the only point of view to eyes fatigued with weeping, which had so long sought, without being aware of it, a light-house that should guide them into port. Thirty days only had elapsed since Bonaparte had landed at Fréjus, and already he had overthrown the shameful Government by which France was weighed down, and had given it a new one, of which the wheels commenced their movement from the first day. He had calmed all inquietudes, dissipated all alarms, and revived all hopes.

There is one report, spread by malevolence, which the friends of Bonaparte have disdained to combat, and which has been finally adopted by credulity and folly,—it is the alarm with which Bonaparte is alleged to have been seized on entering the Hall of the Five Hundred,* at Saint Cloud on the 9th of November. This absurd story would fall to the ground of itself if it were not found in some works which appear to offer a guarantee for the faith they demand.

With respect to the emotion observed in General Bonaparte in the Hall of the Five Hundred at Saint Cloud, the following is its true explanation. On the General's entering the orangery, violent outcries were raised against him: "Down with the new Cromwell!" "No Dictator!" "Outlaw him!"

General Bonaparte knew very well that the Council of Five Hundred was composed of ultra-republicans and of enthusiastic partisans of the current constitution; but he had relied too much upon the success of Lucien's exertions, who had laboured all night to strengthen his brother's party.

Surprise at this reception deprived him for a time of the power to reply. His resolution was speedily taken. It was necessary to decide the question instantly, which could not have been done had the Five Hundred entered upon discussion. He might even have been assassinated; and if he had run the risk, it would not have been a display of valour, but of folly.

With an eagle's glance he saw through the circumstances which surrounded him. This self-consultation lasted perhaps some minutes, and the untalented, judging by themselves, attributed this silence and inaction to fear. But he was not surrounded by those only who were

* The Five Hundred, the lower House of the French Parliament, was known to be anti-Bonapartist.

thus incapable of appreciating his sentiments. I have also collected the opinions of eye-witnesses, who, capable of judging calmly, and possessing, perhaps, as much merit as he whom they looked on, have read his great mind without doing it injustice.

It is difficult to believe all the things reported to be said and done in the very short space of time which General Bonaparte passed in the Hall of the Council of the Five Hundred; it was but an apparition. And, with the same frankness with which I have defended him from the imputation of cowardice, I will add that I do not believe that a poniard was raised against him; it was Lucien who, after his brother's departure, was in real danger.

My brother-in-law was on the Palace steps when Bonaparte came down. His friendship for Lucien made him extremely anxious for the fate of the young Tribune. He saw his brother making his harangue and his tortuous promenade, without taking any step to provide assistance for the President of the Council, who, meanwhile, might be murdered in his curule chair. He approached Bonaparte and mentioned Lucien; the General immediately turned towards an officer who was a few paces distant from him. "Colonel Dumoulin," said he, "take a battalion of grenadiers and hasten to my brother's deliverance."

At length we possessed a Government which promised some sort of security for the future. My mother, whose heart always saw the fair side of everything that was done by a Bonaparte, at first considered this action of Napoleon only as that of a young enthusiast desirous of liberating his country from the evils by which it was desolated.

Never thinking seriously upon politics, she knew the Revolution only by its horrors and its noise. That of the 8th of November, therefore, which was accomplished without firing a gun, she could not understand to be a revolution; though, perhaps, there never had been one more important for us and for Europe. It was the ninth change in seven years, not of the Government, but of the pilot at the helm. Lucien was almost immediately called to the Ministry of the Interior.

Madame Lucien was not pleased with her husband's change of fortune; all this grand display alarmed her. She was obliged now to give up her time to duties which, with reason, she thought far less important than those she had hitherto fulfilled with so much pleasure. She frequently came in a morning to enumerate her troubles to my mother, and to take her advice upon the new and difficult position in which she was placed. But a circumstance which she was far from foreseeing gave her comfort and happiness: it was the change in her favour which took place in the sentiments of her brother-in-law. The penetration of the First Consul discerned the excellent qualities of Madame Lucien's heart; and he soon attached himself to her with a truly fraternal regard.

I must not omit to mention a visit which, a short time before these great events, we made to Lucien's villa of Le Plessis Chamant. All Napoleon's family at that time possessed fine country houses, which they filled with guests. Joseph had Morfontaine, Lucien, Le Plessis Chamant; Madame Leclerc, Montgobert. At Morfontaine, excursions upon the lakes, public readings, billiards, literature, ghost stories more or less mysterious, a perfect ease and liberty, gave charms to the passing hour.

To this must be added that which filled the measure of enjoyment, the most friendly, invariably friendly reception, which was accorded by the master and mistress of the mansion. They did not admit every one, but any person once established as a member of their society was sure of experiencing the most courteous hospitality from Joseph Bonaparte and his lady.

Madame Lucien was very amiable; but her husband's temper was not always the same. That did not lessen the amusement to be found at Le Plessis; perhaps it in some measure contributed to it. I do not remember in my whole life, even in its most joyous seasons, to have laughed so heartily as during the five or six weeks I spent amongst a numerous party of guests at that villa.

M. d'Offreville, from fifty-five to sixty years of age, a man of *great talents,* and of some *pretension* to extreme foppery, was the butt of our mirth and the grand subject of our entertainment. He was a poet, and highly satisfied with his compositions; which, together with the dignity he derived from having held, before the Revolution, the office of cloak-bearer to Monsieur, was the continual theme of his conversation. "It is true," he would sometimes remark, "I have been peculiarly fortunate in my poems: Voltaire, Racine, even Corneille, *have* some feeble passages; my poetry has none." Still, notwithstanding this absurdity, and a figure, countenance, and costume by no means calculated to inspire the respect due to his years, he might have passed well enough in a crowd, if he had had more sense than to expose himself and his follies to the observation and ridicule of a young, gay, and satirical society.

The winter of 1800 was very brilliant in comparison to those which had preceded it. Confidence was restored; every one felt the same sentiments towards General Bonaparte, and at this epoch they were those of attachment. What opportunities has he lost! How much he was beloved at that period! Yes, beloved; and where affection did not exist, admiration and confidence did. The Emigrants returned in great numbers, and had every reason to be satisfied with the reception they met with; if they had vexations to endure from Fouché, on application to the First Consul they were sure to obtain justice.

The First Consul knew too well that the brilliant success of Masséna at Zurich, though it had retarded, had by no means overcome the danger with which we were threatened. Austria, irritated by so many reverses when she had reckoned upon victories, had determined upon a final effort for our destruction, and France was again threatened.

General Masséna, after having resisted a combined Russian and Austrian force of threefold his numbers, had retired upon Genoa, where he was soon shut up with 15,000 men and a population of 100,000 souls; he gallantly sustained a siege of fifty-two days, which should conduce more to his renown than all his victories.

The brave Suchet, separated from his General-in-Chief, effected a retreat upon Nice, and, in concert with Soult and Compans, exhibited prodigies of valour and talent. But almost all the passages of Italy were open, and the Austrians, with General Melas at their head, prepared to make us lament the glory of Zurich; General Otto continued the blockade of Genoa, rejoiced to detain in captivity the conqueror of the Austro-Russian Army.

Napoleon then took one of those resolutions to which genius only is competent. The passage of Saint Bernard was accomplished. Suwaroff had the preceding year declined this enterprise. Napoleon saw its almost impossibility, but saw it only to conquer. His powerful hand no sooner pointed to its glassy summits than the obstacles disappeared. Everything became possible to the exertions of those men, whose talents his penetration had discovered.

General Marmont, commander of the artillery, found means to transport the cannon across the most frightful precipices; he caused the trunks of large trees to be hollowed into the form of troughs, and, placing the cannons and howitzers in them, was thus enabled to have them drawn to the most elevated summit of the pass. The journals have commented largely on this famous passage of Saint Bernard; poetry has celebrated, and the arts have delineated it; but nothing can, at this distance of time, convey an idea of the enthusiasm it communicated to the parties interested in the operation: the letters written from Milan, Suza, Verceil, and La Brunette, by those who, having traversed the Alps, were reconquering Italy, painted in glowing colours the brilliance of this undertaking.

While the French penetrated into Italy by three passes, which the folly of General Melas had left unguarded, General Moreau was acquiring celebrity on the banks of the Rhine. The passage of this river, the taking of Fribourg and Memmingen, the battles of Eugen, Biberach, and Moeskirch, and a multitude of lesser engagements, in which the Austrians lost more than 25,000 in killed and wounded, without calculating prisoners,—all these were the results of a campaign of thirty-three days! Ah! if Moreau had always acted thus, how proud would his country have been of his name.*

During the campaign of Marengo Paris became almost a solitude; from Paris to Turin the road was covered with travellers, who, urged by motives of interest,—some personal, some general,—went to meet the news they were too impatient to await. But this period of expectation was of short continuance. The First Consul crossed Saint Bernard on the 20th of May. On the 21st of June intelligence of the battle of Marengo reached Paris. The effect of this important victory was to raise the funds from twenty-nine to thirty-five francs; six months previous they had been at only eleven.

* The Campaign of the Rhine, which began the 26th of April, 1800, is one of the most glorious military movements of Moreau. Between that day and the 29th of May the Austrians were not only driven across the Rhine, but were obliged to retire beyond Augsbourg.

On that day we had breakfasted and dined at Saint Mandé. The house being solitary, and no one but ourselves arriving in the village from Paris, when we returned to town in the evening we received the news amidst all that delirium of joy which inebriated the people of the Faubourgs, always so vehement in the expression of their sentiments. Two hundred bonfires were blazing at once in the quarter we had to pass through, and the populace, dancing round them, were crying, *"Vive la République! Vive le Premier Consul! Vive l'Armée!"* embracing and congratulating each other as upon a personal and family festivity. A circuitous route home gave us an opportunity of enjoying a truly fine spectacle, that of a great people affectionate and grateful.

"Have you seen," said one to another, "how he writes to the other consuls? That is our man! *'I hope the people of France will be satisfied with its army.'*" "Yes, yes," was exclaimed from all sides. "The people are satisfied;" and shouts of *"Vive la République! Vive Bonaparte!"* were redoubled.

I T was part of the First Consul's policy, not only to bring back prosperity by returning to a gold (as opposed to paper) currency and reviving industry, but also to make Paris the center of pleasure it had been before the Revolution. This was in part to revive the luxury trades—dressmakers, carriage makers, silversmiths, etc. —at which the French had traditionally excelled; but Bonaparte also felt that a revived social life would reflect the solidity of the new regime. Thus, almost as soon as the Consulate began, parties were once more the order of the day. Slowly, at first, the great social round which had characterised Paris before the Revolution revived; only there was a difference. The rich, in whose splendidly decorated houses, the balls, concerts and dinners were given, were mostly men who had made their money supplying the armies during the Directoire and who obviously lacked polish. Thus, the Consul especially depended on Talleyrand, his foreign minister, who not only belonged to one of the oldest and noblest families in France, but had also been a highly fashionable young man before 1789.

Lucien Bonaparte, who occupied, as Minister of the Interior, the Hôtel de Brissac during the winter of 1800, gave there some splendid *fêtes* in the fine gallery which the Duc de Brissac had added solely for this purpose. My mother occasionally took me to these balls; at one of them I remember Madame Bonaparte took her seat at the upper end of the gallery, assuming already the attitude of sovereignty. The ladies all rose at her entrance and when she retired. The good and simple Christine—Lucien's wife—followed her with a gentle smile upon her lips, and the remark was frequently made that if the one was the wife of the First Consul, the Chief Magistrate of the Republic, the other was the wife of his brother, and that Madame Bonaparte might, without derogation of dignity, have accorded the courtesies of society and family intercourse, by giving her arm to Madame Lucien, instead of requiring her to follow or precede her. But Christine was *Madame Lucien,* a name which awoke no good feeling in the mind of Madame Bonaparte, for between her and Lucien a mortal war subsisted.

Apparently, however, she was very friendly both with Lucien and his wife, and it was with an exterior of perfect complaisance that she thus obliged them to follow her. But the amusing part of the business was that Lucien was wholly unconscious of these airs of superiority. The mild Christine often wept in private over the mortification to which she was thus subjected; but she was careful to avoid irritating her husband, who would without a doubt have repaired instantly to the Tuileries, and have there enacted a *scena* before Madame Bonaparte, in which the First Consul would probably have supported him, for he had sincerely attached himself to Madame Lucien since he had learnt to appreciate her excellent qualities.

But a short time afterwards we experienced a heavy affliction in the death of Madame Lucien.* I was affected by it as if she had been connected with us by closer ties than those of friendship. There were not, it is true, between us all the points of contact which constitute an

* She was *enceinte,* and it was said that her death was occasioned by the want of skill of her medical attendant.

intimate connection; but our friendship had strengthened materially since her residence in Paris; our intercourse, if not familiar, was constant; and her matured imagination, the justness of her reasoning, her love for her husband, which taught her to make his gratification her chief object, were all circumstances which daily endeared her to us. My mother, who was tenderly attached to her, bitterly lamented her loss.

We went to see her the day before her death. No visits, it may easily be believed, were permitted; but our intimacy gave us almost the rights of relationship. We found her in a small room adjoining her bedroom. Her apartment had been changed to admit more air, for she was suffocating; and to facilitate her respiration she was lying on a camp bed with two mattresses. This change afforded her some relief, she told us, adding, with a sweet and melancholy smile, but without any accent of complaint, "This bed reminds me of my own bed at St. Maximin,—I can neither sleep nor breathe under those thick curtains and upon those beds of down."

At each word she looked at my mother with a remarkable expression. Her eyes were animated by fever, her cheeks, one in particular, were highly coloured, and varied in tint with every emotion that agitated her, as is always the case with persons suffering under a sudden attack of consumption. "Christine," said Madame Letizia Bonaparte, "you know you must not talk, the physicians have positively forbidden it; and if you mean to recover you must attend to them." The patient shook her head, with the smile so afflicting to those who know that but few days, perhaps but few hours, only are between that moment and dissolution.

"Laurette," said Madame Lucien, "come near me, for I am sure that a death-bed does not alarm you." She took my hand; she perceived the effect which its burning pressure made upon me. "Ah!" said she, "I meant your mother; to you I am but a stranger, and I frighten you, do I not?" I wept, and only replied by embracing her. She pushed me gently away, saying, "No, no; do not embrace me, the air I breathe is poisonous. When I recover, as mamma says—"

We took leave, and this adieu was the last. We saw her no more. She died the following day. As soon as my mother received the intelligence she ordered her horses and hastened to the Hotel of the Interior; Lucien was at Neuilly. My mother went there to seek him, but we were not permitted to see him. My brother-in-law came to our carriage to tell us that he was not in a state to speak even to his sisters or his mother. "I have torn him from that unfortunate house," said he, "where everything reminds him of the loss he has just experienced. He was in the most violent despair."

Madame Lucien was buried in the park of the mansion at Le Plessis Chamant. Her husband erected there to her memory a monument of white marble, surrounded by an iron palisade. When he went to Le Plessis he took his daughters there, that they might pray with him, young as they were. I have heard these notions ridiculed; but for my own part, being of opinion that the dead may be long lamented, I can easily believe that Madame Lucien was a character to excite such regret, and that it might be great and enduring. I shall never forget when my mother was on the point of death in 1799, Madame Lucien was with Madame Bonaparte the mother, and that they came to seek and comfort the poor young girl whom both believed an orphan!

My mother, at the same time, was very unwell; the cruel malady under which she at length succumbed had already taken possession of her. She went out but little, reclined the greater part of the day upon her sofa, and received in the evening the friends who came to bear her company. One of the most assiduous of these was Madame de Caseaux, who was sincerely attached to her. I was myself intimately connected with this lady's daughter, and few days passed that did not bring us together.

My mother at that time had a marriage for me in contemplation; probably it might have conduced to my happiness, but Madame de Caseaux thought not, on account of the great difference of age between my mother's intended son-in-law and myself. "Laurette, Laurette," said she, enforcing her words with her extended finger, "it is not wise, my child, to marry one's grandfather."

My mother did not like contradiction in the most trivial matters; and it may be easily conceived that the very reasonable opposition of her devoted friend on an affair of so much importance irritated her extremely. Her displeasure proceeded to the extent of preventing my visits to Madame de Caseaux when she was unable to accompany me herself; on this point I must say she was unjust to her friend, who would speak her mind to her, or to me before her on the subject of this marriage, but never permitted herself to mention it except in her presence, her rigid principles absolutely interdicting such an interference in the relations of mother and child.

Junot, who had been briefly a prisoner of the English, only returned to Paris after the beginning of the Consulate. Naturally, he hastened to pay his respects to his General, who was then at Malmaison. Junot, in approaching him, was oppressed by a thousand sentiments, in which, no doubt, joy preponderated; but it was chastened by a profound respect, which, "far from diminishing," he has often said to me, "his affection for Bonaparte, had no other effect than to increase it."

"Well, Junot," said the First Consul to him with an enchanting expression of goodness: "Well, and what do you propose to do? I have always told you that I would give you proofs of my friendship as soon as I was in a condition to do so. What are your views? Are you inclined for the service?" and he looked askance at Junot with an air of good-humoured malice. "Have you a mind that I should send you to the Army of the Rhine?"

Junot's colour heightened to crimson, which always happened when he was strongly affected. "Do you already wish to relieve yourself of me, General? However, if you command it, I will go and let General Moreau know that the officers of the Army of Italy have lost none of their courage in Egypt." "There now, my youngster, off at a word!" said the First Consul. "No, no, Monsieur Junot, you do not quit me in such a hurry. I have a great regard for General Moreau, but not sufficient to make him a present of my best friends." And he gave Junot a pull of the ear.

"Junot," continued he, in a more serious tone, "I intend to appoint you Commandant of Paris. It is a place of confidence, particularly at this moment, and I cannot make a better choice. But"—and he looked narrowly round him, as they continued to walk, to observe whether any one was within hearing*—"but you must reflect before you accept this post. You must at once add ten years to your age; for if it be

* This conversation took place in the park of Malmaison, and lasted above an hour; it was the second time that Junot had seen the First Consul, and not the first, as I have said above.

necessary that the Commandant of Paris should be attached to my person, it is equally so that he should be extremely prudent, and that he should pay the utmost attention to whatever concerns my safety." "Ah! General!" exclaimed Junot.

"Be quiet," said the First Consul, "and speak low. Yes, you must watch over my safety. I am surrounded with dangers. I should make no effort to avoid them if I were still the General Bonaparte vegetating at Paris before and even after the 4th of October. Then my life was my own—I cared little for it; but now it is mine no longer; my destiny has been exalted, it is connected with that of a great nation, and for this reason my life is menaced. The Powers of Europe, who would divide France, wish me out of their way." He knit his brow, drew his hand across his forehead as if to banish an importunate idea; then, recovering an air of perfect calmness, he passed his arm under Junot's, and resumed the conversation on State affairs.

"I am about to appoint you Commandant of Paris, as I told you; but you must marry. That is not only suitable to the dignity of the situation you will occupy, but I know you, and require it of you for your own interest."

The First Consul then spoke at length upon the importance which he wished him to acquire in the situation of Commandant of Paris, and gave him such advice on this subject as a father would give to his son. This remarkable conversation lasted above an hour.

On his arrival at Paris Junot had not set up any establishment. Uncertain of his next destination, he thought it useless to make arrangements which an order to depart might compel him to abandon at a moment's notice. He lodged at the house of Méo, a good restaurateur of that period, and whose hotel had some resemblance to the fine establishment of Meurice; but when the First Consul announced to him the remarkable change which the place he was about to occupy would necessarily make in his situation, he desired him at the same time to find a residence suitable to his new dignity; and Junot requested his family, whom he had drawn around him at his hotel, to look out for one. There were, no doubt, great numbers in Paris in the open and cheerful situations of the Faubourg St. Germain or the Chaussée d'Antin, all handsome and newly decorated.

I know not how they persuaded him to fix upon a hotel in the Rue de Verneuil, and even in the dullest and dirtiest part of it; but this house was hired, furnished, and ready for occupation in less than three weeks. Junot installed himself in it as Commandant of Paris in the course of the summer of 1800. With handsome carriages, the finest horses, and the best wines of Burgundy* in his cellars, he then commenced his search for a wife.

The First Consul had especially recommended him to marry a rich wife. "Willingly," replied Junot, "provided she please my taste; but how is that to be done, when almost all heiresses are superlatively ugly?"

He was one morning visiting a lady of his acquaintance, and who happened to be a friend of ours. He spoke of the order he had received from the First Consul to marry, and his own desire to enjoy domestic society. "Have you been to visit Madame de Permon?" inquired the person to whom he spoke. "No; and I reproach myself daily. But why ask?" "Because I believe that her daughter would suit you exactly." "Her daughter!" exclaimed Junot: "she was but a child when I went to Egypt."

"She is young, but no longer a child. She is sixteen. But attend: I have a great inclination to bestow her in marriage at the present moment, but her mother is so bent upon a match she proposes for her, and which has not common-sense, for the intended is old enough to be her grandfather, that she turned a deaf ear when I opened my project to her the day before yesterday; though you must understand that the party in question is a charming bachelor, and one of the first names in France."

"And what would you have me do against all these obstacles?" said Junot, laughing. "You tell me of a woman with twenty admirers; I do not like so many rivals. Mademoiselle Loulou—I believe that is what she was called—must be a little personage of great pretensions, a spoilt child, and thoroughly insupportable. No, no; I kiss your hands;" and, thus taking leave, he hastened out of the house.

From Madame d'Orsay, Junot went to call upon Madame Hamelin,

* A mania which Junot carried to excess was that of being served only by Burgundians. It was natural that his countrymen should have the preference where there was an equality of talent; but if ever so heavy or stupid, the name of Burgundian was sufficient to ensure it. This was the history of the hotel in the Rue de Verneuil; a Burgundian found it for him, a Burgundian furnished it, and a Burgundian was put in charge of the establishment.

another lady also of our acquaintance—an amiable woman who often visited my mother, and was much esteemed by her. Endowed with superior talents, she took pleasure when I was in company with her in bringing me into notice—an unusual mark of kindness which goes direct to the hearts of women in general, and which mine was not backward in acknowledging.

Junot had scarcely entered when his search for a wife became the topic of conversation. "Ah," said she, "there is a young person whom I should like to recommend to you, but she is about to marry and must not be thought of." "So," said Junot, "because she is going to marry, I am not to hear her name." "Oh, with all my heart; you knew her when she was but a child. It is Mademoiselle de Permon."

Junot laughed; it seemed as if I haunted him. However, as Madame Hamelin's frankness and her intelligence were well known to him, and as she had pronounced my name with interest, he asked her some questions concerning me which she answered with the feeling of an amiable and sensible woman.

"Why have you not paid your respects to her mother since your return?" she inquired, seeing his eyes fixed upon the garden with an absent air. "I do not know, but it appears that I have done wisely," he replied, smiling; "for suppose I had fallen in love with your young friend." "Well! you would have married her. Are you not wishing to marry?" "But you have told me yourself that Madame de Permon has a strong desire to marry her to M. de V——, and if she wills it, it will be, for she is not one to yield; I have seen instances of that which I shall not forget."

The same day, Junot, bearing in mind his conversation with Madame Hamelin, found out a person whom he knew to be intimate with my mother and me, and made himself acquainted with all that concerned me, and also with my mother's intentions respecting M. de V——; they were not doubtful, for she had no stronger desire than to conclude the marriage. Junot took his resolution at once; he had engaged to wait upon my mother with Madame Hamelin the following evening; however, he excused himself upon some pretext, but said nothing of the true cause.

At this time, my mother, much out of health, did not quit her sofa. My brother and I exerted ourselves to the utmost to lessen the ennui of her retirement. All her friends, and a crowd of acquaintances, assisted us in endeavouring to make her forget that she was condemned to seclusion for the cure of a complaint from which she might never recover. Thanks to the care and advice of Dr. Backer, she was now mending; as she did not suffer, we were gay. We had music and singing, and when we were not afraid of too much noise we danced to the sound of our own voices. We laughed and enjoyed ourselves; in short, we were happy.

Thus the summer of 1800 passed. The end of September arrived. A great change, meanwhile, had taken place in our family. The two marriages which my mother had proposed for me were broken off: one for pecuniary reasons; the other because I had thrown myself at her feet, entreating her, by her love for me, not to make me a sacrifice and my life miserable.

My mother was perfectly amiable, and she loved me; she therefore broke off a marriage, which in other respects was suitable enough, but to which I had so thorough an antipathy that I should have doomed myself and my husband to misery by saying *Yes.* I was delighted with this change in my lot. My friends—whether from attachment to me, or whether from that sentiment which makes a young girl always unwilling that her companion should marry before her—rejoiced in seeing me at liberty for the following winter.

One evening—it was the 21st of September—about a dozen persons were assembled in my mother's drawing-room, chatting, deciphering charades, and laughing, when suddenly the door opened, and the *valet-de-chambre* announced General Junot. In an instant, as by a stroke of magic, all was silence. This effect was so sudden and so striking that the General was a little embarrassed; but my mother's reception reassured him. She held out her hand to him, reproached him in the most friendly manner for the long delay of his visit, made him sit down by her side, and attended only to him.

The General could not have chosen a worse day for his visit to my mother; no individual of his acquaintance was present. The whole party belonged to the Faubourg St. Germain, and the sort of welcome a General of the Republic would find amongst a circle of emigrants returned within the last six months may be easily imagined. But my mother could act the mistress of the house to perfection. She saw that

General Junot might find himself in a constrained position, and she exerted herself so effectually that he was very soon as much at his ease by her side as if he had been one of our most intimate associates.

The distinctive character of Junot's mind was acuteness and rapidity of penetration. He understood that this was not the place for speaking of the First Consul. He was determined to hear nothing to his prejudice; but neither would my mother, though she was no longer partial to him, have suffered anything to be said against him in her house.

Junot spoke of Egypt, of what he had seen there which was foreign to our manners, with that ability which all who knew him are so well aware of. Albert, who had been spending the evening at Madame Leclerc's, soon came in, and his presence emboldened Junot to propose to my mother that she should, on the following day, go to the Hôtel de Salm to witness the procession which was to pass the Quai de Voltaire.

The occasion was worth the trouble; it was the translation of the body of Turenne from the *Jardin des Plantes,* where it had been deposited since the violation of the tombs of St. Denis, to the *Musée des Augustins aux Invalides.* As Junot was to superintend the ceremony in his quality of Commandant of Paris, he was desirous that we should see him in his glory, and I believe this was the true motive of the zeal he manifested in overcoming my mother's objections on the score of her health.

"Well, then," said she at length, "I will go and see our two heroes pass, the living and the dead: but the living soldier must promise to come and dine with me after he has seen M. le Maréchal installed in his new habitation, or I shall not go." Junot promised, and retired, leaving a most advantageous impression on a party which, with the exception of my mother and brother, were certainly by no means predisposed in his favour.

The following day we repaired to the Hôtel de Salm; we were conducted to a drawing-room, in which Junot had placed a large armchair, with pillows and a footstool, for my mother; the *valet-de-chambre* of the General said he was ready to execute any orders that might be given to him.

"Does your master," replied my mother, "suppose I am one of those invalids to whom he is conveying the body of Turenne?" She was,

The First Consul at Malmaison, 1802 by Jean–Baptiste Isabey.
(COL. MALMAISON, MUSÉE NATIONAL)

The Coronation of Empress Josephine in the Cathedral of Notre Dame in Paris, 1804 (Detail) by Jacques–Louis David.

(COL. MUSÉE DU LOUVRE, PARIS)

Marriage of Prince Jérôme Bonaparte and Princess Catherine of Wurtemberg, 1807 (Detail) by Jean–Baptiste Regnault.

Letizia Bonaparte (Madame Mère) by Baron François Gérard.

Joseph Bonaparte, King of Spain by Baron François Gérard.
(COL. VERSAILLES, MUSÉE NATIONAL)

Pauline Bonaparte, Princess Borghese, 1808 by
Marie–Guilhelmine Benoist. (COL. VERSAILLES, MUSÉE NATIONAL)

Caroline, Queen of Naples, and Her Four Children by Baron
François Gérard. (COL. VERSAILLES, MUSÉE NATIONAL)

Portrait of Hortense by Baron François Gérard. (COL. VERSAILLES, MUSÉE NATIONAL)

however, very sensible of the attentions paid to her, and when Junot passed, he saluted us in so marked a manner as to draw the attention of every one; a person in the crowd was heard to say, on seeing the General bow to my mother repeatedly: "No doubt that is the widow of the Marshal Turenne!"*

Ten days had elapsed from the 21st of September, when Junot first presented himself at my mother's, and now regularly every night he repeated his visit. He never spoke to me, but placed himself beside my mother's sofa, chatted with her, or with any of his acquaintance who happened to be present, but never approached the group to which I belonged, and if at this epoch he had ceased to come to our house I might have affirmed that I scarcely knew him.

But, however undistinguished I had been by any attention on his part, the society in which we moved had already decided that I was his destined bride; the report was brought to me by my friend Laure de Caseaux, and, with great indignation, I repeated it to my mother and brother; they partook of my feelings upon the subject, and, having received a summons to attend my drawing-master, I left them in my mother's bedroom still discussing the steps to be pursued, for it was yet but noon, and, on account of the weak state of her health, she did not rise before that time.

While we were thus respectively engaged, a carriage drove up to the door, and a waiting-maid came in to inquire if General Junot could be admitted. "Yes, yes, let him come up," said my mother; "but, good God! what can bring him here at this hour?" Junot had scarcely entered the chamber before he asked permission to close the door, and, seating himself by the bedside, said to my mother, as he took her hand, that he was come to present a request, adding, with a smile: "And it must be granted." "If it be possible, it is done," said my mother.

"That depends upon you and him," replied the General, turning to Albert. He stopped a moment, and then continued, in the tone of a person recovering from a violent embarrassment: "I am come to ask the

* Turenne died in 1684.

85

hand of your daughter; will you grant it me? I give you my word," and he proceeded in a tone of more assurance, "and it is that of a man of honour, that I will make her happy. I can offer her an establishment worthy of her and of her family. Come, Madame de Permon, answer me, with the frankness with which I put my request, Yes or No."

"My dear General," said my mother, "I shall answer with all the frankness you have claimed, and which you know to belong to my character; and I will tell you that a few minutes before your arrival I was saying to Albert that you were the man whom, of all others, I should choose for my son-in-law."

"Indeed!" exclaimed Junot, joyfully.

"Yes; but that says nothing for your request. First, you must understand that she has no fortune; her portion is too small to be of any value to you. Then, I am very ill, and I am not sure that my daughter will be willing to quit me at present; besides, she is still very young. Reflect well upon all this, and add to it that my daughter has been educated amidst a society and in habits which it is very possible may displease you. Reflect for eight or ten days, and then come to me, and we will enter further into your projects."

"I will not wait twenty-four hours," said Junot, firmly. "Listen, Madame de Permon. I have not taken my present step without having fully made up my mind. Will you grant me your daughter? Will you, Permon, give me your sister? I love her, and I again swear to you I will make her as happy as a woman can be."

Albert approached General Junot, and, taking his hand, said in a voice of emotion, "My dear Junot, I give you my sister with joy; and believe me, the day when I shall call you brother will be one of the happiest of my life." "And I," said my mother, extending her arms to him, "am happy beyond description in calling you my son." Junot, much moved, threw himself into her arms. "Well," said he, "and what will you think of me now?—that I am very childish and weak, I fear;" and, turning to my brother, he embraced him several times in a delirium of joy. "But now," said he, after a few moments, "I have still another favour to ask,—one upon which I set a high value, for it is most interesting to me."

"What is it?" asked my mother. "I desire, extraordinary as it may appear to you, to be myself permitted to present my petition to your daughter." My mother exclaimed against this demand; such a thing had never been heard of—it was absolute folly. "That may be," said Junot, in a firm but respectful tone; "but I have determined upon it; and since you have received me, since I am now your son, why would you refuse me this favour? Besides, it is in your presence and her brother's that I would speak to her." "Ah, that makes a difference," said my mother; "but why this whim?" "It is not a whim; it is, on the contrary, so very reasonable an idea that I should never have believed myself capable of it. Do you consent?"

My mother answered "Yes," and a messenger was despatched to my study, where I was drawing with M. Vigliano, to summon me to my mother,—an order which I obeyed immediately with the greatest tranquillity, for I supposed General Junot to be long since gone.

It is impossible to describe my sensations when, on opening the chamber-door, I perceived General Junot seated by my mother's bed-side, holding one of her hands, and conversing in an animated manner with her. The General rose, offered me his place, took a seat beside me, then, having looked towards my mother, said to me in the most serious tone:

"Mademoiselle, I am happy enough to have obtained the consent of your mother and brother to my solicitation for your hand; but I have to assure you that this consent, otherwise so valuable to me, will become void unless at this moment you can declare here in their presence that you willingly acquiesce in it. The step I am at this moment taking is not perhaps altogether consistent with established forms—I am aware it is not; but you will pardon me if you reflect that I am a soldier, frank even to roughness, and desirous of ascertaining that in the most important act of my life I am not deceiving myself. Will you, then, condescend to tell me whether you will become my wife, and, above all, whether you can do so without any repugnance?"

Since I had been seated in the chair in which General Junot had placed me, I felt as if in an extraordinary dream. I heard distinctly, and understood what was said, but no part of it seemed to affect me; and yet it was necessary to give an immediate answer in one word, upon which the fate of my whole life was to depend.

The most perfect silence reigned in the apartment. Neither my mother nor my brother could with propriety interfere, and the General could only wait my answer. However, at the expiration of about ten minutes, seeing that my eyes still continued fixed on the ground, and that I did not reply, General Junot thought himself obliged to construe my silence into a refusal, and, always impetuous, still more so, perhaps, in his feelings than in his will, he insisted upon knowing his fate that very instant.

"I see," said he, with an accent of bitterness, "that Madame de Permon was right when she told me that her consent was nothing in this affair. Only, Mademoiselle, I entreat you to give me an answer, be it *yes* or *no.*"

My brother, who saw the change in Junot's manner, inclined towards me and whispered in my ear, "Take courage, love, speak out; he will not be offended, even if you refuse him." "Come, come, my child! you must answer the General," said my mother. "If you will not speak to him, give me your answer, and I will repeat it to him."

I was sensible that my situation began to be ridiculous, and that I ought to speak; but all the power upon earth could not have made me articulate a word nor raise my eyes from the carpet. From my first entrance into the room my emotion had been so violent that the palpitation of my heart threatened to burst my corset. The blood now mounted to my head with such violence that I heard nothing but a sharp singing in my ears, and saw nothing but a moving rainbow. I felt a violent pain, and, raising my hand to my forehead, stood up and made my escape so suddenly that my brother had not time to detain me.

He ran after me, but could nowhere find me. The fact was that, as if started by an invisible power, I had mounted the stairs with such rapidity that in two seconds I had reached the top of the house, and, on recovering my recollection, found myself in the attic. I came down again, and, going to take refuge in my brother's apartments, met him returning from a search for me.

He scolded me for being so unreasonable. I wept, and reproached him bitterly for the scene which had just taken place. He excused himself, embraced me, and drew me into a conversation which calmed my spirits; but he could by no means persuade me to return to my mother's room. I was resolute not to appear there again till General Junot was gone.

My brother on his return addressed the General, whom he found still much agitated. "I was," said he, "my dear General, for a moment of your opinion, and permitted my sister to be brought here; but I now see that we have acted in this matter like children, and she, young as she is, has convinced me of it." "Where is my poor Loulou, then?" said my mother; "I told you, my dear Junot, that such a step was absurd. Where is she?" "In my room," said Albert, "where I have promised her that she shall not be molested." "And my answer?" said Junot, with a gloomy air. "Your answer, my friend, is as favourable as you can desire. My sister will be proud to bear your name—I repeat her own words; as to any other sentiment, you cannot ask it of her without disrespect." "I am satisfied!" exclaimed Junot, embracing my brother. "She will be proud to bear my name, and I am content."

The conversation now became more calm, and after a short interval my mother said to Junot: "But tell me how you have achieved the greatest of your victories; how you have induced the First Consul to give his consent to your marriage with my daughter?" "He does not know it yet," replied Junot. "He does not know it!" exclaimed my mother; "you are come to ask my daughter in marriage, and the First Consul does not know it? Permit me to observe, my dear General, that your conduct has been very inconsiderate." "I request you, madame, to inform me in what respect my conduct can be blamable," Junot replied, with some *hauteur*.

"How can you ask such a question? Do you not know the coldness, and even disunion, which has succeeded to the friendship that once existed between the First Consul and myself? Do you think that he will consent to my daughter becoming your wife, and especially without fortune? And what, let me ask, would you do if when you communicate your intended marriage to him, and ask his assent, he should refuse it?"

"I should marry without it," answered Junot, very resolutely. "I am no longer a child; and in the most important transaction of my life I shall consult my own convenience only, without listening to the petty passions of others." "You say that you are no longer a child, and you reason as if you were but six years old. Would you dissolve your connection with your benefactor and friend because it pleases you to make what he will call an imprudent marriage—that is to say, a marriage without fortune? For that is the reason he will give you; for you may easily suppose he will not tell you that it is because he does not like me. What will you do, what will you answer, when he gives you the option between my daughter and himself?"

"But he will never do so!" exclaimed Junot; "and if he could to such an extent forget my services and my attachment, I should always remain a faithful son of France; she will not repulse me; and I am a general officer." "And do you think us capable of accepting such a sacrifice?" said my mother. "And though my daughter is but sixteen years old, can you have formed so unworthy an opinion of her as to suppose that she would thus abuse her power over you?"

"My dear General," said Albert, who had not yet uttered a word during this discussion, "I believe that all this will be easily arranged; but permit me to observe, in my turn, that you have been a little too hasty in this affair; nevertheless, I have no doubt that all will be right, for I do not think with my mother that the First Consul will interfere as a party, and still less as a judge, in a question of such a nature as this."

Junot listened attentively; then, looking at his watch, he suddenly took up his hat, and said to my mother: "I am going to the Tuileries. The First Consul is not yet in council. I will speak to him, and in an hour I shall return." He pressed Albert's hand, kissed my mother's, descended the staircase at two steps, jumped into his carriage, and cried out to the coachman, "To the Tuileries at a gallop, only do not overturn us, because I have important business there."

"Where is the First Consul?" was his salutation to Duroc. "With Madame Bonaparte." "My friend, I must speak to him this very instant." "How agitated you are!" said Duroc, observing his flushed cheek and trembling voice. "Is there alarming news?" "No, no; but I must see the First Consul; I must this instant; I will tell you by and by why I am so peremptory."

Duroc pressed his hand, and as he understood that he could oblige him, he lost no time in acquitting himself of his commission; and in a few moments Junot was introduced to the cabinet of the First Consul. "General," said he, entering at once upon the subject, "you have testified a desire to see me married; the thing is settled—I am about to marry." "Ah! ah! and you have run away with your wife? Your air is perfectly wild." "No, General," replied Junot, endeavouring to calm his feelings for the crisis; for all my mother's objections started at once to his mind, and he felt fearful of a rebuff. "Whom are you going to marry, then?" said the First Consul, seeing that Junot did not speak. "A person whom you have known from her childhood, whom you used to love, General, of whom every one speaks well, and with whom I am distractedly in love,—Mademoiselle de Permon."

The First Consul, contrary to his custom, was not at that moment walking while he conversed. He was seated at his desk, which he was notching with his penknife. On hearing the name, he leapt from his seat, threw away his penknife, and seized Junot by the arm, asking, "Whom did you say you meant to marry?" "The daughter of Madame de Permon, that child whom you have so often held upon your knee when you yourself were young, General." "That is not possible; Loulou is not marriageable: how old is she?" "Sixteen years within a month." "It is a very bad marriage you would make; there is no fortune; and, besides, how can you determine to become the son-in-law of Madame de Permon? Do you not know that woman as she is? You must mind what you are about. She is a spirit——" "Permit me to observe, General, that I do not propose to marry my mother-in-law; and, moreover, I believe——" Here he stopped short and smiled. "Well, and what do you believe?" "That the discussions which had arisen between yourself and Madame de Permon have blended a shade of prejudice with the judgment you have formed of her. What I know perfectly well is, that she is surrounded by numerous friends of long standing, and I have seen the love which her children bear her. Her daughter lavishes such care upon her as only the heart of a devoted child is capable of, and has done so for two years past, to the injury of her own health. Her son——" "Ah, that is a brave youth!" "Well, General, and do you believe that he could be what he is to his mother if Madame de Permon were not herself not merely a good mother, but an excellent woman? Children are respectful and attentive to their mother, but to be to her what Mademoiselle Laurette and her brother are to Madame de Permon, she must deserve their respect. Ask Madame Bonaparte, Madame Joseph, Madame Murat;* these ladies will tell you

* Caroline Bonaparte was married to Joachim Murat, a brave and brilliant general.

how meritorious has been the conduct of Madame de Permon's children from the commencement of her severe illness." "Is she so very ill, then?" inquired the First Consul, with interest. "Very ill; and the utmost care is necessary to her recovery, and to the relief of her sufferings."

The First Consul walked the room without speaking; he was serious, but not out of humour. At length he said, "But without fortune, I suppose; what portion has this young person?" "I have not inquired." "You were right in saying just now that you were distractedly in love. What extravagance! Did I not particularly recommend you to seek a rich wife? for you are not rich yourself." "I beg your pardon, my General, I am very rich. Are you not my protector, my father? And when I inform you that I love a young girl who is poor, but without whom I should be miserable, I know that you will come to my assistance, and portion my betrothed."

The First Consul smiled. "Oh, is that it? But how has this illness happened? Have you long been a visitor at Madame Permon's?" "Eleven days, General; but it is two months since my attention has been attracted towards her daughter. I have been spoken to about her, and one of our mutual friends wished to promote this marriage; but Mademoiselle Laurette was then destined to another husband, and after all that I had heard of her, I would not visit the mother lest I should fall in love with the daughter. In the interval, the projected marriage was broken off. I went, accordingly, to pay my respects to Madame de Permon, and my resolution was soon taken. But now, sir, I am about to give you still further advantage over me—I have acted more madly than you can imagine." Here he repeated the scene of the morning in its minutest details. The First Consul listened in silence, with great attention, and when Junot's narrative was ended, he replied:

"Though I recognize in all that you have just said the character of Madame de Permon, I cannot but approve her arguments as they respect me, and the sacrifice you have offered in the true spirit of a Paladin of the Crusades could not be accepted either by her, or Permon. You have, however, cut me off from the power of even remonstrating against this rash act by the confidence you have just reposed in me; besides, you will not, as you say, marry your mother-in-law, and if the young person be really such as you describe, I see no reason for being severe on the article of fortune. I give you 100,000 francs for your bride's portion, and 40,000 for her wedding-clothes. Adieu, my friend; I wish you happiness!" So saying, he pressed Junot's hand warmly, and said, laughing, as he resumed his seat, "Oh, you will have a terrible mother-in-law!" then added with a more serious air: "But an amiable and worthy brother-in-law."

The preparations for my marriage were proceeding with activity; General Junot was extremely desirous that it should take place immediately. He had induced Madame Bonaparte the mother and Madame Leclerc to persuade my mother, and the 20th of October was the day already fixed upon before I had been consulted upon the subject. It was on the 10th of that month that my mother proposed to me this speedy separation, to which no arguments she could use had any effect in reconciling me. M. de Caulaincourt, an old and faithful friend of the family, was summoned to the conference. Seated between my brother and myself beside my mother's sofa, he earnestly enforced my mother's plea of the impatience of my lover, and, finding this insufficient, began to explain that to his knowledge Junot was at present the object of much intrigue at the Tuileries; that Madame Bonaparte, always apprehensive of the influence which early intimacy and a sentiment of gratitude for early favours might give my mother over the mind of the First Consul, had seen their mutual coldness with great complacency; had never attempted to widen the breach by irritation, judiciously considering that in such cases total oblivion is the most eligible result, and was now extremely disconcerted to find that Junot's marriage was likely to bring the family again into notice. To obviate this, she had attempted to produce a change in his views, and to direct them towards Mademoiselle Leclerc. To this, which was equally new to all his auditors, he added that delays are dangerous, that the First Consul might be induced by the influence of his wife to withdraw his consent, and that Junot himself might be worked to her purpose. My mother's pride now began to take the alarm, and her kind friend was obliged to soothe it to the utmost; and, finally, the result of all this consultation was that I gave my consent to fix the day for the 30th of October; sooner than this I positively refused to quit my mother.

My own marriage has so much occupied my attention that I have neglected to mention that of Madame Murat, which took place soon after, the 8th November. Caroline Bonaparte was a very pretty girl, fresh as rose; not to be compared, for the regular beauty of her features, to Madame Leclerc, though more pleasing perhaps by the expression of her countenance and the brilliance of her complexion, but by no means possessing the perfection of figure which distinguished her elder sister. Her head was disproportionately large, her bust was too short, her shoulders were too round, and her hips too thick; but her feet, her hands, and her arms were models, and her skin resembled white satin seen through pink glass; her teeth were fine, as were those of all the Bonapartes; her hair was light, but no way remarkable. As a young girl Caroline was charming; when her mother first brought her to Paris, in 1798, her beauty was in all its rosy freshness. I have never seen her appear to so much advantage since that time. Magnificence did not become her; brocade did not hang well upon her figure; and one feared to see her delicate complexion fade under the weight of diamonds and rubies.

It has been asserted that when Murat demanded Mademoiselle Bonaparte in marriage, the First Consul made great difficulties in giving his consent.

The true cause of Napoleon's little regard for Murat (for, notwithstanding their alliance, he never was attached to him) was Murat's imprudent conduct when he came to Paris to present the banners taken by the Army of Italy and after his return to headquarters. Those who know the character of Napoleon as I know it will easily understand that Murat would lose much ground in his General's favour by whispering a boast of his credit with the Directory and the War Ministry through the means of Madame Bonaparte and Madame Tallien. I will here give an anecdote which occurred soon after he had rejoined his General, and which reached the ears of the latter on that very day. Junot was at that time wounded and in his bed, and could not have been the informer upon a fact of which he was himself ignorant for some time.

Murat gave a breakfast to Lavalette, some other officer of the general staff, and many of his friends, chief young men belonging to the cavalry, whose company Murat preferred to associating with officers of his own rank; perhaps from that habit of boasting, for which he afterwards became so remarkable, and to which he would find his inferiors more complaisant than his equals.

The breakfast had been very gay. Much champagne had been drunk, and there seemed no occasion for a supplement; but Murat proposed punch, adding that he would make it himself.

"You never drank better," said he to his companions, "I have learned to make it from a charming Creole; and if I could add all the circumstances of that education, you would like it still better." Then, ringing for his valet, he ordered not only all that was necessary for ordinary punch, but a number of accessories, such as tea, oranges instead of lemons, etc., and said aloud: "And be sure not to make a mistake; bring that Jamaica rum which was given me at Paris."

He went to his travelling-case and took from it a beautiful utensil of silver gilt, made purposely to extract the juice of lemons or oranges without squeezing them with the hand. He then proceeded in the whole affair in a method which proved that he had been under a good instructor. The punch was found excellent, so excellent that the bowl was emptied and filled again several times; confidence increased with each renewal; the guests wished to know how such good things were to be learned, and Murat, who perhaps was not quite clear-headed, replied that the finest and prettiest woman in Paris had taught him this and many other things.

Then, as may be supposed, questions multiplied; with the mirth and folly of childhood, they desired to hear the whole history. It appears Murat could not resist, but related much that was unsuitable to the breakfast-table of a party of hussar officers. But the most unlucky part of the affair in its consequences was that, without pronouncing any name, he indicated so plainly the personages concerned that inductions were speedily drawn, and commentaries followed. A breakfast, a dinner, and a supper, all in the same day, in the country, that is to say, the Champs-Élysées, formed the principal facts of this boastful tale, and the finest woman in Paris (the prettiest was not quite so clear), all this told the name; and these young heads translated it with much more ease than at that moment they could have construed a line of Virgil.

Further explanation was unnecessary; when one of the party, taking up the lemon-squeezer, discovered in his examination of it that it had a cipher upon the handle which was not that of Murat. "Ah," exclaimed the young madcap, "now for full information; here we may learn to read as well as to make punch;" and, brandishing the little utensil which Murat, who retained sense enough to see that this was going too far, wished to snatch from him, he looked again at the handle, and began, "Ba, be, bi, bo; Bo,—bon,—bona!" Murat at length succeeded in quieting him, and, the breakfast finished, the chief of the guests forgot the particulars of the morning's entertainment. But two or three, who felt that they might speak without indiscretion, since nothing had been confided to them, repeated the whole history of the punch; on a theatre so fraught with wonders as Italy was at that moment the tale made little impression generally, but all the circumstances of the bacchanalian scene reached the ears of the General. His jealous humour was awakened, and for a moment he proposed requiring an explanation from Murat, but reflection showed him how unwise such a proceeding would be, and he abandoned all thoughts of inquiring into the true circumstances of the case; whether they ever came to his knowledge I know not.

The silver lemon-squeezer disappeared. Murat professed to regret its loss extremely, and reported that some of his giddy companions had thrown it out of the window in sport, and that it had never been recovered. He averred also that the young man who pretended to have read the cipher had his eyes so dazzled by the fumes of the punch that he had, in fact, mistaken M for B, and that the letter J stood for his own name (Joachim).

This scandal was talked of for twenty-four hours, but offered only vague conjectures to those who were but imperfectly acquainted with the parties concerned, which was the case with almost all the guests except Lavalette and Duroc, who thought it advisable not to take further notice of it, and thought, indeed, that the cipher might have been J. M. For my own part, I believe so too; but General Bonaparte, I have reason to think, was not so credulous; and the favour shown Murat on occasion of the expedition to Egypt—a favour which certainly his General had not solicited for him—seemed to confirm his impolitic boasting, and to indicate that his interest with the Directory was supported by a protector who could not please Napoleon. With respect to the fact itself, I apprehend that there was more of levity in it on Murat's part than of reality. I have known the opinion of members of the family respecting it, who perhaps saw things in their worst light, from being in a degree inimical to Josephine. They excused Murat on account of his youth, but were not so indulgent towards Madame Bonaparte.

When, therefore, Murat requested the hand of Caroline Bonaparte, the First Consul was very much disposed to refuse it.

Murat's good looks and the nobleness of his figure is a matter which will bear discussion. I do not admit that a man is handsome because he is large and always dressed for a carnival. Murat's features were not good, and I may even add that, considering him as detached from his curled hair, his plumes, and his embroidery, he was plain. There was something of the negro in his countenance, though his nose was not flat; but very thick lips, and a nose which, though aquiline, had nothing of nobleness in its form, gave to his physiognomy a mongrel expression at least. I shall speak again of his person and of his talents.

During the month of October Junot looked in upon us every morning, and then came to dinner, having his coach or his cabriolet always filled with drawings, songs, and a heap of trifles from the *Magazine of Sikes,* or the *Petit Dunkerque,* for my mother and me; and never forgetting the bouquet, which, from the day of our engagement to that of our marriage, he never once failed to present me. It was Madame Bernard, the famous *bouquetière* to the Opera, who arranged these nosegays with such admirable art; she has had successors, it is true, but the honour of first introducing them is her own.

On the 11th of October Junot came early in the morning, which was not usual. He was still more serious than on the day of the conversation about conspiracies. We were to go this evening to the first representation of *Les Horaces* of Porta and Guillard.

My mother was better, and I looked forward to the evening as a great treat. It was then with no very pleasant emotion that I heard Junot ask my mother not to go to the Opera. His reasons for making this request were most singular. The weather was bad, the music was bad, the poem was good for nothing; in short, the best thing we could do was to stay at home.

My mother, who had prepared her toilet for all the magnificence of a first representation, and who would not have missed it had it been necessary to pass through a tempest, and listen to the dullest of poems, would not attend to any of Junot's objections; and I was delighted, for I placed full confidence in the Abbé Rose, who said that the music was charming. The General, however, still insisted; so much obstinacy at length made an impression upon my mother, who, taking the General's arm, said to him anxiously, "Junot, why this perseverance? is there any danger? are you afraid?"

"No, no," exclaimed Junot. "I am afraid of nothing but the ennui you will experience, and the effect of the bad weather. Go to the Opera. But," continued he, "if you decide upon going, permit me to beg you not to occupy the box you have hired, but to accept mine for the night."

"I have already told you, my dear General, that it is impossible. It would be contrary to all established customs, and I am particular in supporting them. Would you have my daughter, your betrothed bride, but not yet your wife, appear in a box which all Paris knows to be yours? And for what reason am I to give up mine?" "Because it is at the side, which is a bad situation for the Opera; and it is, besides, so near to the orchestra that Mademoiselle Laurette's delicate ear will be so offended she will not, for the next fortnight, be able to perform herself."

"Come, come," said my mother, "there is no commonsense in all this. We will go and hear this second Cimarosa, who, no doubt, will not equal his prototype; but at all times a first representation is a fine thing. Do you dine with us?" "I cannot," answered the General, "I cannot even come to offer you my arm; but I shall certainly have the honour of seeing you at the Opera."

On quitting my mother, the General went up to Albert's apartment, and found him in his study, surrounded by those peaceful labours which so usefully filled his time. He earnestly recommended him not to lose sight of my mother and myself throughout the evening. "I have endeavoured," said he, "to persuade your mother not to go out this evening, and especially against going to the Opera, but without any effect. There may be trouble there, though there is no actual danger to fear; but I confess I should be better pleased if persons in whom I am interested were at home. Your prudence, my dear Albert, guarantees your silence; you understand my situation;" and he left him, promising an explanation of what he had just said the next morning, if not that very night.

My brother came down to my mother, and the thoughtfulness of his air struck us immediately. "Ah!" said my mother, "what means all this? Junot would prevent our going to the Opera; and here is another preparing to accompany us there as if he were going to a funeral. It is worth while, certainly, to lay plans for gaiety if they are to be executed in such solemnity." My brother could not help laughing at this petulant sally, and this restored my mother's good-humour. We dined earlier than usual, and took our seats at the Opera at eight o'clock.

The boxes were already filled. The ladies were all elegantly dressed. The First Consul had not yet taken his place. His box was on the first tier to the left, between the columns which separate the centre from the side-boxes. My mother remarked that the eyes of all persons in the pit, and of nearly all in the boxes, were directed towards it. "And," said Albert, "observe also the expression of interest and impatience on the part of the audience."

"Bah!" said my mother, "though I am near-sighted, I can see very well that it is but curiosity. We are always the same people. Lately, at that *fête* of the Champ-de-Mars, when the Abbé Sieyès"* (she never used any other denomination) "wore feathers like the canopy of the Holy Sacrament under which he formerly carried the Host, did not every one, and myself amongst the first, strain our necks to obtain a better sight of him? And the chief of the *band of sharpers,* was not he also the point of attraction for all eyes in the day of his power? Well, this man is now master in his turn, and he is gazed at as the others have been before him."

My brother persisted in saying that the First Consul was loved, and that the others had only been feared. I was quite of his opinion, and my mother only replied by shrugging her shoulders. At this moment the

* Then one of the five Directors.

door of the First Consul's box opened, and he appeared with Duroc, Colonel Savary, and, I think, Colonel Lemarrois. Scarcely was he perceived, when, from all parts of the theatre, arose simultaneously plaudits so unanimous that they appeared to constitute but one and the same sound.

The stage was thought of no more; all heads were turned towards General Bonaparte, and a stifled hurrah accompanied the clapping of hands and stamping of feet. He saluted the audience with much smiling grace; and it is well known that the least smile enlivened his naturally stern countenance, and imparted a striking charm to it. The applause continuing, he inclined his head two or three times without rising, but still smiling.

My mother observed him through her glass, and did not lose one of his movements. It was the first time she had seen him since the great events of Brumaire, and he so entirely occupied her attention that General Junot came into the box without her perceiving him. "Well, do you find him changed since you saw him last?" said he.

My mother turned hastily round, and was as much embarrassed as a young girl who should be asked why she looked out of the window when the person who most interested her was passing. We all laughed, and she joined us. Meanwhile, the orchestra had recommenced its harmonious clamour, giving the diapason to Laforet and Lainez, who both screamed in emulation who should be best, or rather who should be worst; and Mademoiselle Maillaret chimed in with lungs worthy of a Roman lady of ancient times, making us regret that Madame Chevallier no longer occupied the scene. My mother, whose Italian ear could not support such discord, often turned towards General Junot to speak of the enchanting songs of Italy, so soft and so sweet.

At one of these moments Andoche slightly touched her arm, and made her a sign to look to the First Consul's box. General Bonaparte had his glass directed towards us, and as soon as he perceived that my mother saw him, he made two or three inclinations in the form of a salutation: my mother returned the attention by one movement of her head, which was probably not very profound, for the First Consul, as will be shortly seen, complained to my mother herself of her coldness towards him this night. Junot would also have reproached her at the instant had not one of the officers of the garrison of Paris tapped at the door of the box to request him to come out. It was an adjutant named Laborde, the most cunning and crafty of men. His figure and his manner were at this moment indescribable. Albert, who now saw him for the first time, wished for a pencil to make a sketch of him.

General Junot was absent but a few moments. When he returned to the box, his countenance, which all day had been serious, and even melancholy, had resumed in a moment its gaiety and openness, relieved of all the clouds which had veiled it. He leaned towards my mother, and said very low, not to be heard in the next box:

"Look at the First Consul; remark him well." "Why would you have me fix my eyes on him?" said my mother; "it would be ridiculous." "No, no, it is quite natural. Look at him with your glass; then I will ask the same favour from Mademoiselle Laurette." I took the opera-glass from my brother, and looked at him in my turn. "Well," said the General, "what do you observe?" "Truly," I replied, "I have seen an admirable countenance; for I can conceive nothing superior to the strength in repose, and greatness in quiescence, which it indicates." "You find its expression, then, calm and tranquil?" "Perfectly. But why do you ask that question?" said I, much astonished at the tone of emotion with which the General had put this question.

He had not time to answer. One of his aides-de-camp came to the little window of the box to call him. This time he was absent longer, and on his return wore an air of joy; his eyes were directed towards the box of the First Consul with an expression which I could not understand. The First Consul was buttoning the gray coat which he wore over the uniform of the Consular Guard, and was preparing to leave the box. As soon as this was perceived, the acclamations were renewed as vehemently as on his entrance.

At this moment, Junot, no longer able to conquer his emotion, leaned upon the back of my chair and burst into tears. "Calm yourself," said I, leaning towards him to conceal him from my mother, who would certainly have exercised her wit upon him. "Calm yourself, I entreat you. How can a sentiment altogether joyful produce such an effect upon you?" "Ah!" replied Junot, quite low, but with an expression I shall never forget; "he has narrowly escaped death! the assassins are at this moment arrested."

I could hardly restrain an exclamation, but Junot peremptorily silenced me. "Say nothing; you will be overheard. Let us hasten out," said he. He was so much agitated that he gave me my mother's shawl, and her mine; then, taking my arm, made me hastily descend the staircase which led to a private door opening upon the Rue de Louvois, reserved for the authorities and the diplomatic corps. My mother, conducted by my brother, rejoined us at the glass door, and jestingly asked the General if he meant to carry me off. Junot, though cheerful, still had his mind too much fixed on important subjects to reply to her raillery; my thoughts were wholly occupied by the few words he had said in the box, and the silence and haste imposed upon me alarmed and seriously affected me. Junot observed my paleness, and, fearing that I should faint, ran into the street, though it rained in torrents, without listening to my mother, to find our carriages and servants.

He met with his own first; my mother did not perceive it till she was already on the step, but immediately made an effort to withdraw. Junot, reminding her of the rain and her health, with a gentle pressure compelled her to get in; then whispering to me, "All is right; for Heaven's sake compose yourself, and say nothing!" called to his coachman, "Rue Sainte Croix." Then, taking Albert's arm, they went together to seek my mother's carriage, in which they followed, or rather preceded us; for we found them at home on our arrival.

My mother was throughout her life a sort of worshipper of etiquette, and of the usages which should form the code of elegance and good-breeding. If she ever failed in them herself, it was from an excessive vivacity which she could not always command; not from ignorance of what was correct, or any intention of neglecting it. Notwithstanding her acute and amiable disposition, she attached an extreme importance to these trifles; more so than can be conceived, without taking into consideration the education she had received, and the seal of indelible prejudice which the circumstances of the times had impressed upon them.

No sooner were we alone and in the carriage than she began to dilate upon the dissatisfaction Junot had caused her.

"What is the meaning of all this hurrying backwards and forwards, and in gala costume too? Who would ever have believed that I should give my arm to an officer in uniform to leave the Opera? It is too ridiculous. I will tell him not to go to the Opera again in uniform. He will understand the propriety of it; he has sense and good taste. And then to leave us hanging upon Albert's two arms, making him resemble a pitcher with two handles! Who ever saw a man of fashion give his arm to two women at once? It is very well for Sikes's first clerk to gallant the wife and daughter of his master to the theatre in that manner. But a more serious fault which I have to reproach him with is putting me into his carriage. It is to be hoped no one of distinction was near. Did you observe whether any of our acquaintance were in the corridor?"

I had seen several persons whom I knew just before I got into the carriage, but I should have been very unwilling to increase her displeasure by telling her so; I had not time, however, to answer before we stopped at our own door, and Albert and Junot, already arrived, received us there. Junot led my mother to her apartment, placed her on her sofa, surrounded her by those thousand and one little things which are necessary to the comfort of an invalid; then, seating himself upon a stool at her feet, and taking her hands in his, assumed a tone suitable to the important event he was about to relate. He informed her that Ceracchi and Aréna—the one actuated by Republican fanaticism, the other by vengeance—had taken measures to assassinate Bonaparte.

As General Junot proceeded in his account his voice became stronger, his language more emphatic; every word was a thought, and every thought came from his heart. In painting Bonaparte such as he saw him daily,—such, in fact, as he was at that time,—his masculine and sonorous voice assumed a tone of sweetness: it was melody; but when he proceeded to speak of those men who, to satisfy their vengeance or their senseless ambitions, would assassinate him who was at that moment charged with the futurity of France, his voice failed, broken by sobs, and, leaning his head upon my mother's pillow, he wept like a child; then, as if ashamed of his weakness, he went to seat himself in the most obscure corner of the room.

My mother's heart was formed to understand such a heart as Junot's; and, open as she was to all the tender emotions, she was violently agitated by the state in which she saw him. In her turn she burst into tears. "How you love him!" said she.

"How I love him!" answered he, firmly joining his hands, and raising his eyes to heaven. "Yes, I love him! Judge," continued he, rising, and promenading the room as he spoke— "judge what I suffered a few days ago, when your daughter, with an eloquence foreign to her sex and age, convinced us that all barriers, all precautions, would fall before the poniard of an assassin, provided he were but willing to sacrifice his own life. But what more particularly hurt me was to hear her represent this same assassin as becoming great by his crime."

My mother looked at me with a countenance of dissatisfaction. Albert, who was sitting near the fire, said nothing; but I was sure he did not blame me.

"All that," said my mother, "comes of Laurette's speaking upon subjects which are not in the province of women. I have often told her how much that habit impaired her power of pleasing; but she pays no attention to what I say on the subject. In my time we only knew that the month of May was the month of roses, and our ignorance did not make us the less agreeable. For my scientific education, I never read any book but Telemachus, and yet, I believe, I can converse without being tiresome. I hope, my dear child, that you will correct that error."

"Ah, I hope not!" answered General Junot. "You have misunderstood me: it was not what Mademoiselle Laurette said which gave me pain; but I immediately considered that you were acquainted with Aréna, that he often visited here; that you also knew Ceracchi; that these men might have heard your daughter speak in the same strain; and that the soul and the head of the latter especially was capable of replying to the appeal which he might fancy to be thus made to him through the lips of a young girl, and might in consequence develop a few moments sooner his diabolical intentions. All this is very ridiculous, very senseless, is it not?" continued the General, seeing my brother smile at the last words, "but I cannot help it; for the last week I have not, in fact, been master of my own thoughts. You may judge if they were likely to be calmed by the First Consul's resolution of going to the Opera this evening to expose himself to the poniards of assassins! We have yet only taken Ceracchi, Aréna, and, I believe, Demerville. They are just taken; but they were not the only conspirators. It is pretended that England and the English committee are concerned,— always the English! There are really only two motives: one is the hatred of the family and of Corsica, the other a fanaticism of liberty carried to madness. This is what should alarm the friends of the First Consul. The most active police has no power in such a case, and no means of prevention."

When tranquillity was restored by the arrest of the other conspirators (Topino-Lebrun, Demerville, etc.), the ceremony of my marriage was hastened. The First Consul had said to Junot, "Do you know that your marriage has been held by a very slender thread, my poor Junot? For I believe if these rascals had killed me, the alliance with you would have been little cared for." Bonaparte would not have uttered such a sentiment three or four years before; but on attaining absolute power he took up an idea which was perhaps the cause of his ruin, but to which he always attached great importance, that men are governed and led by motives of interest or fear.

On the 27th of October all the family of Junot arrived at Paris, and were presented to my mother; and never till this day had I duly appreciated the virtues of his heart. Sensible of the wide difference which a Parisian education and constant intercourse with the best society of Paris made between our manners and those of his mother and sister, who knew nothing beyond the towns of Burgundy, he dreaded to perceive in me a contemptuous ridicule, which would have rendered him miserable; and never shall I forget the expression of tenderness and respect with which he presented his mother to mine, and the action which seemed to entreat, though he never used the words, that I would be a daughter to his parents. He had no reason to fear. They were too good and too respectable not to demand and to secure my duty and love.

The next day the marriage contract was signed, and it was not till that moment that I learned that my brother, from his own means, endowed me with 60,000 francs, in satisfaction, as the marriage settlement expressed it, of my claims on the paternal inheritance. My claims! when we all knew that none of my father's property ever had been or ever would be realized; the greater part of it was in the English funds; but it would not have been agreeable to General Junot to receive my dower as a gift from my brother, and therefore this clause was introduced. Fifty thousand francs more were added by M. Lequien de Bois-Cressy, an old friend of my father, and who was to be my mother's second husband; he gave me his dower as his future step-daughter, secured upon an estate in Brittany. He was rich and generous; I was not, therefore, surprised at this present; but that my brother, who, from the proceeds of his own industry, had maintained my mother's house, and furnished my expensive education, should now act so generously, was even more than my gratitude could express; nor was this lessened by the affectionate terms in which he replied to my insufficient thanks.

"Do not speak thus," said he, embracing me with that fraternal tenderness which he had always shown me; "do you not know that my mother and yourself are the sole objects of my affection and of my happiness? I live only for you. It is, then, quite natural that the produce of my labours should be employed for your benefit. A great and an unhoped-for marriage is offered you; the money is my own, and how could I dispose of it better than in making your fortune some way proportionate to the establishment you are about to form?"

A circumstance arising out of this will show the First Consul's prodigious memory, even in matters of the smallest importance to himself. The following day, the 29th of October, Junot, accompanied by my brother as my nearest relation, attended at the Tuileries for the signature of the marriage contract. The First Consul received my brother with great kindness, questioned him upon his prospects and his intentions, spoke of my mother with friendship, and of me with an interest which affected me much when Albert repeated the conversation.

But for the singular part of the interview: he desired the contract to be read to him. When the 60,000 francs from my paternal inheritance were named, he made a movement indicative of surprise, and another, though less marked, at the mention of the 50,000 francs of M. de Bois-Cressy, but made no remark upon either. When the reading was completed, he took my brother by the arm, led him to the recess of a window, and said to him, "Permon, I remember that when your father died he left nothing. At that period I visited your mother daily, and you no doubt know," added he, with an embarrassed air, "that at the same time I was desirous of marrying you to my sister, Madame Leclerc, and of arranging the future marriage of Mademoiselle Loulou with that *mauvais sujet,* my brother Jerome." (He did not speak of the principal marriage he planned at that period!) "Well, Madame Permon then told me that her husband left nothing. What, then, does this mean?"

Albert repeated to the First Consul what he had already said to me, entreating him not to mention it. Napoleon looked at him with an indefinable expression, and said, "You are a generous fellow, my dear Permon; you are a generous fellow; I shall take care of you. But you allow yourself to be forgotten. Why do you never come to the Tuileries? Your brother-in-law will now remind you of me, and will also remind me of you." Accordingly, a few days afterwards, Junot solicited for Albert a situation in which he might give proofs of his attachment to the cause of the 9th of November, and the First Consul appointed him to one of the three then existing posts of Commissary-General of the police of France.

The day preceding my marriage, a circumstance at once trifling and serious had nearly caused its rapture. A friend of Junot's, M. Duquesnoy, was Mayor of the 7th arrondissement; the General, as Commandant of Paris, not belonging more to one mayoralty than another, wished his marriage to be performed before M. Duquesnoy; and he inquired of my mother whether she supposed it would make any difference to me. My mother replied that she was herself perfectly willing, and did not believe that I should be otherwise, but that she would send for me to answer for myself. On General Junot's putting his request to me, I answered, that in this, as in everything else, my mother was mistress of my actions on so solemn a day. I only observed that the distance to the mayoralty of M. Duquesnoy in the Rue de Jouy, Quartier Saint Antoine, was long, and that I should not fear fatiguing my mother if it were no farther off than our church of St. Louis, which, being at the extremity of the Rue Thiroux, was directly opposite our house. I did not at that moment remark General Junot's astonishment; but, having embraced my mother, left the room.

I was no sooner gone than the General asked my mother if I expected to be married at church.

"To be married at church!" she cried; "where, then, would you have her expect to be married? Before your friend with the sash,* I suppose? But, my dear boy, you have surely lost your wits. How could you

---

* Mayors wore—indeed, still wear—a tricolor sash on formal occasions.

entertain the idea that not my daughter only, but myself and her brother, could consent to a purely civil marriage? As for Laurette, I promise you she is capable of thanking you for your intentions if you should propose this to her!" General Junot walked about much agitated. "Will you permit me to speak upon the subject to Mademoiselle Laurette in private? Situated as we now are, there can be no objection to my request."

My mother shrugged her shoulders. "You know not what you are talking of," said she; "until you become her husband, you are but a stranger, and what you wish to say is not likely to make her your friend: why do you want to make a secret of it? Why am I not to be present?" "Because calmness is necessary in treating of such a matter; but I can speak to Mademoiselle Laurette here, with the door of your chamber open."

I was called: nothing could exceed my astonishment, my grief I may say, in hearing this strange proposition. I did not conceal it: the General replied that, situated as he was, it was impossible he could be married at church, "to make a show of myself," added he; "for you could not prevent all the beggars and low people of the Chaussée d'Antin from surrounding the house, and even filling the church. And I am to appear in uniform amidst such a crowd!"

"I do not know," I answered, "what you should find disagreeable in being seen to perform an act which is the duty of every Christian (I am not speaking as a devotee), in entering upon the engagements which we propose to take upon ourselves to-morrow. The very Pagans sought the sanction of this act, the most important of their lives, in the temples of their gods. The Turks only are content with the Cadi, and I hope it is not from them you have taken arguments in support of your extraordinary proposition." "I am much hurt by your obstinacy," said Junot; "how can you, with your sense, persist in a formality which your education ought to have taught you to consider a nullity?"

"I am very young, General, to discuss so serious a question. I understand nothing of the controversy, except that I was born in the Christian religion, and that, very certainly, I shall not stir a step from this house if it be not to go where my duty calls me. Be assured, General, that notwithstanding the advanced state of the preparations our marriage will not take place unless the Church shall bless it."

I stood up to go away. The General took my hand, and saw that my eyes were full of tears. He stamped his foot with violence, and let slip a very unusual expression. "Junot! Junot!" cried my mother from her chamber, where she heard all that passed—"Junot! is that proper language to use?"

"You afflict me greatly," said the General. "It distresses me to give you pain; but, after all, this is a mere childish whim on your part, which you persist in because you have been told to do so; while to me it is a matter of serious consequence. Do you know that it is nothing less than a confession of faith?"

"And suppose it is?" said I; "what was the religion of your fathers? You have been baptized, you have been confirmed, you have received you first communion, you have confessed: here, then, are four sacraments of which you have partaken, and when that of marriage comes in its course, suddenly you turn renegade, apostate, perhaps! No, no, General, it must not be."

Having said this I went to my mother's room, where I found my brother. Junot followed me, and addressing himself to Albert, submitted to him the question which caused this debate; he was in despair; what I insisted upon was of no importance whatever, he said, and would seriously compromise him. "Well!" said I, standing up, "I can say no more upon the subject, of which I ought never to have permitted the discussion. I only regret that General Junot should for a moment have believed that my principles would suffer me to accede to the proposition he has this morning made."

I retired to my chamber, and was just then informed that Mademoiselle L'Olive and Mademoiselle de Beuvry were in the salon, and that they had brought in two coaches the articles which composed my *trousseau* and *corbeille;** the two baskets which were to contain them followed on a large cart—that of the trousseau, in particular, was so large that no coach could contain it.

I sent to request my brother's presence, and he came to me immediately. "My dear Albert," said I to him, "this affair will become serious if the intervention of your friendship and excellent sense does not

* We have no words exactly synonymous with these; both signify the bridal paraphernalia. The "trousseau" is that part of it which is furnished by the bride's family. The "corbeille" is the bridegroom's present. —*Translator.*

prevent it. Not that I request your advice, because my resolution is irrevocably taken, and if General Junot is equally determined a rupture is inevitable; to you, therefore, I refer to render it as little as possible painful to our poor mother. The blow will be terrible to her."

Albert took my two hands in his and embraced me tenderly, wiping away my tears, which flowed abundantly. He walked up and down the room in silent meditation, then stopped some time before the window; my maid, Josephine, came to require my attendance in my mother's room. "I cannot go," said I to Albert; and I begged him to go to my mother, whose apartment was only separated from mine by a very small drawing-room, which had no door towards my chamber. He went, and I had scarcely been ten minutes alone when my mother's room door opened, and she came to me. "My child," she said, "here is one who does not ask your pardon, which, nevertheless, I hope you will grant."

Those who were well acquainted with General Junot know how much the expression of his countenance varied when he was particularly agitated. At this moment he was scarcely recognizable; he advanced behind my mother, leaning on Albert's arm, changing colour so rapidly that he appeared to be ill. "Your brother," said he, "has been showing me how much I have distressed you; he will now explain to you that I am not so much to blame as you may suppose; and if you will take into consideration the character of a soldier full of honour and frankness, but who could not entertain the same ideas with you upon the subject we have been discussing, you will be indulgent and pardon me."

My brother then affectionately taking my hand, and holding his other hand to Junot, said to me: "Our friend has been explaining to me that being the Commandant of Paris, and invested with the confidence of the First Consul, he objects to appearing in open day on an occasion so solemn as his marriage, to perform in a church a sacred act of religion, because, on account of his political position, it would make him a sort of spectacle to the whole town. You know me, my sister; you know that my heart is devoted to you and to honour. Well, after what he has said, I have engaged to persuade you to comply with his wishes. The General does not desire to wound any of your religious convictions; he acknowledges that you are right in requiring the religious ceremony, but he requests that it may take place at night. I believe that this mutual concession will remove all obstacles on both sides."

I looked at my mother, and receiving a sign of approbation from her, had nothing further to object except my dislike to a nocturnal ceremony. It recalled those days of terror when the bridal pair received by stealth the benediction which the priest accorded at the risk of his life. It was necessary, however, to be reasonable; and I consented, as my mother and brother approved it, that the ceremony should take place in the manner proposed.

I afterwards learned that this sudden opposition was caused by the First Consul. This may appear extraordinary to those who remember that two years afterwards he signed the Concordat; but all fruits do not ripen in one season. He had just escaped from the dagger of a man who accused him of attempting to overturn the institutions of Republicanism, and he was not willing that the Commandant of Paris, known to possess his entire confidence, should perform a public act which might point to a new system of action on the part of his patron. He therefore particularly required of Junot that he should only go to church at night, supposing the family to insist upon the religious ceremony. Junot, in his zeal to obey, exceeded his instructions. His religious notions—having passed his youth in an army where none such existed— were not those of incredulity, but of perfect indifference, and he had no suspicion of the effect his proposition would have upon me; in the first instance, then, he did not even speak of a nocturnal marriage, which in fact supplied all the conditions absolutely required by either party.

"At length, then," said my mother, when she had heard me pronounce my consent, "this grand affair is settled;" and turning to Junot, she added, "It has been all your fault. Who would ever have thought of coming on the eve of marriage to say 'I will have nothing to do with the Church'? Come, fall on your knees, and beg pardon of your betrothed. Right. Now give him your hand, or rather your cheek, in recompense of that graceful act of submission. It is the last; to-morrow he will be your master. But what now, is it not all settled?"

The fact was that this nocturnal ceremony, which did not please me at all, had moreover the inconvenience that it would be unaccompanied by a wedding Mass; I whispered this new objection to the General, and it was presently removed by the promise that it should take place at twelve o'clock, the hour of midnight Mass. My mother laughed on overhearing this discussion. "And now that we are all at length agreed," said she, "do me the favour, Monsieur my son-in-law, to take your leave for the present; I must show the young lady her *trousseau,* and hear her opinion of my taste; we shall afterwards both sit in judgment upon yours."

On entering the salon, though it was large, I found myself much in the situation of Noah's dove, without a place of rest for my foot. From an immense basket, or rather portmanteau, of rose-coloured gros de Naples, embroidered with black chenille, made in the shape of a sarcophagus, bearing my cipher, an innumerable quantity of small packets, tied with pink or blue favours, strewed the room; these contained full-trimmed chemises with embroidered sleeves, pocket-handkerchiefs, petticoats, morning-gowns, dressing-gowns of Indian muslin, night-dresses, nightcaps, morning-caps of all colours and all forms; the whole of these articles were embroidered, and trimmed with Mechlin lace or English point. Another portmanteau of equal size, of green silk embroidered in orange chenille, contained my numerous dresses, all worthy in fashion and taste to vie with the habiliments already described.

This was an hour of magic for a girl of sixteen. Time passes away; mature years have already arrived; old age will follow; but never can the remembrance of my mother as she now appeared be effaced from my mind. How eagerly did she watch my eyes; and when the peculiar elegance and good taste of any article of her own choice elicited my admiring exclamations, how did her fine black eyes sparkle, and her smiling rosy lips display the pearls they enclosed! Who can describe a mother's joy on such an occasion, or the effect it produces on the heart of an affectionate daughter! Taking my head between her two hands, and kissing my eyes, my ears, my cheeks, my hair, she threw herself on a settee, saying, "Come now, *mathia mou,** seek something else that will please you."

* Greek words, meaning *light of my eyes;* a most caressing expression, which my mother habitually used towards me.

The *trousseau* being fully examined, the *corbeille** next demanded inspection. At this time the custom of giving a basket or case for the articles of the *corbeille* was not yet exploded; fifty or sixty louis were spent upon a species of basket covered with rich silk or velvet, and highly ornamented, which stood for six or twelve months on the dressing-table of the bride, till, becoming tarnished and worn, it was no longer ornamental, and was consigned to the lumber-room, to be eaten by the rats in spite of its finery. Now they do things with more sense, and lay out the money upon a valuable chest of longer duration. Mine, then, was an immensely large vase, covered with green and white velvet, richly embroidered with gold. Its foot was of gilded bronze; its cover of embroidered velvet, surmounted by a pine-apple of black velvet, transfixed by an arrow, from which were suspended on each side a crown, the one of olives, the other of laurel, both cut in gilt bronze.

This *corbeille* contained Cashmere shawls, veils of English point, gown trimmings of blond and Brussels point, dresses of white blond and black lace; pieces of Indian muslin and of Turkish velvet which the General had brought from Egypt; ball-dresses for a bride; my presentation dress, and Indian muslin dresses embroidered in silver lama. Besides all these, there were flowers bought of Madame Roux, of Lyons; ribands of all sizes and colours; bags (or as we now say, reticules), which were then all the fashion, one of them of English lace; gloves, fans, and essences. At each side of the *corbeille* was a "sultan," or scented bag.

The first contained all the implements of the toilette in gold enamelled black; the apparatus of the work-table—thimble, scissors, needle-case, bodkin, etc., all in gold, set with fine pearls. The other "sultan" contained the jewel casket, and an opera-glass of mother-of-pearl and gold set with two rows of diamonds. The casket contained settings for an entire suite of ornaments without the stones; six ears of golden corn and a comb (which, on account of the immense quantity of my hair, was as large as those which are now worn), set with diamonds and pearls; a square medallion set with large pearls, containing a portrait of

* Mademoiselle L'Olive, being dressmaker to Madame Bonaparte, had been charged by Junot to prepare the *corbeille*, under the instructions of Madame Murat.

General Junot by Isabey, for the resemblance of which the artist's name will vouch, but of a size more fit to be affixed to the wall of a gallery than to be suspended from the neck; but this was the fashion of the day, and Madame Murat had one of her husband, also painted by Isabey, and even larger than mine. The casket contained also a number of superb topazes brought from Egypt, of an incredible size, Oriental corals of extraordinary thickness, which I have since had engraved in relief at Florence by M. Hamelin, and several antique cameos; all these were unset. The bridal purse of gold links, connected together by delicate little stars of green enamel, the clasp also enamelled green, contained too weighty a sum of money had it not consisted of banknotes,* except about fifty louis in pretty little sequins of Venice.

All these elegant presents had been completed under the direction of Madame Murat, and did infinite honour to her taste. At this time such a *corbeille* was a treasure of great rarity; for the first time since the Revolution it had reappeared at the marriage of Mademoiselle de Doudeauville with M. Pierre de Rastignac. Madame Murat's marriage followed after a considerable interval, and her *corbeille* was very rich; but as mine took place nearly a year later, not only was the *corbeille* more beautiful, but it was composed with more conformity to ancient customs, and in a more refined taste. After this time the *corbeille* and *trousseau* again became common, but were copies, not models, like Madame Murat's and mine.

But of all these beautiful gifts, nothing delighted me so much as Junot's affecting attention to my mother. She longed for a Cashmere shawl, but would never purchase one, because she said she could not afford one so good as she wished for; and I had determined that my wedding gift to her should be a red one, because that was the colour she preferred, but I had never whispered my intentions. However, together with my *corbeille* came a small basket covered with white gros de Naples, embroidered in silks with my mother's cipher on the draperies, from which the first thing that presented itself was a superb scarlet Cashmere shawl. The basket contained, besides, a purse like mine, except that the enamel was a deep blue, and within it, instead of money,

* The Bank of France was established in the month of February, 1800; I think it opened the following month. The two purses were made by Foncier, a very celebrated jeweller at that period.

was a topaz of a perfect oval round, the size of a small apricot; gloves, ribands, and two magnificent fans. I cannot describe how I felt this amiable attention. When I thanked the General for it with an effusion of heart which I rather repressed than exaggerated, he replied, "I foresaw what you now express; and if I had not loved her who is about to become my mother with filial tenderness, I should have done what I have for the pleasure I enjoy at this moment."

At nine o'clock in the morning of my wedding day my toilette was commenced in which I was to appear before the Mayor. I wore an Indian muslin gown, with a train, high body and long sleeves that buttoned at the wrist, and which were then called *amadis;* the whole was trimmed with magnificent point lace. My cap, made by Mademoiselle Despaux, was of Brussels point, crowned with a wreath of orange flowers, from which descended to my feet a veil of fine English point, large enough to envelop my person. This costume, which was adopted by all young brides, differing only according to the degree of wealth of the parties, was in my opinion much more elegant than the present bridal fashion.

I do not think that it is prejudice for the past which makes me prefer my own wedding-dress—that profusion of rich lace, so fine and so delicate that it resembled a vapoury network, shading my countenance and playing with the curls of my hair; those undulating folds of my robe, which fell round my person with the inimitable grace and supple ease of the superb tissues of India; that long veil, which in part covered the form without concealing it—to the robe of tulle of our modern brides, made in the fashion of a ball-dress, the shoulders and bosom uncovered, and the petticoat short enough to permit everyone to judge not only of the delicacy of the little foot, but of the shape of the ankle and leg,* while the head, dressed as for a ball, is scarcely covered by a veil of stiff and massy tulle, the folds of which fall without ease or grace around the lengthened waist and shortened petticoat of the young bride; no, this is not elegance.

---

* Prince Talleyrand began life by saying what are called "witty things." Being one day present at the Tuileries, when several ladies were to take an oath of fidelity to the Emperor on their new appointments, he particularly noticed the beautiful Madame de Marmier, who wore remarkably short petticoats in order to show the delicacy of her feet and ankle. Some one present asked Talleyrand what he thought of the *tout ensemble.* "I think," said the witty minister, "that her dress is too short to take an oath of fidelity."

At eleven o'clock the General arrived, with the rest of his family. His mother had preceded him by half an hour. This excellent woman had seen me but twice; but she had made a correct estimate of the mutual tenderness which subsisted between my mother and myself. Her perfect goodness of heart and excellent judgment had inspired the thought of placing herself between us at the moment of a separation which she foresaw would be so painful. Alas! she knew at that moment better than I did what were my poor mother's feelings; and I was far from understanding the full force of the words which, with tears that could not be restrained, she addressed to her, "I will supply your place to her!"

When we set out for the Rue de Jouy, the Rue de Sainte Croix near our house was filled with people, mostly strangers in our quarter; and among them nearly all the principal *Marchandes de la Halle*. Junot was extremely considerate to the people of Paris, and was very popular with them; and I am convinced that in a commotion the mere sight of him would have restored tranquillity; he was very open-handed to them, giving alms very freely. He could, moreover, speak the language of the *Dames de la Halle* admirably, when any occasion arose.

Four of the group requested permission to pay their compliments to me. It was granted, and they entered the salon carrying each a bouquet, certainly larger than myself, and composed of the finest and rarest flowers, the price of which was greatly enhanced by the lateness of the season. They offered them to me with no other phrase than the following: "Mam'selle, you are about to become the wife of our Commandant, and we are glad of it, because you are said to be kind and good. Will you permit us?" And the women embraced me heartily.

Junot ordered some refreshments for all those who had been good enough, he said, to remember him on the happiest day of his life. We set out for the municipality amidst their loud acclamations and the repeated cries of "Long live the Bride and Bridegroom!"

On arriving at the mayoralty of the Rue de Jouy, Faubourg Saint Antoine, where it was Junot's whim to be married we were received and married by M. Duquesnoy, Mayor of this arrondissement. He spared us a long discourse, and only uttered a few well-chosen words, which I have never forgotten.

We returned to my mother's, and the day passed off much as all similar days do. When the hour of midnight struck we crossed over to the church, and at one by the clock of the Corps Législatif I entered the Hôtel de Montesquieu to the sound of the most harmonious music.

With the installation of the Consulate, Bonaparte moved from the Palace of the Luxembourg, where the Directors had resided, to the much larger and grander Palace of the Tuileries, whose last occupants had been Louis XVI and Marie Antoinette. As if that had not already been clear enough the Citizen First Consul moved into the King's Apartment while the Citizeness Bonaparte took over the Queen's. Soon, the first elements of a court etiquette began to appear; and it seemed therefore normal to have the new Madame Junot officially presented to the Consul and to Mme Bonaparte, even though she already knew them both. It was, of course, a first step to the imperial pomp which was decreed in 1804.

My official presentation to the First Consul and Madame Bonaparte was a great affair for my mother; she occupied herself upon my toilet with more minute care than I imagine she had ever bestowed upon her own in the highest tide of her vanity. One thing disturbed her much, no ceremonial. "Nevertheless, he acts the King," said my mother. The truth was that at this time the interior of the First Consul's family was like that of a very rich man, with no more etiquette; Madame Bonaparte had not even yet ladies in waiting.

We went to the Tuileries after the Opera, leaving the ballet of *Psyché* in the middle, that we might not be too late, and arrived at ten o'clock. My heart beat as we alighted at the Pavilion of Flora, at the door which precedes that in the angle so long called the entrance of the Empress. As we ascended the five or six steps before the door on the left, leading to the apartments on the ground-floor, we met Duroc and Rapp. "How late you are!" said Duroc. "It is near eleven o'clock." "Ah!" added the brave Alsatian, "Madame Junot is a worker of marvels; she is about to make an infidel of our good Junot." And he burst into a loud laugh.

I was desirous of turning back; but Junot replied, "Madame Bonaparte desired me to come here after the Opera." "Oh!" said Duroc, "it

117

is quite a different thing if Madame Bonaparte has appointed the hour."

At this moment the folding door of Madame Bonaparte's apartment opened, and Eugène de Beauharnais ran down. He was sent by his mother, because, having heard the wheels of a carriage within the Court, and finding that no one came up, she began to fear lest by mistake, arising from the lateness of the hour, I might be told that she could not receive me.

I was sensible of this attention, and the more so as the messenger was himself very fit to dispel apprehensions of a doubtful reception. M. de Beauharnais gave me his arm, and we entered the large salon together. This fine apartment was so obscure that at first entering I saw no one in it; for it was lighted only by two chandeliers placed on the mantel-piece, and surrounded with gauze to soften the glare. I was very nervous on entering; but an observation from Eugène de Beauharnais contributed wonderfully to restore my composure.

"You have nothing to fear," said he; "my mother and sister are so kind!" These words made me start; no doubt I might experience that emotion which a young woman is so liable to feel at a first presentation to strangers, especially when she has some reason to imagine that she may not be very cordially received; but my spirits recovered surprisingly.

Madame Bonaparte was in the same place which she then occupied as mistress of the house, and where afterwards she was seated as sovereign of the world; I found her before a tapestry frame prosecuting a work, three-fourths of which was performed by Mademoiselle Dubuquoy, whose ingenious hint that Marie Antoinette was fond of such employments had inspired Josephine's inclination for them. At the other side of the chimney sat Mademoiselle Hortense de Beauharnais, an amiable, mild, agreeable girl, with the figure of a nymph and beautiful light hair. Her gracious manners and gentle words were irresistibly pleasing.

The First Consul was standing before the chimney with his hands behind him, fidgeting, as he had already the habit of doing; his eyes were fixed upon me, and as soon as I recovered my self-possession, I found that he was closely examining me; but from that moment I determined not to be abashed, as to allow myself to be overcome by fantastic fears with such a man would be ruin.

Madame Bonaparte stood up, came forward, took my two hands and embraced me, saying that I might depend upon her friendship. "I have been too long Junot's friend," she continued, "not to entertain the same sentiments for his wife, particularly for the one he has chosen." "Oh, oh! Josephine," said the First Consul, "that is running on very fast! How do you know that this little pickle is worth loving? Well, Mademoiselle Loulou (you see I do not forget the names of my old friends), have you not a word for me?"

He had taken my hand, and, drawing me towards him, looked at me with a scrutiny which for a moment made me cast down my eyes, but I recollected myself immediately. "General," I replied, smiling, "it is not for me to speak first." The slight contraction of his brow would have been imperceptible to any other person, but I knew his countenance well: he smiled almost instantly, and said, "Very well parried. Oh, the mother's spirit. Apropos, how is Madame Permon?" "She suffers much; for two years past her health has altered so seriously as to cause us great uneasiness." "Indeed! so bad as that; I am sorry to hear it, very sorry; make my regards to her. It is a wrong head—a devil of a spirit;* but she has a generous heart and a noble soul."

I withdrew my hand, which he had held during this short colloquy, and took my seat near Madame Bonaparte. The conversation became general and very agreeable. Duroc came in, and took part in it. Madame Bonaparte said little on subjects she did not understand, and thereby avoided exposing her ignorance. Her daughter, without saying more than is becoming in a young girl, had the talent of sustaining the conversation on agreeable topics.

M. de Cobentzel was expected at Paris, and his arrival was spoken of. Madame Bonaparte said that she had heard some one observe upon the astonishing resemblance between Count Louis de Cobentzel and Mirabeau. "Who said that?" asked the First Consul, hastily. "I do not exactly recollect. Barras, I think." "And where had Barras seen M. de Cobentzel? Mirabeau! he was ugly; M. de Cobentzel is ugly—there is

---

* I have already said that I shall preserve the turn of Napoleon's phrases and his manner of speaking; it was original, and at once Oriental and *bourgeoise*.

all the resemblance. *Eh, pardicu!* you know him, Junot; you were with him at our famous treaty, and Duroc, too. But you never saw Mirabeau. He was a rogue, but a clever rogue! he himself did more mischief to the former masters of this house than the States-General altogether. But he was a rogue." Here he took a pinch of snuff, repeating, "He was a bad man, and too vicious to be tribune of the people; not but in my tribunate there were some no better than he, and without half his talent. As for Count Louis de Cobentzel—"

He took another pinch of snuff, and was about to resume his observations, but stopped as if struck by a sudden reflection. He thought, perhaps, that the first magistrate of the Republic should not so lightly give his opinion upon a man just named by a great Power to treat with him. He stopped then with a sentence half uttered, and, turning to me, said:

"I hope that we shall often see you, Madame Junot. My intention is to draw round me a numerous family, consisting of my generals and their young wives. They will be friends of my wife and of Hortense, as their husbands are mine. Does that suit you? I warn you that you will be disappointed if you expect to find here your fine acquaintances of the Faubourg Saint Germain. I do not like them. They are my enemies, and prove it by defaming me. Tell them from me, as your mother lives amongst them—tell them that I am not afraid of them."

This sentence, spoken with harshness, gave me uneasiness from two causes: it was disobliging both to Junot and to me; it seemed to reproach him for taking a wife from a hostile society, and to hint that I came into his own with unfriendly dispositions. I could not forbear answering, perhaps hastily:

"General, excuse me if I cannot consent to do what is not in the province of a woman, and particularly in that of General Junot's wife; and permit me to carry from you to my friends only messages of peace and union; I know that they desire no others."

I would not interrupt the relation of this interesting interview to describe the person and manners of Mademoiselle de Beauharnais, but I think it would be an injustice both to her and my readers to omit to describe her as she appeared at my first introduction to her. Hortense de Beauharnais was at this time seventeen years old; she was fresh as a rose, and though her fair complexion was not relieved by much colour, she had enough to produce that freshness and bloom which was her chief beauty; a profusion of light hair played in silky locks round her soft and penetrating blue eyes. The delicate roundness of her figure, slender as a palm-tree, was set off by the elegant carriage of her head; her feet were small and pretty; her hands very white, with pink, well-rounded nails.

But what formed the chief attraction of Hortense was the grace and suavity of her manners, which united the creole languor with the vivacity of France. She was gay, gentle, and amiable; she had wit, which, without the smallest ill-temper, had just malice enough to be amusing. A careful education had improved her natural talents; she drew excellently, sang harmoniously, and performed admirably in comedy. In 1800 she was a charming young girl; she afterwards became one of the most amiable princesses of Europe. I have seen many, both in their own courts and in Paris, but I never knew one who had any pretensions to equal talent.

She was beloved by every one, though, of all who surrounded her, her mother seemed to be the least conscious of her attractions. I do not mean to say that she did not love her, but certainly she did not express that degree of maternal affection which Hortense de Beauharnais merited. Her brother loved her tenderly: the First Consul looked upon her as his child.

My mother had determined to give a ball on the fifteenth day after my marriage; it was an ancient custom, and though not now the fashion, she would by no means forgo it. One evening when we had dined with her, she required our assistance in arranging her plans: "For this ball," said she, "must be one of the prettiest that has been given this long time past; my house, it is true, is very small, but it must be turned into an enchanted parterre of flowers. Come, take your place at the desk, Madame Laurette, and make out our list of invitations, for all your husband's friends must be of the party." Junot thanked her, and kissed her hand.

Junot took the pen, and wrote down all the names of the ladies, beginning with Madame Bonaparte and Mademoiselle de Beauharnais.

He then waited for the name with which my mother would commence the list of gentlemen.

"The First Consul of the French Republic, One and Indivisible; is not that the style?" said my mother. "The First Consul!" we exclaimed together. "Yes, the First Consul; is there anything astonishing in that? I am tired of being on bad terms with any one, and besides—" "And besides," said Junot, laughing, "you think that perhaps you were more in the wrong than he."

"No, no," said my mother; "that is quite another affair. He was in the wrong altogether; but I considered that, as Laurette might be daily in his society, these sort of quarrels might produce disagreeable effects for her, and I wished to prevent that—was I not right?" We embraced her. "But the invitation," she added, "is not all. Do you think he will accept it? do you think he will come?" "I am sure of it; only name the hour that will suit you best, and I will come to fetch you," said Junot, enchanted at this prospect of reconciliation between his mother-in-law and his beloved General.

My mother looked at him with an air of astonishment perfectly laughable. "Fetch me! to go where?" "Where!" returned Junot, as much surprised in his turn; "to the Tuileries, to tender your invitation to the First Consul and Madame Bonaparte." "My dear Junot," said my mother, with the utmost seriousness and sangfroid, "you are quite, nay, perfectly mad." "It seems to me that what I say is, nevertheless, very sensible; that nothing, in fact, can be more reasonable," replied Junot, somewhat disconcerted by the apostrophe. "And I tell you, you are mad. Would you have me go to request General Bonaparte to come again to my house, after having forbidden his appearance there?"

"How, then, do you propose to invite him?" asked Junot, with an accent impossible to describe. "Truly, how should I invite him? Precisely in the same manner as I do every one else, except that the card shall be all in writing, and I will write it all in my own neat hand, which he knows perfectly well."

Junot strode up and down the room, exclaiming, "But that cannot be! You had better not invite him at all! He will think that you intend him a disrespect." "He would be much mistaken, then. But he would think no such thing; and you will see that, after having received my note of invitation, he will do as all well-bred men would; he will call on me before the ball, or at least he will have a card left at the door." "Do you think, then," said Junot, in the utmost surprise, "that he keeps visiting cards?" "And why not? My dear child, because Bonaparte gains battles, is that any reason that he should not visit?"

For a long time my inclination to laugh had been suppressed with the utmost difficulty; Albert, throwing himself back in his arm-chair, had given way to his from the first; and this last observation, together with the stupefied astonishment of Junot, who, with his mouth half open, could not find words to answer, was altogether too much for my gravity, and I burst into one of those fits of wild mirth which one only enjoys at sixteen. My mother and Junot were still no less serious, my mother at intervals murmuring, "I do not see why he should not visit, and certainly I shall not go first."

My brother and I became by degrees more reasonable, seeing that she was perfectly in earnest, and certainly intended that the First Consul should come first to her. Now, it is true that not even a thought of royalty was yet attached to his name, but already for twelve months he had exercised the supreme authority of the State; and this power had placed him on an elevation which appeared quite natural and becoming to him; he was there because it was his proper place.

Albert knew my mother's character, and that by further opposition we should irritate without persuading her; he therefore sat down to the desk, and requested her to dictate her list, which she did with as much self-possession and composure as if the First Consul had never existed. The list consisted of seventy men and forty ladies—a large number for so small a house; but then, as now, it was a pleasure to be crowded, and the greatest approbation that could be expressed the day after a ball was, "What a charming *fête!* we were almost suffocated!"

The next morning Albert breakfasted with us, and it was resolved in our little council that we should all three proceed immediately to the Tuileries, and, in my mother's name, make our personal request to the First Consul and Madame Bonaparte to honour with their presence the ball my family were to give on the occasion of my marriage, taking good care to say nothing of the written invitations which had been entrusted to me for delivery.

Madame Bonaparte received us in the most gracious manner; it was in such cases that she appeared to the utmost advantage. She had already gone through all that a royal novitiate demanded, and it can scarcely be imagined with what ease she stepped into the station of Queen. She accepted our invitation for herself and Mademoiselle de Beauharnais; the latter, she said, was absent from the Tuileries. She seemed, however, by no means willing that we should extend our invitation to the First Consul. "He has been," she said, "but to two *fêtes* since his entry upon the Consulate—the one at Morfontaine, where policy led him to meet the American envoy; the other was the *fête* given him by the Consul Cambacérès on his return from Marengo; and besides," added she, "he dances but little."

"My sister," said Albert, with his natural mildness of manner, "will not readily admit that; the First Consul has often, *very often,* danced the *Monaco* and *Les Deux Coqs* with Laurette, to the sound of my eldest sister's piano. Do you know, madame, that we may claim almost the rights of fraternity with General Bonaparte?" "Yes, he has often told me so," she replied, with an affectation of friendliness. But this was not true, for I know that the First Consul never spoke of my mother to Madame Bonaparte, except when she herself led to the subject, which she was not fond of doing.

After taking leave of Madame Bonaparte, we proceeded by the staircase of the Pavilion of Flora to the apartments of the First Consul. The aide-de-camp in waiting observed that the hour of admission was past. "But I have an appointment," said Junot. "And madame?" asked the aide-de-camp. He was the unfortunate Lacuée, killed at Austerlitz, nephew of the Comte de Cessac, and cousin of M. de Beausset.

"We are too recently married, my friend," replied Junot, "to be more than one and the same person; therefore announce me, if you please; and though ladies do not often come to trouble your hermitage, show that you know how to be gallant, and give my wife your arm." When the door was opened, and the First Consul saw me, he said, smiling very good-humouredly, "What means this family deputation? —there is only Madame Permon wanting to its completion. Is she afraid of the Tuileries, or of me?" "General," said my husband immediately, "Madame Permon would gladly have joined us, but she is very ill, and finds it impossible to leave her chamber to come to request a favour of you, which she is very desirous to obtain. My wife is charged to address to you her petition in form."

The First Consul turned towards me with a smile, saying, "Well, let me hear. What do you wish for?" It is difficult, if not impossible, to describe the charm of his countenance when he smiled with a feeling of benevolence. His soul was upon his lips and in his eyes. The magic power of that expression at a later period is well known; the Emperor of Russia had experienced it when he said to me, "I never loved any one more than that man!"

I told the General what had been agreed upon, and had scarcely ended my little harangue, when he took my two hands, and said, "Well, I shall certainly be at this ball. Did you expect I should refuse? I shall go most willingly." Then he added a phrase which he often repeated: "Though I shall be in the midst of my enemies; for your mother's drawing-room, they tell me, is full of them."

Junot now made a sign to us to take leave; we accordingly made our parting salutations, and the First Consul, after pressing my brother's hand with as much cordiality as if we were still in my father's house, inquired on what day this ball should take place. "Next Monday, General; it is, I believe, the 10th of November."

"What! the 10th of November," said the First Consul, going to his escritoire; "that seems to me to be some particular day; let me see;" and as he spoke he found the calendar he was seeking. "I thought so," he added, on consulting it. "The 10th of November is the anniversary of the 18th Brumaire, and I cannot join a party on that day. Your mother will have no company; your acquaintance of the Faubourg Saint Germain will certainly not quit their retreats to make a festival of the anniversary of the re-establishment of the Republic. What concerns me personally," and his countenance as he spoke assumed an expression serious and severe, "is of little consequence, but I must see the Republic respected; it would not, therefore, be suitable that the anniversary of the day which restored it to us entire should be celebrated otherwise than as a family festival. I do not refuse Madame Permon's invitation if you will name another day."

The change was immediately resolved upon, and he himself named the 12th of November. "Do you receive Josephine?" he inquired. I answered that Madame Bonaparte had accepted for herself and her daughter the invitation which my mother, to her great regret, had not been able to give in person.

"Oh, I have no doubt but Madame Permon is ill," said the First Consul; "but there is idleness, if not some other motive, which I will not mention in her absence. Is there not, Madame Loulou?" And so saying, he pulled my ear and hair till he made my eyes water, which I was not sorry for, as it furnished an excuse for not answering this blunt interpolation, and for the colour which flushed my cheeks. While this was passing between us and the future master of the world, another scene took place in the apartments of Madame Bonaparte below-stairs.

M. de Caulaincourt paid his court very attentively to Madame Bonaparte; an old friendship or relationship between them was connected with a remembrance of protection on his part, and of gratitude on hers. She was, in consequence, on very good terms with my adopted godfather, and almost every morning the pony, with its velvet saddle and gilded bridle, trotted from the Rue des Capuchins to the Tuileries.

Here it arrived on the morning of our visit, just as we had left Madame Bonaparte, and the conversation naturally falling upon the invitation we had brought, M. de Caulaincourt, to whom my mother had related all that had passed on the preceding night, glorying in the firm stand she had made in favour of a written invitation, unceremoniously accused me of having mistaken my instructions, and very innocently repeated to Madame Bonaparte all that he had learned from my mother, of whose plans he perfectly approved. This unlucky incident produced a rather awkward dénouement on our return to the salon; but our apologies were graciously accepted, and whether or not the truth ever reached the ears of the First Consul it produced no visible result.

My mother easily perceived that it would be ridiculous for her to celebrate the anniversary of the 18th Brumaire; the change which we had made in the day consequently received her perfect acquiescence, and passed off without any observation.

All was preparation in my mother's house for the expected ball, which she intended should be one of the most agreeable to be given this year in Paris. Our friends also looked forward to it with impatience. My mother had already refused the requests of above forty men and twelve women for tickets. She was delighted when such requests were made to her. The arrangements for ornamenting the house were perfect; and when at length all the trees, plants, and flowers assumed the places her taste appointed them, and innumerable lights shone among them from lamps of every colour, the staircase and hall perfectly resembled an enchanted palace.

Madame Bonaparte arrived about nine o'clock, accompanied by her son and daughter, and led by Colonel Rapp. My mother met her in the middle of the dining-room; the other ladies she received at the door of the salon. She was polite and gracious to every one, as she so well knew how to be. She conducted Madame Bonaparte to the arm-chair on the right of the fireplace, and begged her, with the hospitable grace of the South, to make herself perfectly at home. She must have appeared to her, what she actually was, a very agreeable and charming woman.

My mother was, perhaps, the prettiest woman in the room, after the First Consul's two sisters. She had been for some time in better health, and the respite from suffering had restored to her features that harmony and regularity in which her beauty consisted. She wore on this evening a dress, made by Madame Germon, of white crape, trimmed with bunches of double jonquils. Its form was Grecian, folding over the bosom, and fastened on the shoulders with two diamond clasps. Her head-dress had a degree of eccentricity in its composition, which became her admirably.

As she could not, or rather did not, choose to appear on the occasion of my marriage with her hair wholly uncovered, she had a toque of white crape (made by Leroi, who then lived in the Rue des Petits-Champs, and had already acquired some reputation), through the folds of which her fine black hair appeared, resembling velvet, intermingled with bunches of jonquil, like those which trimmed her gown. She wore in her bosom a large bouquet of jonquils and natural violets, furnished by Madame Roux, but exhibited neither necklace nor jewels of any kind except two very fine diamond drops in her ears. This attire was set off by a person whose elegance of figure and manner were at least her most striking ornament.

At a quarter before nine o'clock Junot went to the Tuileries to be ready to attend the First Consul to my mother's, but found him so overwhelmed with business that it was impossible for him to name the hour at which he could arrive; but he was desired to request as a favour that the dancing might commence, the First Consul giving his assurance that he would certainly come, however late he might be compelled to make his visit.

The ball, then, was opened at half-past nine. Junot danced with Mademoiselle de Beauharnais, Eugène de Beauharnais with me, Hippolyte de Rastignac with Mademoiselle de Caseaux, and Mademoiselle de P—— with M. Dupaty. M. de Trénis was not yet arrived, nor M. Laffitte. These gentlemen were at this time in the extreme of everything that is inconceivable, and to join a party at two or three o'clock in the morning was nothing unusual with them.

I had this evening, in the opinion of my mother and all our old friends, an important duty to fulfil: it was to dance the *minuet de la cour* and the *gavotte*. For three weeks Gardel's long lessons had been renewed, that this minuet, which with my whole soul I detested, might be executed in perfection. I had entreated my mother to spare me this painful exhibition, but to no purpose. Not to dance the *minuet de la Reine* at a bridal ball would have been a dereliction of all established customs, which she could not by any means sanction.

M. de Trénis belonged to our society: he was a worthy man, and far from meriting the character which he gave himself of being nothing but a dancer. He possessed much information and some wit; natural good sense and a correct judgment, very capable of appreciating the ridiculous extravagance of his own words; that of his dress, though in the height of fashion, was by no means so exaggerated. As of all the fine dancers of the day, he was the one with whom we were the most acquainted, I had engaged him to dance the *minuet de la cour* with me, hoping to be less timid with him than with M. Laffitte or M. Dupaty.

At half-past ten General Bonaparte was not arrived; every one else was, and the five rooms in my mother's suite of apartments were much more than conveniently crowded. All the Bonaparte family except Joseph, who, I believe, was then at Luneville, came early.

Madame Leclerc, always beautiful and elegant, had taken her seat at a distance from her sister-in-law, whose exquisite taste in dress never failed to put her out of conceit with her own appearance, how carefully soever her toilet had been performed. "I do not understand," said she to me, "how a person of forty years old can wear garlands of flowers!"

Madame Bonaparte had a wreath of poppies and golden ears of corn upon her head, and her dress was trimmed with the same. I was afraid that she would foolishly make the same compliment to my mother, and unwilling that a stupid remark should spoil the pleasure of the evening, I answered that my mother, who was older than Madame Bonaparte, had also flowers on her head and round her gown. Madame Leclerc looked at me with an air of astonishment. "But it is quite different—quite a different thing," said she.

At a few minutes before eleven the tramping of the First Consul's horse-guards was heard. Very soon afterwards the carriage drove up to the door, and almost immediately he appeared at the entrance of the dining-room with Albert and Junot, who had received him in the hall. My mother advanced towards him, and saluted him with her most courteous obeisance, to which he replied, with a smile:

"Eh, Madame Permon, is that how you receive an old friend?" and held out his hand. My mother gave him hers, and they entered the ballroom together. The heat was excessive. The First Consul remarked it, but without taking off his gray overcoat, and was on the point of making the tour of the room, but his searching eye had already observed that many of the ladies present had not risen at his entrance; he was offended, and passed immediately into the bedroom, still retaining my mother's arm, and appearing to look at her with admiration.

Dancing had been discontinued as soon as he appeared, and Bonaparte soon perceived it by the stillness of the salon, from whence issued only the murmuring sounds produced by the observations made upon him in an undertone.

"Pray, Madame Permon," said he, "let the dancing be resumed; young people must be amused, and dancing is their favourite pastime. I am told, by-the-by, that your daughter dances as well as Mademoiselle Chameroi.* I must see it. And if you will, you and I will dance the *Monaco*—the only one I know."

"I have not danced these thirty years," replied my mother.

---

* Mademoiselle Chameroi was the finest dancer at the Opera. At this period Eugène Beauharnais much admired her. It was on the occasion of her funeral that the singular history of the refusal of the Curé of St. Roch to bury an actress took place, which is related further on. She died very young.

"Oh, you are jesting. You look to-night like your daughter's sister."

M. de Talleyrand was of the party. The First Consul, after having spoken to us all in the most agreeable manner, entered into a conversation with him in my mother's bedroom, which lasted without interruption for three-quarters of an hour. Towards midnight he returned to the salon, and appeared determined to make himself perfectly agreeable to everyone.

It was then he met my eyes fixed upon him, and called me to him, to make me a compliment on my mother's ball; his praises seemed almost a reproach. My mother had been perfectly polite to him; but it appeared to me that she should have been more cordial.

I went to her, and, persuading her to walk with me, led her towards her own chamber, where I found the First Consul on the spot where I had quitted him; but Junot and M. de Villemanzy had replaced M. de Talleyrand. As soon as the First Consul saw my mother, he went direct to her, and said, "Well, Madame Permon, what have you to say to one of your old friends? It seems to me that you easily forget them. Do you know, I thought you very hard the other evening, and at the very time one of your friends held his knife in readiness?"

"Oh, horrible!" exclaimed my mother; "how can you, Napoleon, say such things?—*Per Dio tacete! tacete!*"

"But why would you not return my friendly salute? I took the first moment of recognizing you to make it."

My mother alleged the weakness of her eyes, and not without cause, for they became very useless in the last years of her life; but General Bonaparte would not be put off with this excuse. "What am I to think?" said he; "are we no longer friends?"

"*Non posso dimenticare, caro Napoleone, che siete figlio dell' amica; fratello del mio buon Giuseppe, del caro Luciano, e di Pauletta.*"—The First Consul made a movement, which I noticed, and replied with a bitter accent:

"So, then, if I still hold a place in your regard, I owe it to my mother and my brothers. It may well be said that to expect friendship from a woman is to expect the sands of the desert to remain fixed."

This discussion gave me pain; it seemed that my mother remembered that unfortunate quarrel excited by one of our cousins, who never could indemnify us for the affection which we lost through his means.

The First Consul walked in silence towards the fire. My mother was seated upon a sofa opposite to him, her arms crossed upon her bosom, and shaking her foot in the fashion which usually preceded a violent scene. Albert, going to and fro between the chamber and the salon, at this moment approached General Bonaparte to offer him an ice.

"I assure you," said he, "that neither Madame Permon nor myself require ice—indeed, I believe we are petrified; I knew very well that absence deadened remembrance, but not to such a point as this." He touched an unlucky string.

"Truly!" said my mother, with a constrained smile, but with her lips sufficiently opened to show her two-and-thirty pearls (on which General Bonaparte cast his eyes; he spoke of them to me the following day);—"truly! one may be permitted to forget after an interval of some years. Did you not wish to persuade me that it was difficult to remember, after a few days, an action which affected the fate of an entire life?"

"Ah!" exclaimed the First Consul, and his countenance darkened in an instant. He knit that brow, the movement of which already agitated the universe; his under lip pressed strongly against the other; and, joining his hands behind him, he walked a few paces without speaking; but all this was scarcely visible, as Junot and my brother told me, when I returned from joining in a country-dance. The First Consul promptly resumed his air of serenity, and, seating himself beside my mother, looked attentively at her hand, which he had taken to kiss.

"It seems to me that you do not correct any of your faults, Madame Permon?" and he pointed to the bitten nails of her fingers.

"No," said my mother, "they and I have grown old together. Leave all in its place; it is only you who are forbidden to remain as you are; you have still so many steps to climb before you reach the summit of your glory that to wish you repose would be to wish harm to ourselves."

"Do you really think as you speak?"

"You know my sincerity. I do not always say all I think; but I never say what I do not think. Have you forgotten my frankness?"

Bonaparte took my mother's hand and pressed it affectionately. At this moment the clock struck two. He asked for his carriage.

"Will you not stay to supper?" asked my mother.

"I cannot possibly," said he, with an accent of regret; "but I will come and see you again."

My mother smiled, and shook her head gently.

"Why that smile? do you doubt me, Madame Permon? If in this evening either of us has doubted the friendship of the other, I do not think it is I who should be accused of having caused that suspicion. Yes, I shall come and see you again. The Signora Letizia shall bring me, since I must rest my claim to your regard upon her, or upon Joseph, or upon Lucien, or even upon Paulette; who knows? perhaps upon Jerome. Speaking of that brave little citizen, you brought him up well while I was far off. I find him wilful, and wilful in bad things. The Signora Letizia spoils him so totally that I much doubt whether he will mend where he now is."

To speak of Jerome was to touch another chord which vibrated very sensibly on my mother's ear. "He is an excellent lad," said she—"all warmth of heart, and good sentiments. Jerome is a true sailor; let him tan himself in the sea air, and he will return to you a Duguay-Trouin, or at least a Duquesne."

This was not the only time in the course of the evening that my mother had advanced an opinion with which she was not perfectly satisfied; but she loved Jerome, I believe, almost as well as she loved me, and her partiality really went a great way. The First Consul was right when he said that at his return he found his brother singularly educated. The seniors of the family had taken care that everything should be in good order—that is to say, Jerome was at the College of Juilly, and was frequently visited there by his family; but he still more frequently visited Paris himself to offer the respects of a young gentleman of fourteen to Mademoiselle Emilie and Mademoiselle Hortense de Beauharnais; then believing himself a man, the studies went on as they might.

Jerome and I were of the same age; my mother, who coupled with his birth the unhappy circumstances of the death of M. Charles Bonaparte, loved him so much the more. In general, she had a warm affection for all the brothers, but had her preferences amongst them as amongst the sisters. Madame Leclerc was her favourite, and to such a degree that I, who could not share her prejudice, often had warm discussions with her on the subject, in which perhaps jealousy might have its share.

At that time I loved Madame Murat the best of Napoleon's sisters, and Joseph and Lucien were, with the First Consul, those of the whole family whom I preferred. Jerome had been very much loved, very much spoilt, not only by my mother, but by my brother, and, indeed, by all of us. I did not find that when he advanced in life, and consequently when his sentiments might be expected to develop themselves, he was to my mother in particular what he ought to have been. I do not accuse him, but I shall have future occasion to prove that I was not mistaken. But this, after all, is no crime.

The First Consul told us, while speaking of Jerome, that he had contracted one of the oddest debts that could be imagined for a youth of fifteen. The First Consul was at Marengo: his brother was already in the service, but, being too young to take part in the campaign, was left in Paris. On the return of the First Consul, Bourrienne was presented with a number of bills, amounting in the whole to a considerable sum, the payment of which was pressing. Amongst others Biennais figured for eight or ten thousand francs. Great inquiries were made, and many reports were spread, as to how so large a debt could have arisen.

At length it was discovered that M. Jerome Bonaparte had purchased of M. Biennais, Rue Saint Honoré, at the sign of the Singe Violet, a magnificent travelling-case, containing everything that could be invented by elegance and luxury, in gold, mother-of-pearl, silver, and ivory, the finest porcelains, and the most beautifully executed enamels; in short, the whole was a jewel. But one very essential thing was wanting to this dressing-case, and that was a beard to make it useful; for whatever it contained would admit of no other application. Razors, shaving-pots of all sizes in silver and china; combs for the moustaches; in short, every article of convenience for shaving, but the beard was wanting; and, unfortunately, the young man, who was but fifteen, had some long years to wait for it. The First Consul told this little history in a very entertaining style.

Madame Bonaparte, whom I often visited, occupied the whole ground-floor of the Tuileries, which was afterwards her residence as Empress, and also that of Marie Louise. Adjoining her dressing-room was the small apartment of Mademoiselle de Beauharnais, consisting of her bedchamber, and a study scarcely of sufficient dimensions to render the smell of her oil paints endurable, when she this winter* painted her brother's portrait. The apartments of Madame Bonaparte were furnished tastefully, but without luxury; the great reception-salon was hung with yellow draperies; the movable furniture was damask, the fringes of silk, and the wood mahogany. No gold was to be seen. The other rooms were not more richly decorated; all was new and elegant, but no more. The apartments of Madame Bonaparte, however, were destined only for private parties and morning visits.

The larger assemblies were held upstairs. As yet there was neither Chamberlain nor Prefect of the Palace; an old Counsellor of State, formerly Minister of the Interior, M. de Benezeck, was charged with the internal administration of the palace, which was at first a little difficult to introduce amongst what remained of true Republicanism. The functions of M. de Benezeck embraced those afterwards divided between the Grand Chamberlain and the Master of the Ceremonies. The *maîtres d'hôtel* and ushers performed the subaltern offices, and the *aides-de-camp* supplied the place of chamberlains.

The First Consul was in the habit of inviting two hundred persons every ten days to dine with him. These dinners were given in the Gallery of Diana, and the guests were of all ranks and classes, always including the Diplomatic Corps, which at this time was become tolerably numerous. The wives of civil functionaries, of generals and colonels, formed the society, for as yet no one ventured to say the Court, of Madame Bonaparte. The General was rigid in the choice he made, not for his quintidian routs, but for the private and frequent invitations to Malmaison, and afterwards to Saint Cloud. It is a fact, which only prejudiced minds will dispute, that the First Consul wished to perpetuate, as far as lay in his power, the amelioration of morals produced by the Revolution. This will perhaps excite a smile in the perusal; never-

---

* This same winter of 1800 the Tuileries caught fire, and Mademoiselle Beauharnais' portrait of her brother, which was a speaking likeness, was consumed. The fire was falsely imputed to incendiaries, but was occasioned by ill-constructed flues.

theless, it is certain that the morals of the existing generation have been retempered by the Revolution.

In 1800, when the Court of the Tuileries was formed, society wore an appearance of morality and domestic virtue which it had never before displayed in France. The Noblesse, or what was at length by common consent denominated the *Faubourg Saint Germain,* was constrained to follow the general current, although here again some exceptions were known in ladies who founded their fame on the importation of follies from Brussels, Coblentz, etc., and afterwards from England.

Eventually, the Imperial Court, like all else pertaining to sovereignty, spread its malign influence. It was, however, comparatively but little open to censure, as the Emperor exercised a magical sway over every woman admitted to his Court.

Anyone who had witnessed the removal from the Luxembourg to the Tuileries on the 30th Pluviose of the year viii., if he had then fallen asleep to the sound of military music, playing all our patriotic airs, and had been awakened by the thunder of cannon on the morning of the 2nd December, announcing that the Emperor Napoleon was about to be crowned by the Pope in Notre Dame, would have discovered a curious contrast between the two processions. In the first, on account of the scarcity of private carriages at that time in Paris, it was necessary to engage for councillors of state and senators hackney-coaches, whose numbers were covered with white paper, producing an effect far more ludicrous than if the numbers had remained visible.

On the day of his installation at the Tuileries, scarcely had the First Consul arrived before he mounted his horse and held a review in the court of the palace, which was not then surrounded by a railing, but enclosed by ill-jointed boards; and the Place du Carrousel was then small and very irregular. The change was rapid; a word from Napoleon was sufficient.

The First Consul admitted that he was happy during his reviews. "And you, too, I am sure, are well content while I am with your conscripts," said he one day to General Lannes. "You do not grumble because the parade retards our dinner for an hour." "Oh dear, no!" replied General Lannes, "it is all alike to me, whether I eat my soup warm or cold, provided you will set us to work at making a hot broth for those rascally English."

He had an aversion for the English that I have never observed in any other general of the Emperor's army, even of those who had fought under the Republic.

The quintidians* (for we must speak the language of the period) were chosen for reviews, or rather for parades, in the court of the Tuileries. These parades were a spectacle worth seeing, especially during the Consulate. Under the Empire they might be more magnificent; but in 1800 their splendour was wholly national. It was the glory of France that we contemplated in those squadrons and battalions, which, whether composed of conscripts or veterans, equally impressed with fear the foreigner who surveyed them from the windows of the palace; for the ardour of the young troops was fostered by constantly beholding the old musketeers of the Consular Guard covered with scars.

The First Consul took pleasure in these reviews, which would sometimes occupy him for five hours together, without a moment's interval of repose. All the regiments in France came alternately to Paris and passed in review with the Guards every fortnight at noon. The First Consul was on these occasions always attended by the aide-de-camp on duty, the Minister of War, the General commanding the First Division, and the Commandant of Paris, the Commissary-General, the Commissaries of War attached to the city of Paris; in short, all persons to whom orders must be immediately transmitted, in case the First Consul should, in the course of the inspection, find any alteration or improvement requisite. By this means no delay could arise in the communication of orders: everything was done instantaneously and satisfactorily, for it was well understood that the eye of the chief closely superintended all, and that if punishment were awarded to negligence, punctuality would be duly appreciated.

Sometimes he galloped along the ranks, but this was rare; he never, indeed, sat his horse unless the troops had already passed in review and he was satisfied that nothing was wanting. Even then he would address a few questions to two or three soldiers casually selected; but generally after riding along the ranks on his white horse *(le Désiré)* he would alight, and converse with all the field-officers, and with nearly all the subalterns and soldiers. His solicitude was extended to the most minute

* The fifth day of the week as redefined by the still used revolutionary calendar.

particulars—the food, the dress, and everything that could be necessary to the soldier, or useful to the man, divided his attention with the evolutions. He encouraged the men to speak to him without restraint. "Conceal from me none of your wants," he would say to them; "suppress no complaints you may have to make of your superiors. I am here to do justice to all, and the weaker party is especially entitled to my protection."

These words he one day addressed to a demi-brigade (I believe it was the 17th), aware that the regiment before its removal to Paris had suffered deprivations in the department where it had been in garrison. Such a system was not only attended with immediately beneficial results, but was adroitly adapted to answer a general and not less useful purpose. The Army and its Chief thus became inseparably united, and in the person of that Chief the army beheld the French Nation. Thus the State, through him, dispensed both blame and commendation. Besides, Paris by this means became acquainted with the army; and the troops, in turn, visiting the capital, ceased to regard it as another world, and themselves as foreigners in it.

My mother's health was strikingly improved since my marriage. Contrary to my brother's inclinations, as well as mine, she had called in a new physician, named Vigaroux, the son of a skilful surgeon of Montpellier, and he seemed to work wonders. He engaged to cure her in six months, and she was surely enough relieved from pain. She dined with me, went to plays, was going about on visits the whole morning, and, far from feeling fatigued, she was the better for all this exertion.

Garat, one of my mother's oldest and most assiduous acquaintances, came one day to entreat our attendance at the Opera on the 23rd December to hear Haydn's fine oratorio of the "Creation," which he, jointly with Steibelt, had arranged, and in which he was to take a part. My mother, who was passionately fond of good music and of Garat's singing, readily promised a compliance. She was to sit in my box; and as Junot dined with Berthier, the new Minister of War, it was settled that I should dine with her ready dressed, and Junot would join us after dinner.

My toilet completed for the evening, I entered the carriage with my brother-in-law, and we found my mother beautiful, gay, and enchanting. She was splendidly dressed in black velvet and diamonds, and no one would have supposed her of the age of sixty-two.

We dined early; my mother ordered her horses while we took coffee, and we set out immediately afterwards. It was seven when we arrived at the Opera. The house was crowded, and being well lighted, and the ladies in full dress, the spectacle was very brilliant.

We distinguished Garat with his opera-glass in his hand earnestly surveying the boxes to recognize his acquaintances. He was more ridiculously dressed than usual; no very easy matter. His coat collar stood higher than his head, and his rather monkeyish face was difficult to discern between ells of muslin by way of cravat below and a forest of curls above.

The instruments were tuned, and this immense orchestra, more numerous than I had ever seen it before, was preparing to render Haydn's *chef-d'oeuvre* more perfectly than he had ever the gratification of hearing it himself.

Junot found my mother and me in high spirits, occupied in looking round this magnificent house, and returning the friendly and smiling salutations of our acquaintance. He was himself in a peculiar state of mind. Berthier had been repeating to him a conversation he had held with the First Consul respecting Junot; and his words were so full of kindness and friendship that Junot was sensibly affected, and his eyes watered, while happiness played in smiles on his lips.

Scarcely were thirty bars of the oratorio played before a violent explosion was heard, like the report of a cannon.

"What means that?" said Junot with emotion. He opened the box door, and looked about for one of his officers or aides-de-camp. "It is strange!" said he. "How can the guns be fired at this hour? Besides, I should have known it! Give me my hat," said he to my brother; "I will go and see what it is." Instantly Chevalier's machine occurred to me, and I seized the flaps of Junot's coat; but he looked angrily at me, and impatiently snatched it from my grasp.

At this moment the door of the First Consul's box opened and himself appeared, with General Lannes, Berthier, and Duroc. He smilingly saluted the immense crowds, who mingled frantic yells of pleasure with their acclamations.

Madame Bonaparte followed in a few seconds, accompanied by Colonel Rapp, Madame Murat (who was near her confinement), and Mademoiselle Beauharnais. Junot was re-entering the box to convince himself of the First Consul's serenity, which I had just remarked upon, when Duroc presented himself with a discomposed countenance and an excited air. He spoke in whispers to Junot, and we heard nothing of his communication; but at night Junot repeated it to me. "I love Duroc; he is almost as much attached to the First Consul as Marmont and myself."

Duroc's words sufficiently explained the disturbed condition in which he appeared. "The First Consul has just escaped death," said he hastily to Junot; "go to him; he wishes to speak to you, but be calm. It is impossible the event should remain unknown here a quarter of an hour; but he wishes to avoid being himself the means of spreading such intelligence; so come with me and let me lean on your arm, for I tremble all over. My first battle agitated me less."

During the short conference of the two friends the oratorio had commenced; but the fine voices of Mesdames Branchu and Walbourne, and that of Garat, could not absorb the attention of the audience. All eyes were turned towards the First Consul, and he alone at this moment occupied our attention. I felt a presentiment of some misfortune.

The moment Duroc spoke to Junot the latter turned pale as a spectre, and I perceived him raise his hand to his forehead with a gesture of surprise and despair; but, being unwilling to disturb my mother and the people in the adjoining boxes, I contented myself with whispering to Junot to ask for intelligence. But before his return we had heard all. A subdued murmur began to spread from the stage to the orchestra, the pit, and the boxes. "The First Consul has just been attacked in the Rue Saint Nicaise."

The truth soon circulated throughout the theatre, when simultaneously, and as it were by an electric shock, one unanimous acclamation was heard. How tumultuous was the agitation which preceded the burst of national resentment! for in the first quarter of an hour the nation was represented by that crowd, whose indignation against so foul an attempt no words are capable of expressing.

Meanwhile I was engaged in observing the First Consul's box, which, being immediately below me, enabled me to see and hear nearly all that passed in it. He was calm, and appeared only warmly affected when the general murmur conveyed to his ear any strong expression of the public feeling. Madame Bonaparte was not equally mistress of her feelings. Her whole frame was agitated; even her attitude, always so graceful, was no longer her own. She seemed to tremble, and to be desirous of sheltering herself under her shawl,—the very shawl which had saved her life. She wept: notwithstanding all her efforts to repress her tears, they were seen trickling down her pale cheeks, and when she looked towards the First Consul her shivering fit returned. Her daughter too was greatly upset. As for Madame Murat, the character of the family shone in her demeanour; although her situation might have excused the display of anxiety and distress so natural in the sister of the First Consul, she was, throughout this trying evening, perfectly composed.

Junot, having received the orders of the First Consul, returned to desire we would not wait for him, and hastily said: "Go with your mother; after setting her down, borrow her carriage to convey you to Madame Bonaparte's; I shall be there, and will take you home;" and away he ran. In spite of the excessive cold he was covered with perspiration.

My brother-in-law accompanied us, and having set down my mother we proceeded to the Tuileries. The First Consul was returned from the Opera, and everything appeared as calm as if nothing had happened; but in the salon things wore a different aspect. Several of the authorities were assembled, the Ministers, the Consuls, the Commandant of Paris, General Mortier, Commandant of the Division, etc. The First Consul, who had hitherto appeared indifferent to all the attempts against him, showed this time no indulgence, and he had good reason.

Madame Bonaparte was quite overpowered; she cried incessantly. Independently of the danger the First Consul had so narrowly escaped, she had herself nearly fallen a victim to the explosion. As she was stepping into the carriage, General Rapp, who was not usually so observant of the perfect agreement of colours in a lady's dress, observed to her that her shawl matched neither her gown nor her jewels. Her perfect elegance in the adjustment of all the accessories of the toilet is well known, and she returned to repair the oversight. Scarcely did it detain her three minutes, yet these sufficed for separating her carriage from that of the First Consul, which it was to have followed close. This delay saved her!

The explosion took place just as Madame Bonaparte's carriage reached the Carrousel: its windows were broken, and pieces of the glass fell on the neck and shoulders of Mademoiselle Beauharnais, who sat on the front seat of the carriage, and her shawl did not protect her from some slight cuts.

It is well known that the barrel containing the powder and charge (and which resembled those borne by the water-carriers) was placed on a crazy little cart, drawn by a mare, and so stationed as to impede the road. It was intended, while in the act of removal by the guards, to explode by internal machinery, and destroy everything within reach. It was afterwards said that the rapidity of his carriage alone had saved the First Consul.

Soon afterwards, I was engaged to breakfast with Madame Bonaparte at the Tuileries. Her custom of inviting young married women, too timid to make themselves agreeable in the society of superior men, was delightful to me. Chatting with Madame Bonaparte, during the perfectly unceremonious repast, upon fashions, and all the little interests of society, these young ladies acquired confidence, and threw off that reserve which the presence of the First Consul was calculated to inspire.

Madame Bonaparte did the honours with grace and vivacity; we were generally five or six, and all of the same age, the mistress of the house excepted. At Malmaison the number was sometimes twelve or fifteen, and the breakfast was served in a small circular salon looking into the court, and which is now present to my imagination, though I have not entered it these sixteen years.

One day, at the Tuileries breakfast, I met Madame Vaines, who was high in favour both with the First Consul and Madame Bonaparte, and another person, whose name I forget; all I remember is, that it must have been a female, for men were never admitted to these morning *fêtes,* the First Consul positively prohibiting it. Madame Bonaparte told us she was going to make a visit to a lying-in lady, and inquired if we would accompany her. We acceded, but begged to know in our turn who was the object of our visit. She answered, that to be sure it was a personage who might eat us, but that at present she was in a gentle mood; in short, it was the lioness of the Botanical Garden, who had been delivered at her full time of three whelps, all living. The First Consul had been already there; but as Madame Bonaparte had informed him of her proposal, he had promised to join us if his engagements would permit.

The lioness was doing well, but was, as Madame Bonaparte had told us, in a languishing mood. Félix Cassal, her keeper, entered the cage, took the cubs from her, and the poor beast, without moving, turned her eyes on him with an expression of softness and affection. She was extended in her cage on a good litter, and her little ones lay rolled in thick coarse carpets, as warmly as in the African sands.

Madame Bonaparte took one of the cubs in her hands, which drew forth a growl from the mother; but Félix spoke to her, and acknowledging his voice by a momentary glance of more fierceness than the former, she again turned to the offender, and renewed her growl. Madame Bonaparte was alarmed. "Oh! never fear," said Félix; "she is behind a strong grating, and, besides, she has not yet recovered her strength; she would not hurt much." "Oh!" said Madame Bonaparte, "I can dispense with the trial of her strength; there would be quite enough remaining to make me repent having caressed her son."

This Cassal was an extraordinary man in his way. He was a great traveller, and had made interesting observations, even on the common habits of the country he had passed through; and though he pretended to have seen marvels altogether incredible, yet all he said was not false, and both amusement and instruction might be extracted from him. He had himself purchased the lioness of some Arabs, who had taken her in the environs of Constantinople. While she was *enceinte,* a child having wounded her in the eye with a stone, she threw herself into so violent a passion as to produce abortion; and as she brought forth the present litter a hundred days afterwards, that must have been the utmost extent of her parturition, which disproves the conjectures of Pliny and Buffon; the latter, I believe, asserts that the lioness is six or seven months with young.

She littered on the 18th Brumaire, and Félix named the first-born whelp Marengo. "Was not I a good god-father?" said he to Madame Bonaparte.

He made me touch one of the whelps; but the lioness, who had turned away and appeared to think no more of the matter, suddenly started up to her full height, and uttered a roar that shook the very walls.

Félix soothed her, and took the cub himself. He told us that the First Consul, on his visit to the lioness, had caressed her, and was very well received. "He inquired the hour of her delivery," said Félix; "the nature of her food, and especially of her beverage; and the General who was with him gave me a bright piece of gold, that the lioness might drink to the health of the Republic, a direction I have obeyed. Oh, he thinks of everything, the Citizen Consul!" While he spoke, I was meditating on the fortunes of this extraordinary man, which seemed to be mysteriously linked with all the wonders of his age.

The First Consul met us on horseback before we had quitted the gardens, and Félix no sooner perceived him than he hurried forward to report the bulletin of the lioness; assuring him that she had drunk to his health, and that she was wonderfully well. Napoleon caressed her, and talked with Félix of all his beasts, with as much ease, and as perfect a knowledge of their properties and habits, as if this branch of science had been his particular study.

Félix, finding such encouragement, entered upon one of his best stories; but just as he arrived (on his own showing) at the most astonishing point, Napoleon patted him on the head with:

"Félix, you lie, my boy; there are no crocodiles in the place you speak of, nor ever were; but it is all one—proceed with your story."

This was more easily said than done. Félix was so thoroughly disconcerted by the First Consul's apostrophe, that it was impossible to recover the thread of his adventure.

"Well, it will do for another day," said Napoleon good-humouredly; "only remember that crocodiles do not devour those who bathe in the Bosphorus, otherwise it would have been much easier to kill Leander by that means than by drowning, as he had no boat, poor fellow!"

We promenaded for some time in these beautiful gardens and their fine greenhouses. They are greatly improved since; yet the Botanical Gardens were even then the most complete institution of the kind in Europe. Other museums were richer in particular articles, but ours alone possessed that superiority in all, which has since rendered it the universal rendezvous for the study of natural history. Napoleon observed that day, "It is my wish to render this the most attractive spot to all learned foreigners in Paris. I wish to draw them here to see and admire a people in their love of science and the arts. The museum of natural history shall be what those of sculpture and painting, and of ancient monuments, will be. Paris should be the first city of the world. If God grant me a life long enough, I would have her become the capital of the universe, in science as well as power. Our painters are already the first, the best in Europe. Excepting Canova and Appiani, Italy herself cannot boast talents equal to ours in painting and sculpture. Their poets also are inferior to ours. Cesarotti and Alfieri cannot dispute the palm with our young writers. In short," added he, "I am proud of my country, and I would have her always mindful of what she is and may be."

For some months after my marriage not a day passed that Junot did not introduce to me several of his friends, and a multitude of acquaintances. I was accustomed to see much company at my mother's. Her circle was a wide one, but it sank into insignificance compared with ours. This perpetual distraction was at first extremely fatiguing, and my mother, who came to install me in my new dignity of mistress of my house, giving me credit for the manner in which I acquitted myself of my arduous functions, added that, for her part, as a spectator only, one of these soirées more than satisfied her, and had its arrangement fallen on her it would have cost her a week's illness.

For some time I was of her opinion, but before a month had elapsed I was sensible of a growing inclination for company, and in a short time, aided by a disposition to view all things on the brightest side, and a lively interest in seeking out, and associating with a visible form, all circumstances relating to the life and character of men whose names had long struck my ears in society, and my eyes in the journals, I began to feel real pleasure in my new situation. Junot, to whom I imparted my change of sentiment, sincerely congratulated me upon it, and promised to assist me whenever my researches should require his aid.

There were at that time few open houses at Paris, the privilege being confined to the ministers and authorities; and even they received only large and formal parties. I was anxious to effect a reformation in this respect, and once expressed my wish to the First Consul, when he was mentioning his own desire to see a more free communication between the society of Paris and the members of the Government.

"Accomplish that, and you will be a charming little woman," said General Bonaparte. "If you make the attempt you will succeed, for you know what it is to hold a drawing-room. Let Citizen Cambacérès see that for this purpose it is not sufficient merely to give a dinner."

The Consul Cambacérès received company every Tuesday and Saturday, and for the first six months of the year 1800 no other house could stand a comparison with the Hôtel Cambacérès; it was soon, however, not only imitated, but excelled. The principal members of his household were Messieurs de Lavollée and Monvel, secretaries, and Messieurs de Chateauneuf and D'Aigrefeuille, who had no appointed functions, but voluntarily acted as chamberlains, and the moment a lady was announced, one of these gentlemen went to the door to receive and conduct her to a chair.

I had a great friendship for Cambacérès, which neither absence nor distance ever impaired; yet I must acknowledge that, notwithstanding the host's peculiar elegance and superior powers of pleasing, and notwithstanding even that friendly welcome and perfect politeness which, under the influence of the master's example, extended itself to the very lowest domestic of the household, no sooner had you passed the gate of the Hôtel Cambacérès than the very air seemed impregnated with ennui, sleep took possession of the eyelids, and a sort of lethargy suspended every faculty as completely as in the temple of Morpheus.

The dinner-party never exceeded five-and-twenty, and of these the proportion of ladies was small; there were never, indeed, more than two of such consideration, from the offices of their husbands, as that their pretensions to precedence might have occasioned jealousies. There was an excellent cook; and the carving fell to the department of the *maître d'hôtel,* Cambacérès himself never doing the honours, except of a dish of rare game.

This was a great innovation in the etiquette of French society, but I found it agreeable; I cannot, however, say as much for his custom of entertaining the guests nearest to him with an enumeration of all his maladies of the day, assuring us he was too ill to eat, yet always concluding by making an excellent meal. He had great conversational powers, and his narratives acquired novelty and grace from the turn of his language. His evening drawing-room was crowded with judges, registrars, and other officers of all the courts in France, who seemed already to anticipate the future Arch-chancellor;* he bore, indeed, even at that period, the character of the ablest civilian in the country.

The Third Consul,** too, had already entered upon his future department, the Financial and Administrative; and he also had his two evenings appropriated weekly. How many original figures have passed before my eyes in these two houses! How often, when my eager scrutiny has been awakened by the announcement of a name which had figured conspicuously in the Revolution, have I been disappointed by an insignificant or repulsive exterior! how often, seated beside such a one the whole dinner-time, which with Cambacérès was never short, I have been stupefied by the utter nullity of his ideas! but on communicating my feelings to Cambacérès, he would answer, "This man's reputation was the result of chance; opportunity fell in his way, and instinctively he seized it by the forelock."

The conduct of Cambacérès during the Revolution has been much talked of, and I do not pretend to excuse it. I hate the sanguinary years with which his name is connected, and everything that recalls them; but, difficult as the task may be, I would fain see him exempted from the censures which attach to the men of that period. Napoleon did not approve of the events of 1793, but he excused the famous vote of Cambacérès by the reflection that the thing once done—that is to say,

* When, in 1804, Napoleon became Emperor, he made Cambacérès Arch-Chancellor and created him a prince.
** Lebrun, who became Arch-Treasurer and Duke of Plaisance.

the King once condemned—the interests of France, and especially of Paris, demanded the immediate consummation of that terrible drama.

He disapproved of the sentence, which he characterized as a resolution unjustly adopted towards a man who was guilty only of the crimes of others; and I never heard him pronounce the name of Louis XVI without the additional epithet of *"the unfortunate King."* I record his opinion here, because I conceive that on a matter so momentous, and which so nearly concerns his own destiny—since it still influences that of France—it must be of the highest interest to us.

Cambacérès was originally Councillor in the Court of Finances of Languedoc. When the Comte de Perigord presided over the states of that province, of which he was commandant in 1786, Cambacérès was in misfortune. M. de Perigord, always benevolent and ready to assist the needy, asked and obtained for the almost indigent Councillor a pension of two hundred francs, and for his father one of two thousand francs, out of the royal lotteries.

The courtesy of Cambacérès was general, but his countrymen from Languedoc he welcomed with a peculiar urbanity, the more invaluable that it had none of the varnish of fashionable politeness. Many Languedocians went direct to the Hôtel de Cambacérès on alighting from the diligences; he received them with kindness, examined their petitions, and if he could not assist them, unhesitatingly told them the truth, pointing out at the same time how they might obtain other advantages, and never failed to forward their interests. I may be allowed to call Cambacérès an honest man; for, looking around on all his equals in power, I have never found one of such absolute good faith and probity, to which many others can testify.

His figure was extraordinarily ugly, as well as unique. The slow and regular step, the measured cadence of accent, the very look, which took three times as long as another's to arrive at its object—all was in admirable keeping with the long person, long nose, long chin, and the yellow skin, which betrayed not the smallest symptoms that any matter inclining to sanguine circulated beneath its cellular texture.

The same consistency, though probably unstudied, pervaded his dress; and when demurely promenading the galleries of the Palais Royal, then the Palais Egalité, the singular cut and colour of his embroidered coat; his ruffles, at that time so uncommon; his short breeches, silk stockings, shoes polished with English blacking, and fastened with gold buckles; his old-fashioned wig and queue; and his well-appointed and well-placed three-cornered hat, produced altogether a most fantastic effect.

Even the members of his household, by their peculiarities of dress, served as accessories to the picture.

He went every evening to the theatre, and seldom failed to make his appearance afterwards with his suite, all in full costume, either in the gardens of the Tuileries or of the Palais Egalité, where everything around exhibited the most ludicrous disparity with this strange group, whose solemn deportment and deliberate and circumspect discourse might serve to personify the disciples of Plato following their master to Sunium.

The First Consul was sometimes annoyed that the ridicule attached to his colleague appeared to recoil upon him, and I remember once seeing him enraged as he listened to the translation of a passage from the English journals. The Second Consul was caricatured, and from the Second to the First the transition is so easy that the journalist made no scruple of it. The First Consul stamped his foot, and said to Josephine:

"You must interfere in this matter—do you hear? It is only a woman that can tell a man he is ridiculous; if I meddle I shall tell him he is mad."

I know not whether Madame Bonaparte achieved her commission to the Consul Cambacérès; but this I know, that although always highly distinguished for his knowledge, his politeness, and his dinners, he yet always remained that which had so highly discomposed the First Consul.

Before quitting the Consul Cambacérès, I must relate an adventure which happened about this time. A Portuguese, named Don Alexander de Souza, had just arrived in Paris, on his road to (or from) an embassy at Rome.

M. de Souza was a very little man, about four feet ten or eleven inches high, and the whole of his delicate person cast in a most diminutive mould: he was not only thin, but absolutely shrivelled; yet he had the air of a gentleman, and his manners were those of a person of quality. The authorities received him with something more than the cordiality due to the friend of our enemies, and M. de Souza had nothing to complain of on his passage through Paris. The Second Consul would not let slip such an opportunity to give a sumptuous dinner. All the authorities were invited, and many of his friends; Junot and I were of the number, as were Duroc, Lannes, and Mortier, now Duke of Treviso, and then Commandant of the First Military Division.

I have not before mentioned this excellent man or his wife, all goodness, simplicity, and gentleness. He was Junot's superior as Commandant of the Division, while Junot was only Commandant of Paris; but we lived on the best and most friendly terms; for General Mortier was, and still is, the best and most worthy of men; but at this period he would laugh like a child, and his mirth sometimes compromised the dignity of the General Commandant's epaulettes.

M. de Souza, on occasion of this dinner, wore a magnificent coat of Segovian cloth, embroidered in gold with a perfection we cannot attain in France. A frill of fine cambric rose almost imperceptibly at the top of his well-buttoned coat, in the English fashion, and his head displayed a peruke *à la Pitt,* more fully to exemplify that Portugal was not only the very humble servant of England, but equally the submissive slave of her minister.

M. de Souza was seated at table between me and Madame Jolivet, wife of a Councillor of State. All the civilities lavished on the foreign traveller failed to banish the ennui with which this republican land seemed to inspire him. I was obliged to stifle my yawns in answering some trifling questions, and had little hope of a gayer termination of the repast, when an incident, certainly not included in the instructions of Cambacérès to his *maîtres d'hôtel,* gave a new turn to the aspect of affairs.

Cambacérès had for some time placed his household on a very respectable footing: his domestics had all the superb livery of the Consuls, and the *maîtres d'hôtel* had exchanged their black dresses for maroon cloth, with wrought gold buttons. There were always two courses at the Second Consul's, and as each course consisted of eighteen or twenty removes, it may be supposed the arm of the *maître d'hôtel* intruded pretty frequently between each of the guests; but poor little Souza's stature presented no obstacle; the dishes passed over his head;

and on one of these occasions, one of the purveyor's gold buttons, being loose, hitched in the little gentleman's wig and carried it off.

The catastrophe was sudden, and no one knew how it had happened; even the *maître d'hôtel* himself had moved some distance before he discovered his involuntary theft; meanwhile the bewildered eyes of M. de Souza were seeking his wig in the direction of the ceiling, as if he imagined it had really taken wings, and those of the thirty persons around him, fixed on his startled figure, caused him an embarrassment which completed the burlesque of his appearance.

Yet we should all have behaved decently had he taken the accident in good part; but, wishing to be dignified under his misfortune, he thought, perhaps, to impress us vastly by saying, with the utmost seriousness, to the *maître d'hôtel*, who came in all haste to apologize:

"Sir, will you restore me my wig?" And he set to work to replace it; but the discomposure which was evident through all his studied calmness prevented his accurately distinguishing the position of the tuft *à la Pitt*, and the wig, to my inexpressible satisfaction, was put on all askew, so that the tuft just surmounted the right ear, till Madame Jolivet, in a tone of more than usual acerbity (for she was offended at the incivility of her neighbour, who had not addressed a word to her since he had conducted her to her seat), said to him, "Sir, your wig is awry;" and as she spoke she obligingly raised her hand to the head of the little gentleman, who bounded away from her friendly assistance with a vivacity that had nearly dashed me to the ground.

I had avoided looking at either my husband or General Mortier, certain that my suppressed laughter must have burst forth; it became, however, at length uncontrollable, and appeared equally to master the whole company; for no sooner had mine exploded than a mad and inextinguishable peal resounded from every side; but General Mortier's was loudest, and so violent as to oblige him eventually to rise from table. The polite host, on whose imperfect vision this by-play was lost, no sooner understood the matter than he exhausted himself in apologies to M. de Souza, who, while panting with rage, replied, bowing, that it was of no consequence; and the unfortunate wig, in spite of Madame Jolivet's officious care, remained awry. General Mortier, I am sure, will to this day remember that dinner and the hearty laugh it afforded him.

W H I L E Bonaparte was in Egypt, Josephine, who was anxious to have a country house, purchased the small chateau of La Malmaison. A simple eighteenth century stone house with two wings, La Malmaison is easily reached* from Paris; it had the added advantage of being situated in a large, splendidly-designed English-style park, but badly needed redecorating. This, too, Josephine now arranged, all at immense cost, all on credit.

Napoleon, who hated being in debt, found on his return that he owed over half a million francs for a house he had never even seen and had a fit. He announced immediately that Malmaison would have to be sold; but, as usual, Josephine won out in the end: when Napoleon saw the house, he fell in love with it.

All through the four years of the Consulate, it remained his favourite residence. It was considered a great favour to be invited there, and being a guest meant, not only that you were privy to much that was going on, but also that you were greatly envied by all those who yearned to be asked. Naturally, as the wife of one of the Consul's most trusted aides, Mme Junot was often invited, and soon grew to be on an intimate footing with the Bonapartes and Josephine's two Beauharnais children, the handsome Eugène and the charming Hortense.

The park of Malmaison was enchanting, notwithstanding its proximity to the barren mountain on one side. The river, though running far below, imparted strength and luxuriance to its vegetation; and nothing could be greener, more fresh, or umbrageous, than the field from which it was separated only by a ha-ha, and that part of the park itself which is bounded by the road. The extent of the park did not exceed a hundred acres; and Bonaparte, on his return from Egypt, endeavoured to persuade Mademoiselle Julien, a rich old maid of the village of Ruelle, as an act of good neighbourship, to sell him, at her own price,

* Malmaison, which has been admirably restored, is now open to the public.

151

an adjoining garden, or small park, by which addition Malmaison would have been placed on so respectable a footing that he need no longer have blushed to compare it with the magnificent estate of his brother Joseph.

The First Consul had a small private garden, separated only by a bridge from his private study. It was here that he took the air, when labour rendered moderate exercise necessary to him; for at that time, and for two years succeeding, he allowed himself no repose but what nature imperatively required. The bridge was covered in and arranged like a small tent; here his table was carried, and he would employ himself with State papers, saying that he felt his ideas become more elevated and expansive in the air than when seated beside a stove and shut out from communication with the sky.

Yet Bonaparte could not endure the smallest degree of cold; had fires lighted in July, and wondered that others did not suffer like himself from the first breath of a north wind.

Our life at Malmaison resembled that usually led when much company is assembled together at a château in the country. Our apartments consisted of a chamber, a boudoir, and a room for the chambermaid, all very simply furnished. That occupied by Mademoiselle Hortense differed from the others only by a folding-door; and this apartment was not assigned her till after her marriage. All opened on a long and narrow paved corridor, looking into the court.

We chose our own hour of rising, and until breakfast our time was at our own disposal. At eleven the ladies all met for breakfast in a small low salon of the right wing, opening to the court; but, as in Paris, gentlemen were never admitted to the party, unless, occasionally, Joseph, Louis, or one of the family. Breakfast was followed by conversation, or the reading of the journals, and someone always arrived from Paris to have *an audience,* for already Madame Bonaparte gave audiences, contrary to the express orders of the First Consul, and patronized petitions, though his anger at her interference had already caused her abundance of tears; but when a beautiful pearl necklace or bracelet of rubies was offered, through the hands of Bourrienne, or of any other friend, the elegance of a present so wholly unconnected with the matters in hand suppressed all curious speculations into the nature of the mine which produced it.

The First Consul was never visible till dinner-time. At five or six in the morning he descended to his cabinet, and was there occupied with Bourrienne, or with the Ministers Generals, and Councillors of State, till the dinner-hour of six, when the party was generally joined by some invited guests. All the suite of the First Consul were at this time enlarging his household by marriage; Colonel Savary had just married a relation of Madame Bonaparte (an unhoped-for happiness to a man whose life knew no other impulse than the desire of advancement); his wife was pretty, but had bad teeth.

Madame Lannes was really handsome, and in high favour at Malmaison, of which she was every way worthy; gentle, unconscious of envy, and never sacrificing to a jest the peace or reputation of another. In person she might have formed a model for the most beautiful Madonnas of Raphael or Coreggio; such was the symmetry of her features, the calmness of her countenance, the serenity of her smile. I first saw her at a ball, where she scarcely danced, although her figure was light and elegant. In the dignified station to which fate exalted her after the death of her husband, the Duchesse de Montebello's conduct was perfectly irreproachable; and she was ever ready to oblige or serve others as far as was consistent with the severity of the Emperor, who would inevitably have discouraged and opposed any affair recommended by a woman.

But to return to Josephine and her morning audiences. This was the only time that the surveillance of the First Consul left her at liberty, and he then committed the duty to Bourrienne, who tells us "he would have deemed it disgraceful to act as a spy on the wife of his friend," and therefore contented himself with concealing from the First Consul such acquisitions of jewellery, etc., as made no claim on the public finances. I must, however, do Madame Bonaparte the justice to say that she saw nothing of all these intrigues, but confined herself to writing a few lines to Berthier, who had much more consideration for her than any of the other Ministers; so little interest, indeed, had she with them, that importunity alone could not give any weight to her requests; the influence of Mademoiselle Hortense, had she exerted it, would have been far more effective.

But if Madame Bonaparte's credit with the authorities was at a low ebb, her reputation for it was also injured by her own proceedings; for example, amongst her most attached friends was Madame d'Houdetot, and her interposition was for once successful in recommending that lady's brother, M. de Céré, to the First Consul's favour, in which sense, good manners, and a pleasing address rapidly advanced him. He was becoming a familiar on the establishment when he was sent on a mission, and a certain day fixed for his return, after which he was to receive the appointment of aide-de-camp. But, alas! youth is heedless, and M. de Céré exceeded his appointment by a whole fortnight.

Napoleon, doubly incensed by the neglect of his orders and by his own error of judgment, a circumstance not very common, would listen to no solicitations for pardon, and peremptorily prohibited the young man's reappearance before him; while Madame Bonaparte observed that "a volcanic head, leading into follies for want of reflection, should not be associated with the indolence of a creole."

After many months had elapsed, determined on a new effort to recover his lost ground, he solicited, through the medium of his sister and of Savary, who was also his friend, an audience of Madame Bonaparte, and to his great joy was desired to repair on the morrow to Malmaison, furnished with a very clear and explicit memorial, which Josephine promised to forward. Arriving at the château, he found Madame, as usual, gracious and enchanting; she told him that the First Consul, already predisposed by her, would easily overlook an irregularity which M. de Céré promised to obliterate by future good conduct, and concluded by receiving his memorial, and recommending him to come himself in a few days for the answer.

The poor young man, intoxicated with the success of his overtures, demanded by anticipation the congratulations of his friends; but he discovered, before retiring to rest, that the memorial was still in his pocket, and he had left as its substitute in the hands of his patroness a long bill from his tailor. In despair at an incident which threatened annihilation to all his new-raised hopes, he passed a sleepless night, and early in the morning was again on the road to Malmaison, determined, as his last chance, to explain the whole affair to Madame Bonaparte. His consternation may be imagined when, advancing with outstretched hand to meet him, she anticipated his explanation with:

"How happy I am! I have delivered your memorial to the First Consul, and we read it together; it was admirably drawn up," added she, with an approving smile, "and made a great impression upon him. He told me Berthier should report it, and within a fortnight all will be settled. I assure you, *mon cher,* this success, for I consider the affair as concluded, made me the whole of yesterday the happiest woman in the world."

If the actual memorial had not been at that moment in his pocket he would have persuaded himself it was really in the hands of the First Consul, and that his unhappy carelessness was all a dream!

From this instance it may be inferred that Madame Bonaparte, though perfectly good-natured, and with the utmost disposition to oblige, could not be entirely depended upon in the management of any affair. She desired to confer favours, but this desire yielded to the smallest apprehension of the First Consul's displeasure.

Bonaparte was very partial to Malmaison, and insisted on all the visitors being entirely at their ease; it was always he who opposed the restraints of etiquette, which already Madame Bonaparte liked, and would fain have introduced, although as burdensome to herself as to others.

Every Wednesday there was a grand dinner at Malmaison. The Second Consul was always of the party, with the Ministers, the Counsellors of State, some particularly esteemed Generals, and a few ladies of unspotted reputation; for Napoleon was then rigorous in the choice of Madame Bonaparte's society. We acted plays in the evening, and the part of the abigails fell to my lot. Madame Savary was also of our company; Junot was our best actor, and Bourrienne, Eugène Beauharnais and Lauriston had talent. It was no trifle to play before, not only an audience of three hundred persons, but the First Consul in particular; for my part I should have preferred doubling the number, could he have been by that means excluded.

It was singular enough that I, certainly the most free with him of the whole establishment, and the most ready to answer his pleasantries —I, in short, who already gave indications of the woman who, according to his own confession of St. Helena, treated him as a boy *(en petit garçon),* the day that he addressed to my ears words to which it did not become me to listen—I could not endure his criticisms, just or unjust, on my performance, however convinced that he was mistaken, and that I best understood my own business with the assistance of Dugazon, my prompter.

The dinner-hour, as I have before said, was six; and when the weather was fine the First Consul ordered the table to be laid in the park on the left of the lawn; the dinner was soon despatched, and he found it wearisomely protracted if we sat more than half an hour.

When he was in good humour, the weather fine, and he had a few minutes' leisure from the labour which even at that time was killing him, he would play at barriers with us. He cheated us as at *reversis,* * would throw us down, or come upon us without crying *barre!* but these tricks were only calculated to raise a laugh. His coat was on such occasions laid aside, and he ran like a hare, or rather like the gazelle, which he would feed with a boxful of tobacco, and tell her to run after us, and the tormenting animal tore our clothes, and sometimes our legs.

One fine day after dinner he exclaimed, "Let us play at barriers!" Off went his coat, and the next moment the conqueror of the world was racing like a schoolboy. The park at Malmaison was not then as complete as it now is, although the most shameful vandalism has spared no efforts to extinguish the remembrances attached even to a few plants. It was separated only by a ha-ha from an open field, afterwards purchased for a plantation, and the curious could observe from this field all that passed in the park.

Madame Bonaparte had been leaning with Madame Lavalette on the iron railing which overlooked the ha-ha, when, advancing a few steps, they were alarmed by the sight of two men, of rough manners, shabby dress, and very suspicious appearance, who were eyeing the First Consul and whispering to one another. I had ceased playing, and at this moment approached Madame Bonaparte, who took my arm, and sent Lavalette to seek her husband or Eugène, but charged her to be careful that the First Consul did not discover her errand, for he detested any precautions.

She met Rapp, who required no stimulating whenever the shadow of danger threatened his General; in a few seconds he was beside the

* A game of cards still in vogue with the dowagers of the Faubourg Saint Germain.

men, and, accosting them somewhat roughly, demanded their reason for standing there frightening ladies, and threatened them with arrest. They stoutly maintained their right to look at their General, who, they were certain, would not drive them away, and appealed to Eugène, who, coming up at that moment to see what was the matter, recognized one of the intruders for an old chasseur of his regiment. The veteran explained in humourous and military phrase that the loss of his arm having disabled him for further service, his brother wished to be accepted as his substitute; and to arrange this affair, they were come in search of their commander, when the sight of the First Consul at full play had arrested their steps; and, having finished this explanation, they turned away.

Bonaparte, with his eyes which saw without looking, and his ears which heard without listening, had from the first word been in possession of a key to the whole scene: he remembered the old quartermaster of his chasseurs, who at Montebello or Marengo had lost an arm while defending the life of a wounded officer. The First Consul had himself caused him to be carried off the field, and as the veteran had since been presented to him on parade, he recalled his features. "Oh! oh!" said he, "there are the *Invalides* in retreat. Good-day, my boy. Well, you are come to see me, then? Come! face about! march once more at the command of your general. Conduct him, Eugène."

And passing his arm round Josephine's waist, he led her to the entrance of the château, where we met the two brothers, Eugène, and Rapp. The old chasseur presented his brother to the First Consul, reminding him at the same time that no legal obligations demanded his services. "It is a voluntary engagement, General," said he, "and you are his Recruiting-Captain."

"Since I am the Recruiting-Captain," said the First Consul, "the recruit must drink my health and that of the Republic. Eugène, take charge of your soldier, my boy; you will pledge him in my name."

The old chasseur watched the departing steps of his General, and, when he disappeared from his sight, burst into tears.

"Come, come, my old comrade, a little more self-command," said Eugène; "why, the deuce, you are like a woman!"

"Ah! talking of women, a pretty mess I have made," said the maimed veteran; "why, I have spoken to the *Générale Consule* as if I were speaking to Nanny and Peggy. And yet she seems all goodness, yonder brave *Citoyenne.*"

Whenever the First Consul played at barriers we all walked, and both cards and chess were superseded. This evening, therefore, he retired to his cabinet, and we saw no more of him. Madame Bonaparte had been so frightened by the sight of the men that nothing could rally her spirits. Eugène, Bessières, and Junot were all returned to Paris, and, no one remaining to cheer her, we spent the evening in enumerating and recounting all the vain attempts made within the last year against the life of the First Consul.

His wife loved him; the influence of gratitude on a good heart had bound her to him. She cried, and embracing me, said, "The figure of this man has made such a terrible impression on me, that I am certain I shall not sleep to-night; and Bonaparte, if he hears me complain, he is angry. He never has anything to fear, according to his own account."

We all retired to our chambers with the nervousness that pervades a party of children who have been listening to ghost stories, and midnight had not struck before the whole château, buried in sleep, might have resembled that of Beauty in the Sleeping Wood, if the moon-beams had not been occasionally seen to glimmer on the arms of those faithful guards, those *chasseurs à cheval,* who silently paraded the park, watching over the safety of him who was the safety of all.

Suddenly a report of firearms was heard from the ditch of the château, and instantly, before we could recover our breath, suspended by fear, everyone was on foot. The First Consul was already in the corridor in his dressing-gown, holding a taper, and crying with his powerful and sonorous voice, "Do not be frightened; there is nothing the matter."

He was as calm as if his sleep had not been disturbed: this I can answer for, because my glance of inquiry was fixed upon his countenance; he was calm without indifference, but he was evidently a thousand cubits above the apprehension of danger. His destiny was not fulfilled, and he knew it!

The alarm arose from the carbine of one of the chasseurs having gone off in consequence of his horse stumbling on a mole-hill.

When the First Consul heard the report of his aide-de-camp he laughed, and called through a little door at the foot of the grand staircase:

"Josephine, dry your eyes; a mole has done all the mischief; no great wonder, for it is an ugly animal. As for the chasseur, two days' arrest, to teach him and his horse not to pass again over my lawn. As I suppose he has had a fine fright himself, his punishment shall not last longer. Good-night, ladies; go to bed again, and sleep well." In passing by my door he added: "Felice notte, Signora Loulou, dolce riposo." "Felicissimo riposo, Signor Generale."

Air and exercise were necessary to Napoleon's existence, and the privation of them, from rain or any other cause, chafed his temper, and made him not only disagreeable, but really ill, so that his humour at dinner was a pretty good index to the state of the weather. Alas! I can but too easily perceive that he sank under the double misery of a scorching sun and a compulsory seclusion. The quintessence of barbarity was exhausted in the conduct of that monster in human shape delegated by England to St. Helena.

The First Consul was soon tired of retracing his own steps through the park at Malmaison, which was not sufficiently extensive to admit of his riding as he might have done at Morfontaine; and he often regretted not having an equally fine estate. Mademoiselle Julien decidedly refusing to sell, he sought elsewhere the means of enlarging his park, and entertained at one time the singular notion of purchasing the Île Channorrier, which is very considerable, well planted, containing fine lawns, and situated in the middle of the Seine. When Josephine pointed out the impracticability of his scheme, he replied:

"At Morfontaine the lakes are on the other side of the road; a subterranean passage may easily be made, and by buying all the tract between the road and the river, and planting it as an English garden, it seems to me that it might be done."

M. de Channorrier, however, refused to sell his island, and Napoleon purchased the woods of Butard, which made a delightful addition to his park; and so enchanted was he with his new acquisition that on the second or third day afterwards he insisted on taking us all there, that Madame Bonaparte might inspect the pavilion, which he was disposed to make a rendezvous for the chase. Josephine was suffering under one of those dreadful headaches which so often tortured her, poor woman! and for which there was no other remedy than sleep.

"Come, come! go with us," said the First Consul, "the air will do you good. It is the sovereign remedy for all pains."

Madame Bonaparte dared no longer refuse; she sent for a hat and shawl; and she, Madame Lavalette, and I mounted an open carriage. Napoleon preceded us, with Bourrienne; the aide-de-camp on duty had not been summoned for this excursion, with which the First Consul was as much delighted as a boy enjoying a holiday. He was on horseback, and sometimes galloped before us, then came back and took his wife's hand; as a child running before its mother returns to embrace her and then renews its race.

No words can describe the terrors of Madame Bonaparte in a carriage, and it is as difficult to express my own impatience, when I see a want of compassion for such weaknesses; they are troublesome, it is true, but are fruits of education, and no fault on the part of their victims, on whom they inflict a sort of martyrdom. Napoleon was not of my mind; he had no pity for his wife, and made no allowance for her.

As this was the first time of our going to Butard, the postilion did not know his way, and the road we followed brought us to a rivulet with banks sufficiently steep to render the passage somewhat difficult for a carriage. The moment Madame Bonaparte descried "this precipice," as she called it, she forbade him to proceed a step further. The pricker, knowing her nervousness, answered, when interrogated, that the passage might really be dangerous.

"See there!" cried she; "I will not go to Butard this way. Go and tell the First Consul that I am returning to the château, unless he knows some other road;" and ordering the postilion to turn his horses, we retraced our way, but had not driven many yards before the First Consul rejoined us.

"What is the matter?" said he, with that expression of countenance peculiar to himself when anything displeased him; "what is this new whim about? Return whence you came," added he, slightly touching the shoulders of the postilion with his hunting-whip; and, setting spurs to his horse, he galloped off again. We found him beside the fatal rivulet, examining its pretty high banks, but as he had just crossed it on horseback, everyone else must pass it too.

"Come," said Napoleon to the little lad who drove the carriage, "a good plunge, then draw in the reins, and you are over."

Madame Bonaparte uttered a piercing shriek, to which the forest re-echoed. "You shall never keep me in the carriage. Let me out!—Bonaparte!—I entreat you in mercy!—Let me out!" Weeping, and clasping her hands, she was truly an object of pity. Napoleon looked at her, but, far from relenting, he shrugged his shoulders and roughly commanded her to be silent. "It is absolute childishness; you *shall* pass, and in the carriage. Come, did you hear me?" said he, swearing, to the postilion.

I saw it was time to interfere for myself, not without hope that the diversion might convince him of his error.

"General!" said I to the Consul, beckoning the pricker to come and open the door for me; "I am responsible for another life; I cannot stay here. The jerk will be violent, and may not only injure but kill me in my present condition," said I, smiling; "and you do not wish that, do you, General?"

"I," cried he, "do you the smallest harm! You! Alight; you are in the right: a jolt might do you much harm." And approaching the carriage, he himself assisted me to descend, for he had dismounted from his horse at the commencement of the scene. Encouraged by the kind expression of his countenance, I ventured, perhaps ridiculously enough, to say, as he supported me to alight:

"And a jolt may be very injurious to Madame Bonaparte, General, for if she were as I am—"

The First Consul looked at me with an air so amusingly stupefied, that, instead of jumping down, I stood on the step, laughing like a young fool as I was; and all at once he responded to my laugh in a tone so shrill and clear that it made us start. At length I jumped down, and Napoleon, who had instantly resumed his former gravity, reproved me for the imprudence of such an exertion. Then, as if fearful he had not been bitter enough in testifying his discontent towards his wife:

"Put up the step and let the carriage proceed," said he, with a tone which admitted of no reply. Madame Bonaparte was so pale, and suffered so acutely, that I could not avoid saying to Napoleon:

"General, you appear cruel, and yet you are not so. Madame Bonaparte is ill, she is in a fever: I conjure you, suffer her to alight!" He looked on me with an expression which made my blood curdle.

"Madame Junot, I never loved remonstrances even when a child; ask Signora Letizia and Madame Permon, and consider whether I am likely to be tamed since." Then, perceiving that his words, and still more his look and tone, almost frightened me, he added, "Well, come, let me help you over *this formidable stream, this frightful precipice.*"

When we had crossed, Napoleon saw that the carriage did not stir, for Josephine, crying as if her execution was preparing, entreated the postilion to stay another minute, as a condemned criminal would beg a reprieve.

"Very well, sir," said the First Consul; "do you choose to obey my orders?"

And this time it was not lightly that he applied a stroke of his whip to the postilion's back, who instantly whipping both his horses, made them take the plunge, and the carriage crossed the brook, but with such difficulty that one of the springs was broken and a pin loosened.

Madame Bonaparte's whole frame was disordered with pain, fear, and rage, and conscious that such passions give an interesting expression only to young faces, she wrapped herself in a large muslin veil, and we were sensible only of her sobs till our arrival at Butard; when her husband, incensed at finding her still in tears, pulled her quite roughly out of the carriage, and dragging her to a short distance in the wood, we could hear him scolding the more angrily because he had set out prepared for a joyous excursion. It would appear that Josephine had other reproaches to make him than concerned the passage of the rivulet, for I heard Napoleon answer her:

"You are a simpleton, and if you repeat such a word I shall say a wicked simpleton, because you do not think what you are saying. And you know that I have a mortal antipathy to all these jealousies that have no foundation for them. You will end by putting it into my head. Come! embrace me and hold your tongue; you are ugly when you cry: I have told you so before."

Our return was melancholy, in spite of the reconciliation. Madame

Bonaparte let fall a few spitefully honeyed words upon my special favour in being permitted to quit the carriage. This leads me naturally to a circumstance which occurred the following year, and the remembrance of which has served me as a clue to many mysteries.

Madame Bonaparte was gone to Plombières without her daughter, who remained behind to do the honours for the ladies at Malmaison. Plays were acted every Wednesday; we had hunting-parties, and the evenings were spent in laughing and chatting. Madame Louis Bonaparte, who was just married, was the most engaging of brides as she had been of girls, and Madame Bessières formed a very agreeable addition to our select society; she was gentle and witty, sensible and good. Never did I see the First Consul so agreeable as during that fortnight; he was amiable, constantly good-humoured and joyous, amused himself with making me recite Italian verses, and then we played at *reversis,* at which we laughed incessantly.

The First Consul was sure to have all the hearts in his tricks, and when anyone tried to force Quinola, not a single heart could be found in the other three hands, so that he carried off all the stakes, crying:

"I have all the fish!—all the fish! Who will buy all the fish in the house?"

At other times he played chess, and as he was not expert at the game, he had recourse to stratagem as at *reversis.* The game could never be finished because there were always found two bishops commanding either the white or the black squares. He was the first to laugh at these contrivances, but was annoyed if they were too seriously noticed; and as he never played for money they were a subject for joke rather than for resentment.

Thus we led a merry life, and the summer slipped pleasantly away; yet some of us wished to return home. I was particularly desirous to be mistress of my own house, though only seventeen, and to see my husband's recent gift to me, the produce of his wedding portion from the First Consul; this was the estate of Little Bièvre. I wished also to visit my mother and friends, whom I had not seen for some months; but we were obliged to abandon our projects; we could not even go to Ruelle, for our carriages and horses were at Paris; we saw our husbands, to be sure, every day, and might have returned with them, for it must not be supposed that we were prisoners; yet the Consular Court was already a cage, the bars of which were indeed veiled with flowers, —nevertheless, it was a cage. Eventually, the flowers became more scarce, but the bars were gilt.

One morning I was in a profound sleep, when suddenly I was awoke by a slight noise near me, and perceived the First Consul beside my bed. Thinking myself in a dream, I rubbed my eyes, which produced a laugh from him.

"It is really I," said he; "why so astonished?"

One minute had sufficed to wake me entirely, and by way of answer I extended my hand towards the open window, which the extreme heat had obliged me to leave open. The sky was still of that deep-blue which succeeds the first hour of dawn. The sombre green of the trees showed that the sun was scarcely risen. I looked at my watch, and found it was not yet five o'clock.

"Really!" said he, when I showed it to him; "no later than that? so much the better, we are going to chat," and taking an arm-chair, he placed it at the foot of my bed, seated himself, crossed his legs, and established himself there as he used to do, five years earlier, in my mother's easy-chair at the Hôtel de la Tranquillité. He held in his hand a thick packet of letters, on which was written in large characters, "For the First Consul, for himself; for him alone, personally:" in short, every form of secrecy and security was adopted, and successfully, for the First Consul reserved for himself alone the letters superscribed with those words; and when I told him that such an employment must be troublesome to him, and he should refer it to some confidential person, he answered me, "By-and-by, perhaps; at present it is impossible. I must answer all. At the commencement of the return of order I must not be ignorant of any want, any complaint."

"But," said I, pointing to a large letter, which by its bad writing, and the awkward position of the seal, showed that its author was not much accustomed to epistolary labours, "this letter probably contains only a request which might have been made through the intervention of a secretary." Napoleon opened the letter, and read from one end to the other, three long pages, filled with very indifferent writing. When he had finished he said to me, "Well, this letter itself proves that I do right in seeing with my own eyes. Here, read it."

It was from a woman whose son had been killed in Egypt. She was the widow of a soldier who died in the service, and having no means of subsistence she had written, she said, more than ten letters to the Minister of War, the First Consul and his secretary, and had received no answer.

"You see it is necessary I should myself see all that is especially recommended to my attention." And he rose to fetch a pen from a table, made a sort of mark, probably agreed upon between Bourrienne and himself, and again sat down as if in his cabinet. "Ah! here is a trap," said he, taking off one, two, three, four envelopes, each highly scented with essence of roses, and inscribed in a pretty handwriting, with the talismanic words, *for the First Consul only*. He came at length to the last envelope, and a laugh soon burst from him, of which I, who knew the rareness of such hilarity, expected no common explanation.

"It is a declaration," said he, "not of war, but of love. It is a beautiful lady, who has loved me, she says, from the day she beheld me present the treaty of Campo-Formio to the Directory. And if I wish to see her, I have only to give orders to the sentinel at the iron gate, on the side of Bougival, to let a woman pass dressed in white, and giving the word *Napoleon!* and that [looking at the date], this very evening."

"Mon Dieu!" cried I; "you will not be so imprudent?" He looked attentively at me; then said, "What is it to you if I do? What harm can it do me?"

"What is it to me! What harm can it do you! Really, General, those are strange questions. May not this woman be bribed by your enemies? The snare, you will say, is too palpable. For all that it may be perilous; and you ask me what does your imprudence signify to me!"

Napoleon looked at me again, and then began to laugh. "I said it in joke; do you think me so simple, so stupid, as to nibble at such a bait? I am receiving such letters every day, with meetings appointed sometimes at the Tuileries, sometimes at the Luxembourg, but the only answer I make to such worthy missives is that which they deserve;" and stepping again towards the table, he wrote a few words, referring it to the Minister of Police.

"The deuce, there is six o'clock!" he exclaimed, hearing a timepiece strike, and approaching the bed he collected his papers, pinched my foot through the bedclothes, and smiling with the graciousness which sometimes brightened his countenance he went away singing, with that squalling voice, so strongly contrasted with the fine sonorous accent of his speech—

> "Non, non, *z'il* est impossible
> D'avoir un plus aimable enfant.
> Un plus aimable! Ah! si vraiment," etc.

It was his favourite air. Madame Dugazon, in the character of Camilla, must have made a great impression on him, for this was the only song he repeated; but, from the first day of singing it, he said *z'il est,* etc. Junot, who heard him say it at Toulon, could never cure him of the habit; he never sang this song, however, unless in excellent humour. I thought no more of this visit; and neither I nor my waiting-maid took any notice of the quantity of envelopes he had left on the ground.

About nine in the evening the First Consul drew near me, and whispered, "I am going to the Bougival Gate." "I do not believe a word of it," said I in the same tone. "You know too well the irreparable loss to France should any evil befall you. If you say another such word I will tell Madame Hortense, or Junot."

"You are a little simpleton," said he, pinching my ear; then threatening me with his finger: "If you think of telling one word of what I have said to you, I shall not only be displeased but pained." "The last consideration would suffice, General." He gazed at me: "The mother's head, the mother's head, absolutely!" I made no answer; and, perceiving that I kept silence, after waiting some minutes, he passed to the billiard-room.

The following morning I was again awakened in surprise by the same knock at my maid's chamber-door, and the First Consul entered, as before, with a packet of letters and papers in his hand. He again begged my pardon for waking me three hours too early, but added: "Why do you sleep with your window open? It is fatal for women, who, like you, have teeth of pearl. You must not risk the loss of your teeth; they resemble your mother's and are real little pearls." And he began to read the journals, making marks under several lines with his nails. He sometimes shrugged his shoulders, and muttered a few words, which I did not hear. He was reading, I think, a foreign gazette, written in French; from a question he put to me, I think his subject was the Prince of Württemberg, eldest son of the Duke, and now King of Württemberg.

This young Prince had been found in Paris, almost in disguise, with a young lady of good birth, whom he had not run away with, but seduced. The ear of the Duke, it appears, was not easily gained, and Mademoiselle Abel could not obtain the only reparation which can be offered to a credulous girl. Junot had been concerned in finding the young people. Having no interest in the story, I had but a confused knowledge of it, but what I heard was not to the credit of the young Prince. His countrymen, it appears, did not judge more favourably, for the article was vehement.

"Have you seen this young lady?" asked the First Consul. I replied in the negative. "Ah! I remember, when I wished Junot to take her home, that you might take charge of her, he leaped several feet high. And the young Duke?" said he. I had not seen him either, or did not remember to have met him, and was quite unacquainted with his person.

"He is one of those young fools who think themselves privileged in all things *because they are princes,*" said the First Consul; "he has behaved ill in this affair, and the father of the girl, being known as a diplomatist, should have insisted more strongly on the reparation." Then striking the journal with the back of his hand: "Here is a man who will never incur a syllable of reproach! the Archduke Charles.* That man has a soul, a golden heart. He is a virtuous man; and that word includes everything, when spoken of a prince."

After running through some journals and letters, the First Consul again pinched my foot through the bedclothes, and descended to his cabinet, uttering a few false notes. I called my waiting-woman, who had not been long in my service, and without explanation prohibited her ever opening the door to anyone who might knock so early in the morning. "But, Madame, if it be the First Consul?" "I will not be awakened so early by the First Consul or anyone else. Do as I bid you."

The day resembled others, except that in the evening we took an

* The brother of Emperor Francis of Austria, the Archduke Charles was a gifted general.

airing towards Butard. As we passed near the spot which had so alarmed Madame Bonaparte the First Consul praised my courage.

"Nay," said I; "I think I was rather cowardly to alight."

"That was a precaution for your situation, and does you credit; I saw, nevertheless, that you had no fear."

Perhaps it never happened to Napoleon to say so long a compliment twice in his life, and it so surprised me that I could not answer; but it reached other ears than mine, and the surprise was not for me alone. "I should like to give you a breakfast here the day after to-morrow," said the First Consul, when we were in the Pavilion; "we will have a little hunting before and after; it will do me good, and amuse us all. The day after to-morrow, Tuesday, I give you all the rendezvous here, at ten."

Entering my apartment, I gave orders to the waiting-maid, and went to bed much wearied, without knowing why. I was depressed; I wished to see my friends; that home so happy, so animated, the charm of my life, was not for me at Malmaison. I was treated with kindness, but I lived amongst strangers. Besides, I scarcely saw my husband, and I knew I was necessary to him, and was yet too young to guess that this necessity would not be eternal.

I spent the night in tears; I would have given years of my life—that life yet in its morning, and whose day promised such beauty and brilliancy—to the familiar spirit who would have transported me to the side of my mother and husband. At length I fell asleep, like children when their eyes are fatigued with weeping. But my sleep was agitated, and the first light of morning scarcely penetrated my Venetian blinds before I awoke, fancying I had heard a noise near my door; but, on listening, I heard nothing. Suddenly it occurred to me that I ought to take the key, for my maid would certainly not dare to refuse the First Consul, and I was determined these morning visits should not be repeated. I saw no harm in them, but knew enough of the world to avoid the construction that might be put upon them. I rose, therefore, very gently, and crossing my maid's room, was not a little surprised to find the door as unsecured as when we went to bed; the key was outside, and the bolt unfastened.

For a moment I was enraged, but, restraining myself, gently opened the door, withdrew the key, double-turned the lock, and, carrying the key with me, returned to my bed, without the power of sleeping; my watch was at hand, and I followed the motion of the fingers until, as they pointed to six, I heard the First Consul's foot in the corridor. He stopped at the door and knocked, but much less loudly than the preceding days. After waiting a moment he knocked again, and this time awoke my maid, who told him I had taken the key. He made no answer, and went away.

When the sound of his steps died away on the stairs leading to his cabinet, I breathed freely, and burst into tears. I looked on the First Consul as a brother, or perhaps rather as a father, since my sentiments towards him were always founded on deep admiration. He was the protector and support of my husband; and Junot himself had the tenderest affection for him; in what light would he view this gross distrust which deprived him of a moment's distraction in conversing with a child he had known from her birth? But having taken my resolution, I became more tranquil; and desiring my maid to shut the door from her room, I was again in a sound sleep, when the door opened violently and I saw the First Consul.

"Are you afraid of being assassinated, then?" said he, with a sharpness that relieved me of all fear; for when any attempt is made to curb me I grow restive, and he might read in my countenance that I was more offended than repentant. I told him, that having risen very early, I had taken the key out of my maid's room, choosing my chamber to be entered only by my own door. Napoleon fixed on me his eyes of the falcon and eagle together, and made no reply: a foolish timidity prevented my telling him my resolution; and I bitterly repented it.

"To-morrow is the hunting-party at Butard," said he; "you have not forgotten it since last night, have you? We set out early, and, that you may be ready, I shall come myself to wake you, and, as you are not amongst a horde of Tartars, do not barricade yourself again as you have done. You see that your precaution against an old friend has not prevented his reaching you. Adieu!" and away he went, but this time without singing. I looked at my watch, and found it nine o'clock, which distracted me, for at that hour all the chambermaids were about in the house, and it was impossible but some of them must have seen him go in or out. "But how did he get in?" I asked myself.

I called my maid Caroline, and asked her why she had departed from my orders. She told me that the First Consul had opened the door with a master-key, and that she dared not hinder his entering my room.

Hereupon I reflected on the course I should pursue. My first suggestion was to demand a carriage of Madame Louis Bonaparte, but what reason could I assign? Ten years later I should have gone to the stables and ordered a carriage, but at seventeen, a timidity, not of character, but of manners, deterred me. I dressed myself, therefore, and went to breakfast with a determined purpose, but great irresolution as to the manner of executing it. Duroc, who would have been my adviser, my friend, and, above all, my means of acting, was absent in Lorraine, and never was I in so much need of his friendship. There was not an individual in the château whom I deemed capable of comprehending my situation.

Madame Louis Bonaparte was kind, sensible, and sufficiently acquainted with the world to know what was due to its observances, but an all-powerful consideration arrested me as I was rising to consult her. I fell back almost stunned, and uncertain what course to adopt. I was determined to return to Paris, and knew that by writing at once to Junot that I was ill and wished to return home, my carriage would arrive in the course of the next day; but it was the same day, Monday, that I resolved to go, not Tuesday, and still less Wednesday. Then again, I was unwilling to appear uncivil to Madame Louis Bonaparte, or to wound the First Consul's feelings.

"*Mon Dieu!*" I exclaimed, dropping my head on my hands; "what can I do?" At the same moment I felt myself pressed in a gentle embrace, and a well-known voice inquired: "What is the matter, then, my Laura?" It was my husband; I threw myself into his arms, folded my own around him, embraced him, kissed his hair and his hands, and so eagerly caressed him that my cheek was scratched by one of his epaulettes, and the blood flowed.

"What is the matter, then?" repeated Junot, stanching the blood and drying my tears. "What is the matter, my poor little one? Look at me, then: do not you know four days have elapsed since I saw you?" "My love, I want to go away—to return to Paris." "Oh, you may be assured that as soon as Madame Bonaparte returns I will take you with me." "And why not now?" "Now! before her return? nay, you do not think of it, my darling?"

I insisted no further, for my plan was now arranged. Junot, though, with all the other acting authorities, prohibited from sleeping out of Paris, frequently visited Malmaison, sometimes after dinner, sometimes in the morning, but, in either case, departed not till we had retired for the night.

This day Junot arrived and stayed to dinner by the First Consul's desire, communicated through the aide-de-camp on duty. When we assembled in the dining-room, the First Consul was in high spirits, joked all dinnertime with M. Monge, and made him explain more than ten times over the nature of trade-winds, with which he was himself perfectly well acquainted, but the worthy man had so singular a mode of arranging his hands when speaking, and of running post in his narrative, that he was very amusing, and would have been ridiculous had he not combined the most excellent heart with his great knowledge.

After dinner billiards were introduced as usual; I played a game of chess with the First Consul; and at the usual hour we all separated,— some to their rest, and others to return to Paris. I prevented Junot's accompanying Bessières by telling him I had a commission to give him for my mother; and, as I must write, it would be necessary to return to my chamber.

When there, my earnest and persevering supplications that Junot would carry me home with him inspired him at last with the idea that some one had offended me, and his unbounded rage and resentment against the supposed defaulter absolutely terrified me; but, reassured on this head, no arguments, no entreaties, could prevail with him "to carry me off," as he said, "in the night, like a heroine of romance." I am now sensible that he could not sanction so ridiculous an act, but I was then very young.

Our discussion had been very long, and at half after twelve, finding Junot resolute, there remained no other expedient than that of persuading him to stay. Here I was much more strongly armed, and after some resistance he said with a smile: "Happily, there are no longer arrests to fear, but you will procure me a scolding;" and he remained.

I double-locked my maid's door, carefully drew the bolts, and took away the key; my own door I left simply shut, with the key outside, and all thus disposed I went to bed, very foolishly convinced that I had adopted the best means of making the First Consul understand that since he was pleased to honour me with his visits, I should prefer any other hour for receiving them to that which he had chosen.

As the village clock was striking five, I awoke; all was quiet in the château, as in the middle of the night. The weather was beautifully serene, and the fine foliage of the park plantations gently undulated in the wind, while a golden ray already tinted the upper branches. All this silence and repose formed so striking a contrast with my own mental uneasiness that I could not avoid starting when my eye fell on Junot sleeping by my side. His sleep was tranquil; yet was there something at once imposing and picturesque in that fine and manly figure, that countenance embrowned by the suns of Africa, that youthful forehead already ploughed with scars, those marked features, and that fair head encircled with a Turkish turban of red and brown, which had accidentally fallen in his way overnight, and been adopted as a nightcap. He was not strikingly handsome, but it could not be denied that he was good-looking.

The half-hour had just struck when I heard the First Consul's steps resound in our corridor. My heart beat violently; I could have wished Junot at Paris, or concealed; but at that moment a sleeping movement partly opened his shirt, and displayed two wounds received at the battle of Castiglione; a little further, just below the heart, was that given him by Lanusse, when in defence of his beloved General he drew his sword against a brave brother-in-arms. "Ah!" thought I; "I fear nothing: there is an impenetrable buckler," and resting my head on my pillow, I awaited the event.

The door opened noisily. "What! still asleep, Madame Junot, on a hunting-day! I told you that—" The First Consul as he spoke advanced, and now stood at the foot of the bed, where, drawing aside the curtain, he stood motionless at the sight of his faithful and devoted friend. I am almost sure he at first believed it a vision. Junot, on the other hand, scarcely awake, leaning on one elbow, looked at the First Consul with an air of astonishment that would have diverted a less interested spectator; but his countenance expressed no symptoms of displeasure.

"Why, General! what are you doing in a lady's chamber at this hour?" He uttered these words in a tone of perfect good-humour. "I came to awake Madame Junot for the chase," replied the First Consul in the same tone; "but," after a prolonged glance at me, which is still present to my memory, notwithstanding the thirty years that have since intervened,— "but I find her provided with an alarum still earlier than myself. I might scold, for you are contraband here, M. Junot."— "General," said Junot, "if ever a fault deserved pardon, it is mine. Had you seen that little siren last night exercising all her magic for more than an hour to seduce me, I think you would pardon me."

The First Consul smiled, but his smile was evidently forced. "I absolve you, then, entirely. It is Madame Junot who shall be punished," and he laughed that laugh *which laughs not*. "To prove that I am not angry, I permit you to accompany us to the chase. Have you a horse?"—"No, General, I came in a carriage."—"Well! Jardin shall find you one, and I allow you to lecture me at your leisure" (because he was a bad huntsman). "Adieu, Madame Junot; come, get up and be diligent," and he left us.

"Faith!" said Junot, jumping up in his bed, *"that is an admirable man! What goodness! Instead of scolding, instead of sending me sneaking back to my duty in Paris! Confess, my Laura, that he is not only an astonishing being, but above the sphere of human nature."

When we were all ready and assembled on the stone bridge in the garden, several carriages and saddle-horses were brought. A small phaeton led the way; the First Consul seated himself in it, and beckoning to me, said: "Madame Junot, will you honour me with your company?"

These words were accompanied with a smile whose expression did not please me; I got in without reply; the door was shut, and the little light carriage, inclining to the right, followed an alley that led to one of the iron gates of the park. I knew the First Consul would only remain in the carriage from the château to the rendezvous, where he was to mount his horse; but the drive appeared to me very long, and I would have given anything to escape.

When we were at some distance from the château, the First Consul, who till then had been watching the horsemen as they passed us to go to the rendezvous, turned towards me, and crossing his arms, said: "You think yourself very clever." I made no reply, and he repeated: "You think yourself very clever; do you not?"

As his tone was now positively interrogative, I answered with firmness, "I do not give myself credit for extraordinary sense, but I think I am not a simpleton."—"A simpleton, no; but a fool." I was silent. "Can you explain the reason why you made your husband stay?"—"The explanation is clear and brief, General. I love Junot; we are married, and I thought there was no scandal in a husband remaining with his wife."—"You knew I had prohibited it, and you knew, too, that my orders ought to be obeyed."

"They do not concern me. When the Consuls signify their will as to the degree of intimacy that shall subsist between a married couple, and the number of days and hours that should be allotted to their interviews, then I shall think of submitting; till then, I confess, General, my good pleasure shall be my only law."

Here I was growing uncivil, for I was angry, and probably my manner put him out of humour too, for he resumed with asperity, and a sort of irony: "You had no other reason, then, but love for your husband in making him stay?"—"No, General."—"You have told a lie there."—"General——"—"Yes, you have told a lie," repeated he in an irritated tone; "I understand the motive of your proceeding. You have a distrust of me which you ought not to have. Ah! you have no answer," said he, in a tone of triumph.

"And if I have been impelled by a different motive from the distrust you speak of, General,—if I have perceived that your visit at such an hour in the chamber of a young woman of my age might compromise me strangely in the eyes of the other inhabitants of this house?" I shall never forget Napoleon's expression of countenance at this moment; it displayed a rapid succession of sentiments, none of them evil.

"If that be true," said he at last, "why did you not tell me your uneasiness? Have I not shown you friendship enough, naughty child, within the last week to obtain your confidence?"

"There I was perhaps in fault. I should have considered that you had known me a child, General; that my relations love you; that you were once tenderly attached to my mother" (he looked on the other side of the road); "and, above all, that there was another and a stronger reason which should have encouraged me to tell you what I thought of this visit on the second or the third day: this is that I am the wife of Junot, —of the man who loves you best in the world. This morning when I heard your step when you were about to enter my chamber, I confess I had some fear of your resentment; but looking at the scars upon his bosom, received partly for your glory, I assured myself that you would never be the cause of suffering to the noble and excellent heart which beats perhaps more strongly for you than for me, in the scarred bosom of Junot."

"You are reading me almost a homily. Who talks of afflicting Junot? Why not have spoken to me?"

"And how was I to do so? When yesterday morning you employed a method that might be called unworthy to enter my apartment, after my conduct should have shown you, General, that the morning visit which you had the goodness to make me was viewed by me in its true light, as unbecoming, you entered only for a minute, and in a humour certainly not inviting confidence. I was left then to my own resources, and my judgment has perhaps erred."

"Is there none of your mother's advice in all this?" "My mother, General! how could my mother direct me? My poor mother! I have not seen her this month." "You can write;" and Napoleon's searching glance seemed to pierce me with its scrutiny. "General, I have not written to my mother that I was not in safety under your roof; it would have given her too much pain."

"Madame Junot, you have known me long enough to be assured that you will not obtain the continuance of my friendship by speaking in the manner you are now doing; there is nothing wanting to your proceedings but that you should have communicated to Junot the device you have so happily imagined." And again I met the same investigating look.

"I shall not reply to that challenge, General," replied I, with impatience I could not disguise; "if you grant me neither sense nor judgment, allow me at least a heart that would not wantonly wound one whom I know, and whom you know also." "Again!" and he struck the frame of the carriage with his clenched fist; "again! hold your tongue!"

"No, General, I cannot; I shall continue what I would have the honour of saying to you. I entreat you to believe that neither my mother, my husband, nor any one of my friends, has been informed of what has passed within the last week. I must add that, imputing no ill intentions to you, it would have been absurd on my part to complain of a mark of friendship because it might compromise me; but I thought proper to put a stop to it at whatever price; and, in so doing, my youth has no doubt led me into error, since I have displeased you. I am sorry for it; but that is all I can say."

We had nearly arrived; the dogs, the horns, all the clamour of the chase were audible. The First Consul's countenance assumed a less sombre hue than it had worn during my long speech. "And you give me your word of honour that Junot knows nothing of all this foolish affair?" "Good Heaven! General, how can you conceive such an idea, knowing Junot as you do? He is an Othello in the violence of his passions, an African in heat of blood; his feeble French reason would not have had strength enough to judge sanely of all this; and—" I stopped. "Well! what then? Come, do not make these pauses in speaking; nothing is more silly." "Well, General, if I had told Junot what has passed this week, neither he nor I would have been here this morning; you know Junot well enough for that, do you not?"

Napoleon, in his turn, made no answer, but played with his fingers on the frame of the carriage. At last, turning towards me: "You will not believe, then, that I meant you no harm?" "On the contrary, General, I am so convinced that you had no ill intention towards me, that I can assure you neither my attachment for you, an attachment dating from infancy, nor the admiration which I feel even more strongly than others, is at all lessened by it; and there is my hand as the pledge of my words."

I cannot express or explain the movement of his forehead, his look, and half-smile, as, gently shaking his head, he refused my hand. I was hurt at the refusal.

"We are at variance, then," said I, "because it has pleased you to follow a course in which all the blame is on your side, and you will *let the beard grow, and wear the dagger,* * because you have given me pain."

For a minute his eyes were fixed on the road; then turning suddenly to me, he extended his little hand, after having ungloved it: "Be assured of my friendship, Madame Junot; you might, had you chosen, have strengthened it; but early education is not easily eradicated. It

* These are the customs of Corsica, when any one is offended or fancies himself offended, who thereby announces himself as an avenger.

inculcates sentiments, and those with which you have been inspired for me are not friendly; you do not like me, and I am sure—"

"I take the liberty of interrupting you, General, to request that you will not talk thus. You pain me; and so much the more as your arguments and inferences are both false. Tell me that you do not believe them; it would be too painful to me to leave you in such a persuasion."

The First Consul was looking at the dogs which the pricker was leading in couples, and he turned so suddenly round as to derange the motion of the carriage. "You are going?" "On our return from the hunt, General, I have induced Junot to take me home, and here is a letter that, as you will perceive, would have determined me, independently of the incidents of the last few days" (I said this with a smile), "to go to my mother."

It was from my mother, urging my return to her, and I had received it while dressing that morning. "If the First Consul, or Madame Louis Bonaparte, should raise difficulties," added she, "show them my letter, and beg they will not detain a daughter from the bedside of her sick mother."

The First Consul, casting his eyes over it, shrugged his shoulders, and smiled with a sort of disdain which pained me. "And when do you return?" asked he with a tone of derision that might have offended a person better disposed than I was, and accordingly I answered with asperity: "Whenever I am wanted, for my part, General; but you may dispose of my apartment; I shall never again occupy it."

"As you will. For the rest, you are right to go this morning; after all this foolish affair, you and I should not meet with much satisfaction at present. You are quite right. Jardin! my horse." And opening the door himself, he jumped out of the carriage, mounted his horse, and galloped off.

On our return to the château, I told Madame Louis that my mother's health imperatively demanded my presence in Paris, and that I intended to return with Junot. She understood me, and I even believe she entirely understood my motives. She wished to detain me to dinner, but Junot's absence the preceding night required an earlier return, and, declining the invitation, we dined at Paris with my mother.

I visited Malmaison some time after Madame Bonaparte's return from Plombières, where she had passed the season; that is to say, six weeks. The First Consul was tolerably cordial, but I could perceive that he still cherished the notion, equally eccentric and injurious, that I had been prompted in all that had passed during the last week of my stay. It gave me pain; but knowing no human means of defeating this prepossession, I left the task to time,* without changing the line of conduct I had marked out for myself.

A year afterwards I dined one day at Malmaison, while residing at Bièvre; satisfied with my charming home, I left it as little as possible, and always returned the same evening. That day I ordered my carriage at ten, but, as I was preparing for departure, a sudden storm came on, of such terrific violence as to injure the trees in the park. Madame Bonaparte protested against allowing me to go through such a tempest, and said that *my chamber* should be prepared. In answer to my persevering excuses, she promised me both linen and a waiting-maid, and urged the danger of crossing the woods at so late an hour. "I fear nothing, madame," I answered; "I have four men with me. Permit me, then, to take leave of you."

The First Consul was occupied, meanwhile, in pulling the fire about with the tongs, and apparently paying no attention to the conversation, though I could perceive a smile on his countenance. At last, as Madame Bonaparte insisted still more strongly on my staying, he said from his place, without resigning the tongs or turning his head: "Torment her no more, Josephine: I know her; she will not stay."

Every one who has trodden the boards of a private theatre will agree with me that no circumstances of their lives afford reminiscences more abounding in pleasure and gaiety than the rehearsals, and everything, in short, that is merely preparatory. But in candour they must equally admit that the actual scenic representation is absolute torture. I have experienced both, and can speak from practical knowledge.

* I know to a certainty that, at this time, *false reports* envenomed all the words of my mother to the First Consul's ears, and I am nearly sure that this story came to the knowledge of persons who would make a pernicious use of it towards us both. The First Consul long retained a rancour, which he certainly would not have felt had it not been both instilled and carefully nourished.

Mademoiselle de Beauharnais's success at Madame Campan's* in the representations of *Esther* naturally induced her to bring the theatre of Malmaison into use. Eugène Beauharnais was a perfect actor. I may, without partiality, say that Junot had superior talent; M. Didelot was an admirable Crispin; I acquitted myself tolerably in my parts; and General Lauriston was a noble Almaviva, or any other lover in Court dress.

But the cleverest of our company was M. de Bourrienne; he played the more dignified characters with real perfection; and his talent was the more pleasing as it was not the result of study, but of a perfect understanding of his part. Grandménil and Caumont, at that time the supporters of such characters at the *Comédie Française,* could have discovered no flaw in M. de Bourrienne's performance of Bartholo, of Albert in *Lovers' Follies,* of the Miser, or of Harpagène; in *The Florentine* he might, perhaps, even furnish them occasionally with a turn of expression worth seizing and copying.

The First Consul himself was almost the sole manager of our dramatic repertory. It was at first but limited, for we dared not venture on first-rate plays, or undertake parts beyond our capacity. We played a number of charming little witty pieces, which certainly have not been equalled since either in good sense or good style. Afterwards we grew bolder; the First Consul himself demanded longer plays. The repertory was all at once increased by fifty pieces, which were put into our hands with a careful distribution of the several parts in conformity with our individual talents. The theatre of Malmaison had at that time an excellent company; latterly it was open to every one, and was no longer endurable.

The first play acted at Malmaison was *The Barber of Seville,* and in saying that this representation was perfect I do not hazard a word that memory can call in question. We have still many survivors of that merry and delightful period, and I fear no contradiction in asserting again that *The Barber of Seville* was acted at the theatre of Malmaison better than it could now be performed in *any theatre in Paris.*

Mademoiselle Hortense de Beauharnais took the part of Rosina; M. de Bourrienne that of Bartholo; M. Didelot, Figaro; General Lauriston,

* A school for young ladies.

Almaviva; Eugène, Basile; and General Savary sneezed in perfection in the part of the Sleeper Awakened.

I have just observed that Bourrienne played well because he understood and felt his part. The same may be said of Mademoiselle Hortense. Gaiety, wit, sensibility, delicacy, all that the author Beaumarchais meant to infuse into his Rosina, she caught instinctively; she entered into the character of the young and fair Andalusian with all her native grace and elegance. To her fine acting she united a charming figure and an exquisite carriage, especially on the stage. Many years have elapsed since those joyous evenings, but my memory still forcibly recalls the graceful and pleasing image of Mademoiselle de Beauharnais, with her profusion of fair ringlets beneath a black velvet hat, ornamented with long pink feathers, and the black dress so admirably fitted to her small and symmetrical shape. I seem yet to see and hear her.

Her brother Eugène was equally perfect as Basile, and M. de Bourrienne in the part of Bartholo. General Lauriston succeeded well in the various situations of Almaviva, though some fault was found with those of the soldier and the bachelor. He was not altogether perfect till the grandee of Spain reappeared under the mantle of the student. M. Didelot was excellent in Figaro.

But our success was most remarkable in that point which generally reduces the managers of private theatres to despair; that is to say, the perfect correspondence of the whole piece: the parts were thoroughly learned, and everything went off well.

Madame Murat sometimes acted at Malmaison. She was very pretty. Her hands and arms were beautiful, and her fair bosom acquired new brilliancy beneath a black velvet bodice, with a gold stomacher; but she had an unfortunate accent, which was particularly fatal to the parts she selected. Her sisterly relation to the First Consul, however, screened this defect from observation, whereas Madame Louis Bonaparte, had she been but the wife of an aide-de-camp, must have been applauded for the excellence of her acting.

This reminds me of an incident which befell me, partly through the instrumentality of Madame Murat, or, at least, through her want of acquaintance with the stage. There was a sort of rivalry between

Marie Louise and the King of Rome, 1811 by Joseph Franque.
(COL. VERSAILLES, MUSÉE NATIONAL)

Portrait of Laure Junot in her wedding dress, engraving after
J. Champagne. (COL. BIBLIOTHÈQUE NATIONALE, PARIS)

Portrait of General Junot, engraving after Baron Gros.
(COL. BIBLIOTHÈQUE NATIONALE, PARIS)

Napoleon and Marie Louise arriving at the Tuileries the day of their wedding, April 2, 1810 by Etienne-Barthélemi Garnier.
(COL. VERSAILLES, MUSÉE NATIONAL)

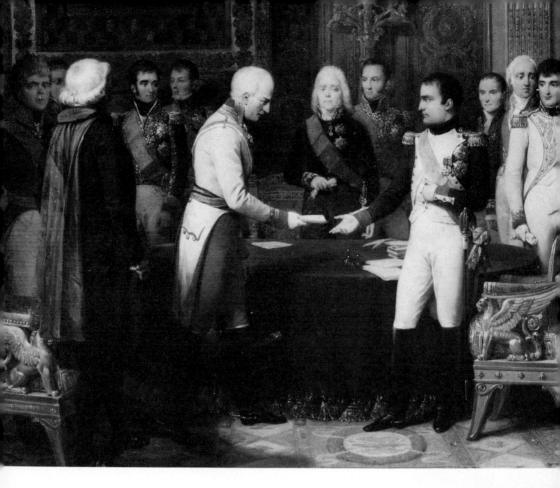

The Battlefield of Austerlitz, December 1805
by Baron François Gérard.
(COL. VERSAILLES, MUSÉE NATIONAL)
Count Rapp bringing the banner of the
defeated Russian Imperial Guard to
Napoleon. To the right is Junot on his
horse, with white plume head gear.

The Congress of Erfurt, October 28, 1808 by Nicolas-Louis-François Gosse. (COL. VERSAILLES, MUSÉE NATIONAL) An Austrian general is presenting a letter from his Emperor to Napoleon. To the left of Napoleon in the foreground is Talleyrand, and, to the right, King Jerome (facing) and Tsar Alexander I (in profile).

The Malmaison Palace, a view from the garden, engraving by
Perdoux. (COL. MALMAISON, MUSÉE NATIONAL)

Malmaison and Neuilly.* Lucien frequently acted both in tragedy and comedy with his eldest sister, Madame Bacciochi. Lucien acquitted himself admirably, and declaimed to perfection. His only failing, and that not altogether dependent on himself, was the modulation of his voice, which was too shrill and in too elevated a key for a tragic tone. But this inconvenience was slight, and Lucien gave great satisfaction as Zamora. I have heard his performance criticized; in my own judgment I did not perceive the defects attributed to him, and I was delighted with him almost throughout the part.

Not so with Madame Bacciochi. Her acting was irresistibly laughable. The First Consul found it so, and, far from flying into a rage, as M. de Bourrienne represents, he did nothing but laugh during the whole play whenever his sister appeared on the stage, and when we returned to the drawing-room, he exclaimed: "I think we have seen Alzira beautifully parodied." He repeated the same thing to Madame Bacciochi herself, who was not the best pleased with it.

To form a just conception of the nervousness (that is the proper word) felt by us *Comedians in Ordinary* of Malmaison, it should be premised that on the day of our representation, which was generally Wednesday, it was the First Consul's habit to invite forty persons to dinner, and a hundred and fifty for the evening, and consequently to hear, criticize, and banter us without mercy. The Consuls, the Ministers, the Diplomatic Corps, Councillors of State, Senators, their wives, and all the members of the then Military Household of the First Consul, formed our audience. But the most terrible was the First Consul himself. There he sat in his box, close beside us, his eyes following us and accompanying their glances with a smile more or less arch at the slightest departure from the piece.

The morning of the representation of *Lovers' Follies,* Dugazon said to me, after hearing Bourrienne rehearse Albert admirably: "Well, take courage, my pupil, you will save the State. You two may do wonders. Crispin is good, too. As for the General, his part is nothing."

In the part of Agatha the dress is changed five or six times. I had requested Madame Murat, and Dugazon also had charged her, not to enter the stage to commence the third act without first ascertaining that

* Where the Murats had their country house.

I had completed my officer's dress under my black domino as the old grandmother. The two first acts had passed off tolerably, with the exception of a few errors of memory and some little deficiency of spirit; but the piece still marched—it was soon destined to *limp*.

Whether from misunderstanding or forgetfulness, Lisette appeared upon the scene without troubling herself about me. The question whether or not I was ready was, however, deserving of attention, for but a very short scene intervenes between that in which I receive the money from Albert and my return as an officer. It was therefore imperatively necessary that I should be in full costume underneath my great black cloak, and I was accordingly putting on my boots when I heard the first lines of the act; I cried out directly, but in vain; I had not yet come to the end of my troubles. The day was suffocatingly hot: agitation and fear threw me almost into a fever, which did not accelerate matters; the boots would not come on, and while my waiting-maid pulled till she almost broke my leg, my ankle began to swell. At length I heard the speech preceding my own, and throwing the boot ten feet off, I hastily assumed my black domino, and entered upon the scene; but my poor head was wandering. I mechanically repeated the words assigned me, but my feet at the moment occupied my whole attention.

In an interval between the couplets I whispered to Junot: "What can I do? I cannot get my boots on!"

"Hey! What?" said he, for he could not hear. I repeated the same thing to Bourrienne, but as I spoke very low and quickly neither of them understood; this little by-play, however, so puzzling to them, began to excite more notice than I wished in other quarters. At last I made my exit, ran to my boots, and endeavoured to draw them on—impossible; the foot was still more swelled, and I might as easily have shod the Colossus of Rhodes as have driven my feet into either of them.

At this moment Dugazon, who was roaming about behind the scenes, arrived to witness my despair. He ran up to me, and, embracing me, said: "All goes on well, but what the deuce were you looking for under your feet just now?" As my brain at the moment retained but one fixed idea, I answered, staring at him in utter consternation: "I cannot get my boots on!" "You have not your boots on?" said he, swearing—"you have not your boots on?"

At that moment my husband's valet, who was to bring me a very small sabre that I had ordered, tapped at my room door, and presenting a sword as large as Mahomet's Damascus blade, told me in his German jargon that my sabre was not ready, but that he had brought me the smallest of the *Cheneral's,* and it was necessary to be cautious in using it, for it would cut like a razor.

"Here is a new trouble!" I exclaimed.

"Eh! do not be uneasy," said Dugazon, capering; "it is all very well. You have a greatcoat; never mind black shoes, keep on your white ones. Agatha is mad: it is no disguise. All those about her know that an access of her malady has just seized her, and that she has assumed a military dress because her head is unsteady. Well, she has forgotten her white shoes. Really, upon my honour, this is not amiss."

Saying this, he pushed me on the stage, and it was fortunate that he did so, for my turn was come, and I should never have had the courage to appear thus as an officer of dragoons in white satin slippers. I took good care not to look towards the First Consul's box; to have seen his smile or frown would have struck me mute.

The result of this fine story is that I played the last scene like a true maniac. But, owing to those unlucky boots, I forgot the Turkish sabre and its sharpness, and when at the conclusion Agatha flourishes it about the ears of Albert, and then suddenly falls into a swoon, the point of the unfortunate Damascus penetrated my white slipper and made a deep cut in my foot, of which I still bear the scar.

But let me ask, Was any one ever seen to enter a theatre in the dress of a dragoon officer and in white satin slippers?

The First Consul was for six months unmerciful upon those unlucky white slippers. I verily think he would have dragged them into a discussion even upon the bull *Unigenitus.*

The First Consul should have been seen in his functions of stage manager to be known under an aspect entirely different from all his portraits. "The First Consul at Malmaison, the First Consul at St. Cloud, and the First Consul at the Tuileries," said Mr. Fox to me, "are three men forming together the *beau idéal* of human greatness; but I could wish to be a painter," added he, "to take his portrait under these different characters, because I should have three resemblances of the same face with three different aspects."

The statesman was right; I had remarked it before him, and was pleased at hearing my own idea so strikingly expressed by the man whom, of all Englishmen, I at that time most highly appreciated. It was perfectly true, and Bonaparte at Malmaison was admirable in extreme simplicity.

One of our best actors was Isabey,* perhaps the very best, Queen Hortense excepted. He, however, ceased to form often a member of our *corps comique* rather than *dramatique,* for reasons which were but imperfectly explained.

One day the First Consul, on dismounting from his horse, and traversing the gallery adjoining the centre salon at Malmaison, stopped to examine a portfolio of engravings which had been placed upon a table at the park end of the gallery. Isabey is said to have entered a moment after him from the theatre, and by the opposite door at the end next the court. The First Consul was then slim, and wore the uniform of the *guides* or *horse chasseurs* of the Guard,—that beloved uniform, the very sight of which makes the heart beat. Eugène Beauharnais, as I have before observed, was colonel of that fine regiment.

Isabey, who had not heard the First Consul return from his ride, seeing a small slender figure at the end of the gallery, dressed in the uniform of the *chasseurs,* and observing the two epaulettes, supposed it to be Eugène, with whom he was extremely intimate, and determined to take him by surprise. Dexterous, light, active, and supple as a cat in his movements, he advanced softly, without the slightest sound, to within a short distance, then, taking a spring, leaped at one bound upon the First Consul and alighted on his neck. Napoleon imagined the house was falling, or that the *old gentleman* was come to strangle him. Rising up, he disengaged himself by main force from his new-fashioned collar, and threw poor Isabey in his turn upon the ground, and, presenting to his dismayed view a countenance for which he was certainly little prepared, demanded in a severe tone:—

"What is the meaning of this buffoonery?"

"I thought it was Eugène," stammered out the luckless youth.

"And suppose it was Eugène," replied the First Consul, "must you needs break his shoulder-blades?" And he walked out of the gallery.

* A highly successful portrait painter specializing in miniatures.

This story was soon bruited about. The First Consul had too much tact not to perceive that his was the ridiculous share of the adventure; Isabey understood it to the full as well, and both would willingly have kept the secret. But whether the one in the first moment of his panic related the whole to Eugène himself, or the other in his resentment could not withhold it from Madame Bonaparte, the affair got wind. I know that a short time afterwards its truth was denied. At all events, if it caused the departure of Isabey and his loss to our company, I must call it an act of useless injustice.

General Lallemand, at that time aide-de-camp to my husband, was also one of our best actors. I have seen but few good comedians, and of those very few indeed were his equals. His talent was natural, but had been improved by the instructions of Michau, from whom he imbibed a portion of that ease and humour which was the principal charm of Michau's own acting.

This excellent man once said to me, "It is always useful to make people laugh," and in illustration of this truth related an anecdote of himself. Passing once quietly along the streets, he encountered one of those disorderly mobs that were in the habit of parading Paris in those happy days when the lamp-posts served for hanging up our gallant citizens; they would have made him join their march, but he resisted, and demanded in the name of that liberty, whose scarlet ensign was as usual conspicuous in the foremost group, that he should be suffered to continue his route in pursuance of his own affairs. The discussion was brief, the lamp was shattered, and poor Michau, already stripped of his coat, was on the point of being hoisted in its place, when a fat fellow, with his plump arms bare, and a red and jolly face, rushed into the midst of the banditti and snatched Michau from their grasp, exclaiming:

"What are you about, simpletons? don't you know 'Punch of the *République*'?" The *Comédie Française* was at that time called the *Théâtre de la République*.

And thanks to his title of "Punch," with which his deliverer, the butcher's boy, had invested him, Michau found himself at liberty, and accepted the apologies which two hundred rascals offered for their design of hanging him, as coolly as if they had simply trodden on his toes!

AFTER the victories of 1800 and 1801, it seemed as if the First Consul, far from being in love with war and conquest, had realised that France could only find a new stability within the framework of a European peace. Treaties were signed with Austria, Prussia, Spain and, finally, even with England.

This new policy was greeted with rapture: not only had Paris become, once again, what it had been before the Revolution, the place everybody wanted to visit, France itself was being transformed in the most positive way. Building on the achievements of the Revolution, a new civil and criminal code was promulgated; the administration of the country, from the ministries in Paris down to the smallest town hall, was reorganised. A new, and greatly improved, educational system was set up. Credit revived, full employment was achieved, and prosperity reached from the top to the bottom of the social ladder: this, indeed, was the golden age of Napoleon.

Of course, the Consul did have a tendency to be autocratic; but his policies were so successful that no one minded; and the very Constitution gave the illusion of liberty. At the head of the state, there were three consuls—Bonaparte, Cambacérès and Lebrun; but the Second and Third Consuls, it quickly became clear, were little more than ministers of the First. All three Consuls held office for ten years—a period long enough to make the government stable, limited enough to preclude a dictatorship.

Then, there were three parliamentary bodies: The Senate, whose members were appointed by the Consul, was charged with protecting and amending the Constitution, as well as setting up the lists of candidates for the other Assemblies and various other elective posts. The *Corps législatif*, or legislature, voted the laws and the budget, without, however, discussing them. That was done in the *Tribunat*, or House of Tribunes, where debate was free, but no vote was ever taken. This ingenious system provided the regime with the appearance of governing only with the consent of the people, since all bills were debated, then voted on while, in fact, the division between debating Chamber and elected Chamber ensured that the First Consul almost always got his way. That would have been the case with a more democratic system, however: it is impossible to overestimate Bonaparte's popularity during the Consulate.

Nor is it any wonder: after the agony of the Revolution, and the corruption of the Directoire, the country knew it could count on stability and prosperity. True liberty, that of living your life as you chose, was ensured by the new regime. There were no more proscriptions, no more arrests. The émigrés were allowed to return even as the purchasers of confiscated estates were guaranteed their property. And, last but not least, France enjoyed some substantial territorial conquests: today's Belgium, the left bank of the Rhine and most of northern Italy were French. To most everyone, therefore, the future looked truly golden.

A series of victories of the French arms had at length determined Austria to conclude a treaty of peace; it was signed at Luneville* by Count Louis von Cobentzel for the Emperor and Germanic Confederation on the one part, and by Joseph Bonaparte in the name of the French Republic, which might still call itself One, and more than ever Indivisible.

All who had been concerned in the Congress came to Paris to share in the magnificent *fêtes* which the First Consul commanded, that the people might have an opportunity of testifying their joy; and that a free circulation of money might revive commerce, and give work to that multitude of individuals who, to the number of a hundred thousand, exist in Paris by the labour of their hands,—a labour which, though chiefly devoted to objects of luxury, produces those commodities which the higher classes, especially in seasons of festivity, can no more do without than the lower can subsist without bread. The *fêtes* given by the Government were a signal not only to Paris, but to the

* In February, 1801.

187

whole of France, for balls, dinners, and social assemblages of every kind. Hence commenced in Paris, at this period, life and gaiety, which ceased not to animate it till the change introduced in 1814. Each succeeding day brought ten invitations for the evening.

The almost Oriental luxury which the Emperor afterwards introduced into his Court was not then known. Madame Bonaparte, who possessed in the highest perfection the art of dressing, set the example of extreme elegance. No sight could be more charming than a ball at Malmaison, composed of the numerous ladies connected with the Military Household which the First Consul had just formed, and who constituted, without having yet received the name, the Court of Madame Bonaparte.

All were young, many were pretty, and I know but one ugly enough to merit the epithet. When this beautiful group was attired in robes of white crape trimmed with flowers, and their hair ornamented with garlands as fresh as the complexion of their merry faces, smiling with happiness and good-humour, it was a charming and striking spectacle to see the animated dance which derived its zest from their gaiety in the same room in which the First Consul and the most eminent persons in Europe were promenading. These assemblies required a continual renewal of dress, and the first year of the Consulate saw the revival of that trade in the manufacturing towns of France, which again became an honour to the country. The Government officers, no doubt, made smaller accumulations, or laid out less money on estates; but shopkeepers sold their goods, domestics procured places, and workmen got into employment through the medium of from eight to ten thousand balls and five or six thousand dinners, which were given in the course of the winter at Paris. It followed that the silk mercers sold a million yards of satin or velvet, crape and tulle in proportion, the shoemakers manufactured their shoes, the artificial florist was called to assist at the toilet with his flowers, the hairdresser and dressmaker with their industry, and the perfumer with his gloves, fans, and essences.

The higher classes of trade were equally indispensable; the jeweller, the goldsmith, the glass and porcelain manufacturer, the upholsterer, the cabinet-maker, all flourished; the money passed through their hands into those of their workpeople, and the immense population of this great town were all employed and all happy, because the superior classes received company, and expended their incomes in an honourable manner.

At the epoch of which I am writing all prospered. The Peace of Luneville, which secured to France the Rhine as the limit, had been signed. The concessions stipulated at Campo-Formio between General Bonaparte and Count Louis von Cobentzel were confirmed; these concessions were the Duchies of Milan, of Mantua and Modena, together with the Ionian Islands, to be added to the Cisalpine Republic. All was glory shed upon France by the First Consul, and sensibly felt by a grateful nation.

All this was not, however, conceded without much hesitation on the part of the Austrians; it was the necessity of retreating on all sides before our cannon which first induced Austria to treat without the consent of England, notwithstanding her recent engagement to the contrary. This was a great victory gained over English gold. But Joseph Bonaparte, after having given some grand dinners at Paris to the Count von Cobentzel, in which department we had given him all the assistance in our power, was obliged to maintain against him at Luneville many long and warm discussions upon every point to be surrendered, for, alas! we were unreasonable, and asked, the plenipotentiary thought, too much. Happily for the success of Joseph's negotiations, he received, just at the critical moment, a courier from General Brune, bringing a copy of a despatch to the First Consul, announcing a victory in the true Republican style of conciseness:—

"Citizen First Consul,
"I have the honour to inform you that I crossed the Adige yesterday, 1st of January, immediately above Verona; which puts me into a position to announce to you very shortly the occupation of that town.
                                        "I salute you with respect,
                                                        "Brune."

Accordingly, on the 3rd of January Verona was occupied by our troops, as well as Vicenza some days afterwards, and the Brenta was then crossed. In fact, the army was now on the march, and with sufficient rapidity to form a junction with Moreau, who, on his part, encamped at the distance of twenty-five leagues from Vienna, had concluded an armistice with the Archduke Charles, a good prince, an honest man, and a great captain,* but often unfortunate.

An armistice was concluded between M. de Bellegarde, the Austrian commander in chief, and General Brune, and three weeks after the glorious Treaty of Luneville was signed, which wholly restored Marshal Bellegarde's repose, and I may add *en passant* that of some other Austrian Generals-in-Chief, who had had enough of this war.

Count Louis von Cobentzel, who had just signed, at Luneville, the treaty of peace between Austria and France, was the greatest lover of spectacles, *fêtes,* and all kinds of merry diversion, that I have ever met with in my life. The Emperor, his master, had made a judicious selection in appointing him envoy for signing a treaty of peace. He interested himself in the programmes of all the intended *fêtes;* enjoyed them by anticipation, and gave his opinion on the preparations.

I frequently saw him, for, as he was passionately fond of plays, and I had a box at all the theatres, he preferred going privately with Junot and me to appearing in the official box of the Minister for Foreign Affairs.

Count Louis was middle-aged, very ugly, and is truly reported to have resembled Mirabeau. He had the same sallow face, and his eyes, which, however, bore no other resemblance to those of Mirabeau, were equally small. He had also the same enormous head of hair, which gave so singular an effect to Mirabeau's countenance. Count Louis was lively and sensible, but withal had plenty of follies. He had been for a long time Austrian Ambassador at the Court of the great Catherine, and retained a profound and enthusiastic admiration for that Sovereign, who kept a theatre, played herself, and carried the condescension so far as to write comedies for the amusement of her Court. When Count von Cobentzel was once launched on this favourite topic it was a vain hope to extract a word from him that did not bear reference to the theatre at the Hermitage, in which his frightful person would certainly not set off his dramatic talents to the best advantage.

* Who defeated Napoleon at the Battle of Aspern.

The First Consul related to us one evening that M. de Cobentzel had had a temporary stage constructed in the palace of the Austrian Ambassador at St. Petersburg, principally with the object, as you may suppose, of acting himself. One day the Ambassador was to assume the character of the Comtesse d'Escarbagnas. The Empress had promised to be present, and the *Count-Countess* was dressed early to be in readiness for appearing on the stage the moment the Czarina had taken her seat. She arrived, and the Ambassador was sought for, but neither *he nor the Countess* could be found.

At length, after a tiresome search, he was discovered in his cabinet, in male attire indeed, but with his hair puffed, in high-heeled shoes, and so suffocated with passion that he could scarcely articulate the words, "Hang that villain for me!" pointing to a man who was praying all the saints in heaven to defend him from the supposed madman.

This was a special courier from Vienna arrived in haste, with very important despatches, and specially ordered to deliver them into the Ambassador's own hands; for Catherine II made no scruple of violating the seals, not only of her own subjects, but of foreigners, and even Ambassadors, whose diplomatic character is sacred amongst the most savage nations. M. de Beausset, when Ambassador from France, made serious complaints of this gross breach of international law. The courier was a young man, recently attached to the Foreign Office, and had never even seen the Count von Cobentzel. He arrived at seven in the evening, just as the Count, having finished his toilet as Comtesse d'Escarbagnas, was complacently contemplating the reflection in a large looking-glass of a figure which has perhaps never since been paralleled; smiling at his whimsical visage, adding a patch, flirting his fan, enlarging his hoop, and repeating the most striking passages of his part. At this moment the courier from Vienna was announced. The Count replied that he would see him the next morning, but at present he was otherwise occupied; recommending that he should repose himself for the night, and leave business till the morning.

But the young man was a novice in diplomacy, and scrupulously conscientious in discharging his commission. His orders were to use all diligence and at whatever cost to reach St. Petersburg before midnight on this very day. He had arrived, and loudly and pertinaciously insisted on seeing the Ambassador. One of the secretaries informed M. de

Cobentzel of the courier's orders. "Why, what does the obstinate fellow want? Is he possessed? Well, send him in!"

The secretary, accustomed to the fooleries of his master, without an instant's reflection on the necessity of preparing a stranger for the interview, introduced him into the cabinet, saying, "There is the Ambassador." And the courier found himself in the presence of a woman dressed in the fashion of his grandmother's days, who advanced affectedly to meet him, and while putting with one hand an extra patch on a round cheek, already concealed behind a thick coat of rouge, stretched out the other to receive the packet, saying: "Well, sir, let us see these important despatches." The courier turned round instead of answering, to request an explanation of the strange spectacle that thus presented itself. But the secretary had vanished, the door was shut, and he found himself alone with the burlesque vision.

"I wished to speak to the Ambassador," cried the young man, whose brain, somewhat heated by the fatigue of several days' rapid travelling, was nearly overset upon seeing a feminine figure seize the Ministerial packet and endeavour to snatch it from him, saying all the while, "Here is the Ambassador! I am the Ambassador!"

The young Austrian was strong, and retained a firm hold of the despatches confided to him; but, beginning to be frightened, he called for help, insisting on seeing the Ambassador, and refusing to recognise him under this disguise. In vain Count von Cobentzel ran after him round the cabinet, explaining why on this particular occasion he was dressed in his fine brocaded gown and velvet petticoat. Greek would have been more intelligible to his companion. At length the Count exclaimed in despair:

"Well, blockhead, you shall see him, you shall see your Ambassador," and, entering his bedchamber, he threw off his gown and petticoat, and returned to the obstinate courier in white silk stockings, high-heeled shoes, black breeches, and puffed hair,—another edition of my dragoon's dress and white satin shoes.

Accordingly, the young courier, more than ever persuaded of his insanity, persisted in refusing to surrender the Imperial packet, until the Ambassador was growing seriously angry, when, to complete his fury, the Empress's arrival was announced to him. The secretary of the embassy explained this strange scene to the diplomatic messenger, and persuaded him at length to give his despatches into the hands of Count Louis von Cobentzel. The Count read them, and found them indeed a singular prologue to the comedy he was about to perform.

They announced to him that Beaulieu and Wurmser had no better fortune in Italy than the Archduke Charles upon the Rhine. That General Bonaparte, then twenty-six years of age, was taking possession of Italy at the head of 36,000 Frenchmen, and was beating General Beaulieu, notwithstanding (and very probably on account of) his seventy-six years, though he had 50,000 men under his orders. They also warned the Ambassador that it was of the utmost importance to induce the Czarina to give effect to her promises, so long since made, of placing an armament by sea and land at the disposal of the Allies, and pressed him not to lose a moment in communicating this intelligence to the Empress, and in entering upon the question of the armament.

This order admitted of no delay in its execution; Count von Cobentzel felt it, and I may say painfully. England was at this moment about to sign a treaty of subsidy and alliance with Russia; Austria was deeply interested in avoiding the smallest offence to England, and the Count felt that it would be an agreeable compliment to the British Ambassador to consult him on this important occasion. Lord Whitworth was sent for and came. To form a just conception of this interview the two personages should be known.

Lord Whitworth was tall, perfectly well made, and handsome, with a countenance and manner of the highest distinction. I have never known a man better calculated to represent a nation, great, prosperous, and haughty; always magnificently dressed, even at the Consular Court, it may be imagined how particular he would be at that of Catherine II, where Eastern luxury prevailed to a magical extent. Imagine, then, the contrast he would present to the countenance, figure, and manners of M. de Cobentzel, always a little burlesque, and decorated on this occasion, for the amusement of the persons who witnessed the conversation, in the absurd accoutrements of the Comtesse d'Escarbagnas.

The English peer received the Count's communication with the cold politeness habitual to him, and, recommending him not to keep the Empress waiting, went to apologize for a delay which admitted of no apology but the truth. I believe, though I am not quite sure of it, that the Empress, in her impatience to be informed more at length of the details of events of which the English Ambassador could only give the outline, required the immediate presence of the Count von Cobentzel, who came in his gown, hoop, and puffs to the audience.

Count Louis von Cobentzel, though really agreeable, was much less so than he would have been had he permitted his own good sense and information to direct his manners, instead of servilely copying those of Prince Kaunitz and Prince Potemkin, to both of whom he affected to bear a personal resemblance, and whose frivolity and morality, both of the school of Louis XV, he assumed together with an exclusive predilection for the great world. This world was the Court, beyond the luminous circle of which all to him was chaos.

His good sense made him understand that a generation had sprung up in which were to be found names bearing a lustre of renown fully equal to that of heraldic blazonry. He knew this, but to his aristocratic ears the sound of the word "citizen," applied to the Head of the Government, produced discord in all social harmony; and he could not reconcile himself to the necessity of addressing Madame Lannes without the title of Princess. He had talent, however, and was, as I have said, agreeable; he related multitudes of anecdotes about the Court of Russia, all very amusing; that of the Comtesse d'Escarbagnas did *not* come from himself, but was told me at a later period by the Count's cousin, Count Philip von Cobentzel, who very soon succeeded him as Ambassador at Paris, and remained here till our rupture with the Austrians in 1804.

Louis von Cobentzel was fond of joking, especially when he was, as he called it, incognito; that is to say, when he left two dozen ribands and medals in his carriage, and retained but two or three; which, with his black coat, almost French, his silk stockings, diamond shoe-buckles and full-dressed head, made him a personage not very likely to diminish the merriment of such of the frequenters of the Montansier and the Vaudeville as should chance to meet him in the corridors. Our box at the Vaudeville having a private entrance and staircase from the Rue de Chartres, made it particularly agreeable to the Ambassador, and his frequent presence there was an additional attraction and amusement to us.

In the seasons of 1800, 1801, and 1802, the Vaudevilles resumed the gaiety which the stern events of the preceding years had greatly diminished; song was resumed, and farce did not seek its subjects in Plutarch, Livy, or the State Trials. Pero and his friends, Scarron's marriage, and a thousand other such subjects, were more suitable to this temple of gaiety than ambitious names, the very sound of which is sufficient to chase away mirth. At this moment the companies of the Vaudeville and the Théâtre de Montansier were particularly well chosen.

The *Comédie Française* was also in its glory. Talma, Lafont, St. Prix, Monvel—what an admirable constellation of talent! Then Mademoiselle Raucourt, Madame Vestris, Monsieur Fleury, Mademoiselle Georges, Mademoiselle Duchesnois, Mademoiselle Volnais, and Mademoiselle Bourgoin; the recent *débuts* of the four last still divided the society of Paris into rival factions; but greater than all these was Mademoiselle Mars, already the queen of comedy.

Fleury was one of the performers at this theatre who pleased me best; I never heard him assume any character without giving it full effect, by his excellent judgment and good sense. His manners were those of a perfect gentleman, fully imbued with the *ton* of good company, with none of the affectation of the present day.

The Austrian Embassy was not the only one which at this period enlivened Paris; the Emperor of Russia, if he had not an actual representative at the Consular Court, had at least a medium of communication with the First Consul in the person of General Sprengporten. Charmed with the generosity with which Napoleon had treated Russia, in sending home without ransom or exchange, well clothed and provided for, the eight thousand prisoners taken at Alkmaar on the surrender of the Anglo-Russian Army, Paul had charged General Sprengporten with a letter of thanks to the First Consul, but without giving him any diplomatic status.*

* General Sprengporten was not a Russian, but born in Finland of an ancient family. At the period of the famous revolution in Sweden in 1776, he was much attached to the cause of Gustavus III, but he arrived at Stockholm too late to assist the young King; the *chapeaux* had beaten the *bonnets*, and Gustavus was the conqueror. Sprengporten afterwards passed into the Russian service, and although not formally Ambassador at Paris he was treated and listened to as such.

This General gave charming *fêtes;* and though himself of a disposition habitually melancholy, arising from his exile from his native country, to which his engagements in the Russian service were a bar to his ever returning, he so frankly testified his desire to see his guests well amused that it was impossible to avoid being so. He was, moreover, a bachelor; and this circumstance contributed to the freedom of intercourse and mirth which his house offered.

It was here that I first saw Madame Recamier; I had heard her much spoken of, and I acknowledge that my mother had prejudiced my judgment concerning her, in persuading herself, and consequently me, that Madame Recamier's reputation was exaggerated, and that she must necessarily be a person of overbearing pretensions.

Great, then, was my surprise when I beheld that lovely face, so blooming, so childish, and yet so beautiful! and still greater when I observed the timid uneasiness she experienced in her triumph. No doubt it was pleasing to be proclaimed the unrivalled beauty of the *fête;* but it was evident that she was pained by the envious glances of the females, who could not wholly suppress the ill-will with which they witnessed her monopoly of adoration.

Madame Recamier truly deserved that homage; she was really a pretty woman! The expression of her eyes was mild and intellectual, her smile was gracious, her language interesting; her whole person possessed the charm of native grace, goodness, and intelligence. She reminded me at first sight of the Madonnas of the Italian painters; but the resemblance consisted wholly in expression—not in regularity of features.

It was the mind which animated her eyes and blushed in her cheek; the smile which so frequently played upon her rosy lips expressed the unaffected joy of a young heart, happy in pleasing and in being beloved.

At the time when I first met Madame Recamier she was in the prime of her beauty and of her brilliant existence. M. Recamier was at the head of one of the first banking-houses of Paris; his misfortunes were not then foreseen. He had, therefore, the means of giving to his charming consort all the enjoyments of wealth and luxury, as a poor return for her tender attentions and the happiness which she shed over his home and his life. M. Recamier's house was a delightful residence;

nothing was comparable to the *fêtes* he gave to foreigners recommended to him, and whose choice of M. Recamier for their banker was no doubt fixed by the desire of an introduction to his wife. Curiosity attracted them to his house; they were retained there by a charm which acted equally upon old and young, male and female.

Madame Recamier is an indispensable figure in contemporary Memoirs. Not that she either reflected or impressed her era, but because she could have belonged to that era alone. One cannot expect to find, in future times, a woman like her—a woman whose friendship has been courted by the most remarkable persons of the age; a woman whose beauty has thrown at her feet all the men whose eyes have once been set upon her; whose love has been the object of universal desire, yet whose virtue has remained pure; whose unsullied reputation never suffered from the attacks of jealousy or envy; a woman who lost none of the affections which had been pledged to her, because in her days of gaiety and splendour she had the merit of being always ready to sacrifice her own enjoyments to afford consolation—which no one could do more sweetly and effectually—to any friend in affliction. To the world Madame Recamier is a celebrated woman; to those who had the happiness to know and to appreciate her she was a peculiar and gifted being, formed by Nature as a perfect model in one of her most beneficent moods.

Since the 18th Brumaire society had been reuniting and grouping round a Government which offered it at length not only security but prosperity. The peace with Germany, that which was in progress with Russia, and a preliminary treaty already far advanced with Great Britain, afforded a bright horizon to replace those thick clouds which weighed upon the bosoms even of individuals, oppressing all with fears, not only for their possessions but their lives.

Paris once more became the abode of joy and pleasure. In the two first years of the Consulate the finest *fêtes,* except those of the Government, the Ministers, and other authorities, were given by the richest bankers, such as M. Recamier, M. Perregaux, and two or three others; then followed MM. Seguin, Hainguerlot, and other opulent persons, who returned to France in pleasures the wealth she had bestowed upon them.

These *fêtes* were soon rendered more brilliant by the presence of numerous foreigners of distinction, who crowded into France as soon as they were permitted to travel. Italy, England, Switzerland, sent their contributions of visitors who, in exchange for the gold with which they enriched us, were taught the arts of refined entertainments.

The Russians followed the Germans as soon as their new sovereign gave them permission to quit their frozen regions. The Emperor Paul was just dead; and Alexander, the eldest of his sons, had mounted the throne at twenty-three years of age. The despotic domination of the Czars immediately gave place to a paternal government, as much wiser as it was more gentle. I remember that at this period the Russians who came to Paris cherished for their young sovereign a sentiment bordering upon idolatry. Many kept his portrait in their inmost apartment, beside that of the favourite saint, surrounded like it with lights and gems, and as much venerated as St. Alexander Newsky or St. Nicholas.

My poor mother was now suffering under a state of severe illness which neither our cares nor our affection could alleviate, but which she endured with admirable fortitude. Her distressing state added to my indisposition. The final stroke which was to inflict on me this heart-breaking grief was not yet given, but it was threatened, and contributed to my present suffering.

I was at this time far advanced in my first pregnancy, and had suffered much; surrounded by the tenderest attentions, spoiled, as I may say, by my own family, and bearing about me the child who was to make me proud of the name of mother, I ought not, perhaps, to have been sensible of suffering.

At that period the culture of the pineapple was not so well understood as it is at present, and it was consequently a great rarity. In my peculiar situation I became possessed of a longing for this fruit that produced a degree of intense suffering; and in order to gratify my whim Junot, with the affectionate gallantry of a man whose wife is about for the first time to make him a father, ran all over Paris, offering twenty louis for the object I so much coveted. Disappointed in his endeavours, he informed Madame Bonaparte of the circumstance, and she, with her characteristic kindness of heart, sent me the only one that was procurable from the hothouse at Malmaison. From a singular revulsion of feeling this delicious fruit, so eagerly desired by me, and obtained with so much difficulty, became, when actually in my possession, positively distasteful.

No one could be more kind than Madame Bonaparte always was to young women in my situation; she entered into our feelings and interested herself in everything that could be agreeable to us; in these circumstances she was truly amiable. On hearing of the pineapple she prophesied that I should have a daughter, and in support of her opinion proposed a game of patience. I knew by experience all the *ennui* which this unfortunate game promised; but there was no refusing, and in spite of my incredulity I was compelled to sit down and see my destiny settled by the caprice of the cards. It is known that the Empress Josephine was superstitiously credulous in these matters; and, in fact, I was witness, in the years 1808 and 1809, to two events of this kind not a little extraordinary. This time she kept me above an hour, cutting with the right hand and the left, naming days, hours, and months, and ended at length by confirming her prediction of a girl.

"Or a boy," said the First Consul, who came in at that moment, and who always made game of Josephine's cards; "Madame Junot will have either the one or the other, and if I were you, Josephine, I would not risk my reputation for sorcery by a too confident prediction." "She will have a girl, I tell you, Bonaparte; what wager will you lay me of it?" "I never bet," said the First Consul; "if you are sure of the fact, it is dishonest; if not, it is as foolish as losing money at play." "Well, bet sweetmeats, then." "And what will you lay me?" "I will work a carpet to put under your feet at your desk." "Well, now, that is something useful. On such terms I will bet you that Madame Junot has a boy. Now, mind," said he, turning to me, "that you do not make me lose;" and laughing as he looked at me, he added: "But what will become of the wager if you should have both a boy and a girl?" "I will tell you, General, you must give me both wagers."

And there was something so ridiculous in this idea of boy and girl coming at once that even I could not refrain from joining in the laugh, while my look of consternation increased the mirth of the First Consul, my husband, and every one else who was present.

We were now at the period of New Year's gifts and visits, and I was admiring like a child, as I then was, all those brilliant and useless trifles which custom demands should be offered by the gentlemen to a lady whose house they frequent, when two friends came to increase their number and add their good wishes, which were not merely the tribute of etiquette. They were General Suchet and his brother. After the conversation which the occasion demanded, we fell into a discussion upon the merits of those family meetings which this season brought with it; and it was agreed that the celebration of Christmas, of New Year's and Twelfth Days, the birthday and saint's day of the head of the family, and other festivals, were favourable to the maintenance of domestic harmony, and were therefore worthy of being preserved.

In furtherance of these observations the General proposed that we should meet on Twelfth Day, to which I assented with great satisfaction.

"Yes," said Junot; "I engage you to sup here the evening after to-morrow upon a truffled turkey." "Agreed," said General Suchet; "we will come here the evening after to-morrow, and then for the turkey, and truffles, the cake, and plenty of laughter."

I was now in momentary expectation of my confinement, and, notwithstanding the efforts of my mother-in-law to support and comfort me, looked forward to the moment with dread. In the night of the 4th of January we had an alarm, which called up my mother-in-law, who had not undressed for a week past. Marchais was summoned, and pronounced that twenty-four or forty-eight hours would settle the business, and left me, recommending composure and sleep.

I was out of spirits during a part of the succeeding day; I performed my religious duties and wrote to my mother, because she had forbidden me to leave the house; I then arranged my baby-linen and basket, and in this occupation I found the entire dissipation of my fears and melancholy. In the little cap with its blue ribbons, and in the shirt, the sleeves of which I drew through those of the flannel waistcoat, I thought I could see the soft and fair head and fat little mottled arms; in my joy I imagined the pretty clothes already adorning my promised treasure, and pressed them to my bosom, longing to clasp and to see my child, to feel its breath, while I said to myself: "And this little being which I expect will be all my own!" Oh, what days of joy were before me! Junot found me leaning over the cradle in a sort of ecstasy, and when I explained to him the cause of an emotion which his heart was well formed to understand, he embraced me with a tenderness of which I felt prouder than I should have done six months earlier.

My thoughts now took quite a different direction; I not only did not fear, but I desired the decisive moment; and when my friends met in the drawing-room they found me as gay and as happy as any young wife or young girl could be. Madame Hamelin formed one of our party. She was then young, gay, lively, and a most ready assistant in promoting that easy confidence which forms the great charm of intimate association. She had an original and striking wit, bordering a little on the maliciousness of the cat, and sometimes showing that she had tolerably long claws; but I believe that, like puss also, she did not put them out unless attacked.

The evening passed off cheerfully; my mother-in-law was delighted to see me in perfect oblivion of the critical moment, which, however, she knew could not be far distant. We sat down to table, and the turkey, the cake, the madeira and champagne redoubled our gaiety. In half an hour we laughed so heartily that even to this day I think of it with pleasure. General Suchet sat beside me and addressed me in a compliment so absurd that it provoked a violent fit of laughter, with which the room resounded, and which was echoed with equal noise by seventeen or eighteen persons who surrounded the supper-table. I stood up to answer, with my glass of water, for I never in my life could drink wine, to the numerous glasses filled with sparkling champagne which were extended towards me, when I fell backwards into my chair, a cry escaped me, and my glass dropped from my hand. But the sudden attack which had caused this commotion was over in an instant, my cheeks recovered their colour, and I looked up. Junot, still paler than I had been, holding his glass of champagne, was looking at me with an air of consternation.

The rest of the company seemed nearly equally alarmed, and the grotesque expression of so many countenances hardly recovered from a fit of hilarity, while, as in duty bound, they were assuming on the other side of their faces the solemnity which the circumstances appeared to require, resembling at once *Jean qui pleure* and *Jean qui rit,* produced so risible an effect that I relapsed into a fit of uncontrollable laughter. My mother-in-law now came behind my chair, and whispered: "Take my arm, my dear daughter, and come to your room." "No, no!" said Gabriel Suchet, "we cannot spare her!"

Hereupon he began to relate a story so absurd that I laughed again as immoderately as before, and was again interrupted in the same manner; my mother-in-law told her son that I must be removed and a carriage sent for Marchais. Junot came to me, took me in his arms, and almost lifted me from my chair. This time the General interposed, offered to bet upon the sex of my child, and would with difficulty permit my husband to carry me away. He led me, however, to my room, obeying his mother's behests with as much simplicity as any honest bourgeois, any M. Guillaume or M. Denis, of the Rue de la Perle or Rue Saint Jacques. He busied himself in regulating the temperature of my room, in calling my nurses together, giving them fifty orders at once, which neither they nor he understood, ordered the horses, and returned to my side, already expecting to hear the cries of his child; but I was in no such hurry.

During this tedious season of watching and anxiety Junot was almost distracted; he threw himself at intervals on the mattress which had been laid for him in the parlour, then got up, walked the room with hasty steps, crept to my bedroom door and tried to get in, which I had positively prohibited, and returned to his apartment, where his aide-de-camp, General Lallemand, sat up with him all night, endeavouring with arguments and consolations of friendship to calm a little the violence of his agitation and to restore something like composure to his mind.

Junot on leaving me by no means recovered his self-possession; he wandered through the rooms all opening into each other, which at both extremities brought him to one of the doors of my chamber, found repose in none of them, and at length, unable longer to endure his confinement, snatched up a round hat which happened to meet his eye and sallied forth into the street. Without once considering which way he was going, habit or instinct led him to the Tuileries, and he found himself in the Grand Court without knowing how he had got there. Before ascending, however, the staircase leading to the First Consul's apartments, the consideration of his dishabille crossed his mind; "But no matter," said he, as he looked down upon his brown coat, "I am sure of finding here a heart which will understand my feelings."

All his comrades in the antechamber were astonished at the expression of his countenance and the disorder of his dress; but none of them felt any disposition to ridicule; and the First Consul, as soon as he heard that Junot wished to see him, sent for him into his cabinet. "Good God! what is the matter, Junot?" he exclaimed with surprise on seeing him. "General, my wife is in labour and I cannot stay at home," was the answer, but in a voice almost choked with tears. "And you are come to me to seek courage; you are right, my friend. Poor Junot! how you are upset! Oh, women, women!"

He required a relation of all that had happened from my first seizure; and though Junot dared not give utterance to his apprehensions, yet Napoleon gathered from all the facts he described that my life was actually in danger; and his conduct in this moment of anxiety, when his discernment penetrated into a mysterious horror, was that of the tenderest and best of brothers. "My old friend," said he to his faithful and devoted servant, pressing his hand,—a very rare caress,— "you have done right in coming to me at this moment, as I hope to prove."

So saying, he left his cabinet, and, leaning upon Junot's arm, stepped into the salon where the statue of the great Condé stands, and walked up and down, talking of the only subject which interested his companion; for he was too well versed in the management of the human heart to interrogate chords which would certainly have been mute at such a moment. Amongst other things, he asked my husband how he came to the Tuileries. "On foot," was the answer; "a species of desperation drove me from home, though my heart is still there, and I wandered hither without knowing which way I came." "And may I ask you, then," said Napoleon, "why you look out of that window ten times in a minute to see if any one passes the gate? How should they come here to seek you if your servants do not know where you are? if your officers saw you come out in plain clothes? It seems to me that they are more likely to suspect you of throwing yourself into the river than of coming here." He called and gave his orders. "Send a footman immediately to Madame Junot's to learn whether she is yet put to bed, and if not, let the family be informed that General Junot is here."

He again took my husband's arm, and continued to converse with him with such affecting kindness that Junot could not repress his tears. He was attached to his General, to that vision of glory which commanded admiration; but in such moments as the present Napoleon's conduct could not fail to subject to him the whole heart and affections of the individual whose sufferings he thus alleviated, even if he had not been already devoted to him body and soul. This day riveted, if I may say so, the chains which bound Junot to Napoleon.

Seeing him leave the house in a state bordering on distraction, Heldt, his German *valet-de-chambre,* followed him into the Tuileries, and on his return home informed the aide-de-camp Laborde where the General was to be found.

Junot had been three-quarters of an hour with the First Consul, whose arm rested on his, obliging him to remain a prisoner when he would rather have been at large and have had the power to come and learn the result of all his uneasiness. The footman could not yet be returned, when Junot, emboldened by the First Consul's goodness, begged to be allowed to inquire for him. "I should have been told," answered the First Consul, "if he was returned. Remain quiet." Then, dragging him still farther on, they were presently in the gallery of Diana. There Junot's uneasiness became so violent that Napoleon several times looked at him with astonishment, and, with an accent to which it is impossible to do justice, repeated, "Oh women, women!"

At length, at the moment that Junot was about to escape without listening to anything further, M. de Laborde appeared at the farther end of the gallery; he had run with such haste that he could scarcely speak, but his countenance was full of joy.

"General," he said, as soon as he had recovered his breath, "Madame Junot is safe in bed, and is as well as possible." "Go, then, and embrace your *daughter,"* said the First Consul, laying a stress on the word "daughter." "If your wife had given you a boy, they would have told you at once; but first of all embrace me;" and he pressed him affectionately in his arms. Junot laughed and cried, and, thoughtless of everything but the event which had just occurred, was running away, when Napoleon said to him: "Stay, giddy-pate, are you going through the streets without your hat?"

He returned to the First Consul's cabinet, where he had left his hat;

the time was not yet come when the Prince of Neufchatel would not have presumed to enter the Emperor's presence, even at three o'clock in the morning, without his coat buttoned, his ruffles, dress-boots, and his plumed hat under his arm. "Give my friendliest greetings to your wife, Junot, and tell her that I have a two-fold quarrel against her: first, because she has not given the Republic a soldier; and secondly, because she has made me lose my wager with Josephine. But I shall not be the less her friend and yours." And again he pressed Junot's hand and let him go.

It would be impossible to describe the delirium of joy which was painted on Junot's countenance and actuated his manners when he returned to me. He bathed his daughter's little face with tears of delight so soft, so pure, that it was easy to see his happiness without his uttering a word. Then, throwing himself on his knees beside my bed, he took my hands, kissed them, and thanked me for his child, his daughter, his little Josephine.

But notwithstanding his joy, Junot perceived that something weighed upon my heart which was not connected with my past sufferings.

"What is the matter?" said he, embracing me again. "Nothing, but a great deal of happiness." "I know you, Laurette; I see the tears in your eyes: your heart is not at ease. What is the matter?"

I looked at him without answering; the tears rolled down my cheeks, but I would not speak. At this moment M. Marchais came in. "What! again?" he said to me. "My dear General, you should scold your wife, and the way I see you employed gives you additional right to do so!" Junot at this moment had his child in his arms and was embracing it. "You shall hear all, then. Oh, Madame Junot, make no signs to me; I shall not heed them! You must know, then, General, that this young mother, who is a little heroine for courage, as soon as she was safely put to bed, and had learned that you were not at home, sent for your father, that he might give his blessing to your child. I went myself to seek M. Junot, but he refused to come as soon as he learned that the infant was a girl. At length he was persuaded; but when Madame Junot, notwithstanding her weakness, took the babe in her arms to present it to him, saying, 'My father, bless your granddaughter;

it is another heart that will love you,' instead of embracing the child, he replied in a tone of vexation:

" 'It was not worth while to make all this noise about a wretched girl. What is your husband to do with this little crying thing? He will give it a pretty reception . . . and the First Consul too! do you think he does not wish his Generals to have boys?' If I had any authority over your father other than that of a physician in his patient's chamber, I confess I should have used it with some severity. I have frankly told you all this because it is a part of my duty, and because to-morrow, or the day after, a similar scene might have a fatal effect upon Madame Junot. It has affected her seriously, because she believes that the birth of a daughter is a great grievance to you, and it is in vain that I have represented to her that a mother of seventeen and a father of twenty-nine years of age will have time enough to pray for boys without being in despair at a first disappointment, and meanwhile the grandfather may fret as much as he pleases."

Scarcely had M. Marchais' first words struck Junot's ears than he understood the cause of my distress; and he seated himself upon my bed and wept with me, while he dried my eyes with his handkerchief and kisses.

Then, taking up his daughter out of a little basket* of fine embroidered muslin, made on purpose that she might lie in it upon my bed, he placed her in my arms, and embraced us both with an air of such joyful delight as left no doubt of the sentiments of his heart, which, however, never could be doubtful to me. But the first moment of my father-in-law's denunciation was terrible; no doubt he had no intention to injure me, but he might have killed me. "Mamma," said I to my mother-in-law, who just then came in, "you were right, you see; he loves it as well as if it had been a boy."

"Did not I tell you so?" replied this excellent woman. "My son's heart is too good and too noble to entertain the ideas his father would have given him credit for."

* This barcelonnette was the tasteful production of Mademoiselle L'Olive,—in form of a swan, the feathers of which were embroidered in relief with white cotton; the wings, a little spread, made a sort of handle to lift it by; the back was open, forming the cradle, and from its neck and reverted head fell a veil of white Indian muslin for the curtain, which was gathered up in the beak of the swan.

T H E creation, early in 1801, of the Kingdom of Etruria—essentially, the former Grand Duchy of Tuscany—represented a new step in Bonaparte's policy: first Spain was pacified and made into a reliable ally by the cession of territory to the husband of an Infanta. That state, although certainly not French, was nonetheless occupied by the French army: giving it up proved to Europe that Bonaparte, far from being insatiable, wanted no more conquests. Then, conveniently, a vassal state was set up on the border of the French possessions in Italy, thus protecting them from attack. Finally, the visit to Paris of the new King and Queen was supposed to provide the French with an easily understood lesson.

Don Luis, like his wife Maria Luisa, was a Spanish Bourbon who, furthermore, was Louis XV's great-grandson. He was also, as Mme Junot noticed with scorn, astonishingly stupid. At a time when some people still thought that Bonaparte might re-establish the monarchy in France as General Monk had done in England, parading a degenerate Bourbon was a clear indication that the First Consul had no intention of giving up his place to the Pretender. Finally, of course, the visit of the wretched sovereigns of Etruria was a perfect pretext for the display of power and magnificence which, to Bonaparte, was very much the order of the day.

We have now attained a new and memorable epoch in our history, that of the re-establishment of thrones and of religion. The foundation of several republics was the work of General Bonaparte; when at the head of an army, not yet his subjects, his moderation procured him even more renown than his victories. Now that his powerful hand directed the destinies of France, he attempted to set up a petty crown, to place a baby sceptre in the hands of a man incapable of reigning, as if he would say to France, already grown unaccustomed to sovereignty: "See what a king is! Be not afraid of the phantom!"

This monarch, whose new dignity procured for him more ridicule than respect, was the King of Etruria, Don Louis, Infant of Parma, nephew of Queen Marie Antoinette, and husband of the Infanta Marie Louise Josephine, daughter of Charles IV. They came to Paris in the month of May, 1801, to thank the First Consul for their nomination to the crown of Etruria, which was a stipulation of the treaty between France and Spain concluded on the 21st of March, at Madrid. By this treaty France acquired the Duchy of Parma, and ceded Tuscany to the Prince, giving him as an indemnity for his paternal inheritance the territory we had conquered from his uncle. But the King, Louis I, was very possibly ignorant who was the Sovereign of Tuscany before it fell to his share; though had he known it, I am by no means certain that he would on that account have refused the crown.

I never beheld two more extraordinary persons than these new Sovereigns. They assumed the incognito of Count and Countess of Livorno (Leghorn), and brought with them a *Countling,* who, though not quite three years old, was made of more importance than both his illustrious parents put together. Those who have not seen this royal personage at five years of age, in full Court dress, a hat and feathers under his arm; a sword at his side, decorated with a huge bunch of ribands; his poor little locks powdered and frizzed, confined in a bag wig, driven through the streets of Florence on the front seat of a state carriage, and, though fastened to his cushion, rolling from right to left like a little ball; the Queen Dowager, his mother, riding backwards in the most respectful attitude,—whoever has not beheld this spectacle has missed one of those exquisitely ridiculous scenes which prolong laughter till it becomes painful.

At the time I am speaking of, as the King his father was still living, the Prince Royal of Etruria was content to give his little hand to be kissed, whether asked for or not. As for his parents, all who remember their arrival and sojourn in Paris in 1801 will agree with me how totally dissimilar they were from all other human beings, especially if Her Majesty the Queen is to be compared with a woman of even moderate beauty, or the King with a man possessed of a single idea.

Fêtes were given to the King of Etruria, not from any regard to the new-fangled monarch, but from a spontaneous desire to meet the wishes of the First Consul, who well knew how to appreciate the sentiments which dictated the attention. The reception given to his tributary King, who was come to tender to the Republic homage for his crown, was at once magnificent and in good taste. He was, in the first instance, cordially entertained at Malmaison.

The First Consul wished to become acquainted with the character of the man on whom he had bestowed a kingdom, enriched by the noblest monuments of art and science; a very few interviews, however, sufficed to prove that he was nullity personified. Not so the Queen. Her appearance was at first repulsive; but on further acquaintance, when she had thrown aside a timidity partaking in some degree of stateliness, which threw a restraint over her words and actions, she proved to be very agreeable.

M. de Talleyrand was the first of the Ministers who gave a *fête* to the new Sovereigns. The entertainment was given at Neuilly, in the month of June, when the country was in its highest beauty. Taste and ingenuity were displayed in all the arrangements, but both were lost upon him for whose enjoyment the whole was chiefly intended. The *fête* was Florentine, and its illusion complete. The beautiful square of the Pitti Palace was admirably represented, and when their Majesties descended to the garden they were surrounded by crowds of pretty Tuscan peasant girls, offering them flowers, singing couplets, and enticing the royal pair into their groups to hear verses in their own praise. This was followed by the famous improvvisatore Gianni prophesying for them, in fine Italian verse, a long and prosperous reign. All this made no impression on King Louis. The Queen, who alone understood it, made acknowledgments for both.

The finest of these *fêtes* was that given by the Minister of the Interior. He had not, like M. de Talleyrand, the advantage of a villa in the country, but his garden was skilfully laid out to bear the appearance of a park, and the whole scene reminded one of fairyland. Three hundred and fifty ladies found seats in that fine gallery where Lucien in the preceding year had given such agreeable balls, which, pleasant as they were, certainly afforded no presage of M. Chaptal's evening of enchantment. The First Consul was enraptured, and, though seldom known to take notice of such matters, not only expressed his satisfaction at the time, but long afterwards reverted to the invisible singers and the ravishing harmony of M. Chaptal's gardens.

Yet here, as at Neuilly, all the delicate courtesies shown in honour of the Sovereigns were appreciated by the Queen alone; the poor King could not find a word of thanks for so much pains expended on *fêting* and pleasing him; even when, in the midst of a Tuscan village, where Tuscan peasants were singing in chorus the beautiful lines of Tasso and Petrarch, which he could scarcely fail of understanding, a crown of flowers was offered him, accompanied by flattering verses, still not a syllable could he say—the same eternal and unmeaning smile, which seemed to express that he could not comprehend even the language and scenery of Italy, still sat upon his lips.

In the dance his Tuscan Majesty was really amusing. I had the honour of figuring near him at the ball given by the Minister of War on the anniversary of the Battle of Marengo, and congratulate myself on my wonderful self-control in preserving my gravity through the whole country-dance. The King, dancing with Queen Hortense, skipped and jumped about in a manner by no means beseeming the royal dignity. In one of his capers a buckle from his shoe suddenly flew into the air, and alighted in my head-dress; and so highly was the King's mirth excited by its course and final resting-place, that he was nearly choked with laughter. We were little less diverted when, on examining the buckle to ascertain how it had found its way from the royal foot to my head, it was discovered that it had been only glued to the shoe.

This *fête* of the Minister of War acquired a peculiar character from the supper being served in the garden, under tents, with all the military appendages of a bivouac, and from the charm imparted by the glorious day which this *fête* was intended to recall. The fireworks were so designed as to show to the First Consul that the army which surrounded him could honour him alone. A balloon was sent up in the course of the evening, which, against the dark azure of a clear sky, luminously traced as it rose the word "Marengo."

One evening during the King of Etruria's stay in Paris the First Consul accompanied him to the *Comédie Française* to see *Oedipus*. The house was crowded to excess. All Paris was desirous to see, side by side, General Bonaparte, who as a private individual had created republics, and the King he was crowning, now that he was himself Chief of the most powerful Republic in the world. The manners of the new King were especially amusing when contrasted with those of the First Consul, who was always calm, serious, and well calculated to stand the gaze of millions.

When Philoctetes repeated the line, "I have made Sovereigns, but have refused to be one," the noise of the acclamations with which the theatre resounded was almost alarming. The whole house was shaken by applauding feet, while the audience in the boxes, who seldom take part in such scenes, unanimously joined in the cheers of the pit. It was the universal nation expressing to Napoleon the sentiment which filled all hearts.

As for the King, he started at first in his arm-chair, then laughed most complacently on observing all hands and eyes directed towards the box where he sat with the First Consul. But the mirth of those who knew him was complete when, finding the applause prolonged, he thought politeness required some mark of attention in return for such unequivocal proofs of an interest he was quite proud, as he said, of inspiring in so great a people; and he rose to make his best obeisance.

"Poor King!" said the First Consul, shrugging his shoulders. These words, "Poor King!" appear the more contemptuous from his mouth, covered as he was with laurels, and radiant with the glory of his great deeds. But on all occasions a word either of praise or contempt has appeared to me more impressive from him than from other men.

After a visit of some weeks the King and Queen of Etruria quitted Paris and proceeded to their own kingdom of perfumes, where they were received and installed in their throne by Murat. "The rising generation," said the First Consul one day, laughing, "were unacquainted with the face of a King; well, we have shown them one." But his countenance instantly recovered its seriousness, and he added: "Poor Tuscany! poor Tuscany!"

Shortly before the arrival of the King of Etruria in Paris, an aristocratic measure was under discussion,—that of the lists of eligibility relative to elections, the object of which was to fill all official posts with select persons.

Cambacérès, strange as it may seem, pronounced strongly in favour of the lists, and the First Consul held a long discussion with him. Napoleon said that the lists were founded on a bad system, and on false and erroneous principles. "France," said he, "is a great Power, but it is the people who compose that power. This law, although a part of the constitution, is not therefore the less bad and absurd. It is not fifty, sixty, or even a hundred men, assembling together in a moment of tumult and excitement, who have a right to make a constitution and to alienate the rights of the people. The sovereignty of the people is inalienable." These are the very words of Napoleon; they were written in pencil by him who gave them to me, and he wrote them as they fell from the First Consul. Did they truly interpret his sentiments?

It was some weeks previous to this incident that the establishment of the Legion of Honour, one of the most remarkable events of the whole rule of Napoleon, was first talked of. This affair doubtless made an impression, but less than proportionate to the difficulty with which it had been effected.

The creation of the Legion of Honour, when it was first mooted, excited feelings and discussions of which, in the present day, it is impossible to convey an idea. The creation of an order of knighthood in a country filled with republican institutions, and resolved on equality, appeared at first, even to those who, from their reputation in arms, were entitled to be chiefs of the order, a sort of monstrosity. None of them had even imagined that the First Consul would one day assume the sovereignty of the State. I do not think that the Consulate for life had yet been talked of; Napoleon now held the office for ten years only.

"Well, after all," said my mother to Junot, "I assure you, my dear son, a green, red, or blue ribbon is a very pretty thing over a black coat or a white waistcoat. I am fond of these talismans of ambition. The Consular Court is now rising with an *éclat* far surpassing its predecessors. You will agree with me that, unless power possesses both the will and the means to make itself respected, it is indispensable to surround it with a sort of theatrical splendour, to prevent its becoming an object of mockery. Bonaparte is a man of sense and tact; he understands all this, and reduces it to practice. You will see where all this will end——"
And my mother gently nodded her head, as she changed her position on the sofa; for at that time, in compliance with the decree of her physicians, she scarcely ever rose from it.

Junot's demeanour as he listened to her harangue was droll; he saw plainly that she was jesting, but as he did not himself entirely approve this measure at the outset, he was at a loss for an answer. He was much perplexed also to guess how my mother had penetrated the secrets of the Council of State, in which the First Consul had spoken at great length, and with an eloquence the more extraordinary as oratory was by no means his forte; he possessed to an almost irresistible extent the art of compelling his auditors to adopt his views; but that he should speak for an hour together and with real eloquence, was truly astonishing.

This was not the first time that my mother had surprised us by talking politics, in which formerly she never interfered; but a heart like hers must follow the interests of those she loved. Until my marriage no warmer sentiment than a sincere friendship for a few individuals had caused her to look upon public affairs either with pleasure or uneasiness. But in fifteen months her attitude was changed. Her daughter was the wife of a man so intimately attached to the established order of things that the future welfare of that daughter depended on its preservation; her son had a lucrative office in the administration of the Republic; and the personal opinions of my mother were silenced by these strong ties, which bound her to the existing Government.

She who had never busied herself with any political gossip now grew desirous of sounding public opinion; she had two or three journals read to her daily, and such of her friends as were in a situation to give her information were laid under contribution. My good and affectionate mother, all these habits so foreign to her former life were not agreeable to her. But it would have distressed her to be ignorant of anything in which we were interested; and through the elder M. Portalis she frequently learned rumours which did not reach Junot till he heard them from her two or three days later; not through any breach of confidence on the part of the Councillor, but merely because Junot did not attend the sittings of the Council, and their proceedings were not reported in the journals. It happened so in the case of the Concordat, one of those landmarks which denote a great epoch in the history of our Revolution.

ALTHOUGH the Revolution had begun as a demand for liberty, it quickly turned into an authoritarian regime willing and able to suppress liberty in the interest of greater efficiency. Among the first to go was freedom of religion—not unjustifiably, perhaps, inasmuch as the Catholic Church had adopted, as has so often been its wont, the most reactionary positions, and conducted a violent campaign against the new regime.

As a result, Catholic services, by 1794, could only be held clandestinely. With the fall of Robespierre, then the installation of the Directoire, the situation changed somewhat: priests were no longer automatically arrested, services were, on occasion, tolerated; but the laws which forbade them were not rescinded and when the Directors felt the need to conciliate the left, they would have a few dozen priests arrested. Then, as the Consulate got under way, toleration became the order of the day: thus it was possible for Mme Junot to be married religiously. It seemed clear to Bonaparte, however, that so messy a situation could not be allowed to endure. Further, with the kind of Concordat which, like before the Revolution, allowed the Head of State to appoint the bishops, it would be possible to use the Church as a stabilising element, a kind of spiritual police which would remind the faithful they owed obedience to the government.

It made perfect sense, therefore, to open a negotiation with the Pope; and, indeed, on July 15, 1801, a Concordat was duly signed. New bishops were appointed by the First Consul; they received their canonical institution from Pius VII, and the system worked exactly as Bonaparte had expected: the Bishops' pastoral addresses of this period are monuments of subservience and flattery, while elements of the right, until then disaffected, rallied the regime.

It was the First Consul's desire that the promulgation of the Concordat, which had received his definitive ratification, should be attended with a religious ceremony, in all the pomp and circumstance of Roman worship. The Concordat concerning religious affairs, after being signed at Paris on the 15th July, 1801, by the Consuls, was sent to Rome, where it underwent a critical examination in the Conclave, and was then signed and ratified in all its integrity by the Pontiff.

Fourteen prelates, more attached to remembrance of the past than to hope of the future, refused to recognise the Concordat. These fourteen bishops were then in London, where at least they lived in peace and without care; they were right not to change their lot: they would not have been so well treated in France; for the First Consul allowed the bishops only a sufficient revenue for maintaining a creditable establishment. "They should not have reason to blush," said the First Consul, "in fulfilling the highest ecclesiastical functions; they should also have the means of succouring the unfortunate within their dioceses; but archbishops and bishops must not absorb the revenue of a province, excite scandal, and, as in former days, bring religion into disgrace." Forty bishops and nine archbishops were instituted by the First Consul, who imposed the formula of oath to be taken by them on entering upon their dioceses.

From sixty to eighty ladies were invited to accompany Madame Bonaparte to Notre Dame. She had then no ladies in waiting; but four companion ladies had voluntarily taken upon them the duties of that office. We assembled at the Tuileries at half after ten in the morning of Easter Day, in the year 1802. The Consuls occupied but one carriage. The First Consul had issued no orders, but it was intimated to the principal public functionaries that he would be pleased to see their servants in livery on the day of the ceremony. He put his own household into livery on the occasion: it was certainly showy, but, as yet, by no means well appointed. Madame Bonaparte was accompanied by her daughter and her sister-in-law: the rest of the procession followed promiscuously.

Madame Bonaparte and all the ladies were conducted to the gallery to hear the Te Deum, and the gallery of Notre Dame on that day presented an enchanting spectacle: it formed a magnificent conservatory, filled with the choicest flowers.

Madame Murat's fair, fresh, and spring-like face, comparable only to a June rose, was surmounted by a pink satin hat and plume of feathers. She wore a gown of fine Indian tambour muslin, lined with pink satin and trimmed with Brussels point, and over her shoulders was thrown a scarf of the same lace. I have seen her more richly dressed, but never saw her look more beautiful.

How many young women, hitherto unknown, on this day took their degree in the realm of beauty, beneath the brilliant beams of a mid-day sun, rendered more glowing in their passage through the stained windows of the cathedral! The First Consul himself, the same evening, remarked upon the galaxy of beauty which shone in the gallery.

The ceremony was long. Cardinal Caprara, who officiated, was tedious in the extreme; and M. de Boisgelin was equally prolix in his sermon. At near three o'clock we returned to the Tuileries completely tired. One of the most striking circumstances of the day was the military display. The firing of musketry, the troops lining the streets, the salvoes of artillery, which from the earliest dawn had shaken every window in Paris, mingling the sounds of the camp with religious chants, and with that ecclesiastical pomp so justly in accordance with the solemnity, formed a combination truly imposing.

The First Consul was vehemently irritated by the answer of General Delmas to his question, How he liked the ceremony? "It was a very showy harlequinade," said the General, "and, to render it complete, wanted only the presence of the million of men who have shed their blood for the destruction of that which you have re-erected."

A great misfortune had befallen our family: my mother had ceased to exist. Her sufferings were over, but we had lost our friend, our delight. She had occupied all my time and thoughts, and the void produced by the removal of this adored object occasioned an anguish to which I know of nothing comparable. The affectionate and considerate conduct of Junot on this sad occasion sweetened the bitterness of my grief.

A proof that Junot well understood the heart of her he honoured was his liberality to three hundred of the most distressed amongst the poor of Paris. They were relieved and clothed in the name of her whose funeral car they surrounded, and for whom they were mourning and offered prayers of gratitude. How much did this delicacy in giving and administering the consolation of which I should be most sensible endear my husband to me!

The First Consul was very kind at the time of my affliction. He appeared to bury in oblivion his former disagreements with my mother. Junot brought me messages of the most friendly consolation from him, and Madame Bonaparte did me the honour of a visit, with Lucien, who had just arrived from Spain. The sight of Lucien deeply affected me. I knew how dear he was to my mother. She loved him almost equally with my brother Albert; she rejoiced in his success, and suffered in his disasters. His departure for Spain had much distressed her, and in her greatest agonies she made Junot repeat to her all the honourable traits of his mission to Madrid. Junot felt a degree of partiality for Lucien, as did all who were attached to the First Consul.

Meanwhile we had lost Madame Leclerc; she had been strongly urged by her brother to follow her husband to Saint Domingo.* I believe General Leclerc would willingly have dispensed with this addition to his baggage, for it was a positive calamity, after the first quarter of an hour's interview had exhausted the pleasure of surveying her really beautiful person, to have the burden of amusing, occupying, and taking care of Madame Leclerc. In public she professed herself delighted to accompany *her little Leclerc,* as she called him; but she was in reality disconsolate, and I one day found her in a paroxysm of despair and tears, quite distressing to any one who had not known her as well as myself.

"Ah, Laurette," said she, throwing herself into my arms, "how fortunate you are! You stay at Paris. Good heavens, how melancholy I shall be! How can my brother be so hard-hearted, so wicked, as to send me into exile amongst savages and serpents! Besides, I am ill. Oh! I shall die before I get there." Here her speech was interrupted, for she sobbed with such violence that for a moment I was fearful she would have fainted. I approached her sofa, and, taking her hand, endeavoured to encourage her, as one would a child, by talking of its playthings or new shoes: telling her she would be queen of the island; would ride in a palanquin; that slaves would watch her looks to execute her wishes; that she would walk in groves of orange-trees; that she need have no dread of serpents, as there were none in the Antilles; and that savages were equally harmless.

Finally, I summed up my consolatory harangue by telling her she would look very pretty in the Creole costume. As I advanced in my

* Now called Haiti; he was going there to re-establish dominion over this recently emancipated French colony.

arguments, Madame Leclerc's sobs became less and less hysterical. She still wept, but her tears were not unbecoming. "You really think, Laurette," said she, "that I shall look pretty, *prettier than usual,* in a Creole turban, a short waist, and a petticoat of striped muslin?"

Description can give but a faint idea of Madame Leclerc at the moment when her delight at being presented with a new hint for her toilette chased away the remembrance that she was on the eve of departure for a country where she expected to be devoured. She rang for her waiting-maid. "Bring me all the bandanas in the house." She had some remarkably fine ones, which my mother had given her from a bale of Indian silks and muslins brought over by Vice-Admiral Magon. We chose the prettiest amongst them, and as my mother had always worn silk handkerchiefs for nightcaps, I was accustomed from my infancy to the arrangement of the corners in the most becoming manner; Madame Leclerc, therefore, when she examined herself in the glass, was enraptured with my skill.

"Laurette," said she, replacing herself on the sofa, "you know, my dear, how I love you! You preferred Caroline, but we shall see if you won't repent yet. Listen! I am going to show you the sincerity of my affection. You must come to Saint Domingo—you will be next to myself in rank. I shall be queen, as you told me just now, and you shall be vice-queen. I will go and talk to my brother about it." "*I* go to Saint Domingo, madame!" I exclaimed. "What in the name of madness are you thinking of?" "Oh, I know there are difficulties in the way of such an arrangement, but I will talk to Bonaparte about it; and as he is partial to Junot, he will let you go to Saint Domingo."

While I looked at her in perfect amazement, she proceeded, arranging all the while the folds of her gown and the fashion of her turban: "We will give balls and form parties of pleasure amongst those beautiful mountains" (the serpents and savages were already forgotten); "Junot shall be the commander of the capital. What is its name? I will tell Leclerc I expect him to give a *fête* every day. We will take Madame Permon too." And as she said this she pinched my nose and pulled my ears, for she liked to ape her brother, and thought such easy manners had an air of royalty.

But both the ludicrous effect of this scene and the weariness I was beginning to feel from it fled at once before the sound of her last words. My mother, who loved her with a tenderness equal to that of Madame Letizia,—my poor mother, who already lay on a bed of suffering from which she was never more to rise! I felt it possible that I might make an answer harsh enough to awaken the beautiful dreamer from her reverie; therefore, putting on my gloves, I was about to take leave, when Junot was announced; he had seen my carriage at the door, and, stopping his cabriolet, came to my rescue.

"You are just arrived in time," cried Madame Leclerc; "sit down there, my dear General, and let us settle everything; for it is high time," said she, turning to me; "you will have no more than enough for preparing Mademoiselle Despaux, Madame Germon, Le Roi, Copp,* Madame Roux—no, Nattier will do better, Mademoiselle L'Olive, Lenormand, Le Vacher, Foncier, Biennais" (and at each name of these celebrated contributors to the toilette, as she counted them on her finger, she cast a glance of triumph towards us that seemed to say, "See what an excellent memory I have, and how admirably I can choose my ministers!"). "As for myself," she added, "my preparations are made, I am quite ready; but as we set out very shortly, you had better make haste."

Junot's countenance would certainly have diverted any fourth person who might have been a spectator of the scene; his eyes wandered from me to Madame Leclerc, who, perceiving his perplexity, said: "I am going to take you both to Saint Domingo, Madame Permon too, and Albert; oh, how happy we shall all be together!" Junot was for a moment motionless, till a tremendous burst of laughter interrupted the silence,—not very politely, it must be confessed; but I afterwards learned that the explosion was provoked by a wink of peculiar intelligence.

Madame Leclerc was astonished at such a mode of testifying his gratitude, expecting to see him throw himself at her feet; but she reckoned without her host. "Very pretty," said she, pouting; "will you please to explain the meaning of this gaiety? Methinks it is not exactly the way to thank an old friend who intends you a kindness." "Have

* Copp was a famous shoemaker, the same who, after a most attentive examination of a shoe which one of his customers showed him, complaining that it split before she had worn it an hour, detected at length the cause of such a misfortune befalling a specimen of his workmanship:

"Ah," said he, with the air of making a discovery, "I see how it is, madame: you have been walking!"

you had the goodness to mention your intentions to the First Consul, madame?" said Junot, who, though growing more decorous, could not yet entirely overcome his risible propensities. "No, certainly not; for your wife has but just suggested the idea."

Junot turned to me with an astonishment that nearly set me laughing in my turn. "What! my wife go to Saint Domingo?" said he. "And why not? She will be the first person there next to myself; she is used to the world; she dresses well; she is elegant. I will give her some slaves, and Leclerc will make you commandant of that town—the— the——" "The Cape," said Junot. "Exactly, the Cape—the Cape." And she repeated like a parrot the word which in five minutes she would altogether have forgotten.

"I am infinitely obliged to you, madame," said Junot, with comic seriousness; "but really, with your permission, I should prefer remaining Commandant of Paris. Besides, there is a slight obstacle which you do not appear to have taken into contemplation." And, throwing his arms round me, he drew me towards him, embraced me, and hinted at my being in the family way.

Madame Leclerc opened her eyes even wider than was usual with her when surprised, and that was not unfrequently,—a little mannerism that was not unbecoming, and said: "I did not think of that. But what of that," said she the next moment; "what does it signify whether your infant utters his first cry on the waves or on *terra firma?* I will give Laurette a vessel to herself. Ah! what say you to that, M. Junot? Am not I a capital manager? I will write immediately to Brest, where we are to embark, and order a vessel to be expressly prepared. Villaret-Joyeuse is a good-natured man; he will do anything that I desire. Come, let me embrace you both."

"As for embracing you, madame," said Junot, laughing himself almost out of breath, "I am assuredly too happy in the permission not to take advantage of it, but for our voyage we will, if you please, drop that project, which Laure's friendship for you no doubt inspired. Besides," added he, "I do not think the First Consul would consent to it. You know he likes to nominate his Generals spontaneously, and without reference to private feelings, such as would influence this affair." And he laughed anew. "But," he continued, "I am not the less grateful for your intentions, madame, and be assured I am fully sensible of them, only"—and again the unfortunate laugh redoubled—"another time be kind enough to prove them otherwise than by putting my little Laura to bed on the wide ocean, and giving me the command of the Cape instead of Paris, and all this for old friendship's sake."

Junot, kneeling on a footstool beside Madame Leclerc's settee, was kissing her hands all the while that he said this, in a tone which, though certainly of derision, and perhaps of a little innocent impertinence, could not be offensive. Madame Leclerc was not competent to understand the raillery of his expressions, but, by a sort of instinctive cunning, she perceived that he was making fun of her, and, whether really distressed at so peremptory a negative to her project, or at being laughed at in my presence by Junot, of whose former attachment for her she had a thousand times boasted to me, the fact is she repulsed him with such violence as to throw him from the footstool on the carpet, and said, in a voice choked with sobs:

"This it is to attach one's self to the ungrateful—I, who love Laura like a sister!" (and, in truth, that was not saying much). "And you too, Junot, who refuse to accompany and defend me in a country where I am to be deserted!" And her tears rolled in floods.

"I will never refuse to assist a woman in peril," said Junot, rising, and with an expression half in jest and half earnest; "but permit me to say that is not your situation." "Ah!" continued she, still weeping, and without listening to him, "you would not have made all those reflections when we were at Marseilles! . . . You would not so tranquilly have seen me set out to be devoured, perhaps. . . . How can I tell? In short, to face all the dangers of a land filled with savages and wild beasts. I, who have said so much to Laurette of your attachment to me."

This time it was impossible to restrain my laughter. Such an appeal to a husband in the very presence of his wife threw me into such a paroxysm of mirth that Junot, though beginning to be weary of the scene, could not forbear joining. "Come, be reasonable," said he to the beautiful Niobe with the freedom of an old friend; "do not weep; it destroys the lustre of the eyes, the bloom of the cheek, and renders the prettiest woman almost ugly—beautiful as you are!" After our departure we indulged for several minutes in a most immoderate fit of laughter.

"Is it possible," said Junot at length, "that you can have said anything tending to inspire her with the barbarous notion of your inclination to visit the country of the blacks?" I told him the whole story, and he in return explained to me why he had been so excessively amused by the capricious beauty's sudden proposal to carry me off eighteen hundred leagues from Paris, made with as much ease as one invites a friend to a week's visit at a country seat. "She still loves you, then?" said I.

"She!—in the first place, she never loved me, and in the next, supposing her to have returned in the slightest measure a love as passionate as beauty can engender in an ardent mind and volcanic head at the age of twenty-four, she has long ago lost all remembrance of it. No; you visited Madame Leclerc at a moment when she was under the dominion of one of those nervous affections to which women, and especially such women, are frequently subject. The sight of you instinctively redoubled her emotion, simply because it recalled happy days; then you talked to her of dressing *à la* Virginia, and she immediately recollected that at Marseilles, when I was madly in love, when the excellent Madame Bonaparte, the mother, was willing to accept me as a son-in-law, and the First Consul, ever prudent and wary, observed, 'You have neither of you the means of living,' I, in my delirium, answered: 'But, General, think of Paul and Virginie*—their friends preferred fortune to happiness, and what was the consequence?' The First Consul, who was never romantic, did but shrug his shoulders and repeat his usual phrase: 'You have neither of you the means of living.' "

"But," said I, "it could not be the bandana and the fashion in which I turned up its red and green corners that produced this jargon of unconnected folly." "You need seek no deeper for it. Madame Leclerc's imagination is perfectly stagnant on many points, and compensates itself by an incredibly creative faculty in others. Her ignorance is unbounded, and equalled only by her vanity. Well, these two properties, which make up her whole composition, easily open themselves a way which the most sprightly imagination, united with a few grains more of sense, would find it difficult to trace. I know her well; her vanity made her veritably believe that I should be but too happy to

* An enormously successful romantic novel; its author is Bernardin de Saint-Pierre.

222

join this expedition to Saint Domingo." "And you think she would really have spoken to the First Consul if you had not arrived?" "Beyond all doubt, for she is perfectly sincere. She was convinced that all she was arranging, or rather deranging, in her pretty little head was entirely for our interests, and would have requested her brother's permission for my joining her husband's army as a special favour towards me."

I do not know whether it was a suggestion of the female imagination, ever restless, or perhaps more properly jealous, that made me observe on the possibility that Madame Leclerc, tenacious of her project of roaming with me amongst the blacks in a gown of striped muslin and a bandana jacket and turban, might yet mention it to her brother.

"You are very right," said Junot. "Beautiful creature as she is (and good and excellent, moreover, for her heart is free from malevolence), this affair might prove a rehearsal of the story of the bear knocking his friend on the head. We must forestall such favours."

The event proved my sagacity. The same day Junot related to the First Consul all that had passed between his sister and me, taking care, as may be supposed, not to throw in too strong a colouring. As for the picture itself, with all its subordinate attributes, the First Consul knew his sister too well to suppose the relative situation of the parties exaggerated. Three days afterwards he said to Junot with a smile: "You are bent, then, on going to Saint Domingo?" Junot replied only by a bow and a corresponding smile. "I am sorry, but you cannot go at present. I want you here, as I have given General Leclerc to understand, who wanted to persuade me that you would be more useful to me at the Cape than in Paris." Junot assured me that it was amusing to observe the countenance of the First Consul as he spoke this; it exhibited a rapid succession of novel impressions, recalling images of the past.

Yet the whole affair passed over Madame Leclerc's mind without penetrating beyond its surface, for she possessed no solidity, and all her conceptions were as uncertain and fugitive as her head was incapable of methodizing any plan. The next time I saw her she had forgotten everything but the bandana. She had been that very morning to my poor mother's to have her turban arranged by her hands, and my mother, though in extreme pain, had taken a sort of pride in setting it off to the best advantage round a head which in this dress was one of the prettiest imaginable.

The squadron at length set sail in the month of December, 1801. The dresses, hats, caps, and other frivolities which Madame Leclerc took out with her, were innumerable. Thirty-five ships of the line, twenty-two frigates, and an immense number of gunboats followed the vessel which bore the lovely Cleopatra, and which had been furnished with every appurtenance of luxury, elegance, and utility, that the fair voyager might have no desire ungratified. The General was disposed to refuse admission to so many useless indispensables; but Madame Leclerc, at the first sound of objection, assumed a tone that instantly reduced her spouse to silence for the sake of peace during the exile to which he was condemned.

Haiti, in itself, only mattered because it had been a source of sugar for France; but what was far more important to Bonaparte is that it might serve as a base from which to attack, or at least frighten, the British West Indies. Then, too, abandoning a colony because the colonised objected to being enslaved seemed like a bad precedent, something no great power should allow. As it turned out, however, Haiti was not as easy to reconquer as Bonaparte had supposed. In an age when medicine was virtually non-existent, and when nothing was known about tropical diseases, the "fevers", as they were known—malaria, typhoid, cholera—were usually deadly; and since the source of infection remained a mystery, Europeans usually fared very badly in the tropics. Sure enough, General Leclerc, along with most of his men, caught the "fevers" and died; oddly enough, the fragile, often sickly Pauline came through it all unscathed; thus it was as a less than desolate widow that she returned to Paris in 1803.

Peace with England was definitely signed. The Treaty of Amiens had confirmed the preliminaries of reconciliation with our great rival on the 25th of March, 1802. On this occasion, which terminated all the differences of Europe, Joseph Bonaparte was again our messenger of peace. The temple of Janus was at length closed, and France exalted to a higher pinnacle of glory and real power than she has ever since attained, for she had emerged from a struggle with united Europe victorious, aggrandized, and respected. The colonies captured by England were restored to us. The course of the Scheldt was left in our hands, as well as the Austrian Netherlands, part of Brabant, Dutch Flanders, and a number of cities, as Maestricht, Venloo, etc.

Paris now realized the vision of the First Consul for his great city; it had become the capital of the civilized world. Such was the concourse of foreigners that exorbitant prices were charged for the most inferior lodgings, and paid without hesitation. My situation as wife of the Commandant of Paris introduced me to all strangers of any celebrity, and I confess my most interesting recollections belong to this portion of my life. Russians and English were the principal actors on this scene. The English, greedy of travelling, and so long shut out from their European tour—for Italy, Switzerland, and part of Germany had, since 1795, been as inaccessible to them as France—gave loose to their joy with all the frankness and sincerity of their national character, which is so totally in opposition to the sophistry and artifice of their Cabinet. They flocked in crowds to Paris, and entered with ardour into the pleasures which France offered them in abundance, which they felt too happy in repaying with their gold. Society, too—the best society— then beginning to reorganize itself, presented attractions which their acute and judicious perceptions were equally capable of appreciating.

Among the English arrivals of that day were some names whose undying reputation fills the memory nearly to the exclusion of all others. Mr. Fox,* for example, was one of those beings whom it is impossible to see, though but once, without remembering forever, as a happy epoch in one's life, the day of introduction. His fine talents and noble character were the adoration of a majority of our countrymen.

Mr. Fox's aspect did not at the first glance seem to justify his prodigious fame—his demeanour was even ordinary—and the first time that I saw him, dressed in a dark gray coat, and with his head somewhat inclined, he gave me the idea of a good Devonshire farmer—a man incapable of any pretension. But how rapidly were these opinions put to flight when the course of conversation brought the energies of his mind into view. His countenance became animated with the first sen-

* The great English Whig.

tence of interest that passed his lips, and gradually brightened with increasing intelligence till it was absolutely fiery and sparkling. His voice, subdued at first, rose in modulation till it burst upon the ear like thunder; and the same man, who but a few minutes before had appeared the most commonplace of mortals, was now an object of intense admiration.

I first saw him at a distance; he was next introduced to me at the Tuileries, where, in the midst of a multitudinous and noisy throng, it was impossible to put in operation any of the plans I had concerted for drawing forth the sentiments of one of the most distinguished and most justly celebrated men of the eighteenth century. At length he dined at my house, and the conversation, having first been of a general kind, turned afterwards on such topics as were more especially adapted to the illustrious stranger. The entire concurrence of opinion between Mr. Fox, Junot, and some of his other guests, precluded debate, but the affairs of England and the Ministry which had replaced Mr. Pitt were long under discussion, and the conversation, though tranquil, was of a remarkable character; when one of the company, who had been of the Egyptian expedition, and had returned with his mind violently exasperated, brought forward the awkward subject of the events in that quarter, freely indulging his rancour against England. Mr. Fox's countenance changed with a rapidity it is impossible to describe; we no longer beheld the leader of the English Opposition, but the advocate of Mr. Pitt, defending him with his eloquence amidst a circle of enemies. The conversation grew warm, and Junot soon took an unfortunate part in it. He had been made prisoner on his return from Egypt by a Captain Styles, conducted to Jaffa, and introduced to Sir Sidney Smith, who was negotiating there with the Grand Vizier the Treaty of El-Arich for the evacuation of Egypt; thence he accompanied Sir Sidney on board the *Tiger* to Larnaka, in Cyprus; here Junot, as I have before observed, contracted for Smith one of those chivalrous friendships which he was very capable of feeling and the brave English Commodore well calculated to inspire. He had more than once laid lance in rest as the champion of his friendly foe; and now, believing him compromised in something that was said respecting the infamous infraction of the treaty which he had guaranteed, and satisfied in his own mind that his gallant friend was the most honourable of men, "It was not his doing!" cried Junot, animated by a sentiment of truth and justice, "he would never have said, with Mr. Pitt, 'The destruction of that perfidious army is a matter of rejoicing; the interests of human nature require its total annihilation.' No. Sir Sidney Smith would be incapable of uttering such a libel on his profession and on human nature." Mr. Fox turned crimson, then pale as death; passed his hand over his eyes, and made no immediate answer; at the end of a minute that striking voice, which, with its sonorous tone, could overpower all others, murmured rather than articulated: "I beg your pardon; Mr. Pitt never used such words. No," answered the statesman, to whose upright and patriotic soul the imputation was truly painful; "those terrible words never fell from the lips of Mr. Pitt; they are Mr. Dundas's."

Paris was also at this time the rendezvous of a multitude of English, who, though less celebrated than Mr. Fox or his brother, proved very agreeable acquaintances. Those whom I chiefly preferred were Lord and Lady Cholmondeley, Mrs. Harrison, a young widow from India of most simple, unaffected, and fascinating manners, the Duchess of Gordon and her daughter Lady Georgiana, Colonel James Green, and Lady Elizabeth Foster, afterwards Duchess of Devonshire. Lady Cholmondeley had considerably the advantage of me in years, but her manners and those of her lord were courteously polished. She talked to me of the glory of the First Consul and his companions in arms in a tone of perfect sincerity and good-will—she blended so amiably with unqualified respect for the dignity of her own nation a just appreciation of the qualities of those I loved—that I was almost attached to her. The First Consul, who received every morning circumstantial intelligence respecting the English in Paris, had a high esteem for the Earl and Countess Cholmondeley. The Duchess of Gordon is assuredly not forgotten by those who had the supreme happiness of seeing her in Paris in 1802. When I wish to divert my thoughts I call to mind her burlesque appearance and manners, which, as is well known, were, notwithstanding her duchess mania, very far from ducal.

The general aspect of society in Paris at that time deserves a place in contemporary memoirs. The First Consul required all the principal authorities to maintain not only a creditable, but a splendid establishment. Nothing could exceed (and this fact will be attested by all living persons who knew Napoleon as I did) his extreme and rigid economy in all his private concerns, though when circumstances required it he could equal in magnificence the most sumptuous sovereign of the East. I remember his once admonishing Duroc for neglecting to transmit an order regulating the private breakfasts at the Palace which he had given him the evening before; the order, therefore, had been delayed but a few hours. "But an additional day's expense," said the First Consul, "is too much."

A few minutes afterwards one of the Ministers arrived. The First Consul immediately entered into consultation upon a *fête* that was to be given the following week on the 14th July, the anniversary of the destruction of the Bastille, which was observed till the re-establishment of royalty; the Tuileries were illuminated, and, as far as I can remember, the theatres were opened gratis. "Josephine," said he, with the tone of kindness he generally adopted towards her, for he was tenderly attached to her, "I am going to impose upon you a command you will have much pleasure in obeying. I desire you will be dazzling; make your preparations accordingly. For my part, I shall wear my fine suit of crimson silk* embroidered with gold, presented to me by the city of Lyons; I shall then be superb!" This dress was, as he said, presented to him by the city of Lyons on the occasion of the *Helvetic Consulta* in the month of January preceding; and, to say the truth, he had already worn it and made a most singular appearance in it, which instantly occurred to my recollection when he talked of his *fine suit,* and I could not suppress a laugh. He perceived it, for nothing escaped his observation, and, coming up to me, said as he surveyed me with a half-angry and half-smiling air: "What do you mean by that sarcastic smile, Madame Junot? You think, I suppose, that I shall not be as smart as all those handsome Englishmen and Russians who look so sweet upon you and turn all your young heads. I am sure I am at least as agreeable as that English Colonel—that dandy who is said to be the handsomest man in England, and whom I can compare to nothing but the Prince of Coxcombs."

This expression, a dandy,** was a favourite word with Napoleon for designating men who displeased him. In the present instance he

* It can be seen today at the Musée Napoléon in the Palace of Fontainebleau.
** *Godelureau.*

alluded to a tall Englishman called Colonel or Captain Matthews, and who passed for a devourer of hearts—English ones, be it observed. I could not avoid laughing still more heartily at this idea of the First Consul and his pretensions to elegance and fashion; whereas he had at that time an utter antipathy to everything that is called fashionable, and showed it in the most unqualified dislike of such young men as had the misfortune to pass in the world for agreeable and elegant. Soft speeches, graceful attitudes, and all other qualifications of a beau, he treated with even more bitterness and contempt than he generally bestowed on the persons he most disliked. Madame Bonaparte presently afterwards made an observation in praise of M. de Flahaut, who, she said, possessed a variety of talents. "What are they? Sense? Bah! who has not as much as he? He sings well—a noble talent for a soldier, who must be always hoarse by profession. Ah, he is a beau! that is what pleases you women. I see nothing so extraordinary in him; he is just like a spider with his eternal legs. His shape is quite unnatural; to be well shaped——" Here his speech was broken in upon, for being at that time much given to laughing, I could not restrain a second fit on seeing the First Consul look with complacency at his own small legs (which, like his whole person, were then very shapely), covered with silk stockings, and a shoe sharp-pointed enough to have pierced the eye of a needle. He did not finish his sentence, but I am certain he meant— "to be well shaped his leg should be like that."

And yet no being could have less vanity than Napoleon; he was neatness itself, and extremely particular in his dress, but made not the slightest claim to elegance. For this reason the movement which approached his hand to his leg as he mentioned the spider legs of M. de Flahaut set me laughing by its *naïveté*. He both saw and heard the laugh, and, what is more, he understood it, and coming towards me again said: "Well, you little pest! What do you find to laugh at? So you must make game, in your turn, of my legs. They do not figure as well to your fancy in a country dance as those of your elegant friends. But a man may both sing and dance without being a dandy. Let me ask yourself, Madame Junot, if Talleyrand's nephew is not a pleasing young man?" My answer was ready. The person he alluded to was Louis de Perigord, who, as well as his brother and his sister, now

Madame Justus de Noailles, had a large fortune; he was then nineteen years of age and already united to the acuteness of his uncle a sound judgment, sprightly wit, polished manners, and a vivid resemblance to his father's person. The last is a eulogium in itself.

Napoleon, then addressing Josephine, said: "I desire you will be dazzling in jewellery and richly dressed; do you hear?" "Yes," replied Madame Bonaparte; "and then you find fault, perhaps fall into a passion, or you erase my warrants of payment from the margin of my bills." And she pouted like a little girl, but with the most perfect good-humour. Madame Bonaparte's manners possessed, when she chose it, a seducing charm. Her graciousness might be too general, but undeniably she could be, when she chose, perfectly attractive and lovable. When the First Consul announced his wish regarding her toilette, she looked at him so prettily, walked towards him with such graceful sweetness, her whole manner breathing so evident a desire to please, that he must have had a heart of stone who could resist her. Napoleon loved her, drew her close to him, and embraced her. "Certainly, my dear love; I sometimes cancel your warrants of payment because you are occasionally so imposed upon that I cannot take it upon my conscience to sanction such abuses; but it is not, therefore, inconsistent to recommend you to be magnificent on state occasions. One interest must be weighed against another, and I hold the balance equitably though strictly."

By 1802, the First Consul's ambition had grown: he no longer thought it enough to have a ten year term; so the ever-obedient Senate offered him, first a second ten-year term, then, later in 1802, tenure for life. Having thus become a republican monarch, Bonaparte soon wanted more. In May, 1804, the Senate went the whole way and made him, not King, but Emperor of the French Republic. At the same time, the *Tribunat*, whose occasional opposition annoyed the new monarch, was dissolved. Although both Senate and Legislature remained, they were so slavishly compliant as to count for nothing: from then on, Napoleon ruled absolutely.

Fittingly, perhaps, the new Empire was soon baptised in war. The peace with England ended first, with responsibility on both sides, and the other European powers (Spain always excepted) soon followed

England. They had reason to regret it: on December 4, 1805, the first anniversary of his coronation, Napoleon won the most dazzling of his victories at Austerlitz, beating the armies of Russia and Austria whose emperors were forced to sue for peace.

PART III

The Glories of

Empire

I T   W A S   I N the spring of 1802 that the first appeal was made to Napoleon's ambition to reign, by his nomination as Consul for another ten years, after the expiration of the ten years fixed by the constitutional act of the 13th of December, 1799. Very little attention was at that time paid to this renewal or prolongation of power; and the *Senatus Consulte,* which appointed Napoleon Consul for life, conveyed the first warning to the French people that they had acquired a new Master.

It declared that "the French Republic, desirous of retaining at the head of her Government the Magistrate who had so repeatedly in Europe and in Asia conducted her troops to victory; who had delivered Italy; who had moreover preserved his country from the horrors of anarchy, broken the revolutionary scythe, extinguished civil discords, and given her peace; for it was he alone who had pacified the seas and the Continent, restored order and morality, and re-established the authority of the law: the Republic, filled with gratitude towards General Bonaparte for these benefits, entreats him to bestow on her another ten years of that existence which she considers necessary to her happiness."

The First Consul's reply is admirably conceived in the style of true simplicity and noble elevation, and is, besides, pervaded by a tincture of melancholy, the more remarkable as the expressions are for the most part prophetic: "I have lived but to serve my country," replied he to the Senate—"Fortune has smiled on the Republic; but Fortune is inconstant; and how many men whom she has loaded with her favours have lived a few years too long! As soon as the peace of the world shall be proclaimed, the interest of my glory and my happiness will appear to point out the term of my public life. But you conceive that I owe the people a new sacrifice, and I will make it," etc.

The important decree I have cited above was presented to the First Consul, and his answer returned on the 6th of May, 1802. Junot, who felt for him that passionate attachment which makes everything a matter of ardent interest, which affects the happiness or honour of its object, said to me: "We must celebrate at the same time this memorable event in the life of my General which testifies the love of a great nation, and our gratitude to the First Consul and Madame Bonaparte for their generous favours. You must invite Madame Bonaparte to breakfast at our house in the Rue des Champs-Élysées, before it is completed. She must even see it in its present state; to wait till it is furnished would delay the project too long, and would, moreover, deprive us of a new opportunity of inviting her. Arrange the matter with Madame Bonaparte, and I will undertake for the First Consul."

I waited then on Madame Bonaparte and preferred my request: she received it with extreme kindness. She was gracious whenever an opportunity allowed, and with a charm of manner that enhanced her favours. She accepted my invitation, therefore, conditionally.

"Have you mentioned it to Bonaparte?" said she. I told her that Junot was then with the First Consul making his request, and she replied: "We must wait his answer, then; for I can accept no *fête* or dinner without Bonaparte's special permission."

This was very true; I had myself been witness to a sharp lecture she received from the First Consul for having breakfasted with a lady for whom he himself entertained the highest esteem, Madame Devaisnes, only because he had had no previous notice of it. I believe he was actuated by prudential motives, and a knowledge of Madame Bonaparte's extreme facility in accepting everything offered to her; at the Tuileries it was difficult to approach her, as no one could visit there without authority; yet even there a few intriguing old ladies paid their respects to her regularly three or four times a week, with petitions, demands for prefectures, seats in the Senate, commands of military divisions, places under the Receiver-General; in short, nothing was forgotten in this long list, except the good sense which should have prevented such unbecoming interference.

The First Consul was aware that her favours were so unsparingly and indiscriminately distributed that she would sometimes make fifteen promises at a single breakfast, dinner, or *fête;* he was consequently extremely particular where he allowed her to go. He knew, however, that at our house she would meet only the same persons who visited at the Tuileries.

Junot was delighted at the kindness with which the First Consul had received his request; he had granted it, but with the singular addition of desiring that no other men should join the party except Duroc and Junot, while the women were to be twenty-five. The breakfast took place, but was not honoured by the presence of the First Consul. Madame Bonaparte and Madame Louis came without him. Madame Bacciochi and Madame Murat were also present, and all my young married comrades, if I may apply that term to the wives of Junot's brothers-in-arms.

Some were very agreeable, and all in the beauty of freshness and youth, so that no spectacle could be prettier than that our table exhibited, when surrounded on this occasion by from twenty-five to thirty young and cheerful faces, of which not more than one or two could be called ordinary. Madame Bonaparte was an astonishing woman, and must have formerly been extremely pretty, for though now no longer in the first bloom of youth, her personal charms were still striking. Had she only possessed teeth, she would certainly have outvied nearly all the ladies of the Consular Court.

The breakfast passed off very well. When it was disposed of, Madame Bonaparte chose to visit every part of the house, and in this amusement the morning passed rapidly away. At three Madame Bonaparte proposed a drive to the Bois de Boulogne. General Suchet and his brother accompanied us, and did not take their leave till we re-entered Paris. During the drive Madame Bonaparte conversed with me respecting our new establishment, and concluded by saying that she was commissioned by the First Consul to inform Junot and myself that he presented us with the sum of a hundred thousand francs for furnishing our house. "It is ready," added Madame Bonaparte; "Estève has orders to hold it at your disposal. For it is of no use, Bonaparte says, to give them a house unless it be made habitable."

Some time afterwards I gave a ball for my housewarming, when its newly-finished embellishments appeared to great advantage. The whole ground-floor was opened for dancing. The First Consul, whom the Republic had just called to the Consulate for life, did us the honour to be present. Madame Bonaparte had said to me the preceding day: "I am determined, in compliment to your ball, to dress in the very best taste; you shall see how charmingly I can perform my toilette."

She made good her promise. She personated Erigone; her head was adorned with a wreath of vine leaves interspersed with bunches of black grapes; her robe of silver llama was trimmed with similar wreaths; her necklace, earrings, and bracelets were of fine pearls. Hortense accompanied her mother, and was on that occasion, as on all others, and in all places, graceful and fascinating. She danced like a sylph, and I seem to see her still, slender as an aërial nymph, and dressed after the antique in a short tunic of pink crape, embroidered in silver llama, her fair head crowned with roses.

I see her, as she always was, the life of the party; her gaiety, good-humour, and spirit of pleasing, imparting the same qualities to all around her. The young people grouped about her, looked at her, and loved her, as the crowd would now and for ever follow and love her. As for the First Consul, he insisted on seeing every part of the house, and Junot, at his desire, acted as his cicerone to the very cellars and garrets. He stayed only till one o'clock, but for him that was a very late hour, and we were proportionately grateful.

The *Senatus Consulte,* requiring rather than declaring the prolongation of the Consulate, did not appear sufficiently satisfactory; another was presented to the First Consul on the 31st of July, or the 1st of August. Junot went early that morning to the Tuileries, and had a long interview with the First Consul, and on his return assured me that

Napoleon was still undecided whether or not he should accept the Consulate for life. It was two months after the requisition for the prolongation of the Consulate for ten years that the nation, sensible of the necessity of preserving to the utmost possible extent that protection under which France had seen her prosperity revive, demanded the Consulate for life. But Napoleon, great as was his ambition, desired that the will of France should justify it. An appeal was ordered, registers opened. The citizens were at liberty to sign or not without fear of proscription, for it is remarkable that Napoleon never revenged any political offence.*

"The life of a citizen belongs to his country," replied the First Consul to the deputation of the Senate; "as it is the wish of the French nation that mine should be consecrated to her, I obey her will." Surely he had a right to say that it was the will of the people, for of three millions five hundred and seventy-seven thousand two hundred and fifty-nine citizens who voted freely, three millions five hundred and sixty-eight thousand eight hundred and ninety gave their vote in the affirmative.

The opinions in which Junot had been educated were so entirely and purely republican that the *Senatus Consulte* declaring Napoleon Consul for life was by no means so agreeable to him as might have been expected from his attachment, at a time when indifferent observers saw in this event only the present and future welfare of France. One day when we dined with the First Consul at Saint Cloud, I remarked that Junot's countenance on returning to Madame Bonaparte's drawing-room, after half an hour's interview with Napoleon, was altered, and wore an expression of care.

In the carriage, on our way home, he was thoughtful and melancholy. At first I asked in vain what had affected him, but eventually he told me that, having been questioned by the First Consul as to the opinion of the better circles at Paris respecting the Consulate for life, he had answered that it was entirely favourable, which was the truth; and that the First Consul had observed thereupon, his brow becoming stern and gloomy as he spoke: "You tell me this as if the fact had been

---

* Mme d'Abrantès who was, very naturally, a Bonapartist, did not hesitate to ignore the truth now and again. This is one such occasion.

just the reverse. Approved by all France, am I to find censors only in my dearest friends?"

"These words," said Junot, his voice failing so much that I could scarcely hear him—"these words almost broke my heart. I become my General's censor! Ah, he has forgotten Toulon!" "But it is impossible that the expression of your countenance should have been the sole cause of his uttering such words." Junot was silent for some time, then, without turning towards me, said: "No; I certainly spoke of our regret —I may use the word—on reading the new *Senatus Consulte,* which overthrows the Constitution of the year viii.—in reducing the Tribunate* to a hundred and fifty members! The Tribunate is a body much valued by the friends of liberty and of the Republic; then the mode of election is absurd—those two candidates for the Senate; in short, all this has been found great fault with in the country, particularly what has been done for the Council of State." I asked Junot what he meant had been done for the Council of State.

"It has been recognized as a constituted body," said he; "I told the First Consul that this measure had been ill received in many of the provinces. I have been, as I always shall be, an honest and loyal man—I shall neither betray my conscience, the interests of my country, nor those of the man whom I revere and love above all things—but I believe that I am serving him better in speaking the truth than in concealing it. I then explained that any expression of dissatisfaction which he might have remarked upon my countenance was not to be attributed to his nomination as Consul for life, but to the unfavourable impressions very generally produced by the numerous *Senatus Consultes,* which for the last fortnight had daily filled the columns of the *Moniteur.* The nomination for life of the two other Consuls is also spoken of in terms that I do not like to hear applied to anything which relates to the First Consul. I have much friendship for one of them, and a high esteem for the other; but why should two magistrates be imposed upon the nation, which certainly has not raised its voice for them as for my General? In fine, my poor Laura, I spoke as I thought, and I

---

* The Constitution provided for a three house Parliament; the Tribunat debated bills, but did not vote on them; the Corps législatif voted but did not debate; and the appointive Senate was limited to constitutional questions.

begin to see that we have got a Court in earnest, because one can no longer speak the truth without exciting displeasure."

This journey to Saint Cloud caused Junot a fit of illness. His affection for the First Consul was so great that whatever tended to disturb it went directly to his heart. Some days afterwards I received an invitation from Madame Bonaparte to breakfast at Saint Cloud, and to bring my little Josephine. I went alone, because Junot was confined to his bed by indisposition. Napoleon, it is well known, never breakfasted with Madame Bonaparte, and never appeared in her room in the morning, except occasionally, when he knew he should meet some persons there to whom he was desirous of speaking without exciting observation.

This morning he came into the room just as we were rising from the breakfast-table, and on advancing towards us, at once descried in the midst of the group the charming figure of my little Josephine, with her pretty light hair curling round a face that beamed with grace and intelligence, though she was only eighteen months old. The First Consul, immediately on seeing her, exclaimed:

"Ah! ah! here is our god-daughter, the Cardinaless! Good-morning, m'amselle—come, look at me!—there, open your eyes. Why, the devil! do you know that she is prodigiously pretty—the little thing resembles her grandmother—yes, faith, she is very like poor Madame Permon. And what a pretty woman she was!—she was really the most beautiful woman I ever saw." As he was saying this, he pulled the ears and nose of my little girl, who did not approve of it at all; but I had taken the precaution to tell her that if she did not cry at Saint Cloud we should stop at a toy-shop on our way home, and she should have whatever she liked. Napoleon, who did not know this promise, remarked how very good-tempered the child was, while I was secretly reminding her of the toy-shop ten times in a minute.

"That is what I like children to be," continued Napoleon, "not perpetually crying or fretting. There is that little Letizia, who is as beautiful as an angel—well, she cries so violently that I make my escape as if the house was on fire."

As he was talking, the party had removed to the blue salon, which was Madame Bonaparte's morning-room.

A circular balcony upon which this room opened passed along the whole suite of apartments. The First Consul stepped out of the window, and made me a sign to follow. I was about to give the child to her nurse, but he prevented me, saying:

"No, no; keep your daughter; a young mother is never as interesting as when she has her child in her arms. What is the matter with Junot?" he added, as soon as we were out on the balcony.

"He has a fever, General, and it is so violent as to oblige him to keep his bed."

"But this fever is of some kind or other; is it putrid, malignant, or what?"

"Neither the one nor the other, Citizen Consul," I replied, with a little impatience, for I was provoked at the petulant tone of his questions; "but Junot is, as you know, very susceptible, and a pain which goes to his heart affects his health. You know, General, that such complaints are beyond the power of medicine."

"I see that Junot has been telling you of the sort of quarrel we had the other day. He made himself quite ridiculous."

"You will give me leave, Citizen Consul, not to confirm what you have just been saying with my assent; you are no doubt jesting. All that I can do is to affirm that, having probably misunderstood Junot, you have given him serious pain. That he has suffered severely has been manifest to me, because neither my cares nor this child's caresses have been able to calm his mind. Also I conclude, General, that, in reporting to me the conversation you are speaking of, he did not tell me the whole." This, as I afterwards learnt, was the truth.

The First Consul looked at me some moments without speaking— took my right hand, which held my little girl upon my left arm, then suddenly rejected it with a very singular movement; seized Josephine's little white and mottled arm, kissed it, gave a pretty hard tap upon her cheek, pulled her nose, embraced her, all in a minute, then disappeared like a flash of lightning. I repeated this little scene to Junot, whom, on my return, I found very ill. He was not only very irritable, but his temperament itself was opposed to his reasoning tranquilly upon anything that agitated him. His adventure at Saint Cloud had quite upset him.

This very morning he had suffered the application of thirty leeches, and though the loss of so much blood ought to have weakened him, he was in no degree more composed, because his nerves were strongly agitated, and he had not slept for three days. However, about seven in the evening, after taking some mutton broth, he threw himself upon the sofa in my apartment, and fell fast asleep. The night soon drew on, I was left in darkness, and, fearing to wake my husband, I was resting in an armchair by his side, without any lights. My head began to nod; the strong and regular, but monotonous breathing of Junot gradually sent me to sleep also.

Suddenly I heard a quick step on the little staircase which led from the breakfast-room into the court. Accustomed to watching by a sick-bed, I was on foot in an instant, and heard Heldt, the first *valet-de-chambre,* running upstairs and calling, "Madame! madame!"

A light struck upon my still half-closed eyes, a well-known voice effectually roused me, and the First Consul appeared.

"Good-evening, Madame Junot; you did not expect me, I imagine; well, where is your dying patient?"

As he spoke, he entered the small cabinet which served as an ante-room between Junot's apartments and mine, and in which Andoche had just been sleeping.

"Well, M. Junot, what is the matter with you, then? Hey? What does this fever mean? Well, what are you crying for, great baby? Ay, I shall mimic you presently myself." Here he pulled his ears and his poor nose, pinched his cheeks, and lavished all his expressions of favour on him. Junot meanwhile was suffocating; I perhaps never knew him so deeply affected. He took the First Consul's two hands alternately, pressed them to his bosom, and looked at him with an expression of affection.

He could not speak. He next took the hand of the good Duroc—who had accompanied the First Consul candle in hand—that excellent friend, whom for some time he misunderstood, but who never ceased to be the truest and most valuable of his brothers-in-arms.

"I imagine you are no longer ill," said the First Consul, taking the chair I had been offering him ever since he came in. "Hey! hot-brain?"

He was scarcely seated before he stood up again, and began walking round the room, saying:

"Ah! so this is what they call your palace; I should be glad to see it: they all tell me it is a marvel and a folly; but this room seems simple enough."

Hereupon he went into Junot's room and his cabinet, then returned and passed into my apartment. "Ah! ah! so this is the sanctuary," said he, in a tone of kindness, though rather banteringly. "But what the devil is this? Do these happen to be your grandmothers?"

"They are not even relations, General," I replied. "It is a piece of Junot's gallantry, who chose to ornament my room with portraits of all the celebrated females of antiquity and of the last century; he was willing that I should not be too humble in my character of a woman."

"Oh! he might have dispensed with the portrait-gallery for that purpose. But he was right not to admit into it the women of the present day, for all pretend to be celebrated; it is the folly of all countries."

He continued to walk on as he talked; while I looked at him with attention, and a smile which I could not wholly suppress. At first he did not remark this, but in the end guessed the cause, which was the singular style of his costume, always absolutely laughable, when he assumed the dress of a private citizen. From what cause I can scarcely tell, but all the illusion of glory which surrounded him could not make his appearance imposing when not attired in military uniform. It might arise from his being wholly unaccustomed to this undress; but at all events he was totally different in it, even in its very eccentricity, from other men. On this occasion his great-coat was of superfine cloth, and his hat was a remarkably fine beaver, but it was still of the same unfashionable make, and was set on the head in the same peculiar manner, with the difference only from his former appearance, that his hair was not powdered, and the curls had disappeared.

"Well, M. Junot," said he, after having made the tour of my apartments, the only portion of the house yet furnished, "I hope this little journey round your domains has quite cured you?" Junot seized the hand which the First Consul presented to him, pressed it between both his, and wept without answering. At this moment he was neither the man of strong mind nor the courageous soldier, but a feeble child. "To prove that you are quite cured," continued the First Consul, "you will breakfast with me to-morrow at Saint Cloud. Good-night, my old friend. Adieu, *Madame la Commandante.*"

We attended him to the street door. No one knew that the First Consul was in our house; he had imposed silence upon Heldt, the only one of our servants who had seen him; and it is well known that Napoleon was not one of those persons who might be disobeyed. He was right in his privacy; the knowledge of his visit would but have created jealousies. He had crossed the Tuileries on foot, and at the entrance of the Champs-Elysées a chaise, or sort of cabriolet drawn by two horses, which Duroc generally used, was waiting for him.

Junot slept badly that night; his mind was so ardent that happiness and sorrow were equally inimical to his bodily health. He was, however, quite recovered the next morning, went to Saint Cloud, and returned perfectly enchanted. But a new storm was already threatening. Fouché, whose rank should have made him the friend, as he was the equal of his brother-in-arms, but who was, in fact, his most active enemy, and the more dangerous because unsuspected, took advantage of the extreme irritability of Junot's character, to which it was so easy to give a sinister colouring.

The first distribution of Crosses of the Legion of Honour took place at Boulogne on the 15th of August, 1802. I was a witness to that ceremony, which is still fresh in my memory. When the creation of the Legion of Honour was first proposed, it excited violent opposition. Over this opposition the First Consul triumphed; but he deemed it advisable to show some regard to deeply-rooted opinions, and to avoid lacerating wounds which time had not yet healed.* For the space of two years, therefore, the Legion of Honour was not talked of.

It was not until the period when the Empire was declared that the Emperor made his *classification* of the different Crosses. This classification excited no small degree of surprise, for it had been supposed that the rewards would be uniform. Junot was created a Grand Officer of the Legion of Honour, and almost immediately after he was appointed Grand Cross. After this followed the appointment of the twenty-four Grand Officers of the Empire.

The Emperor now announced his intention of coming to review the

* Since the Legion of Honour was an order of chivalry, it seemed to some like a return to the customs of the Ancien régime.

troops. During the ten months that Junot had been on duty at Arras, preparatory to the scheduled invasion of Great Britain, Napoleon had not even sent Berthier to him, except perhaps for a few hours. The Emperor wished Junot to form the corps according to his own judgment, unassisted by any directions. This, he afterwards acknowledged, was intended as an experiment on the capability of his old aide-de-camp. It was fortunate for Junot that he acquitted himself so satisfactorily.

The Emperor arrived on the Wednesday at noon, and took up his abode at the house of the Prefect, of whom he made minute inquiries as to the manner in which the troops behaved to the country-people, and whether the grenadiers cantoned in the little neighbouring villages had been guilty of any pillage. On the following day he reviewed the troops, and during the seven hours occupied by their manoeuvres he was constantly on foot.

Escorted by M. Maret, I advanced to the group surrounding the Emperor. He was in the act of remounting his horse to see the troops defile. He recognized me, although I was still at some distance, and sent Colonel Lafond to ask me to advance nearer, that I might have a better view. When the evolutions were over, I observed the Emperor directing his horse towards the place where I stood. He rode up, and kindly inquired how I was, how I liked Arras, and whether I did not wish to return to Paris. To all these gracious questions I dare say I replied very foolishly, as I did not expect such courtesy, and I was taken by surprise. The truth, however, is that the embarrassment I felt at the novelty of pronouncing the words "Sire" and "your Majesty" was the principal cause of my *gaucherie*. Maret, whose arm I held, afterwards told me that I trembled exceedingly.

After the review Junot and all the officers of his division dined with the Emperor, who paid them very handsome compliments. "Junot," said he to my husband, "mention in to-morrow's order of the day that I am satisfied, extremely satisfied, with my brave grenadiers of Arras."

Napoleon had been Emperor about three months when he determined to inaugurate the Order of the Legion of Honour* by a public solemnity, the first since Napoleon had enjoyed his new title. It took

* Created by the law of the 19th of May, 1802.

place in the Eglise des Invalides at Paris on the 14th of July, 1804. It was a happy idea to consecrate a military reward, by such a ceremony, in that venerable pile which is the last asylum of the wounded soldier.

Preparations were made at Boulogne for another brilliant ceremony. The Emperor had distributed the first Crosses to the Dignitaries of the Order, then in Paris, on the day of the inauguration. He now wished to distribute with due formality those which were to supersede the "Arms of Honour."* Every individual to whom "Arms of Honour" had been awarded received a summons to Boulogne. The camps of Saint Omer, Bruges, Arras, Montreuil, and Amiens sent deputations, and seventy thousand men assembled at this imposing ceremony.

Junot and I set off for Boulogne: a place was reserved for me in Berthier's pavillion, which was the best situation for witnessing the magnificent spectacle which took place on the 15th of August. The Emperor had chosen that day with the view of celebrating at once his own birthday and the festival of his brothers-in-arms. Near the Tour d'Ordre, on the most elevated point of the hill, a throne was constructed, around which waved two hundred banners that had been taken from the enemies of France. On the steps of the throne were ranged the twenty-four Grand Officers of the Empire whom Napoleon had selected from amongst the most distinguished military commanders.

On the throne was placed the ancient chair known by the name of the *Fauteuil de Dagobert,* and near the Emperor was the helmet of Bayard,** containing the crosses and ribbons which were to be distributed. The shield of Francis I was also brought into requisition.

In a valley cut by the hands of Nature there were stationed sixty thousand men, in several ranks, and in *échelon.* The valley was so formed that they seemed to be ranged in an amphitheatre, and could be seen from the sea, the waves of which broke against the foot of the Tour d'Ordre, or rather at the foot of the hill on which it was erected. In front of the men was the throne, which was ascended by a few steps. There was seated, in all the splendour of his glory, the man whose genius then ruled Europe and the world. Over his head a multitude of

* "Arms of Honour" were given as a distinction to especially brave or successful soldiers and officers.
** A famous 16th century knight.

247

banners, tattered by cannon-balls and stained with blood, formed a canopy appropriate to the occasion. Though the day was fair, yet the wind blew with extreme freshness, so that these trophies of victory waved in full view of several English vessels then cruising in the straits.

I had the pleasure of meeting, on this occasion, Madame Ney, who was one of the pupils of Madame Campan, and had received a most finished education. She was remarkable for an air of simplicity, and I may even say a certain degree of timidity, which was the more attractive inasmuch as it formed a contrast to the manners of most of the ladies by whom she was surrounded at the Court of France. Those ladies were, it is true, for the most part perfectly amiable and well-bred, but they were young and inexperienced; and having seen little of the world, especially of that courtly world upon which they had recently entered, they were easily dazzled by the illusions of fortune, and were sometimes betrayed into gross absurdities.

The fine ladies of the Faubourg Saint Germain, who at first formed part of the Empress Josephine's Court, thought they would produce a wonderful impression by assuming airs of hauteur, though from them better manners might have been expected. To all this ill-breeding of various kinds, the manners of a woman *comme il faut,* such as Madame Ney, formed a delightful relief. The softness and benevolence of Madame Ney's smile, together with the intelligent expression of her large dark eyes, rendered her a very beautiful woman; and her lively manners and accomplishments enhanced her personal graces. It may easily be imagined that I was not a little delighted to meet this charming person at Boulogne.

The ceremony of the distribution was exceedingly long. Each legionist ascended the twelve steps leading to the throne, and after receiving his Cross and ribbon from the Emperor's own hand, made his bow, and returned to his place. When Napoleon presented the Cross to one of his old comrades, who had fought with him in Italy or Egypt, there seemed to be a glow of feeling which carried him back to his early and most brilliant glory.

It was five o'clock, and for a considerable time I had observed the Emperor turning frequently and anxiously to M. Decrès, the Minister of the Marine, to whom he repeatedly said something in a whisper. He then took a glass and looked towards the sea, as if eager to discover a distant sail. At length his impatience seemed to increase. Berthier, too, who stood biting his nails, in spite of his new dignity of Marshal, now and then looked through the glass, and Junot appeared to be in the secret, for they all talked together aside. It was evident that *something* was expected. At length the Minister of the Marine received a message, which he immediately communicated to the Emperor, and the latter snatched the glass from the hand of M. Decrès with such violence that it fell and rolled down the steps of the throne.

All eyes were now directed to the point which I had observed the Emperor watching, and we soon discerned a flotilla, consisting of between a thousand and twelve hundred boats, advancing in the direction of Boulogne from the different neighbouring ports and from Holland. The Emperor had made choice of August 15 as the day for uniting the flotilla with the other boats stationed in the port of Boulogne, in sight of the English vessels which were cruising in the straits; while at the same time he distributed to his troops rewards destined to stimulate their courage, and to excite their impatience to undertake the invasion of England.

But the satisfaction Napoleon enjoyed at the sight of the flotilla was not of long duration. An emphatic oath uttered by M. Decrès—who, it is well known, made a liberal use of these ornaments of speech— warned the Emperor that some accident had occurred. It was soon ascertained that the officer who commanded the first division of the flotilla, disregarding the advice of the coasting pilot, had, just as he was on the point of landing, run foul of some works newly erected along the coast. The shock swamped some of the boats, and several of the men jumped overboard. The cries of the people at the seaside, who hurried to their assistance, excited much alarm. Fortunately, it happened to be low water at the time, and I believe one man only was drowned.

The accident was exceedingly mortifying, happening as it did in the full gaze of our enemies, whose telescopes were all pointed towards us, and it threw the Emperor into a violent rage. He descended from the throne and proceeded with Berthier to a sort of terrace which was formed along the water's edge. He paced to and fro very rapidly, and we could occasionally hear him utter some energetic expression indicative of his vexation. In the evening a grand dinner and ball took place in honour of the inauguration. About six o'clock, just as dinner was about to be served for the soldiers, under the tents, a heavy fall of rain came on. This served to augment the Emperor's ill-humour, and formed a gloomy termination to a day which had commenced so brilliantly.

On the evening of the festival at Boulogne, Junot received orders from the Emperor requiring him to set out for Calais next morning. He told me I might accompany him if I chose, but that, owing to the little time he had at his disposal, he could not pass the whole day in Calais, "Unless," said he, "you consent to set out to-night immediately after the ball." I accepted this proposition, and we arrived at Calais next morning at seven o'clock. Consequently, we had ample time to look about us. On my return the Emperor asked me how I liked my nocturnal journey, what I thought of Calais and Dessein's Hotel, and put to me many questions respecting what I had observed in several places on our route.

I mention this fact, though unimportant in itself, because I wish to seize every shade, however trivial, which belongs to the portrait of Napoleon. Certainly he had no need of my opinion, nor my remarks upon anything which referred to that part of the French coast; but I had eyes and ears, and, being free from prejudice, I could judge impartially of what I saw, and that was enough for him. He would sometimes question a child, and would often interrogate women on subjects to which they were not, perhaps, in the habit of directing their attention. On these occasions he always liked to have a ready answer.

On our return to Arras I observed a twofold activity prevailing in all that related to the manoeuvers of the army. Junot was several times summoned to Paris. In his absence the command devolved alternately on Generals Dupas and Macon, who were both attached to the Imperial Guard. On his return from one of these journeys Junot informed me of a circumstance which at the time I thought very extraordinary: this was the introduction of a sort of sumptuary law, regulating the Court dress of the ladies. This dress was then nearly what it still remains. The *chérusque,* * which, however, was speedily retrenched, was exceedingly

* A Gothic ruff with long points, composed of tulle embroidered with gold or silver to correspond with the dress.

becoming. The robe and petticoat were as they are now, with this difference, that the embroidered border of the robe was not to exceed four inches in depth. The princesses alone had the privilege of wearing the robe embroidered all over. Such were, at first, the commands of the Emperor, and they were dictated by good sense and paternal feeling. He did not wish that in his Court, which was composed of men who had rendered honourable services to the country, but many of whom were comparatively poor, the extravagance of a young wife should compromise the happiness of her husband. This sumptuary regulation was at first rigidly observed.

The mention of embroideries reminds me of a curious circumstance. Every one who frequented the Tuileries about the period I allude to must recollect a certain coat composed of red taffety, and richly embroidered in gold in a symbolic pattern, consisting of branches of olive, oak, and laurel. This coat was worn by the First Consul, with boots, a black cravat, and all the accessories of a military costume. It was known by the name of *l'habit de Lyon.*

M. Levacher, an eminent silk mercer in Paris, observing the decline which had taken place in a considerable branch of the silk trade, owing to the disuse of embroidery, resolved to endeavour to revive it. For this purpose he consulted with some of the principal embroiderers, and sent them the design I have above mentioned. As soon as it was finished, he took it to M. Chaptal, the Minister of the Interior. The Minister was struck with the beauty of the work. "But," said he, "how can you expect that the First Consul will wear an embroidered coat—he who never even wears the uniform of a general officer?" "I will not despair of gaining my object," said M. Levacher. "I am Madame Bonaparte's silk mercer; she has always been very friendly to me, and I will see what she can do."

Madame Bonaparte was struck with the beauty of the garment, but candidly informed M. Levacher that there was no hope of prevailing on the First Consul to wear it. The silk mercer, not a little disheartened by this assurance, had folded up the coat, and was putting it into the box, when the door leading to the First Consul's cabinet suddenly opened, and Bonaparte appeared. M. Levacher was at first somewhat embarrassed; but, immediately recollecting that his success depended on seizing the present opportunity, he opened the box, and submitted the coat to the inspection of Napoleon, at the same time warmly urging the necessity of reviving the drooping prosperity of the unfortunate city of Lyons which was dying amidst the regeneration of France. The First Consul listened to him with marked interest: Bonaparte had already entertained plans for ameliorating the trade of Lyons, and the offering now presented to him afforded a fair excuse for wearing embroidered coats, and causing them to be worn—a fashion which could scarcely have been introduced without very good reason in a Court which was yet entirely Republican.

"I will not deny," he remarked, "that I have some repugnance to equip myself in this fantastic costume, but for that reason my resolution will be the better appreciated." Such is the history of the *habit rouge,* which every one thought so singular when Bonaparte first appeared in it.

Bonaparte expressed a decided dislike to the *percales* and muslins,* which were then much worn by ladies in France. But he was always pleased whenever he saw any of us in a leno dress. I recollect one day wearing a leno dress of which Madame Bonaparte had made me a present. I was then very slender, and my figure would very well admit of my wearing a stiffly-starched gown, but, as it was then the fashion for the ladies' dresses to fall like the draperies of the antique statues, I must have looked ridiculous. However, the Emperor thought proper to applaud my taste. "That is the way you should all dress, *en négligé,* ladies," said he. "I do not like to see you in those English muslins, which are sold at the price of their weight in gold, and which do not look half so well as a beautiful white leno. Wear leno, cambric, and silk, and then my manufactures will flourish."

Napoleon's coronation was to take place on 2nd of December, 1804, and Junot was summoned to Paris to attend the ceremony. General Oudinot took the command of the division of the grenadiers at Arras, whither Junot did not afterwards return. On my arrival in town I found my house filled with different members of Junot's family, who had arrived from the country to be present at the coronation. It is impossible to form an idea of the bustle and gaiety which prevailed in

---

* *Percales* and French muslins were exceedingly fashionable and expensive at the time here alluded to. With the exception of leno, all the white worn by ladies was brought from England.

Paris at this time. From morning till night the streets were thronged by a busy and joyous multitude. Some were seen hurrying to procure tickets to witness the ceremony, others were engaging windows to see the procession pass, and, to afford some idea of the ardent curiosity that prevailed, I may mention that a family of my acquaintance from Artois, having arrived too late to procure tickets for the interior of Notre Dame, paid the sum of three hundred francs for a second-floor window near the gate of the Cathedral.

The sight hunters first visited Dallemagne, the famous embroiderer, who was preparing the Emperor's mantle, for which Levacher had furnished the velvet; thence they proceeded to Foncier's, to see the crowns of the Emperor and Empress, and the Emperor's sword, the hilt of which was adorned with the famous diamond known by the name of the Regent, and lastly, they went in search of tickets to view the interior of Notre Dame, where the most splendid preparations were making for the approaching ceremony. Embroiderers, tailors, florists, jewellers—in short, tradesmen of every description—were busily at work, and all joyfully anticipating a rich harvest of profit.

At this instant of universal joy the Pope arrived in Paris. His Holiness was lodged in the Pavillon de Flore,* and the Emperor himself set the example of showing him the honours due not only to his dignity as a Sovereign and the Head of the Church, but also to his personal virtues. The countenance of Pius VII. has never been faithfully represented in any of his portraits; none that I have seen accurately portray his mild and intelligent features.

His extremely pallid complexion and jet-black hair, together with his white robes, produced altogether a singular effect. When I was presented to him, his venerable appearance inspired me with a feeling of interest, independent of the respect which I, as a Catholic, owed to the Head of the Church. He gave me a very beautiful chaplet with a relic, and seemed pleased to hear me thank him in Italian. On the Pope's arrival in Paris all the authorities, primary and secondary, paid their formal respects to him. The generals were not the last to observe this ceremony, though several among them had evinced a reluctance which gave umbrage to the Emperor.

* One of the wings of the Palace of the Tuileries, the sovereign's residence.

On the occasion of the generals paying their visit to the Pavillon de Flore, a question arose as to which of them should harangue the Holy Father. Several among them spoke Italian very fluently, and General Sebastiani, who always had a taste for making speeches, offered his services, but he was considered too young in the scale of commanders, and the choice fell on General Cervoni.

This selection, which was to all appearance perfectly suitable and proper, gave rise to a droll incident. At the time when the French entered Rome with Alexander Berthier, Cervoni, who was then a brigadier-general, was Military Commandant of the city. It was even said he ordered the arrest of Pius VII. That, however, was not the fact; but it was nevertheless believed at the time, and consequently Cervoni was an object of terror in Rome. The Pope feared him as he would his evil genius.

When Cervoni delivered the address in the name of the generals, the Pope was struck with the pure and elegant accent with which he spoke Italian. *"Come lei parla bene l'Italiano. . . ."* said his Holiness. *"Santo Padre, sono quasi Italiano." "Oh! . . ." "Sono Corso." "Oh! . . . Oh! . . ." "Sono Cervoni." "Oh! . . . Oh! . . . Oh! . . ."* And at each exclamation the Holy Father retreated a few paces backwards, until at length he got close to the chimney and could go no farther. The Pope probably thought he was going to be seized and sent to prison.

It was irresistibly humorous to hear Cervoni himself describe this scene, the drollery of which must have been heightened by the contrast between the voices of the interlocutors. Cervoni had a clear, sonorous, and powerful voice; while the Pope, on the contrary, spoke in a shrill soprano, and somewhat nasal tone. In person, Cervoni was not unlike the Pope: he had the same pale complexion, and the same form of countenance; but at the period alluded to he was a young and handsome man.

W I T H the new Empire went a proper Court. Already under the Consulate, a fairly strict etiquette prevailed at the Tuileries and at Saint Cloud, the palace just outside Paris which Marie Antoinette had redecorated just before the Revolution. Now the etiquette of the old monarchy was revived; chamberlains, ladies in waiting and other court positions were created anew. There were some differences, though: titles of nobility remained in abeyance —until 1808, anyway. Certain court functions—First Gentleman of the Bedchamber, for instance—were dropped. Still, the Bonaparte family was given princely titles and the style of Imperial Highness. Ball, suppers, and other court entertainments were revived. Unfortunately, neither the Emperor nor his courtiers quite knew how to go about it all, so the ceremonies were stiff, and the atmosphere was one of often paralysing dullness.

Napoleon himself was no help. He was given to walking rapidly up and down the two lines of his courtiers, stopping to tell the women they looked old, or overdressed, or underdressed, blaming the men for shortcomings and occasionally flying into a rage. As for the fêtes, they were just as frozen: with the Emperor's eagle eye watching it all, no one could relax. Of course, Napoleon noticed that as well, so one day, in exasperation, he accused his court of being morose, adding; "I order you to have fun". For once, he was not obeyed.

As part of his reconciliation of the various factions in France, the Emperor also tried to bring about a fusion of the old Society with the new. Members of the great aristocratic families were given court functions once again and a few genuinely rallied the regime; but most kept up a discreet opposition. In the houses of the nobility, many a snicker could be heard about the lack of manners at the new court. Napoleon knew all about that; and few things annoyed him more.

The formation of the new Court about to be established now occupied the attention of every mind. The influence which such a circumstance is sure to engender had already manifested itself in active intrigue. Madame Bonaparte, who was of easy temper and kind disposition, was applied to on all sides for the presentation of a *dame du palais,* * a chamberlain, or an equerry; in short, she was assailed by that numerous troop composed almost exclusively of those whose influence was so fatal to the Emperor in 1814. At the time of the coronation this crowd of expectants was still endurable by the true friends of Napoleon, for among them were the wives of those men who had shed their blood for France, and who were devoted not only to their country, but to the Emperor.

Napoleon, however, was then dreaming of the accomplishment of an impossibility, viz., *the system of fusion,* ** about which he said so much at Saint Helena; and this statesmanlike but unsuccessful policy is the only excuse for the grievous error he committed, in surrounding himself by individuals who, but a few years before, had spoken of his downfall as one of their dearest hopes. The men who were really attached to him saw the error and pointed it out, but the Emperor was deaf to their remonstrances, wishing to make allies rather than enemies, and vainly endeavouring to reunite all parties for the good of France.

The *dames du palais* were, at the period of the coronation, selected from among the wives of the generals and Grand Officers of the Empire. Madame de Lavalette was appointed *dame d'atours,* or Mistress of the Robes, and Madame de La Rochefoucauld, Lady of Honour.*** The new Court was refulgent with a species of glory, which women regard with the same solicitude as men pursue theirs, viz., elegance and beauty. Of the Princesses and the young women who formed the Court of the Empress, it would be difficult to mention one who was not distinguished for beauty.

Among these were Madame Maret, whose lovely face and finely-turned figure were equally admired with her purity of taste and elegance of manner, and Madame Savary, who possessed a countenance and form of equal beauty, but had one fault, which was, that, though she dressed well, there was always some part of her costume which did not harmonize thoroughly with the rest. Madame Lannes' fine features resembled Raphael's or Correggio's most exquisite Madonnas. But perhaps the brightest star in this dazzling constellation was Madame de

* lady in waiting.
** between the new men and the old aristocracy, that is.
*** At this time, the head of the Empress' Household.

Ca . . . y. I often thought she might be compared to one of the Muses. In her were combined perfect regularity of features with an indescribable charm of expression, a profusion of soft, rich silken hair, and a shape replete with grace and elegance.

Madame Durosnel's attractions consisted in her fine blue eyes, overhung by long and glossy lashes; in her fascinating smile, which discovered a set of the finest ivory teeth in the world; a profusion of fair hair, a hand and foot cast in the finest proportion, and a general elegance of manner which indicated a cultivated mind. Madame Durosnel was married some years later than I, and her husband was old enough to have passed as her father.

The Households of the Princesses were formed with a more direct view to the *fusion system* than even that of the Empress Josephine; for the individuals about them, being Heads of Families, carried with them considerable influence, and gave a colouring to the whole establishment. For instance, the Princess Caroline had for her Chamberlain M. d'Aligre, whose name and fortune sufficed, in the Emperor's opinion, to form a banner round which the most adverse parties might rally. Indeed, the Faubourg Saint Germain at this period had reason to be indebted to the Princess Caroline, for it was through her mediation that the life of the Marquis de Rivière was saved, as the Empress Josephine saved the two Polignacs.*

The Princess Elisa, whose austere temper rendered her less pliant to her brother's will than other members of the family, was surrounded by persons not so exclusively attached to the Faubourg Saint Germain, with the exception, perhaps, of one of her ladies, Madame de Br . . . n, who, however, did not remain long with her, but entered the service of the Princess Borghèse. Madame Laplace, the wife of the geometrician, was disposed to join the Princess in the pursuit of science.

The drawing-room of Saint Cloud presented on one occasion a scene which subsequent circumstances rendered remarkable. Madame Leclerc lost her husband at Saint Domingo; she had his body embalmed, and she returned home with his remains on board the same vessel which had conveyed him to the island a few months before in perfect health. The Emperor, who thoroughly knew her disposition,

* All three had been arrested in 1801 for plotting against the First Consul.

and who was anxious that she should wear her weeds with decorum, consigned the young widow to the care of his brother Joseph and his amiable spouse.

Madame Leclerc was consequently lodged in the Hôtel Marboeuf, in the Rue du Faubourg Saint Honoré, then occupied by Joseph Bonaparte. Here I saw her on her return from Saint Domingo. She had then a frightful sore upon her hand, which, though it was healed for a time, appeared again in spite of all the efforts of her physicians. She looked most angelic in her weeds, though she was evidently impatient of the retirement they imposed on her! "I shall certainly sink under this, Laurette," said she to me one day. "If my brother determines to shut me out from the world, I will put an end to my existence at once."

Junot observed that, though we had a Venus de Medicis, a Venus of the Capitol, and a Venus Callipyge, we had never before heard of a "Venus Suicide." At this compliment the features of Madame Leclerc instantly brightened up, and extending her hand to Junot, she said: "Come and see me often, Junot; you are one of my old friends. Laurette, you need not be jealous, for you know I am going to be married."

Accordingly, a short time after, Napoleon, who was then only First Consul, arranged a marriage between her and Prince Camille Borghèse. When I saw the Prince I was struck with his handsome appearance; I was not then aware of his complete absence of intellect.

I reckon myself fortunate in having been a witness to the wedding visit of the Princess Borghèse to her sister-in-law, Madame Bonaparte. I was well aware of the rivalry which existed between these two ladies, and had observed many instances of the jealousy which Madame Leclerc entertained of Madame Bonaparte. I well knew Madame Leclerc's character, her excessive vanity, her constant endeavour to be thought not only the most beautiful, but the most brilliant of her sex. How often have I seen her shed tears of vexation at beholding her sister-in-law covered with diamonds and pearls of regal splendour!

On the evening of her introduction as Princess Borghèse to Madame Bonaparte at Saint Cloud she exhibited one of the most striking traits in her character. It may well be conceived that her toilette that day was an affair of the utmost importance. After considering every colour, and consulting the opinion of all about her, she at last fixed upon a robe of green velvet, upon which, with no great regard to taste, were displayed all the diamonds of the house of Borghèse, forming what was then called a *Mathilde*. Her head, her neck, her ears, and arms, were loaded with diamonds; in short, she was a dazzling mass of jewels, and the satisfaction she enjoyed in this gaudy display was most amusing. When she entered the room she observed the sensation she created, and the flush of triumph which overspread her countenance certainly made her look extremely beautiful.

Her intention was obviously to mortify her sister-in-law, and she seemed to revel in her triumph. She was a Princess, the most beautiful of her sex, possessing a collection of jewels more splendid than was possessed by any private gentlewoman in Europe, and a settlement of two millions a year. After she had passed round the room, she came and sat next me. "Laurette, my little Laurette! only look at them," said she; "they are ready to burst with envy! But 'tis no matter: I am a Princess, and a real one."

I could not help recollecting this last expression when I was at Rome in 1818; I then saw her at the Borghèse Palace, enjoying the protection which the Pope had extended to the Princess Borghèse. Thus she was not only the first Princess of her family, but she contrived to retain her rank amidst all the disasters of her relatives.

Although a general joy pervaded all minds at this moment, Junot was vexed that the name of his friend Marmont did not appear on the list of appointments which had been made on the formation of the Empire; he was neither created a Grand Officer of the Empire nor a Grand Officer of the Crown. Such a sincere friendship attached Junot to his old college companion, and his first brother-in-arms, that he was distressed at this evidence of neglect.

Junot assured me that he knew the author of it, though from motives of prudence he would not inform Marmont. I pressed him to tell me, and though I was shocked I was not surprised; to accuse others was the constant practice of the individual in question, who, holding as he did the very highest rank in the army, should have preserved a noble and honourable line of conduct instead of earning for himself an odious reputation. Some time after the coronation, when Prince Eugène was appointed Grand Chancellor of State, the rank of Colonel-General of Chasseurs was given to Marmont.

On the 1st of December the Senate presented to the Emperor the votes of the nation. It is worthy of remark that for the Empire there were only two thousand five hundred and seventy-nine negative votes, and three millions five hundred and seventy-five affirmative, while for the Consulate for life there were, I believe, nearly nine thousand negative votes. I breakfasted with the Empress on the very day of the presentation of the registers to the Emperor, and I can positively affirm, whatever may have been said to the contrary, that Josephine had no gloomy presentiments either as regarded herself or Napoleon.

She was in excellent spirits, and she told me that the Emperor had that morning made her try on the crown which next day he was to place on her head before the eyes of France; and she shed tears of joy while she mentioned this. She also spoke feelingly of the disappointment she had experienced on receiving the Emperor's refusal to her solicitation for the return of Lucien.* "I wished to make to-morrow a day of grace," said she; "but Bonaparte" (for she continued to call him by this name long after his elevation to the Empire, "impatiently rejected my suit, and I was compelled to be silent. I wished to prove to Lucien that I can return good for evil. If you should see him let him know it."

I was astonished at Napoleon's inflexibility towards his brother, and one, too, to whom he owed so much. His marriage with Madame Jauberthon was alleged to be the unpardonable offence he had committed; but I am of opinion that the republican sentiments entertained by Lucien formed the real objection to his recall to France. Another circumstance which augmented the hostility of the Emperor towards his brother was the conduct of Madame Letizia Bonaparte. She warmly espoused the cause of her exiled son, and quitted Paris for the purpose of conveying to him assistance and consolation.

The elder Madame Bonaparte's maternal feelings were painfully lacerated at this period of general joy and festivity. Her youngest son, Jerome, was excluded from the family circle which Napoleon had collected around him, and to which he looked for the consolidation of his future power. Jerome had married Miss Patterson in America.

* After a series of disagreements with Napoleon, worsened by his marrying a woman of whom his brother disapproved, Lucien had moved to Rome, then part of the Pontifical States.

Though he was at the time a mere boy, yet the marriage was nevertheless valid, since it took place with the consent of his mother and his elder brother. But the First Consul was furiously indignant at the conduct of the young midshipman, conceiving that as head of the Government he was also the head of his family.

Jerome had left America to return to Europe. Madame Letizia informed the Emperor of his departure; and Napoleon immediately took measures to prevent his landing, not only in any of the ports of France, but also those of Holland and Belgium, and wherever he had power to exclude him. I make no comment on this severity; subsequent events may or may not have justified it; of that the reader will presently be able to judge. Be this as it may, Madame Letizia Bonaparte was, at the time of the coronation in Rome, without either title or distinction. She was, however, introduced in David's picture of the coronation. This must have been by command of the Emperor, for I cannot imagine that the idea was suggested by herself.

Before daybreak on the 2nd of December all Paris was alive and in motion; indeed, hundreds of persons had remained up the whole of the night. Many ladies had the courage to get their hair dressed at two o'clock in the morning, and then sat quietly in their chairs until the time arrived for arranging the other parts of their toilette. We were all very much hurried, for it was necessary to be at our posts before the procession moved from the Tuileries, for which nine o'clock was the appointed hour.

I was at that time as intimate with the Duchess of Ragusa* as Junot was with her husband, though she afterwards quarrelled with me, for some reason that I never could discover. We arranged to go together to Notre Dame, and we set out at half-past seven in the morning. Junot was to carry one of the honours of Charlemagne—the ball or the hand of Justice, I do not now recollect which. We accordingly left him busily engaged in arraying himself in his peer's robes.

Who that saw Notre Dame on that memorable day can ever forget

* Marmont's wife—he was (later) created duc de Raguse.

it? I have witnessed in that venerable pile the celebration of sumptuous and solemn festivals; but never did I see anything at all approximating in splendour to the *coup d'oeil* exhibited at Napoleon's coronation. The vaulted roof re-echoed the sacred chanting of the priests, who invoked the blessing of the Almighty on the ceremony about to be celebrated, while they awaited the arrival of the Vicar of Christ, whose throne was prepared near the altar.

Along the ancient walls of tapestry were ranged, according to their ranks, the different bodies of the State, the deputies from every city; in short, the representatives of all France assembled to implore the benediction of Heaven on the sovereign of the people's choice. The waving plumes which adorned the hats of the Senators, Councillors of State, and Tribunes; the splendid uniforms of the military; the clergy in all their ecclesiastical pomp; and the multitude of young and beautiful women, glittering in jewels, and arrayed in that style of grace and elegance which is to be seen only in Paris—all together presented a picture which has perhaps rarely been equalled, and certainly never excelled.

The Pope arrived first; and at the moment of his entering the cathedral the anthem *Tu es Petrus* was chanted. His Holiness advanced from the door with an air at once majestic and humble. Ere long the firing of cannon announced the departure of the procession from the Tuileries. From an early hour in the morning the weather had been exceedingly unfavourable. It was cold and rainy, and appearances seemed to indicate that the procession would be anything but agreeable to those who joined in it.

But, as if by the especial favour of Providence, of which so many instances are observable in the career of Napoleon, the clouds suddenly dispersed, the sky brightened up, and the multitudes who lined the streets from the Tuileries to the cathedral enjoyed the sight of the procession without being, as they had anticipated, drenched by a December rain. Napoleon, as he passed along, was greeted by heart-felt expressions of enthusiastic love and attachment.

On his arrival at Notre Dame, Napoleon ascended the Throne, which was erected in front of the Grand Altar. Josephine took her place beside him. Napoleon appeared singularly calm. I watched him narrowly, with the view of discovering whether his heart beat more unsteadily beneath the imperial trappings than under the uniform of the Guards; but I could observe no difference, and yet I was only ten paces from him.

The length of the ceremony, however, seemed to weary him; and I saw him several times check a yawn. Nevertheless, he did everything he was required to do with propriety. When the Pope anointed him with the triple unction on the head and both hands, I fancied from the direction of his eyes that he was thinking of wiping off the oil rather than of anything else; and I was so perfectly acquainted with the workings of his countenance that I have no hesitation in saying that was really the thought that crossed his mind at the moment. During the ceremony of the anointing the Holy Father delivered that impressive prayer which concluded with these words:

> ". . . Diffuse, O Lord, by my hands, the treasures of your grace and benediction on your servant, Napoleon, whom, in spite of our personal unworthiness, *we this day anoint* EMPEROR *in your name.*"

Napoleon listened to this prayer with an air of pious devotion; but just as the Pope was about to take the crown, called the *crown of Charlemagne,* from the Altar, Napoleon seized it and placed it on his own head. At that moment he was really handsome, and his countenance was lighted up with an expression of which no words can convey an idea. He had removed the wreath of laurel which he wore on entering the church, and which encircles his brow in the fine picture of Gérard. The crown was perhaps, in itself, less becoming to him; but the expression excited by the act of putting it on rendered him perfectly handsome.

When the moment arrived for Josephine to take an active part in the grand drama, she descended from the Throne and advanced towards the Altar, where the Emperor awaited her, followed by her retinue of Court ladies, and having her train borne by the Princesses Caroline, Julie, Elisa, and Louis. One of the chief beauties of the Empress Josephine was not merely her fine figure, but the elegant turn of her neck, and the way in which she carried her head; indeed, her deportment altogether was conspicuous for dignity and grace. I have had the honour of being presented to many *real princesses,* to use the phrase of the

Faubourg Saint Germain, but I never saw one who, to my eyes, presented so perfect a personification of elegance and majesty.

In Napoleon's countenance I could read the conviction of all I have just said. He looked with an air of complacency at the Empress as she advanced towards him; and when she knelt down—when the tears which she could not repress fell upon her clasped hands, as they were raised to Heaven, or rather to Napoleon—both then appeared to enjoy one of those fleeting moments of pure felicity which are unique in a lifetime, and serve to fill up a lustrum of years. The Emperor performed with peculiar grace every action required of him during the ceremony; but his manner of crowning Josephine was most remarkable: after receiving the small Crown surmounted by the cross, he had first to place it on his own head, and then to transfer it to that of the Empress.

When the moment arrived for placing the Crown on the head of the woman whom popular superstition regarded as his good genius, his manner was almost playful. He took great pains to arrange this little Crown, which was placed over Josephine's tiara of diamonds; he put it on, then took it off, and finally put it on again, as if to promise her she should wear it gracefully and lightly. My position enabled me fortunately to see and observe every minute action and gesture of the principal actors in this magical scene.

This part of the ceremony being ended, the Emperor descended from the Altar to return to his Throne, while the magnificent *Vivat* was performed by the full chorus. At this moment the Emperor, whose keen eye had hitherto glanced rapidly from one object to another, recognized me in the corner which I occupied. He fixed his eye upon me, and I cannot attempt to describe the thoughts which this circumstance conjured up in my mind. A naval officer once told me that during a shipwreck, when he had given himself up for lost, the whole picture of his past life seemed to unfold itself before him in the space of a minute. May it not be presumed that Napoleon, when he looked at me, was assailed by a host of past recollections.

When I saw the Emperor a few days afterwards, he said: "Why did you wear a black velvet dress at the coronation?" This question took me so by surprise that I could not readily reply. "Was it a sign of mourning?" continued he. "Oh, Sire!" I exclaimed, and the tears started to my eyes. Napoleon looked at me as if he would scan my very inmost thoughts. "But tell me," said he, "why did you make choice of that sombre, I may almost say sinister, colour?" "Your Majesty did not observe that the front of my robe was richly embroidered with gold,* and that I wore my diamonds. I did not conceive that there was anything unsuitable in my dress, not being one of those ladies whose situations required them to appear in full Court costume." "Is that remark intended to convey an indirect reproach? Are you like certain other ladies, because they have not been appointed *dames du palais?* I do not like sulkiness and ill-humour." "Sire, I have shown no ill-humour; but for that I claim no merit, because I feel none. Junot has informed me that your Majesty does not wish to make double appointments in your Household and that of the Empress, and that when the husband is one of the military Household the wife cannot be a *dame du palais."* "Junot told you so, did he? And how happened he to mention that? Were you complaining? Are you infected with ambition? I hate ambitious women. Unless they are Queens they are intriguers; remember that, Madame Junot. But now tell me, are you not vexed at not being appointed *dame du palais?* Answer me candidly; if a woman can be candid." "I will, Sire; but your Majesty will not believe me." "Come, come, let me have an answer." "Then I am not vexed." "Why?" "Because I am not one of those persons who can easily conform to absolute subjection; and your Majesty would probably wish that the protocol for regulating the Court of the Empress should be framed on the model of a military code." Napoleon laughed. "Not unlikely," resumed he. "However, I am satisfied; you have given me a very good answer, and I shall remember it." Then, after a pause, he said: "Poor Junot! did you observe how his feelings were moved at the coronation? He is a faithful friend. Who could have foreseen, when we were both at Toulon ten years ago, that we should live to see such a day as the 2nd of December?" "Perhaps Junot, Sire."

Here I reminded him of a letter which my husband wrote to his father in 1794, and in which he refuted the objection of the old man who blamed him for leaving his regiment to follow the fortune of an

* The fact is, that black or dark-coloured velvet dresses were much worn at that time, especially with diamonds. There were a great many at Napoleon's coronation.

obscure and unknown general like Bonaparte. Junot replied: "You ask me who General Bonaparte is. He is one of those men whom Nature creates sparingly, and who appear in the world now and then in the lapse of ages." My father-in-law showed this letter to the *First Consul* when he passed through Dijon after the Battle of Marengo, and the *Emperor* appeared quite struck with the recollection which I called to his mind. The conversation between myself and Napoleon, which I have just described, took place at a ball which was given either by the War Minister or M. de Talleyrand, I forget which.

T H E battle of Austerlitz was not only a resounding triumph for Napoleon: it also looked like the proof that no one could withstand him. Together, the Austrian and Russian armies had been greatly superior to the French, in numbers at least; but that made no difference at all. By December, 1805, therefore, Napoleon had every reason to feel like the master of Europe.

Unfortunately, no matter how often its troops, or those of its allies, were defeated, England refused to give up; and as long as it went on waging war, it stood to reason that new anti-French European coalitions financed by British gold would spring up. Napoleon thus found it imperative to defeat England once and for all: neither side even considered the possibility of compromise.

There seemed to be no reason, though, why the war would ever end. In this typical instance of the fight between the whale and the elephant, Napoleon found himself as incapable of defeating the British Navy as England was of defeating the French army; so he invented the Continental Blockade. By preventing British goods from entering Europe, he hoped to drive both the City of London and the British government to bankruptcy, thus putting an end to the war. The problem was that the very merchandise the Emperor had banned was greatly in demand—everything from tropical products like sugar, coffee, tea and spices to cloth and machinery.

In France itself, where cities like Bordeaux were ruined by the Blockade, large-scale smuggling was soon organized; bad as that was, however, there was much worse. Both Holland and Portugal had long been Great Britain's major trading partners, and, indeed, their economies depended heavily on this flow of goods. Holland had been in French hands since 1795 when it had become a protectorate as the Batavian Republic; then, in 1806, Napoleon made it the Kingdom of Holland with his brother Louis as King.

That left Portugal. Way off on the other side of Spain, with its own dynasty, it hardly seemed like a logical conquest; so, at first, Napoleon sent ambassadors—Junot was the last of them—to pressure the country into joining the Blockade. The Portuguese government, feeling rightly that it might as well commit suicide, refused, upon which Napoleon sent an army of occupation under Junot. The craven Charles IV of Spain allowed this army free passage, and John VI of Portugal, with his family, fled to Brazil, then a Portuguese colony.

As it turned out, however, Napoleon had just created his own Achilles' heel: it was in Portugal, after Wellington took over the command of a British expeditionary force, that the French armies suffered their first serious reverses. As for Spain's compliance, it did not do it much good. In 1808, Napoleon seized the Bourbons, emprisoned them and replaced them by his brother Joseph.

In 1805, when Mme Junot crossed Spain on her way to Portugal, all this was still in the future: it was only as ambassador that her husband was going to Lisbon. By appointing a notoriously obedient, brutal and not very bright general as his envoy, however, Napoleon made his threat quite clear: there could be no question of negotiations between Junot and the Portuguese government. What he expected, and demanded, was compliance pure and simple.

Spain in 1807, when the French army marched through it to gain the frontier of Portugal, bore no resemblance to the Spain which I beheld when I entered that ancient kingdom in the month of March, 1805. I scarcely know how to describe the first aspect of a country so strangely different from ours in forms, in language, and in customs. England, separated from France as it is by the Channel, is even less different from our country than is Spain from the last French village upon the banks of the Bidassoa. I left St. Jean de Luz in the morning, and slept at Irun, a miserable town on the opposite side of this streamlet, or rather marsh, in which is situated that Isle of the Conference where the dishonest said to the honest Minister: *"Il n'y a plus de Pyrénées."*

The utterance of such a sentiment in 1660 might have made one expect to find in 1805 at least some vestiges of relationship between the two people. None, however, exist. Nay, notwithstanding the apparent alliance which, since the time of the Directory, was so proudly displayed—notwithstanding the fraternity which seemed to be established between the two nations—I could easily perceive, even on the frontier, that they were not friends. The curiosity we inspired was tinctured with no kindly feeling, and I am convinced that when we put up at a *posada* we were made to pay more for the *ruido de la casa* than would have been exacted from an Italian, or even from a heretic Englishman.

I reached Madrid on the 10th March. Though the approach to Madrid produces so unfavourable an impression, yet the appearance of the city on first entering it is grand and imposing. The streets are long and straight; the Calle de Alcala, where the French Ambassador resided, is one of the finest streets in Europe. It is terminated at one end by the magnificent promenade of the Prado, and the fine palace of the Duke of Alva, and at the other by La Puerta del Sol. The great street of Toledo, of which so much is said in "Gil Blas," and in the Spanish romances, and the street of Atocha, are finer than any in London or Paris.

For a long period Madrid was but a little town of no note belonging to the Archbishop of Toledo. Philip II. first made it a royal residence. He was influenced in his choice by the salubrity of the air of Madrid and its fine waters, of which there is an abundant supply. Fountains are to be seen in every quarter of the city, which, for execution and design, are execrable—a rather extraordinary circumstance, considering that they were erected at the epoch of the revival of the arts, when Spain produced so many splendid works. I can bear testimony to the fine quality of the water they supply. Its excellence arises, I fancy, from the many meanderings it is obliged to make.

Junot, who was advised of my arrival, came to meet me. He was accompanied by General Beurnonville, our Ambassador at Madrid, who informed me that Alphonso Pignatelli had given a very faithful description of his house which he was lending us, and that it was scarcely habitable. "Madame de Beurnonville," said he, "regrets exceedingly that we cannot ask you to come to our house, but we are very badly accommodated ourselves, and are full of complaints." This was said on our way to the Calle de Clavel, in which Pignatelli's house was situated. The two Ambassadors had got into my carriage, and we soon drove up to the door of my new abode.

I beheld a little white house, built exactly on the model of those of England, for many in Madrid are like those in London, whatever difference may exist in other respects between the two cities. The door was furnished with a bright brass knocker, and on entering I found myself in a neat little vestibule paved with marble, and as well sanded as if it had formed part of a Dutch habitation. The staircase was, like the house itself, small but elegant, and in good taste. We passed through an antechamber to the dining-room, and I next proceeded to examine the drawing-room and bedchamber, and was delighted with the neatness and elegance of the furniture. A good collection of pictures, French bronzes, and porcelain, completed the ornaments of this agreeable habitation, which was certainly one of the finest houses in Madrid. Junot and Beurnonville were highly amused by observing my astonishment. This little conspiracy had been got up in order to afford me the pleasure of an agreeable surprise.

After resting a few hours, I proceeded to the French Ambassador's, and was kindly welcomed by Madame Beurnonville. This lady was very much respected at Madrid, where her exalted birth alone would have ensured her a favourable reception. In a country where birth is everything, it is very important that an Ambassador's lady should possess that qualification. The impression produced even by the Emperor's glory, reflected as it was upon his Generals, was not alone sufficient to command the respect of persons of elevated rank. A prejudice so profoundly rooted could not be removed in a day.

When I arrived at Madrid the Court had quitted the Escurial for

Aranjuez. The customs observed at the Spanish Court at this period were the same as those which prevailed in the reign of Philip II.

On my arrival at Madrid I was visited by many ladies of the Court, some of whom manifested towards me much kindness and attention. One of these ladies, the Duchess of Ossuna, had resided long at Paris, and was distinguished for her pleasing manners and gracious deportment. The Duchess's two daughters, the Marquise de Santa Cruz and the Marquise de Camarasa, were highly educated and amiable women. The Duchess's house was furnished in the French style, and in the most perfect taste.

Another lady of high rank, who paid me a visit as soon as she had learnt my arrival, was the Marquise d'Ariza, formerly Duchess of Berwick. Her second husband, the Marquis d'Ariza, was Chamberlain to the Queen Maria Luisa. In her youth she had been very beautiful, and at the time I knew her she still retained her fine figure and graceful deportment. When, on the morning promenade at the Prado, she alighted from her carriage, and walked up and down, attired in an elegant *basquina* and lace *mantilla,* drawing the latter from side to side with her fan to shade the eyes, as the Spaniards say, she resembled one of Andalusia's lovely daughters. She had then a son twelve years of age, who afterwards came to Paris as Duke of Berwick.

I also received much attention from the Marquise de Santiago. A stranger figure than this lady was never seen. The Marquis d'Ariza had laid me a wager that I could not look at her without laughing. The poor woman painted unmercifully. The ladies of Charles II's Court would have looked pale beside her. Her daily operation of painting being ended, she made herself a pair of finely-arched black eyebrows, which she fixed above a pair of immense eyes, which were constantly on the broad stare. These same eyebrows gave rise to a laughable incident which I heard related at the house of the Marquise d'Ariza.

There was a party at Aranjuez, and the company were in the height of gaiety, dancing and laughing, when the Marquise de Santiago was announced. Though she was then somewhat younger, she painted as thickly as when further advanced in life, and she was attended then, as she still was at the age of sixty, by a *cavaliere servente,* or, to use the Spanish term, a *cortejo.*

The Marquise arrived late, and apologized by saying that the beauty of the evening had tempted her to take the air in the Calle de la Reyna. Whilst she spoke a universal titter prevailed through the room. Her appearance, which was at all times singular, was at this moment irresistibly droll. She had but one eyebrow! As Nature had in her case been very sparing of this feature, and as the one which attracted attention was black as jet, the contrast was complete. She herself had no suspicion that anything was wrong. The *cortejo* was equally unconscious. At length the mirth of the company exploded in loud peals of laughter, and the lost eyebrow was discovered to have accidentally fixed itself on the forehead of the *cortejo*.

Junot, who was very anxious to have an interview with Godoy, the Prince of the Peace* saw him on the day after his arrival. The Prince knew that he had to make an important communication from the Emperor Napoleon, and, although the cannon of Austerlitz had not yet been heard, Spain was the most faithful ally of France, as much from interest, it may be believed, as from friendship. The Prince of the Peace wished to please the Emperor, and was exceedingly gracious during this interview with Junot, who came home quite captivated by him.

"Berthier was talking nonsense," he said, "when he spoke ill of this man. He is described as being insolent, but I consider him merely a courtier, such as I can imagine the gentlemen of the Court of Philip V to have been. He does not like the Prince and Princess of the Asturias, and he informs me that we shall not meet with a good reception in that quarter. He says that France has no greater enemy than the Prince Royal, and added that it is his wife, the daughter of the King of Naples, who has excited him against us, merely because France is the ally of Spain." Junot informed me that the Prince exclaimed:

"Ah, monsieur, Spain will some day have in him a King who will render her very unfortunate. This double alliance with the House of Naples forms a bond which connects us with Austria, to whom a third daughter of the King of Naples is married. All these women have combined against France. Her new glory mortifies them, and perhaps you will scarcely believe that this new league is planned and directed by the Queen of Naples** herself. Our gracious Queen, whom

* Godoy had risen rapidly from the ranks of the Bodyguard by becoming Queen Maria Luisa's lover. In 1805, he was, and had been for some time, Prime Minister.
** Maria Carolina, Queen of Naples, was born an Austrian archduchess.

Heaven preserve! opposes this influence with all the powers of her mind and her natural affection for her son; but, General——" And he struck his breast with his right hand and shook his head repeatedly.

"I am astonished at what you tell me," said I to Junot; "I have often heard my uncle Demetrius speak of the Princess of Naples, who is now Princess of the Asturias. He knew her at Naples, and described her as a charming creature, beautiful and interesting, able to converse in seven or eight languages, an excellent musician and artist, and, in short, a highly-accomplished woman. The Prince of the Peace must talk nonsense." Junot rejoined: "May not a Princess be accomplished in the sense in which you understand the word, and yet be the most malicious person in the world?"

It would be a mistake to suppose, notwithstanding all that has been said of him, that the Prince of the Peace was utterly devoid of talent. He possessed considerable shrewdness, good sense, and judgment, combined with an aptitude for business, the more remarkable in a Spaniard, as they are usually very inactive. These qualities seemed calculated to render him a good Minister, but, on the contrary, what misfortunes did his administration bring upon Spain!

I believe Godoy's intentions to have been good, as a Minister and a patriot. He encouraged the arts, and by his orders travellers were sent from Spain to different parts of the world, in order to bring back to their native country information on science and manufactures; he constructed bridges and roads; he opposed the Inquisition, and in this conflict—the most serious, perhaps, that was ever maintained between the throne and the altar—the temporal authority was triumphant. How, then, are we to account for the misery which resulted from the government of the Prince of the Peace? On what was grounded the hatred of the whole nation towards that one man? There must have been some good reasons for this, for it seldom happens in such cases that the judgment of the mass of a nation is erroneous.

The Court, as I have already mentioned, was at Aranjuez when we arrived in Madrid. Junot went there first without me, and it was determined that I should be presented on the 24th of March, *en confidencia*—that is to say, without the formality of a full Court dress and hoop. We set out from Madrid on the 23rd of March at four in the afternoon, in order to sleep at Aranjuez that night, so that I might be

272

presented to their Majesties next day at half-past one—that is to say, immediately after their dinner, and before his Majesty went out to hunt. On leaving Madrid we crossed the Mançanarez by the bridge built in the reign of Philip II. by Juan de Herrera, and in allusion to which a wit of the time observed that "now the bridge is made for the river, it will be well to make a river for the bridge."

At a little distance farther on we again crossed the Mançanarez, but by fording it; after which we found ourselves on the magnificent road leading to Aranjuez, which is bordered merely by a few miserable-looking olive-trees. This road, which is six leagues in length, runs in a straight line, and is so perfectly smooth that the carriage rolled along as swiftly as though we had been flying. In this way we descended into the lovely valley in which is situated the royal *sitio* of Aranjuez. The descriptions which the poets have given us of Arcadia, the valley of Tempé, and all the spots most favoured by Heaven, do not excel the beauty of Aranjuez.

On entering the valley, all trace is lost of the chalky plains of New Castile. Instead of barrenness, the eye dwells on a picture of luxuriant fertility. Nothing is seen but verdure, flowers, and trees laden with fruit. A balmy fragrance perfumes the air. In short, one seems to be transported to another world, and to enjoy a new existence. The palace is not fine; it is nothing more than a small plain country house, such as might be the abode of any wealthy private gentleman. The Tagus surrounds the palace, and forms a very pretty artificial cascade in front of a parterre beneath the windows. The water is so close to the walls that the King can enjoy the amusement of fishing from his terrace.

I was so enchanted with this earthly paradise that I could have wished to spend the whole day in wandering over the grounds, instead of retiring to my chamber to array myself in full dress at broad noon-day. However, I had no choice, and in due time I commenced the important preparations for my presentation. I put on a dress such as I should have worn at the Imperial Court, and a head-dress of diamonds. I should have preferred pearls, for diamonds appeared to me to have too glaring an effect for daylight. But whenever I hinted at the idea of wearing pearls to the Marquise d'Ariza and some other ladies, they were as much shocked as if I had intended to insult their Queen.

These ladies told me one thing which appeared so ridiculous that I thought they were hoaxing me. They assured me that the Queen never received a lady in white gloves. "You must therefore recollect to take them off," said the Duchesse d'Ossuna, "or you will get into disgrace."

I laughed at this, and when I was dressed, never doubting but that what I had been told was a joke, I put on a pair of white gloves. But on arriving at the door of the apartment in which their Majesties were to receive me, the *camarera-mayor* touched my arm, and by signs requested me to take off my gloves. As she could not speak a word of French, and I could scarcely understand a word of Spanish, the dialogue was not very noisy, though our gestures were sufficiently animated. I observed that the old lady was growing impatient, and I felt myself getting a little out of humour.

That I, a Frenchwoman and a foreigner, who held no rank at the Court of Spain, should be subjected to this strange regulation, appeared to me unreasonable and absurd. Perhaps I was equally so in attempting to resist it; but I am one of those persons who like to have their own way, and consequently I found myself in open rebellion against the *camarera-mayor,* and resolutely withdrawing my gloved hands, I exclaimed: "No, no, señora!" to which she replied: "Señora Ambassadress, it is indispensable."

At length, finding that I obstinately resisted, she smiled, and, seizing my arm with her little dingy, shrivelled hands, she began to unglove me by force. I now saw the folly of longer resistance, and I submitted to the ceremony with a good grace. The old lady folded up my gloves and carefully laid them behind a red curtain, near the door of the Queen's apartment, and then, looking at my hands, she exclaimed: *"Jesu! . . . Jesu! . . . how very pretty! . . . Oh! . . ."* She evidently wished to console me and to remove the embarrassment I naturally felt at entering the presence-chamber in a dress with a train, diamonds, and bare arms. The *camarera-mayor* then entered to receive the commands of their Majesties, and on her return I was immediately ushered in.

The King and Queen were standing very near the door, so near it, indeed, that on entering I scarcely found room to make my three courtesies. The Queen advanced to me and received me with pleasing condescension. She entered into conversation with me about my journey with an air of interest which certainly could not be sincere, as she must have cared very little about me; but she appeared to do so, and this appearance is always gratifying on the part of a sovereign.

She seemed to me to be still a fine woman, though she was then growing stout, and was getting a double chin, like Catherine II., which imparted a matronly appearance to her countenance. She, nevertheless, wore a *coiffure à la grecque* with pearls and diamonds plaited along with her hair, or rather her wig. Her dress, which consisted of a slip of yellow taffety, covered with a robe of beautiful English point-lace, was cut exceedingly low on the neck and shoulders. Her arms were without gloves, and adorned with bracelets composed of magnificent pearls, each clasp consisting of a single ruby, the finest I ever beheld.

I could not help thinking of my adventure with the *camerara-mayor* when I saw the Queen's bare arms, which, as well as her hands, were exceedingly beautiful. A smile, which I was unable to repress, apparently revealed to her Majesty what was passing in my mind.

"I suppose," said she, "you were astonished at being required to take off your gloves? It is a custom of which you, madame, at least have no reason to complain, for your hands are made to be seen."

Charles IV's figure and appearance were perfectly original. He was tall, his hair was gray and very thin, and his extremely long nose did not tend to improve a countenance naturally devoid of intelligence, though it had an expression of good-nature and benevolence. His toilette, when I had the honour of seeing him, was not calculated to set off his personal appearance. He wore a blue frock-coat of coarse cloth, with yellow metal buttons, buckskin small-clothes, blue stockings drawn up over his knees, after the fashion of our grandfathers about a century ago, and over the stockings a pair of gaiters. I afterwards learned that this was his hunting-dress.

Hunting was an amusement, or in his case I may more properly call it a fatigue, of which he was exceedingly fond. Like his father, he went out to the chase every day of his life, let the weather be foul or fair. "Rain breaks no bones," he used to say.* Every day after dinner he would get into his carriage and take a drive of seven or eight leagues before he commenced hunting. In conformity with old etiquette, the

---

* When one of his sons was on his death-bed, he went out daily to hunt with as much indifference as though the child had been perfectly well. "What can I do for him?" was all the sympathy he expressed.

Foreign Ministers were admitted to pay their respects to the King twice a week: the day on which I was presented was one of these demi-reception days.

After speaking to me about my journey, and inquiring after the health of my little daughter, the Queen suddenly changed the conversation, and asked me some questions relative to the Empress Josephine. However, she did not say much on that subject, for I managed to change the conversation. From the few words which fell from the Queen, I could easily perceive that the idea she had formed of the Empress was not founded merely on her own judgment.

"How does she dress?" inquired she. "In the most elegant and tasteful style," I replied. "We take her as a model in all that relates to dress, not merely because she is our Sovereign, but because her exquisite taste prompts her to wear everything that is most graceful and becoming." "Does she wear rouge?" I answered "No," which at that time was really true. The Empress certainly rouged at a later period of her life; but I never recollect having seen her wear it during the Consulate or the beginning of the Empire. "And flowers—does she wear artificial flowers?" continued her Majesty. I replied in the affirmative. But these short answers were not satisfactory. I was obliged to be more specific, and accordingly described some of the dresses which the Empress had worn at *fêtes* in honour of the coronation. The Queen then said to me: "Have you seen my daughter, the Queen of Etruria? Do you not think she is very much like me?"

This question quite embarrassed me, and I was at a loss what to say, for it is impossible to imagine a more ordinary woman than the Queen of Etruria. I feared her Majesty was laying a snare for me; I never could have conceived that maternal love was so blind. However, there was something in the Queen's manner which convinced me of her sincerity, and I answered that the Queen of Etruria was remarkably like her Majesty. "Oh!" resumed the Queen, "she is not to be compared to my Carlotta at Lisbon—she presents a strong resemblance both to her father and me; observe her well when you see her. She is like her father in the upper part of the face, and like me in the lower part."

It was curious enough that all this was perfectly true, and yet the Princess was very ugly, and the Queen of Spain possessed the remains of beauty. She certainly could not be called very handsome at the time when I saw her (1804–5). She had then lost her teeth, and the artificial set which replaced them was no very good specimen of the dentist's skill.

As to the King, he nodded assent to all that Luisa said, and looked at me with an air of good-nature. However, he did not seem to be quite pleased at being excluded from the conversation, and when he could find an opportunity of getting in a word, he asked me what I had thought of the *coches de colleras.* He said I must have been much astonished at seeing them drawn by mules, and added that of course I had never seen such animals before.

At this remark I really could not refrain from laughing, for I was then a lively, giddy young woman; but, speedily recovering my gravity, I informed his Majesty that his finest mules were brought from one of our French provinces, namely, from Poitou. I shall never forget the expression of stupid astonishment that was depicted in the King's countenance on hearing this. He stared at me, and looked as incredulous as if I had told him that Peru was in Madrid.

"Did you know that, Luisa?" said he, turning to the Queen. Her Majesty, by a nod, answered in the affirmative. Then, after a pause, and looking earnestly at me, she said, addressing the King: "Is not Madame Junot very much like a Spanish lady? she has the complexion, the eyes, and the hair of a Spaniard." "Yes, yes," said the King, rubbing his hands and smiling, *"La señora es Espanola."* "And yet," resumed the Queen, addressing me, "you are a native of France, are you not? You were not born in Greece? My daughter-in-law, to whom I was speaking about you yesterday, tells me that she saw in Naples an individual of your name, a Prince Comnèna. Is he your father or your brother?" "He is my uncle, madame," I replied, and explained to her that my name was not Comnena, and that I was connected with that family only on my mother's side.

I then took leave of the King and Queen after a long audience. This interview with the King and Queen of Spain left an impression on my memory which time can never efface. At a period not far distant I had an opportunity of evincing my grateful recollection of the marks of kindness their Majesties were pleased to confer on me. This was at the time when they were so cruelly confined at Marseilles by order of the

Emperor. My brother was still in that town, and was impelled by the generosity of his character to alleviate the sufferings of these noble fugitives.

M M E Junot was nothing if not a Parisienne: to be required to wear the fashions of the 1780's struck her as an unparalleled act of barbarism. By 1805, and indeed for ten years before that, the fashion had been for high-waisted, flowing dresses whose straight lines were meant to be reminiscent of ancient Rome. Made of the lightest of materials in 1795, they were now, at Napoleon's behest, markedly more sumptuous. Heavy silks, brocades, lamés, velvets, all lavishly embroidered in gold and silver were the order of the day.

That was nothing like the court dress Mme Junot was now required to wear: a tight, pointed bodice, and vast side hoops, the normal pre-revolutionary court costume, were still compulsory at the court of Lisbon. Even in the eighteenth century, the unwieldy character of this fashion had required young women to take lessons in how to walk, dance and curtsey. Naturally, Mme Junot came wholly unprepared to this costume, hence the comical horror which she displays in the following pages.

It should also be noted that she had no doubt at all as to which was the superior fashion. The French have long had a tendency to consider any customs that differ from their own as wholly comical or repulsive. When Napoleon was on the throne, this feeling was greatly exaggerated: France, it was obvious, ruled the world; French usages, which were superior anyway, must prevail. Thus, Mme Junot's story of the dress with the hoops is also a typical example of French cultural smugness.

On our arrival the Court was at Queluz, and the Queen was as mad as ever. Junot was anxious that his retinue should be as splendid as a retinue possibly could be in Lisbon. His dress was superb, and became him admirably, for he was then a very handsome man. He wore his magnificent full-dress uniform of Colonel-General of the hussars, the same which he had had made for the Emperor's coronation. The dolman was white, with red facings, the pantaloons blue, and the pelisse blue, richly embroidered with gold. The sleeves of the dolman and pelisse were adorned with nine gold chevrons, superbly embroidered in an oak-leaf pattern. The pelisse was bordered with magnificent blue fox-fur.

This dress cost fifteen thousand francs, independently of the heron plume in the shako, which was a present from the Empress Josephine, and was worth more than three thousand francs. He presented a truly martial appearance in this dress. His tall handsome figure and noble countenance, on which five honourable scars were visible, naturally commanded respect. One of these scars was particularly visible, and was caused by a wound received at the battle of Lonato.

Junot proceeded to Queluz in great pomp. The most trivial points of Portuguese etiquette were scrupulously observed, and the equerry in white silk stockings was not forgotten. The carriage in which he rode was one of the finest Paris could produce, having been built by the celebrated coachmaker Leduc; the liveries were rich, and the attendants numerous. Consequently the embassy, consisting of the Ambassador, M. de Rayneval, Colonel Laborde, MM. de Cherval, Legoy, and Magnien, presented a very imposing appearance. Junot went through his part exceedingly well, and was received with a marked degree of favour, for which, perhaps, he was in some degree indebted to our eight hundred thousand bayonets, and also to the fear naturally inspired by such a Minister of Peace as Junot, who was inclined to say with the ancient Roman: "I bear peace or war in the folds of my mantle." The Prince of Brazil by no means realized the idea which Junot had formed of him from what he had heard.

"*Mon Dieu!*" he exclaimed on his return home, "how ugly the Prince is! . . . *Mon Dieu!* how ugly the Princess is! . . . *Mon Dieu!* how ugly they all are! . . . There is not a comely face among the whole set, except the Prince Royal (the late Don Pedro), the Prince de Beira. He is a handsome youth, and he looks like a dove amidst a brood of owls. But I cannot conceive," added Junot, "why the Prince of Brazil stared at me so steadfastly. . . . I did not know that there was anything very extraordinary in my looks, but he never for a moment turned his eyes from me." In the evening we learned what had excited the Prince's curiosity.

M. d'Araujo said: "Do you know, the Prince was quite puzzled to know why the Ambassador did not take off his *cap*, as he called it." "What does he mean by his cap?" inquired I. "Why, he calls the shako a cap. I have affirmed that the shako is never removed, even in the presence of God, and the Ambassador has certainly gone far to confirm that idea. However, I can assure you that but for me the affair would have been made the subject of a note. But you will be surprised when you learn the effect which the General's appearance has produced at Court."

These last words piqued my curiosity, but M. d'Araujo smiled and would not gratify it. However, it was not long before his meaning was explained. On the day after the presentation, the Prince Regent's first *valet-de-chambre* was sent to request that the French Ambassador would be pleased to lend his hussar uniform as a pattern for his Royal Highness's tailor, who was to make one like it for the Prince, and one for the Infant Don Pedro. I had not then seen the Prince of Brazil, therefore I could not laugh, as I afterwards did, when I beheld his corpulent figure, clumsy legs, and enormous head, muffled in a hussar uniform. His negro hair (which, by-the-bye, was in perfect keeping with his thick lips, African nose, and swarthy colour) was well powdered and pomatumed, and tied in a thick queue. The whole was surmounted by a shako, ornamented with a diamond aigrette of great value. A more preposterous figure was never seen. There was the pelisse hanging over his *right* shoulder like a Jew's bag of old clothes, and his clumsy, ill-shaped legs muffled in braided pantaloons and red boots. But the best of all was the shako; it was put on quite straight, and very backward, with the visor resting on his powdered head.

After Junot had made all his diplomatic evolutions, my turn came. This was an anxious moment. Before I left Paris, and during my journey, hoops had been only remote objects of terror, but as the time for wearing them approached I began to lose courage. Twice or thrice I attempted to try them on before my dressing-room mirror, but I turned about so awkwardly that I had nearly fallen flat on my face. . . . And then what a strange figure I cut!

"Heavens!" I exclaimed, almost crying with vexation, "what an absurd thing it is to be obliged to wear these horrible instruments of torture. . . . My dear husband," said I, in the most coaxing tone I could assume, "do pray get me exempted from this infliction. Come, I know you can arrange the matter if you will . . . France is so powerful!" But, within the first fortnight of his embassy—that is to say, when he had fairly entered upon his duties—Junot began to be very grave. He no longer laughed at the whimsical etiquette of the Portuguese Court, and he now talked of nothing but diplomatic notes and the duties which nations owe one to another. When I spoke to him about the hoops, he seemed as astonished as if I had wished him to make a declaration of war.

"Your hoop, Laura . . . go in your hoop, by all means. Recollect that, being an Ambassadress, you, of all persons, are required to observe this etiquette. . . . To think of going without a hoop—the thing is impossible!" What was to be done? there I was like an ass just harnessed with his panniers, swinging to the right and swinging to the left, and in momentary expectation of falling on my nose. I was out of all patience, and openly rebelled. I declared that my name should not mark an epoch in the annals of diplomatic presentations, and that people should not have to say: "Oh! you recollect, it was the year when the French Ambassadress fell down at Court . . . Don't you remember her ridiculous exhibition?"

Among the foreign Ambassadors at the Court of Lisbon was Count Lebzeltern, the Austrian Minister. His lady rendered me the important service of helping me out of my dilemma. I was giving her a history of my trouble, and complaining of the tyranny of Junot, when she said: "But, my dear madame, I cannot imagine how it is that you find the hoop so awkward as you describe. . . . You are slender, and you move as lightly as a fairy; why, then, should you be so clumsy in your hoop? There must be something wrong about it. Let me see it; I dare say I can suggest a remedy." She guessed right. On examining my hoops she found that they wanted at bottom a little iron or brass rod, the use of which was to act as a counterpoise to the enormous weight above it. When I tried them on after this improvement I found that I could walk like other people.

On the day appointed for my presentation, after getting the monstrous mountain properly adjusted, I put on a dress of white silk embroidered with gold llama, and looped up at the sides with large gold tassels, precisely after the manner of a window-curtain. On my head I wore a *toque,* with six large white feathers fastened by a diamond clasp, and I had a diamond necklace and earrings. When thus harnessed, I drew on a pair of white gloves (for the daughter had not the same antipathy as the mother), and I was ready to set off for Queluz. But my troubles were not yet at an end. I had got dressed, it is true, and had made up my mind to look like an ass laden with cabbages, but this was not enough. A fresh difficulty presented itself. How was I to get into the carriage, especially at an hour of the day when the Chafariz de Loretto was crowded with Galegos,* who began to laugh when they beheld my extraordinary figure?

With my foot on the carriage steps, I tried to squeeze myself in, first frontways, then sideways, and at length I stepped back in utter despair, for the vehicle was as much too low for my plume as it was too narrow for my hoop. Junot, who had not to go to Queluz that day, anxious to see me safe off, came down to the door in his *robe-de-chambre* and slippers, and assisted in *packing* me as gravely, and with as much care, as if I had been a statue worth a million. At length we mastered the difficulty, and in I got; but then I found I was obliged to sit slantwise, and with my body bent almost double, for fear of breaking my feathers and crushing my beautiful moire draperies. In this state of purgatory I rode from Lisbon to Queluz, a distance of two leagues!

I was ushered by the *camareira-mor*** into the little suite of apartments belonging to the Princess of Brazil. As it was contrary to Portuguese etiquette for the Prince or King to receive an Ambassadress, this was the only visit I had to make, for all the Princesses were assembled in the drawing-room of the Princess of Brazil. . . . I made my three courtesies, looking all the while very stupid—for this ceremony is in itself exceedingly foolish—and then I waited for the Princess to speak to me.

I had been informed that she would question me about France, and that she wished to render herself agreeable to me; not that *I* personally

---

* Natives of the Spanish province of Galicia, employed as labourers in Lisbon, and extremely industrious.
** The same post as the *camarera-mayor* of the Spanish Court, already mentioned.

was worth that trouble, but I was the representative of *female* France. Accordingly the Princess commenced by observing that she should much like to know the Empress Josephine, and she asked me whether she was as handsome as she was represented to be. I replied that her Majesty was still very handsome, and that her figure in particular was exquisitely fine. "If," added I, "your Royal Highness wishes to see a portrait of her, I can have the honour of showing you a most striking likeness."

I then produced a miniature by Isabey, which was, like all his works, a masterpiece of grace and delicacy. The Princess then spoke of her mother, and laughed very much at the Court regulation respecting gloves. She then asked whether I thought her like her mother. I boldly answered *yes*. Heaven forgive me for the falsehood! for the Queen had really been a fine woman, while the Princess could never have been anything but a most hideous specimen of ugliness.

Picture to yourself, reader, a woman four feet ten inches high at the very most, and crooked, or at least both her sides were not alike, her bust, arms, and legs being in perfect unison with her deformed shape. Still, all this might have passed off in a royal personage had her face been even endurable; but, good heavens, what a face it was! . . . She had two bloodshot eyes, which never looked one way, though they could not absolutely be accused of squinting—everybody knows what eyes I mean. . . . Then her skin! there was nothing human in it; it might be called a *vegetable* skin. . . . Her nose descended upon her blue livid lips, which when open displayed the most extraordinary set of teeth that God ever created. Teeth, I suppose, they must be called, though they were in reality nothing but huge pieces of bone stuck in her large mouth, and rising and falling like the reeds of a reed-pipe.

This face was surmounted by a cranium covered with coarse, dry, frizzy hair, which at first sight appeared to be of no colour. I suppose it was black, for, looking at me, the Princess exclaimed: "She is like us. . . . She is dark-complexioned. . . . She has hair and eyes like Pepita." "Heaven preserve me!" I inwardly exclaimed, while I involuntarily turned my eyes to a mirror as if to assure myself that what she said was not true. Pepita was the Queen of Etruria.

The dress of the Princess of Brazil was in *discordant* unison, if I may so express myself, with her person. This was precisely what it ought to have been. She would have been natural, at least, in a dress of dark-coloured silk, made perfectly plain. However, she had thought proper to array herself in a dress of Indian muslin embroidered with gold and silver llama. This dress, which was wretchedly ill made, very imperfectly covered an enormous bosom, and a chest all awry, while diamond brooches ornamented the sleeves, whose extreme shortness displayed a pair of arms which would have been much better concealed. Her frizzy dingy hair was plaited, and decorated with pearls and diamonds of admirable beauty. The body of her dress, too, was edged with a row of pearls of inestimable value. Her ear-drops were perfectly unique; I never saw anything like them. They consisted of two diamond pears, perfectly round, of the purest water, and about an inch in length. The two brilliants which surmounted the drops were likewise superb. The exquisite beauty of these jewels, combined with the extreme ugliness of the person who wore them, produced an indescribably strange effect, and made the Princess look like a being scarcely belonging to our species. Near her stood two of the young Princesses, one of whom was about ten years old. They were both fine girls, especially the one whose name was, I believe, Isabel—the one, I mean, who afterwards married her uncle, Ferdinand VII. As to the other Princesses, Doña Maria-Anna and the widow, they were both ugly; but it was an amusing piece of coquetry in them to station themselves beside the Princess of Brazil; her singular ugliness gave a comparative touch of beauty to the others.

Let the reader imagine, if he can, this personage dressed, as I have seen her, in a hunting-jacket (made almost like a man's) of green cloth trimmed with gold lace, a petticoat likewise of green cloth, open behind and before, like those worn by our great-grandmothers when they used to ride on horseback in the country, and then the *beaux cheveux,* which I have already mentioned, surmounted by a man's hat stuck on the crown of her head. Such was the hunting costume of the Princess of Brazil, and her Royal Highness, it must be observed, hunted like another Nimrod. Heavens! what a strange being she was!

One day I arrived at Queluz just as she was setting out to the chase, and when I beheld her equipped in her extraordinary costume I fancied I saw a grotesque vision before me. She had a black horse, very small, like all the Portuguese horses, but sufficiently skittish to intimidate a good male equestrian. To my amazement the Princess mounted him *astride,* and giving him two or three smart cuts with the whip, she made him prance round the esplanade in front of the palace, and then set off at full gallop, like a headlong youth of fifteen just broke loose from college. She appeared so ridiculous that I had difficulty in preserving the gravity indispensable to my *diplomatic* dignity.

My presentation audience being over, I went, according to etiquette, to see the *camareira-mor.* This personage was a little thin woman, very dark and very shrivelled, as most of the old women in Portugal are. Her dress, like that of all the ladies of the Court of Lisbon, was the strangest masquerade that Christian women can possibly assume. It consisted of a petticoat of very stiff and thick silk, of deep blue colour, with a border of gold embroidery; and her robe was a piece of some kind of red silk, which dragged behind her by way of a train. I observed that some of the elder ladies of the Court wore a sort of *toque* or cap fitted close to their heads (this, I believe, was peculiar to widows), and the *camareira* had in hers a large blue flower of the same colour as her petticoat.

When I entered the Princess of Brazil's drawing-room, all the *damas de honor* were seated—guess, reader, where? On the floor—yes, on the floor—with their legs crossed under them like tailors, or rather like the Arabs, who have bequeathed this among the many other customs they have left to the Peninsula. The ladies all rose up as I entered, and I almost fancied myself surrounded by a flock of Brazilian birds—those brilliant red and blue feathered paroquets. Their dresses were of the brightest and most glaring colours. The Princess, though blind to the defects of her person, apparently had sense enough to avoid these showy colours, and she never wore a Court dress. If she had done so, it would have been an awful affair to encounter the twofold monstrosity of her person and her apparel.

After my presentation I was looked upon with much consideration at Lisbon. I was the only personage of importance connected with the Diplomatic Corps. There was, to be sure, the wife of the English Minister, Lady Robert Fitzgerald; but, I know not how it was, her manners rendered her intolerable. The good sense and gentlemanly manners of Lord Robert Fitzgerald formed a striking contrast to the qualities which distinguished his lady.

She was quite a virago, with large legs, large arms, and large teeth, the latter making one almost afraid to go near her lest she should bite, an apprehension not unreasonable in those who observed the furious way in which she used to eye even a French hat or cap, looking like a tiger ready to fly at the face of the woman who wore it. The reserve maintained by Lord Robert Fitzgerald previous to our arrival in Lisbon was a proof of his sagacity. He perceived the influence which France, supported by Spain, was about to exercise upon Portugal. That influence was not received by the nation with the ardour which England might have been led to expect; but it was not on that account the less decided; and Lord Robert, who knew the timid character of the Portuguese Government, had no inclination to engage in a conflict which at that moment could not have turned to the advantage of England.

The Queen, Doña Maria was at times raving mad, and was always haunted by the dread of hell-fire. Whenever her confessor, the Grand Inquisitor, entered her room, she would exclaim that he was the devil. She used also to greet her daughter-in-law with the same appellation; in this instance the mistake was less pardonable.

This Queen was the mother of the two Princes of Brazil. One died of the small-pox before he came to the throne; the other reigned in Brazil as he did in Lisbon. Heaven knows how gloriously that was! . . . Her Majesty never left her royal prison except to enter another— namely, one of the little Portuguese carriages, in which she was closely shut up until she got into the country and quite out of reach of the public gaze; then sometimes her keepers would let her get out of the carriage and enjoy her liberty.

One day, when I was strolling in a little romantic valley in the neighbourhood of Cintra, I met three ladies, one of whom attracted my notice on account of her strange appearance and wild stare. It was a windy day, and her hair, which was as white as silver, was blown over her face and shoulders. As this appeared to annoy her, one of the females who accompanied her endeavoured to draw the hair from her face, but for this kind office she received a box on the ear, which I heard.

Three men were walking at some distance to render assistance in case of need. When I was perceived, one of these men came to me, and, addressing me in Portuguese, begged that I would retire. He did not, however, mention her Majesty, and it was not until afterwards that I was informed by M. d'Araujo it was the Queen. I think her attendants must have told her who I was; for as I withdrew I perceived that she was menacing me with clenched fists, and darting at me looks which were absolutely demoniacal. This encounter not only frightened me, but it gave rise to a world of melancholy reflections.

The Sovereign of a great nation wandering in a solitary valley, and consigned to the charge of a few menials, whose impatience and ill-temper being excited by constant attendance on the unfortunate lunatic were likely to increase her malady; her gray head, too, which in its dishevelment seemed to reject the crown it could not support—all presented a picture which made a profound impression on my mind. When, on my return home, I mentioned my adventure to Junot, we could not help remarking the curious fact that all the Sovereigns of Europe—at least, all the *legitimate* Sovereigns—were at that time either mad or imbecile.

W H E N , in 1804, the French Senate offered Napoleon a crown, it was careful, at his secret order, to make him, not a king because that would have smacked of the ancien régime, but an emperor, a title which, like that of Consul, was connected to ancient Rome. What quickly became clear, however, was that Napoleon did not think of himself as a new Augustus: instead, he chose to see the Empire as a modern re-edition of Charlemagne's.

At that time, very little was known about the early Middle Ages; so it was a romantic, and wholly inaccurate notion which prevailed instead: all Europe was to be united under the new Emperor's scepter. France itself, much extended—it reached eventually all the way to Hamburg—was ruled directly by Napoleon, as was the Kingdom of Italy, with Eugène de Beauharnais as Viceroy: indeed, Napoleon was known formally as His Majesty the Emperor and King.

Then came the protected States, most of them ruled by members of the Bonaparte family: Holland, under Louis; Westphalia, under Jerome; Spain, under Joseph; the Grand Duchy of Berg, then the Kingdom of Naples, under Murat, Caroline's husband; the Grand Duchy of Tuscany, under Elisa, while that of Warsaw was attached directly to the French Crown.

The next ring was made up of the allies: Bavaria, Saxony, Austria, Prussia, Russia, the Scandinavian countries, who were allowed to retain their dynasties and their laws, but were expected to be mostly or completely compliant. And finally, outside the pale, was the Enemy: Great Britain, whom the Allied and Protected States were expected to help defeat.

Of course, this impossible structure reflected nothing but Napoleon's growing megalomania: as we know, it all collapsed within less than ten years; and it is, in fact, easy to see that some of the new Bonaparte kingdoms were created, not for political reasons, but simply because it came to seem offensive for any Bonaparte to be deprived of a throne. There were two exceptions, though: the beautiful, frivolous Pauline, although eager to be granted the status of a ruler, had no intention of leaving her glamorous life in Paris; and Lucien, who was in deep disgrace because he had married a woman of whom Napoleon disapproved, and then refused to divorce her. Although Lucien, too, had a title, it was that of Prince of Canino, and had been given him by the Pope. All through the Empire period, he lived in Rome as a private person.

Soon, a mania for royalty possessed Napoleon's soul. His brothers and sisters became Kings and Queens. Madame Murat was called Grand Duchess of Berg; and Joseph Bonaparte was taken from his peaceful and domestic pursuits to reign over the ancient Parthenope. "Leave me to be King of Mortefontaine," said he to his brother; "I am much happier in that domain, the boundary of which, it is true, I can see, but where I know myself to be diffusing happiness." His wife experienced the same regret on quitting her home; but Napoleon had spoken, and it was necessary to obey. He had said: "The House of Naples had ceased to reign, and a new King is given to the Two Sicilies."

The Princess Elisa was the first of his family whom Napoleon preferred to the supreme dignity. He conferred on her the Republic of Lucca, which he erected into a Principality. When the Princess Caroline saw her eldest sister wearing a Sovereign crown, she also must have her ivory forehead similarly decorated. She was made Grand Duchess of Berg; but whether it was that there was no Duc de Nemours in her Duchy, or whether it was that one of her subjects, daughter of a shoemaker at Dusseldorf, but a very great lady notwithstanding at the Imperial Court, had spoken to her on terms of too much equality, she did not much like the lot that had fallen to her, and pleaded hard for a little kingdom.

Then came the turn of the Princess Pauline. The Emperor had actual warfare to sustain on her account. At length she was created Duchess of Guastalla. It was no great thing, to be sure, but even a molehill seemed too much for her to govern. If there had been kingdoms in the air, as in the time of the sylphs, she might have been enveloped in a pink and blue cloud, nicely perfumed, and sent to reign in those fortunate regions where the sceptre of government is a sprig of flowers. This, however, did not suit her; her tears and her pretty airs amused her brother for some time; but as it was not in his nature to be patient, he became angry at last.

The Princess Elisa discovered that Lucca and Piombino were miserable Principalities. She complained; the Princess Caroline complained; the Princess Pauline complained—it was a chorus of grievances. "Ah, çà!" said the Emperor; "what does all this mean? Will these ladies never be content? One would think we were really sharing the inheritance of the late King our father!"

One day I had accompanied Madame* to Saint Cloud, whither she went to dine with the Princess Borghèse, who then occupied the ground-floor of the palace; the Emperor came there in the evening, and, on seeing me, said laughingly: "Well, Madame Junot! so you are not gone yet?" "Sire, I am waiting till my daughters are perfectly recovered, and shall then immediately commence my journey."

"Do you know," said Madame, "that you ought to leave me my ladies; here is Madame Junot, who has been absent from her duties for a

* Madame Mére, Napoleon's mother, to whom Mme Junot had been appointed lady in waiting.

twelvemonth, and you are going to send her to Italy!" "It is not I who send her—it is her own pleasure to go; ask her yourself;" and looking at me with a smile, he made me a significant sign. In such moments as these his countenance was charming. "Well, why do you not say that it is yourself who are positively determined to go to Parma?" "But, Sire, I cannot say what is not true. I have not the smallest inclination to go thither."

He burst into a fit of laughter—a very rare thing with him; for though his smile was becoming, he scarcely ever laughed aloud, if at all. "And why is it not your pleasure to go, Madame Laurette?" and my poor nose was pinched until it almost bled. "A good wife should always follow her husband; it is the Gospel law." "Sire, your Majesty will permit me to say that the Gospel has nothing to do with this case; that I am not a good wife in this particular; and—that perhaps I might be a supernumerary at Parma."

"Ah! ah! these gossips have been putting mischief into your head! Why do you listen to them? Besides, the hen should be silent in the presence of the cock: if Junot amuses himself at Parma, what is that to you? Wives must not torment their husbands, or they may make them worse." This he said, not looking at me, but with his eyes turned covertly towards the Empress, who, like a woman of sense, seemed not to understand him. Scenes of jealousy were becoming frequent; and, to say the truth, not without some cause.

I had opened not only my eyes, but my ears, to what the Emperor had said. I then knew nothing of what I afterwards learned; but the expression of my countenance as I looked at the Emperor had probably something in it extremely comic, for he again did me the honour of laughing at me.

"Well, there you are quite stupefied about a trifle—a trifle which you wives make a great concern when you know it, and which is of no consequence whatever when you do not. Now, shall I tell you all what you ought to say on such occasions? Do you wish to know?" "I listen, Sire." "Just nothing! but if, like the rest of your sex, you cannot be silent—if you must speak, let it be to approve." "Indeed!" cried Madame. "Shocking!" said the Princess Borghèse. "I should like to see Prince Camille expecting me to approve such proceedings!" And she turned round upon her sofa, arranging the folds of her shawl.

The Empress said nothing; but she had tears in her eyes, and I am sure that a single word would have made her weep, which the Emperor did not like. The tears of a woman made a profound impression upon him, and this was why he dreaded them so much. The man who could not, without emotion, hear the sound of the evening bells—and it is well known that he would frequently stop in his walk in the park of Malmaison to listen to the church bells of Reuil or Bougival—the man who often avowed the particular charm he found in seeing a delicate girl dressed in white and wandering among the trees, must needs have naturally possessed a susceptible heart; and no doubt he concealed his feelings under a rude and dry exterior till this rind became a part of his character.

The Court was now very attentive to all the Emperor's proceedings. At the time of the coronation he was in love, as I then stated, and the love was real. During my absence some trouble had arisen about it. The Empress had been annoyed by the conduct of the favourite lady, who, in consequence, had received a recommendation to retire to a watering-place.

The Emperor, while making this concession, was out of humour about it, as the Empress had occasion to feel when any new cause of jealousy arose, which, as report said, was pretty frequently during the journey to Italy on account of the coronation; for the Emperor, though his heart had been really touched in one instance, never denied himself any gratification of the kind, and his wanderings were somewhat various.

Already the departure of the Princess Louis was whispered, and, although she was about to occupy a throne, her absence could not but be regretted in a Court of which she was the life. She reminded me of Henrietta* of England. Not so the Princess Caroline; of all the family she was perhaps the only one who had not learnt to become a Princess; she could not leave off the satirical giggle and sneering of the school-girl, while her manners were undignified, and her walk the most ungraceful possible.

But in self-sufficiency she was perfectly the Sovereign lady; she

---

* Maria Henrietta Stuart, sister of Charles II of England, married the duc d'Orléans, Louis XIV's younger brother. She was remarkably bright and spirited.

spoke of herself and of her person with the highest consideration, and with a contemptuous ridicule of others, which imposed upon unthinking people. Her decisions upon all points were as inexhaustible as they were injudicious. With an incomparable freshness, and that profusion of lilies and roses which were enchanting when she shaded them with a fringe of embroidered tulle lined with pink satin, half enveloped in English point, and tied with ribbons of the same colour, as fresh and charming as her own complexion,—with all this her beauty did not please. Her eyes were small; her hair, which in her infancy had been almost white, was now neither light nor dark; and her unfortunate sneer showed her teeth too much, because, though white, they had not the regularity of a string of pearls like those of the Emperor and the Princess Pauline.

Her mind remained in its natural state, without any cultivation or instruction, and she never employed herself except in scrawling at random some pencil strokes upon white paper, which her flatterers called drawing; as a child she had vivacity and an engaging manner; and as she began to grow into youth just as her brother, as Commander-in-Chief of the army, was drawing worshippers to the star of his family, she had her full share of flatterers; and as some philosophy is required to weed out from the minds of children the seeds of vice and evil habits, hers flourished at their leisure, in spite of the tuition of Madame Campan, with whom she was boarded for two years. Madame Campan, though a woman of very superior merits, had the great fault of never contradicting the daughters of rich and powerful families who were confided to her.

At this period the Court became materially diminished by the departure of the Princesses and the two brothers of the Emperor; and the Princess Borghèse being always an invalid, and occupied solely with the care of her health, though not a very elegant amusement, it was on the Princess Caroline alone, or the Grand Duchess of Berg, as she chose to be called, that all the hopes of fashionable gaiety rested. She then occupied the beautiful palace of the Elysée, where she began to receive the Court *en princesse,* notwithstanding her satirical vein, to which people were becoming accustomed.

J U S T as it seemed to Napoleon that his brothers and sisters must become kings and queens, so he wanted his court to be the most splendid ever seen. He ceaselessly exhorted his dignitaries to live lavishly in splendid houses; he often gave them large sums of money, usually taken from the contributions paid by defeated enemies, and expected them to spend every penny, on the assumption there would always be more where that came from.

So it was that his ministers, marshals and court functionaries moved into the most splendid palaces in Paris: Talleyrand, for instance, bought the Hôtel Matignon, today the residence of the Prime Minister. The Junots had a huge private house on the Champs Élysées; but that still was not enough. It is amusing to note the disdain with which Mme Junot speaks of Bièvre, which was, in fact, a good-sized castle. Raincy, to which she eventually moved, had been nothing less, before the Revolution, than one of the main residences of the duc d'Orléans, the King's cousin, and it was indeed a palatial residence which, after 1795, had become the property of Gabriel-Julien Ouvrard, the richest banker in France, and quite possibly in Europe.

Just as only Raincy would do for Mme Junot, so the Emperor's palaces multiplied: to the Tuileries and Saint Cloud, Fontainebleau and Compiègne were soon added; then came the Grand Trianon; and, at the end of the reign, Napoleon was planning to redecorate Versailles itself.

I had always longed for a country residence. Junot, it is true, had given me Bièvre, but this house had become of very little use since his appointment as Governor of Paris. It was too far distant, and much too small besides for our family, numerous not only by the increasing number of our children, but by the colony of relations it was Junot's hospitality to lodge. He said to me one morning: "You must dine at Raincy to-day; Ouvrard has given me leave to kill some deer there, and I wish you to hunt with me in a calash."

It was in the beginning of October; the weather was charming and the chase fortunate. I looked with delight upon the beautiful groves of Raincy. The *château,* notwithstanding the vandalism which had destroyed three-quarters of it, was still a noble piece of architecture, seated in the midst of fresh verdure, and surrounded by its pretty Russian cottage, its hunting-box, its clock-house, and its stabling; I admired the pretty village at the extremity of its fine alley of poplars, the orangery, and all the other objects which beautify the park. But within the house I found still greater cause for admiration. M. Ouvrard had made it a palace of enchantment. The bathroom was charming. It contained two basins of vast dimensions, each formed of a single block of gray and black granite. Four pillars of the same material, and three curtains of white satin, enclosed each basin as in a cabinet. The floor was in large squares of black, white, and yellow marble; the chimney was of *vert antique,* and the walls of stucco perfectly finished; round them stood an immense circular sofa of green velvet. The ceiling represented mythological subjects admirably executed. A valuable lamp was suspended from the centre. On entering this superb room, I could not forbear exclaiming: "What happiness it must be to possess such a place as this!"

Junot looked at me with a smile, and, taking my hand, led me to the salon, an immense apartment divided into three by pillars, between which stand statues holding candelabras. One extremity is the billiard, the other the music room; the centre is the reception-room. This was formerly the bedroom of the Duc d'Orléans, and forms one of the front wings, its three sides looking upon the home park, reserved for the use of the family, and from which the deer are excluded. The character of this portion of the park is simple and beautiful; a large lawn is terminated by the river, bordered by an orangery and summer-house; on each side of this lawn a grove diverges from the house as far as the eye can reach, the part on the right composed of lilacs, that on the left of acacias. The view from the window was enchanting.

"How do you like this *château* and park?" said Junot. "Oh! it is a fairyland." "And if by a stroke of the wand you were to become mistress of it, what would you say?" "I cannot tell, for that is sure not to happen." "Do you wish that it should?"

I coloured at the mere thought that it might be, and looked at him with an expression which probably pleased him, for he took me in his arms and said: "It is yours."

There are certainly hours of bitterness in life, and no one has had more experience of them than myself; but there are also moments, fugitive in duration, but indelibly engraven on the mind, which are equal to an eternity of happiness.

Amongst the persons now figuring in the Imperial Court was one deserving of notice here, and with whom I was very intimately acquainted, Madame Regnault de Saint Jean d'Angely, of whose husband I have spoken in a former volume. Madame Regnault was well born and beautiful; she had a perfect model of a fine Grecian head, with its exquisite outline and correct proportions. Her glossy black and naturally waving hair never required the aid of the curling-irons. Her teeth were white and regular. Her figure was symmetrical, and she never had recourse to the corset, even when she wore a Court dress; her hand and arm, foot and leg, were small and perfectly formed; in short, she was in all respects, at the time I am speaking of, a beautiful woman. She was also extremely well informed, had read much, and was very witty, but so modest that you must have known her long to become acquainted with these qualities.

In the last moments of her unfortunate husband's life her conduct was beyond praise. Regnault's muscular strength was prodigious when in a state of health; but under the influence of that malady of the brain which brought him to the grave it was terrible, and made it very dangerous to approach him. His wife, without any fear, or rather without showing any, watched him like the most attentive nurse. In this miserable state she wandered with him through Brussels, Mons, Antwerp, wherever the unfortunate exile could obtain the slight favour of some hours' rest for her dying husband. A mutual friend, alas! also proscribed, met her in this painful pilgrimage, and has related to me traits of Madame Regnault which must have obtained for her the friendship of anyone who had not felt it for her already.

The Emperor, who, notwithstanding his immense genius, had always a weak side which chained him to humanity, was liable to imbibe prejudices against particular women. Madame Regnault was one of those who had the misfortune, and it really was one, not to please him. Everyone knows the manner in which his Court circle was formed; the triple row of ladies, behind whom were ranged also a triple row of gentlemen, all listening with as much curiosity as the females to hear the speeches, polite or impolite, which the Emperor should address to them.

It is easy now to speak as we please upon this subject, and to affect courage when the battle is over; but I will affirm that when on a Court-day the Emperor appeared at the door, which was in the angle of the Throne-room, with a cloudy brow, everyone was afraid; first the ladies, then the gentlemen; and last, but not least, that group assembled in the deep window to the left—that group, generally complete with the single exception of England, covered with jewels and orders, and trembling before the little man who entered with a quick step, dressed simply in the uniform of a Colonel of Chasseurs. I have known women, and I have a right to place myself among the number, who preserved in his presence an independence of manner which pleased him better than silly fear or base flattery. When he made an unpleasant speech to a lady, and it was repelled with respect and yet with spirit, he never returned to the charge. For myself, when I have offended him, he has often passed me at two or three successive Court circles without speaking, but he never said a word which could wound my feelings. I have heard him do so to others, and once in particular to Madame Regnault de Saint Jean d'Angely.

It was at a ball given by the Grand Duchess of Berg at Neuilly. The Emperor was out of humour, and was going the tour of the circle somewhat rudely: I believe he did not even trouble himself to know to what lady he was speaking till he stopped opposite Madame Regnault, examining her dress, which was charming. A petticoat of white crape trimmed with alternate tufts of pink and white roses; and not a head-dress worn that night had so beautiful an effect as the lovely roses which Madame Regnault had embedded in the soft velvet of her glossy black hair. If to this elegant attire the recollection of her fine features and exquisite figure is added, and to that the age of twenty-eight years, it must be conceded that no idea but of beauty and interest would be likely to arise from the contemplation of her person.

But all this graceful simplicity seemed to increase Napoleon's ill-humour, and a bitter smile played on his lips as he said to her, in his clear and sonorous, though solemn, bass voice: "Do you know, Madame Regnault, that you are ageing terribly?" The first effect of this speech was painful to Madame Regnault's feelings. To be thus pointed out to the attention of a thousand persons, of whom at least a hundred females were delighted to catch the mortifying words, was a heavy tax upon a lady's philosophy; but a moment's reflection enabled her to give proof of her good sense and spirit.

Looking upon the Emperor with an amiable smile, she replied in a voice distinct enough to be heard by all persons around: "What your Majesty has done me the honour to observe might have been painful to hear had I been old enough to be frightened by it."

The respect and fear which the Emperor inspired could not restrain the low murmur of approbation which ran round the circle. Napoleon possessed tact to an extent which can hardly be conceived by those who did not know him personally. He looked at Madame Regnault and said nothing; but soon afterwards, passing us again—I was standing close beside her—he addressed himself to me with a sort of malicious smile, but with an inflection of voice almost gracious, and said: "Well, Madame Junot, do you not dance? Are you *too old* to dance?" Notwithstanding this prejudice of the Emperor against her, Madame Regnault was always faithful in her attachment to him, which became worship when misfortune reached him.

During the winter of 1807 all the Ministers gave *fêtes*. The Grand Duchess of Berg* was the Queen of them all, because the absence of the Queen Hortense, and the age of the Empress, who no longer danced, left the field open to her. She was at this time very fresh, and indeed very pretty. She dressed very elegantly, opened all the balls with the Governor of Paris, played whist with the Governor of Paris, rode on horseback with the Governor of Paris, received the Governor of Paris alone in preference to all other persons, till the poor Governor of Paris, who certainly was not an angel, and whose head, and even heart, though always attached to me and his children, was not insensible to the impressions of the moment, could no more resist these

* The title then belonging to Caroline Murat

seductions perpetually attacking him than the Christian knights could resist the temptations of the palace of Armida.

He fell in love, passionately in love, with the Grand Duchess of Berg; not that she returned his love—she has assured me that she did not, and I am bound to believe her. The results, however, of this mischievous affair were the misfortunes and death of Junot. How dangerous it is to love Princesses! witness M. de Canouville, to whom it cost his head; M. le Duc d'Abrantès, exiled; for the Vice-royalty of Portugal, as it was called, was but a gilded exile. It is true the predicament was sufficiently embarrassing, for M. de Septeuil lost one of his legs because he could not love the Princess Borghèse. Truly the love of such great ladies is not all ease and delight.

A great misfortune now fell upon our family in the loss of my mother-in-law. To understand Junot's distress upon this occasion it would be necessary to know how much he loved her. To save him many painful hours I had concealed her danger from him, and the stroke consequently came upon him with the shock of an unexpected calamity. Junot loved his mother with so much tenderness that nothing could relieve the weight of grief with which her death oppressed him.

During the days which followed he was ill, but determined to attend the funeral. My mother-in-law was buried at Livry, a small village of which M. Arthur Dillon was Mayor, and the Curé was a particular friend of ours. I knew Junot's excessive sensibility, and I dreaded some accident. In fact, at the moment when the holy water was thrown upon the corpse, he fell down in a swoon, from which he was very slowly restored. For a long time he refused to receive company, and it was only the necessity of fulfilling his duties that induced him to go out. He never afterwards spoke of his mother without tears in his eyes.

The Emperor wrote to him upon the occasion a very friendly letter, full of such words as are sure to go direct to the aching heart when they are used by such a man as Napoleon; and this letter was written wholly by his own hand, although seventeen lines long. It is remarkable that in this letter the Emperor *tutoyait* Junot, and spoke to him as in the days of Toulon or Italy. It concluded with a curious sentence.

My father-in-law was keeper of the forests and waters in the department of the Côte-d'Or. The grief he felt at the separation from the companion of his life unfitted him for business; he felt a distaste for everything, and would not retain his employment; he wrote to his son to this effect, and at the same time requested him to solicit from the Emperor the permission to resign it in favour of his son-in-law, M. Maldan. Junot, in writing to the Emperor, submitted to him his father's petition, saying that he was so overwhelmed with grief by the death of his wife as to be unable to fulfil the duties of his situation. The Emperor's answer, as I have said, was in a strain of friendship and of the truest kindness; but on the subject of M. Junot's petition he wrote:

"I do not see why your father should wish to resign his employment; when I have seen him I have always supposed him a man of energy and strength of mind. What is there in common between his office and his wife? If he is at a loss for a wife to receive company according to his duties, let him marry again." I own that this inevitably leads to the conclusion that Napoleon was not sentimental; nor was he. The objects that engrossed his thoughts were too vast to leave room in them for the ideas of ordinary life. He refused the transfer of the place at that time, but granted it some months afterwards. The Emperor's letter was dated from Warsaw.

It often happens that we commit blunders ourselves which we should think it impossible for another person to fall into. On the evening after Junot had received this letter he went to the Tuileries to pay his court to the Empress. She had already learned from the Arch-Chancellor, who told her all the news that would bear telling, that Junot had received a letter from the Emperor.

Junot, thinking to interest the Empress in his father's wishes, spoke of his grief and his desire to retire; he then repeated the Emperor's answer, and gave it word for word, not in jest, for he was much hurt by it, but in perfect innocence of saying anything that could at all affect the Empress. Nor was it till she made him repeat the whole sentence that he began to discover that this indifference to women and wives was likely to prove painful to the Empress; and that, in fact, she was deeply wounded by it. She was not, however, the less kind and gracious to him.

The Empress, it is well known, was fond of the game of patience. Every evening the packs of cards were placed upon the table, and patience proceeded, while that of the spectators was sorely tried. As her love for the Emperor was sincere, and her solicitude, I am persuaded, was as great for the individual as for the Sovereign whose crown she shared, she had recourse to every means of tranquillizing her anxiety; and as cards proved amongst the readiest, they were continually resorted to. One evening when I was with her, having exhausted her favourite game in every variety of form, the Empress wondered whether a courier would arrive that night: it was nine o'clock. "I cannot make up my mind," said she, "to retire to rest till I am satisfied whether there will be any tidings for me to-night."

She recommended the game of patience, and before it was half accomplished was certain she would succeed, which accordingly she did; and scarcely was the last card placed on the last pack, when the Arch-Chancellor entered, with his usual solemn pace, and delivered to her Majesty a letter from the Emperor—a letter the more agreeable to her as it announced that the army would repose, during the month of March, in cantonments between the Vistula and the Passargue. This last particular is impressed on my mind by the circumstance of an entire line of the Emperor's letter containing the names of the two rivers being utterly unintelligible to the Empress. It was handed to us to decipher, if we could, but with equal ill-success; for my own part, I could as easily have read the inscription on Cleopatra's needle. At length Junot arrived, and as he was even more accustomed to Napoleon's handwriting than the Empress herself, the incomprehensible line was made over to him, and he read it.

"Really," said the Empress, "it is very fortunate for me that you took it into your head to fetch Madame Junot, otherwise we should have seen nothing of you, and I should have remained in ignorance that the army was stationed between the Vistula and the Passargue."

This was mildly spoken, but Josephine was visibly hurt that Junot paid her no other attention than was due to the Empress. She laughingly whispered a few words in his ear; upon which Junot coloured and looked round to see whether I was listening or observing, and replied in a tone which made it apparent that he was piqued in his turn.

I was poorly at this time, without positively knowing the cause of my malady; I guessed it with indescribable joy, for it seemed to give hopes of a boy after my five girls. In consequence, however, of this slight indisposition, I kept my bed somewhat later of a morning, and had not risen from it on the day following the incident of the letter, when I heard several voices in my salon, and suddenly my bedroom door was thrown wide open, and the Princess Borghèse was announced.

"Well, my little Laurette, so you are ill? I can easily believe it. You are vexed: hey? Come, tell me all about it." And, jumping on my bed, she established herself on my feet quite to her satisfaction, and regardless of any inconvenience she might cause me. I rang for some pillows, that I might sit up and offer my duty as a Lady of the Court, instead of thus remaining in my nightcap in presence of so august a personage; but she would not suffer it, and we had the strangest conversation possible.

"So, so, Laurette, tell me why you have not given me a *fête* at your country-house of Raincy?" "Because, as your Imperial Highness can scarcely bear the motion of a carriage, I did not imagine you could hunt, which is the only *fête* we can offer you at Raincy." "And why should not I hunt as well as Caroline? Your *fêtes* are all for her." "But, madame, you do not ride on horseback." "What does that signify? I could follow in my palanquin. Have you seen my palanquin?" "No, madame . . . but that is of no consequence, you cannot hunt in a palanquin." And the idea struck my fancy as so perfectly ludicrous that I could not avoid laughing.

"Very well; they all laugh when I tell them I can follow the chase with my bearers. M. de Montbreton tells me I have not common sense. But we shall see; I want to consult Junot about it: where is he?" I rang and inquired for Andoche: he was gone out. "Ah! ah! gone out already! Really he is very early in his visits. Perhaps it is for the Empress's *fête;* he is Director-in-Chief of everything that is done at the Élysée. You ought not to allow it," added she, with an air of seriousness quite amusing. "I have no control in such matters," I answered, with a heart a little swelled, for I understood her allusion. "But what *fête* do you mean, madame?" "Why, the 19th of March, to be sure— Saint Joseph's Day. We are to *fête* the Empress our sister. We are to perform a comedy at Malmaison; you are one of the principal actresses. What! do you know nothing about it, my dear Laurette?"

A message was at that moment brought me from the Grand Duchess of Berg, desiring to see me, to which I answered that I would hasten to attend her commands; but it was not easy to get rid of such a personage as the Princess Borghèse. I was obliged to listen to the full detail of her projected costume and singing, then to complaints against such of her ladies as had been wanting in respect. Then she talked of the Emperor's victories, of my nightgown, and then again of her dress for Rosina: it was the most discursive *tête-à-tête* imaginable. She was determined to perform Rosina on the occasion; a complimentary song was to be added to the music-lesson, and that affair would be settled. Then followed lamentations sufficiently comic, addressed as they were to me, on Junot's *having forgotten* how beautiful she was. . . . Oh, the strange being! Suddenly she exclaimed in an ecstasy:

"My little Laurette, do you know my new Chamberlain?" "No, madame; who is he?" "M. de Forbin." My brother was well acquainted with him, but I had seldom seen him; though I knew that he was both sensible and agreeable, and that his elegance of manners and distinguished merit naturally fitted him for the situation to which he was appointed. "What, my dear Laurette, do you not know my new Chamberlain?" She leaned over me and pulled at once all the three bell-ropes at the head of my bed. My *valet-de-chambre* and women came running in all together. "Send in the gentleman who is in the salon," said she to the *valet-de-chambre;* and in walked M. de Forbin.

I do not know whether I am infected with the prejudices of persons who are growing old, but I must say that in my opinion the present day does not produce men so attractive for talents, manners, and personal appearance, as numbers who figured at the period of which I am writing, and amongst whom M. de Forbin was eminently distinguished. He was well formed and handsome; his language was remarkable for grace and elegance, and his abilities in painting, poetry, and literature made him the most delightful drawing-room companion in the world. Such was the M. de Forbin whom the Princess Borghèse brought into my chamber while I lay in bed, to show me *her Chamberlain;* for her State Household was as yet a splendid novelty.

The whole establishment had been summoned to deliberate upon the piece that should be selected for the Empress's *fête*. Let it be understood that the two sisters-in-law thought no more of the Empress than if her name had been Saint Lucia. They were determined on a *fête,* and a *fête* in which they should play the principal parts, and attract universal applause. Could the party have been transported to Madame de Genlis's Palace of Truth, this would have appeared as the really actuating impulse.

The Princess Pauline therefore insisted on the representation of the *Barber of Seville.* "Because," said she, "I shall play Rosina to admiration." "But, madame, it is an opera." "I do not mean the opera, but the French piece translated; I have it, and very well translated." "But, madame, it is very long, and, besides, it is for the Empress's *fête.* Nothing could be so suitable to the occasion as—" "Really," said she, quite irritated, "she must be very hard to please; what can she wish for but that we should be amused? Well, it will well suit me to perform the comedy, and take the part of Rosina. How pretty I should look in the black and pink hat, and the little pink satin dress, with an apron of black blonde."

The Princess Caroline, who had far more sense than her sister (although I cannot subscribe to the extraordinary pleasantry of M. de Talleyrand in saying she had the head of Cromwell placed on the shoulders of a pretty woman), had also set her mind on a part contrived expressly and exclusively to show herself off. The two sisters could not, therefore, be brought to agree, and the great Sanhedrim which had just closed its sittings could not betray more irresolution than the present council.

A lucky motion was at length made to consult Junot, whose opinion was fortified by former favour with one sister and present favour with the other. I will not say whether this was wholly attributable to the strength which friendship acquires from the recollections of infancy; but, however derived, he had sufficient influence with both to induce them to abandon the project of performing a great drama, and to play two small pieces composed expressly in honour of the day, telling each that her part might be made as prominent as suited her own inclination.

M. de Chazet was to compose one of these pieces; the witty, agreeable M. de Longchamps, at the command of the Princess Caroline, the other; and he never failed to charm, whether giving parties of pleasure, sketching after the most caustic manner of Teniers the pilgrimage of an old maid, warbling the despairing strains of a patriot on the eve of exile, or simply in the chimney-corner relating some old legend with that grave spirit and interest which is the exclusive gift of Nature, and cannot be acquired by study.* Spontini, known to the musical world by *La Vestale,* was to contribute the music.

No sooner were the pieces prepared than the parts were distributed; and now the eagerness to be *prima-donna* appeared in its full force. The male characters were fairly assigned; but as to the female, it mattered not whether they were or were not suited to the talents of their several representatives, provided those of the two Princesses were carefully worked up and comprised all the interest of the pieces.

Our only resource was in playing something less badly than our Imperial coadjutors, and in that respect we had full latitude. The actresses besides the two Princesses were the Maréchale Ney, Madame de la Vallette, and myself. The gentlemen, Messieurs de Brigode, d'Angosse, de Montbreton, and Junot; besides another who acted a subordinate character, and whose name I have forgotten. The Maréchale Ney acted an old grandmother with the talent she uniformly displayed, for I never knew her to do anything otherwise than well, but her part was not very important.

The pleasure of this comedy was certainly not so great to its ultimate audience as to ourselves during our three weeks' rehearsals; not that the matter was uniformly laughable to us all, or to me, for example, when on entering one of the palaces at which we were to rehearse, an equipage met my eyes with amaranth liveries, turned up with yellow and laced with silver, that is to say, my own; but where was the person the landau had conveyed? Not in the gallery! I found, in short, that a council was being held; but not in the fashion of the *Comédie Française,* to which the dramatic corps were admitted, and each allowed to give an opinion. In our company we had not even the liberty of remonstrance.

The Princess Pauline, as an actress, acquitted herself tolerably well, but her singing was so outrageously out of tune that it was scarcely

* He composed the affecting ballad of *We must depart! Adieu, my Laura!* (so beautifully set to music by Boieldieu) at the moment he was himself embarking for his exile in America, and was also the author of *My Aunt Aurora.*

endurable. It was, besides, sufficiently ridiculous to see her carried into the middle of the theatre (for the state of her health prevented her walking), and there in her armchair rehearsing the part of a young affianced bride. Who was her lover? I do not remember, unless it was M. de Brigode, who in the second piece performed Lolo Dubourg admirably. Madame Ney and Madame de la Valette also performed in the first piece, the former extremely well; as for Madame de la Valette, M. de Chazet, who was her instructor, exclaimed rather angrily: "Cannot you, dear madame, express a little more emotion? rather more tenderness, I conjure you! really, one would suppose you were asleep!"

His reproach was just. It would be impossible to speak or move with more monotony or cold indifference; she was perfectly provoking—an animated statue, but not animated like Galatea, with the sacred fire of the heart. And yet this woman, who appeared so cold, has proved that her soul was warmed by the noblest passions.

In the second piece Junot was a lover, a character not at all adapted to his comic talent. It was love in its utmost passion, in all the vigour of first impressions. I think M. de Longchamps must have been bent on placing his Charles in *recollected situations,* and putting into his mouth words he must pronounce with pleasure; I cannot otherwise account for the parts of Junot and the future Queen of Naples in this piece.

Its plot is simple. The scene is laid at the house of the Mayor of Ruelle; Caroline and Charles, mutually in love, and born the same day, are engaged in marriage. An insufferable coxcomb is desirous of crossing their hopes; but the good genius of the weeping lovers has recourse to Malmaison. The wedding is to be celebrated, and the Empress designs to honour it with her presence. Meanwhile Charles and Caroline sing together to the air of *O ma tendre musette.*

Junot was much affected: those who knew his heart could have no difficulty in divining the nature of his emotions. Not so the lady; she tried to appear moved, but could not succeed. Her feigned agitation was revealed only by the increased *alto* of the tones that came fretfully from her lips, which, however pretty, were never intended for the passage of harmonious sounds.

The Princess Pauline was enchanting in her costume of a peasant bride. The timidity which she really felt, and which a first public appearance cannot fail to excite even in persons of first-rate talent, was most becoming, and enhanced her beauty in an extraordinary degree. The performance was certainly very amusing, both to see and hear. My education in good manners was never more essential to prevent a burst of laughter in the midst of a reply, for though the Princesses might be the two prettiest women in the world, they were certainly two of the worst actresses that ever trod the boards of a theatre.

My part was in the piece of M. de Longchamps, which was by far the prettiest. My dramatic skill was at best but indifferent, and this character quite unsuited to it. I had never aspired beyond the part of waiting-maid, or one of distrust and malice, such as Madame Dervil in the *Rivals*. On this occasion I was to be a very silly, frivolous young girl, goddaughter of the great lady who was expected at Ruelle; and I came to request a compliment for my godmother from the Mayor, whom M. de Montbreton personated to perfection, with an ease and truth seldom to be found in an amateur.

I was quite certain of failing in my performance—a circumstance probably very desirable to others, but quite the reverse to myself. I therefore requested Mademoiselle Mars,* if she had a few minutes to spare, to have the goodness to hear me rehearse; and by the more than urbanity with which she complied, rehearsing with me unweariedly every morning during the fortnight that elapsed before the appointed *fête,* I had an opportunity (of which I perhaps stupidly availed myself far more effectually than of her lessons) of admiring the play of her pliant and charming features, her expressive smile conveying some idea while it disclosed her pearly teeth, and those beaming eyes, which, in accordance with the smile, revealed the coming sentiment before it could find utterance.

Hearing her thus in a private room, divested of all that delusive attraction which the lights, the public plaudits, the whole witchery of the scene cast around an actress on the stage, I mentally exclaimed: "This is the greatest actress in the world! she is pursuing her natural vocation. Here is no appearance of acting; it must therefore be the perfection of the art." From that moment I became a declared and enthusiastic admirer of Mademoiselle Mars, and considered it a public misfortune that she refused to receive pupils.

* One of the best, and most famous, actresses of her time.

In these interviews I had equal reason to appreciate the tone of her conversation, her excellent judgment, and her good taste; I found in Mademoiselle Mars everything that could constitute a woman formed to shine and please in the very best society.

On the important day we breakfasted with the Empress in the stuccoed dining-room on the ground-floor at Malmaison leading to the Emperor's closet. We were five-and-twenty seated at a table, over which the Empress presided with her accustomed grace, and all the simplicity of a hostess in ordinary society. She had desired me to bring my two eldest daughters, Josephine and Constance. Josephine, her goddaughter, was placed beside her. Their English governess accompanied them.

The representation, terminating with a humorous madrigal of birthday congratulation to the Empress, passed off tolerably. The Princess Pauline performed far better than her sister, notwithstanding the vanity of the latter, who is perfectly persuaded that in every word, step, and action she excels all other women.

It was late before we left Malmaison, and our return was rather painful to me, for the Grand Duchess of Berg took it into her head that we should accompany her in her carriage, though I had my own in waiting, and should have much preferred travelling at my ease in it. We had not proceeded far before the Princess was taken ill: it was at Ruelle; I ordered the coachman to stop; the carriage-door was opened, and she alighted, which I would willingly have been excused doing, for the night air, though not absolutely cold, was far from agreeable.

The Princess had had a nervous attack in the course of the day, and had even fainted; when the Empress Josephine, finding a letter entangled in her gown, put it into her hand, which she held closed with her own during her swoon—a trait which deserves publicity. When the Princess recovered and perceived this delicate attention, she said with ill-concealed ill-humour, in reply to a question which no one asked, for the Empress took no notice of the circumstance.

"It is a letter from Murat.

"I very well knew the writer," said the Empress afterwards to me; "for I recognized the hand."

We reached Paris at three in the morning. I set the Princess down, and Junot handed her out of the carriage and conducted her to her apartments; her carriage conveyed me home, but alone.

This little comedy of the 19th of March, 1807, had occupied the whole Imperial Court through the preceding winter, filling it with intrigues, petty hatred, vengeance, and scandal; for, alas! all these existed amongst us, and other bickerings still more despicable. But is not this the secret history of all courts?

One evening the Arch-Chancellor paid me a visit. He appeared thoughtful, and, seating himself beside my sofa, which I could no longer quit, accosted me with: "I bring you strange news; the Emperor is not only re-establishing the ancient *noblesse,* but is creating new titles of rank; and who do you think is the first military Duke? Guess."

"Marshal Lannes?" "Very natural, but not correct." "Marshal Maséna?" The Arch-Chancellor smiled and shook his head. "Well, then, unless it is Bernadotte, who, in spite of his violent republicanism, seems to wear harness as a courtier with perfect docility, I can guess no further."

"It is Lefebvre;* I have just seen his wife." "And not ill chosen. Madame la Maréchale's manner may not be in perfect harmony with her dignity of Duchess, but she is a good wife; besides, you know the Emperor makes no account of us—one difficulty in his choice was therefore obviated; and Lefebvre is one of the most estimable members of our military family. I am sure the Emperor has well weighed his choice."

The Arch-Chancellor, with all his caution, smiled at me, and we understood each other without speaking. It was evident that Napoleon, willing to revive the high nobility and revive the twelve peers of Charlemagne, intended to give additional lustre to his twenty-four Grand Dignitaries of the Empire, which, however, should be the just reward of their services; but it was necessary to feel his way, and to proceed warily with a people who held the very name of King in

* Lefebvre, a brave soldier, had come up from the ranks; his wife had been the regiment's laundress. Napoleon chose him, as his first duke, because no one could have been less like the nobility of the ancien regime.

abhorrence, and had only accepted an Emperor in consideration of the ancient relation of that dignity with a Republic.

Napoleon, surrounded by a thousand perils, never relaxed his precautions; and, though apparently regardless of obstacles, was careful not to shock the men of the Revolution; they were to be gained, but this was no longer a work of difficulty. The temptation was spread before them, and Nature achieved the rest.

No sooner was the bait offered than all, far from repelling it, were eager for a bite, and that which Napoleon presented in the duchy of Dantzic was of the most attractive kind. Aware of this, he would not confer it where it might in any case be liable to abuse, and Marshal Lefebvre, esteemed by the army and all true Frenchmen, and deserving of the highest reward of valour, was the person best adapted to the Emperor's purpose.

The important question which at this time agitated the Imperial Court was how the new Duchess would bear her dignity, and she speedily resolved it. She went to the Tuileries to thank the Empress Josephine for the favour the Emperor had just conferred. The Empress was in the great yellow salon; and as Madame la Maréchale had not demanded an audience, the usher, accustomed to call her by that name, entered to take the orders of the Chamberlain-in-Waiting; he returned and addressed her: "Madame la Maréchale may enter." The lady looked askance at him; but suppressing all audible tokens of indignation she entered the salon; and the Empress, rising from the sofa she usually occupied beside the fireplace, advanced a few steps to meet her, saying with that engaging graciousness she could always assume when it pleased her:

"How is the Duchess of Dantzic?" La Maréchale, instead of answering, winked intelligently, and then, turning towards the usher, who was in the act of shutting the door, *"Hey, my boy,"* said she, *"what do you think of that?"* How was it possible for the most determined gravity to resist such an attack? Towards the end of the Empire the Duchess of Dantzic became tiresome, and almost as rational in her speech as Madame Fabre de l'Aude, who once answered the Emperor's query when she would lie in of her twenty-fifth child: "When your Majesty pleases." But the Maréchale Lefebvre, or the Duchess of Dantzic, as you may please to call her, was very amusing at the time her husband was made a Duke (a year before the other Generals), and for a long time maintained her eccentric character under the ducal dignity.

While we in Paris were celebrating our conquests at five hundred leagues' distance with dancing and various diversions, all Europe was marching at the Emperor's bidding; and already new plans were succeeding to those of which a few weeks had witnessed the accomplishment.

A great misfortune befell the family of the Empress Josephine in the death of the eldest son of Queen Hortense, who died in Holland of the croup. The letters of Madame de Brock described the grief of the Queen as so violent as to threaten irreparable injury to her health. Whatever might be the projects of the Empress, her heart was deeply smitten by this event. She seemed to apprehend the menace of divorce in every tear that was shed over the tomb of the young Prince. "Oh, what a misfortune!" she continually repeated with sobs of distress. It is impossible to speak too highly of the young Prince Louis, who, had he lived to fulfil the promise of his childhood, must have become a distinguished character. He bore a striking resemblance to his father, and consequently to the Emperor, from which likeness the malice which pursued the Emperor even into his holiest affections has invented a calumny so infamous that I should degrade myself by refuting it.

The Queen of Holland left her marshes and aquatic plains to come and seek, not consolation—for what mother consoles herself for the loss of her child?—but an alleviation of the despair which was undermining her health. She went to the Pyrenees, to Cauterets, and from thence made the famous tour of the Vignemale. From her gracious manners and benevolence she was positively adored by the inhabitants of this district.

Queen Hortense came to Paris, after the season for visiting the watering-places, in this same year, 1807, and brought back to us the charming parties where the most distinguished artists of France came to bring their tributes to a Princess whose proficiency in the arts enabled her so perfectly to appreciate them. How delightfully did the hours pass in such gifted society! There, at a round table, sat Gérard, with his immortal pencil; Isabey, whose productions may be imitated but never equalled; Garnery, who, after working long upon a pretty design for an album, ended by sketching the room we were in, with such fidelity that its most trifling articles of furniture might be recognized, and yet with such excellent effect that no minuteness of detail was observable.

But the talents of the mistress of the mansion were worthy to compete with those of her distinguished guests, and were in no way more remarkable than in the extraordinary resemblance and beautiful effect of her portrait sketches. Thus the Queen possessed a unique collection of drawings, if in her adventurous peregrinations she did not lose them. I have seen in her albums faces which no doubt would have been surprised to find themselves in company. It was at this time that she composed *Partant pour la Syrie! Reposez-vous, bons chevaliers, Le beau Dunois, Le bon Chevalier, En soupirant j'ai vu maître l'Aurore,* and many other romances which we still know and sing, and which I always sing with renewed pleasure. Queen Hortense is no longer here to receive flattery; and truly her productions may be praised with a very clear conscience.

Amongst other talents she possessed in a remarkable degree that of attracting friendship. I have always thought that had she succeeded her reign would have been fortunate, because many of the good actions which in other Princes result only from policy would have originated with her in love of her duties and of the public weal. She would have perfectly understood that her peace of mind depended upon the well-being of her people. She would often have pardoned when she had the power of punishing, looking upon vengeance as the attribute of a base mind.

I N spite of Mme Junot's occasional defense of the Imperial court's morality, it was in fact neither more nor less dissolute than any other contemporary ruling group. Napoleon himself had many mistresses; Pauline took one lover after the other, as did Caroline and Elisa; Hortense de Beauharnais, Louis's wife, had children by men other than her husband, and the same went on at every level of Society. Still, the Emperor had one strict criterion: however his relatives actually behaved, there must be no scandal —not for moral reasons, but because he did not want the Bonapartes to become the laughing stock of Europe.

It was no surprise, therefore, that he should have been furious when Caroline took Junot as her lover and proceeded to advertise the fact. As he soon discovered, though, that was still better than what came next.

While Junot was having his affair, Mme Junot (who was not quite the virtuous wife she makes herself out to be) was having an almost equally public affair with Count Metternich, the highly seductive Austrian ambassador (and later Chancellor). What both Caroline and Metternich had in common, as it turned out, was a thirst for knowledge: as Governor of Paris, Junot had access to the latest and most confidential dispatches. Caroline needed to know as much as she could so as to influence her brother; Metternich, who rightly thought Mme Junot would whisper many a secret to her lover, wanted to keep Vienna informed; and both succeeded.

There was a difference, though: whereas Mme Junot had been relatively discreet, Junot and Caroline had flaunted their affair. It was thus easy to get the Emperor to put an end to it; but then, the infuriated Caroline took her revenge by seducing Metternich. For the Austrian, Caroline was obviously better than Laure as a pro-vider of news; and, if we are to judge by his later behaviour, she was also better in bed. Be that as it may, the outcome of this quick change was that Laure, who not unnaturally felt that a faithless husband was bad, but losing a lover was worse, and Caroline, who flaunted her triumph, eventually had a screaming fight, thus causing the greatest scandal of all. And that was fol-lowed by a tremendous scene Junot made when he discovered his wife had been unfaithful. The poor Laure was severely beaten, and when she reappeared in public with a black eye, everyone knew just why.

The Emperor, on his return to Paris from the campaign against Prussia, was received with as much joy as when he came from Marengo. Accla-mations and harangues were not spared, and addresses poured in from all quarters of the kingdom. Adulation did not prompt these addresses.

They were the expression of the enthusiasm of France—an enthusiasm amounting to delirium, and which Napoleon rejoiced to accept. The Emperor returned to Paris about the end of July, 1807, and this event produced results very important to my family.

I had long foreseen them, but unhappily had no power of prevention. I loved Junot, but I had not reproached him on account of his connection with the Grand Duchess of Berg, because I never considered it criminal. I saw, however, the course he was running, and the end to which it would inevitably lead. The Emperor had a peculiar mode of thinking relative to his sisters, which led him to exact from them the strictest propriety in their conduct; and he believed it to be true that none of the Princesses had ever given occasion for the slightest reflection upon their reputations. Up to this period it had been a matter of indifference to Fouché, and to another whom I will not name because he is living, whether the Emperor's sisters caused the world to talk of them or not—whether M. le Comte de Fl——, M. de C——, etc., compromised these ladies, or were compromised by them.

The Princesses were gracious to Savary, Fouché, and others, and the Emperor was the only person who remained in ignorance of what all the world knew. He thought that the Princess Pauline was an inconsistent beauty, wearing a pretty ball-dress in disobedience to Corvisart, and only guilty of not keeping the house when ordered by her physician. Hitherto these ladies had never been betrayed by the superintending authorities; but when it became known that a man they did not like might be ruined by a direct accusation, this complaisance ceased. Alas, I had long foreseen it!

When the Emperor arrived at Paris the storm had already gathered. The clouds had been collecting in Poland. The Emperor had received written intimations that Junot was compromising the Grand Duchess of Berg; that his livery was seen at unsuitable hours in the Court of the Elysée, and that numerous corroborating circumstances might be adduced. It was one of Junot's comrades, still living, who preferred this accusation. Napoleon's heart was wounded by this news, and when Junot presented himself before him on his return he met with a stern reception and constrained language. Junot's fiery spirit could not endure the Emperor's coldness, and he asked an audience. It was immediately granted, and was stormy. The Emperor accused him without reserve, and Junot, sorely wounded, would not answer upon any point, asserting that the Emperor ought to depend upon his care for the honour of his name.

"Sire!" he exclaimed, "when at Marseilles I loved the Princess Pauline, and you were upon the point of giving her to me—I loved her to distraction—yet what was my conduct? Was it not that of a man of honour? I am not changed since that period; I am still equally devoted to you and yours. Sire, your mistrust is injurious to me." The Emperor listened, watching him meanwhile with marked attention; then walked the room in silence, with his arms crossed and a menacing brow. "I am willing to believe all that you say," at length he replied; "but you are not the less guilty of imprudence, and imprudence in your situation towards my sister amounts to a fault, if not to worse. Why, for example, does the Grand Duchess occupy your boxes at the theatres? Why does she go thither in your carriage? Hey! M. Junot! you are surprised that I should be so well acquainted with your affairs and those of that little fool Madame Murat?"

Junot was confounded at finding that the Emperor had been informed of this circumstance, which, nevertheless, was sufficiently important, considering the relative situation of the two personages, to fix the attention not only of the police, but of the public; nothing but the infatuation, which so often blinds those who are entering upon the career of ruin, could have caused his astonishment at the natural consequences which had followed his conduct.

"Yes," continued the Emperor, "I know all that and many other facts which I am willing to look upon as imprudences only; but in which also I see serious faults on your part. Once more, why this carriage with your livery? Your livery should not be seen at two o'clock in the morning in the courtyard of the Grand Duchess of Berg. *You, Junot! You* compromise my sister!" And Napoleon fell into a chair.

Before proceeding further I wish to explain the motives which have induced me to raise the veil which with my own hand I have thrown over the private life of Junot. All the other connections which he formed acted only upon my own happiness, and in no way upon his destiny. Here the case was totally different. I do not hesitate to ascribe all my husband's misfortunes, and even his death, to his unhappy entanglement with the Queen of Naples. I do not charge this connection with real criminality; I even believe that there was only the appearance of it; but the suspicious appearances which really did exist led to the most fatal consequences: they kindled the lion's wrath. Subsequently, circumstances produced an eruption of the long-smothered volcano, and the tempest burst forth.

At present my readers must return with me to the Tuileries, to the closet of Napoleon, and there see him, not alone, but in company with those who poisoned his life by their daily, nay, hourly reports. It was not Lannes, it was not Bessières, it was not Masséna, it was not even Soult, for I must do him justice, though, for what reason I know not, he does not like me; neither was it Duroc, notwithstanding all that has been said again and again upon the subject of his police of the interior of the palace; neither was it Junot, notwithstanding the quantity of reports which he received daily as *active* Governor of Paris, a personage who no longer exists except in memory; it was none of these men: they had notions of honour which would have made them feel an antipathy to such conduct; neither was it Rapp, with his rough exterior but noble soul, who would thus have betrayed the secret of a comrade's heart to soil twenty pages of a scandalous report, which was destined to serve no useful end or political interest, but simply for a moment to engage the curiosity of the Emperor, whose singular turn of mind on these subjects led him to take a real pleasure in knowing how many grains of salt I or anyone else might strew upon a buttered muffin.

The men who played this odious part are well known, and universal contempt has amply recompensed their infamous conduct. Two in particular carried in their countenances sufficient indications for the judgment of the public. The one is dead, and as a Christian I have forgiven him all the evil he did to Junot; but as a widow and mother I have not forgiven him the irreparable wrong which the father of my children suffered from him. The other, as guilty, is not yet gone to give an account of his conduct as a man and a citizen before the tribunal of his Maker. He not only lives, but he still injures; he menaces, he acts, he is influential in evil. Such were the men who filled the poisoned cup which the Emperor compelled his oldest friend to drink!

The Emperor's ignorance respecting the real conduct of his sisters is inconceivable, for his eagle eye penetrated many other mysteries.

Fouché, Junot, Duroc, and Dubois, the four persons in whose hands all the State police of Paris and France was vested, were silent upon what they knew on this subject, because it would have distressed the Emperor; none of them was willing to do this. It came to his knowledge at last, but clandestinely, and through a channel so unusual that he placed but little confidence in the rumour, which he attributed to the imprudence of young women, and said to Madame Mère: *"Le diable!* Signora Letizia, why do you not reprimand your daughters, and warn them against compromising themselves with a tribe of young fops? Let them dance with the officers of my Guard; they are brave men at least, if they are not handsome."

I shall not undertake to answer all the calumnies which have been attempted to be fastened upon the family connections of the Emperor. It is sufficient to have lived in intimacy with Napoleon to know his mode of thinking upon matters of morality; my blood boils when I hear him accused of *corruption.* A scene at Malmaison, recorded in a former part of these Memoirs, will perhaps be brought in evidence against me. I answer by referring to the scene itself. Napoleon employed no manoeuvres to induce me to accede. Had I yielded to his will he would have despised me, for the wife of his friend, failing in duty to her husband through the allurements of the Sovereign, would have appeared infamous in his eyes.

Napoleon was not informed of the indiscretions of one of his sisters until the time of the Portuguese War; and the man who was accused of causing them was almost exiled to Junot's Staff. I know that those who chose to turn everything into ridicule will assert that it is impossible. It is a fact, however; and suspicion once infused into such a mind as his, everything became speedily known to him. Still he would have remained ignorant of the adventures of Messieurs de Septeuil and de Canouville if the histories of the horse and pelisse, and of the explanation, had not come to enlighten him—but these circumstances belong to the year 1810.

Junot's indiscretion, then, was the first which reached the Emperor's ear, and, as I have shown, it violently irritated him. "Suppose," said he, walking up and down the room, "Murat should become acquainted with all these fine stories of the chase at Raincy, the theatres, and your carriage and livery." It seems that the carriage and livery offended him most highly. Junot attempted to excuse himself by observing upon the brilliancy of that of the Grand Duchess; the Emperor stamped with violence, and looked at him for some time without speaking; at length he said in a voice of severity, and an interrogative tone: "And what colour are your liveries, then?" Junot cast down his eyes and said nothing.

The fact is, that the colour of our livery was precisely the same as that of the Grand Duchess; the difference was in the trimming and lace, the Grand Duchess's being turned up with white and gold lace, ours with yellow and silver; the coat of amaranth cloth was of precisely the same shade in both. This similarity was, in truth, the will of the Grand Duchess; I always thought that it was to serve some crafty purpose, and now I found my suspicions proved.

"Yes," said the Emperor, still pacing the room, "if Murat had learned all that I have been repeating, what would he say? What would he do? You would have had a terrible storm to encounter!" Junot's countenance instantly changed; at length, recovering all his energy, he made two steps towards Napoleon, and said firmly: "If Murat should believe himself offended, it is not so long since we were on equal terms, both on the field of battle and elsewhere, but that I should be ready to give him all the satisfaction he could wish for. Though the Cossacks may be afraid of him, I am not quite so easily frightened, and this time I should fight with pistols." "Ah! truly," cried the Emperor, with admirable naïveté, "that is precisely what I feared;" and then he added in a gentle tone: "But I have settled that; I have spoken to him and all is right."

"Sire, I thank you; but I must observe to your Majesty that I cannot consent to an accommodation being arranged between the Grand Duke of Berg and myself; if he believes himself offended, which I deny that he has any right to be, he can easily find me; my hotel is very near the Elysée." "Yes, yes," said the Emperor, "much too near; and à propos of that, what is the meaning of the frequent visits my sister has been making to your wife?" "Sire, my wife is much indisposed, and cannot go out without great care. Her Imperial Highness the Grand Duchess has done her the favour to come and see her two or three times this spring, which is the amount of the numerous visits that have been reported to your Majesty." "That is not true," replied the Emperor, taking a long letter from a drawer near him, and looking it entirely through, while his brow became more and more contracted. Junot cast a momentary glance upon the letter and recognized the writing. "I beg your Majesty's pardon, but if you condemn your sister and your oldest friend and most faithful servant upon the accusations of the writer of that letter, I cannot believe you impartial."

Napoleon seemed surprised, but made no objection to this observation; an almost imperceptible smile seemed to curl his lip, and Junot proceeded: "Besides, Sire, this is not a letter, for he* was with your Majesty; it is therefore *a report, a report of his police,* copied by him! It must be a beautiful production! He ought at least to have respected your Majesty's sister; but there are very efficacious means of teaching people circumspection and politeness; and I shall employ them with him." "Junot," exclaimed the Emperor, "I forbid you to fight Savary." Junot smiled contemptuously. "You have suspected me, you have accused me of treachery, Sire; I cannot ask satisfaction of you for this; I must then go and demand it of him who has caused me all this pain, and, by Heavens! I will. If afterwards Murat has any commands for me, I am at his service; unless, indeed, this paltry fellow should send a ball through my head, which is possible, for I have known very indifferent soldiers kill a brave man. But if I come out of this affair safe and sound I shall be ready to attend the Grand Duke of Berg."

Napoleon rose impetuously, and coming to Junot, who was leaning against the mantelpiece, took him hastily by the hand, and turning him sharply towards himself, said to him in a loud and agitated tone: "Once more I command you to keep the peace! Neither Savary nor Murat; I will not permit you to fight either with the one or the other." Then drawing nearer to Junot and again taking his hand, he pressed it affectionately, saying: "Come, promise your old friend."

With Napoleon such moments were brief, but they were triumphant; he never failed to come off conqueror on such an occasion. There was an irresistible charm in his look and in his voice which was sure to overcome the firmest resolution. Junot felt his anger giving way under their powerful influence; he clasped the Emperor's hand, and pressed it to his heart, which beat violently; and the Emperor, on

* General Savary.

feeling its agitated pulsation, also experienced a moment of indefinable but visible emotion; nevertheless he overcame it, gently withdrew his hand, passed it through Junot's thick light hair, and tapping his head, said with his melodious voice, which vibrated like an Aeolian harp: "Promise me to be reasonable, wrong-head; and come to me again, I have more to say to you."

This conversation had lasted an hour and a half. The waiting-room was full of persons all upon the watch to learn the result of this long conference. One man in particular wished it shorter. He knew the Emperor, and he knew that very long audiences were never accorded to men about to fall under his displeasure; and Junot's countenance, when he at last came out, confirmed his opinion. Junot passed within two paces of him, but affected not to see him: "For I could not have avoided telling him my opinion of his conduct," said Junot to me when we were in Spain eighteen months afterwards, and more united than ever, conversing confidentially upon this period of his life, of which he revealed to me the most minute circumstances.

R I G H T from the beginning of the Empire, Napoleon realized that putting his relatives on thrones was all very well, but that it would not remove the stigma of the parvenu from either them or himself. The solution was obviously a series of intermarriages between the Bonapartes (and Beauharnais) and members of Europe's old ruling families. The first of these took place between Princess Augusta of Bavaria and Eugène de Beauharnais. This, at least, had not been forced on the Bavarian royal family: as France's most faithful ally, the ruler had just been raised from the status of Elector to that of King. By the time it came to Jerome, however, the family of Princess Catherine of Württemberg was given no choice at all.

Princess Catherine was a good match, in the Emperor's eyes, not because of either beauty or virtue—in fact, she was attractive, intelligent and kind—but because she was related to most of the crowned heads of Europe, not least Tsar Alexander's mother.

Thus, at one blow, the Bonapartes became cousins of the most illustrious dynasties.

Of course, there was more to come: when, in 1809, Napoleon divorced Josephine, he chose as her replacement a Habsburg Archduchess who, among other qualities, was Marie Antoinette's grandniece, thus allowing the Emperor to refer casually to his aunt, the late Queen. To be fair, Napoleon also thought that the marriage would consolidate his alliance with Austria; but there he erred badly. If, sometimes, in middle class families, blood is thicker than water, this was not at all the case among European dynasties. In 1813, Francis I of Austria, Marie Louise's father, did not hesitate to declare war on Napoleon; and when, in 1814, his troops entered Paris, he did not scruple to dethrone his daughter and his son-in-law.

It was the 20th of August, 1807; Junot had made all his preparations for his journey back to Portugal, and was gone to dine with M. Lalligant, one of his friends, to whose child he and Madame de Caraman were to stand sponsors. The house was encumbered with chests and portmanteaux, the courtyard with baggage-waggons and carriages; everything announced the approaching departure of the master of the mansion: in fact, in two days Junot was about to set out for Bordeaux, the place of his immediate destination.

I had superintended all that was to make the journey agreeable, and I was fatigued; but at nine o'clock, just as I was going to bed, my *valet-de-chambre* informed me that one of the Emperor's footmen was in waiting to deliver a letter to Junot from the Grand Marshal. I took the letter, which was endorsed, *The Grand Marshal of the Palace;* and beside this signature, in scarcely legible writing, were the words *In great haste;* the whole address was in Duroc's hand. I made two men mount on horseback, wrote a few words for each of them, and sent them in different directions to find Junot; but while they were in search of him he arrived. He had been to a certain hotel, where he had learned the purport of Duroc's letter, which was to the following effect:

"The Princess Royal of Württemberg,* my dear Junot, will arrive at Raincy with her suite to-morrow morning at nine o'clock, and will rest there till seven in the evening. His Majesty has made this arrangement. Will you have the goodness to give orders that everything should be in readiness to receive her? I will send whatever you think requisite for her proper accommodation, and for the kitchen service.

"I renew my assurances of attachment to you.

"Duroc.

"20th—at six in the evening."

"Well!" said I to Junot, after reading it, "a pretty task they are setting us! it is much like one of the orders given to the Princess Graciosa by her tyrannical stepmother; but the misfortune is, we have no Prince Percinet with his wand." Junot walked about with an anxious look. I saw that I had done wrong in complaining, which would but increase his ill-humour, and, going up to him with a smile, I said:

"But standing there like the god Terminus will not forward this business that I am complaining of, and which, after all, is not worth talking about. It appears that her Royal Highness is to spend the whole day with us at Raincy; it will be your affair to dispose matters so that she shall not be weary of us; which is just possible, because neither the dogs nor the stags are packed up, so that you will be able to show her a hunt; and if it should not be quite so agreeable to you as your chase by the light of flambeaux the Princess will understand that, with the best intentions in the world, it is only possible to give what one has. Come, answer Duroc; or do you wish me to do it?" And I went to my desk. Junot looked at me, listened, and seemed to wake up by degrees; his fine countenance, to which gloom was not at all becoming, cleared up, and at last became even cheerful. "Yes, answer him," he replied, embracing me slightly.

I wrote to Duroc that we were about to give the necessary orders for the reception of her Royal Highness, and that Junot and I returned thanks to the Emperor for giving us this new opportunity of proving our devotedness to him. I thanked Duroc for his offer of sending us all

* Who was to marry Jerome, the Emperor's youngest brother.

things necessary for the service, but added: "This would inconvenience rather than assist us; and I engage to be perfectly prepared for the reception of the Princess at the hour appointed."

I then sent for Rechaud. This Rechaud was a clever, and in our present dilemma a most important, personage: he was, moreover, a thoroughly honest man, a qualification not often to be found combined with skill in his profession. He and his brother had been brought up in the kitchen of the Prince of Condé, and afterwards became so expert in cookery that they attained great celebrity in the gastronomic world. Rechaud had previously given me a specimen of his ability in the direction in which it was now wanted, by preparing in a few hours for the reception of the Marquis de la Romana at Raincy in great form. I explained the state of the case, and he instantly understood all that was to be done. "Madame may set out for Raincy," he said with a *sang-froid* worthy of Vatel; "everything shall be ready at the time mentioned."

I knew Rechaud, and, getting into my carriage, set out for Raincy without any anxiety, at ten o'clock at night, and in delightful weather. On reaching the mansion I found carts already arrived with provisions for the morrow. All night the road to Raincy was travelled over by goers and comers transporting thither whatever was needful, not simply for food, but for luxury. The next morning, before I was up, Rechaud tapped at the door of the bath-room, where I had slept to leave my apartment for the use of the Princess of Württemberg, in case she should wish to retire to it upon her arrival; he came to tell me that everything was quite ready.

Neither had I been idle in the department which fell under my superintendence; all the apartments were in perfect order for the reception of the Princess and suite, even to the superb bath-room, which was prepared in case the Princess should choose to leave the dust of her journey in one of its fine marble basins. One thing teased me sadly: it was my curiosity to know why the Princess, on arriving within four leagues of Paris, should be detained there a visitor to the Governor of the City without daring to proceed.

My husband pretty well understood both the Emperor's orders in this matter and his reasons for them. He did not choose that the Princess Royal of Württemberg should make such an entrance into Paris as the Duchess of Burgundy and her sister the fair Gabrielle of Savoy might have made; and when he found that the march of the Princess had been so stupidly calculated that she would arrive within sight of the Barriers at ten o'clock in the morning, he determined that she should not pass them till eight in the evening, and that she should remain in the interim at some private villa which might be hired for the occasion.

The Emperor was going to dismiss Duroc after having given him these orders, when he cried out suddenly: "Oh! *parbleu!*—Junot—Junot has Raincy—the Princess must spend the day at Raincy. It is a charming place, and I hope she will think it a great deal more beautiful than the huge demi-Gothic castles of Suabia and Bavaria. Besides, Madame Junot knows how to speak to crowned heads. Then write to Junot that the Princess Catherine of Württemberg will pass to-morrow with him and his wife."

The Princess arrived at Raincy exactly at nine o'clock, as had been announced. She possessed the German preciseness, even in its minutest details. I was impatient to become acquainted with her. Jerome's fate could not be indifferent to me, for I had loved him from childhood, and though he only had treated me with coldness at the death of my mother, I still continued very much attached to him. He had sworn to me, when we met at breakfast in Estremadura, that he should never forget the mother of his son, her who had given him a paradise in a strange country. I involuntarily thought of that young victim, who was said to be so beautiful, and who was so affectionate! who had had a child! but was that child to become an orphan?

It was therefore with a strong prepossession against her that I approached the Princess of Württemberg with my welcome. She received me with perfect grace, and assured me that if she had known my situation she would have sent me a courier early in the morning to desire me not to rise to receive her.

The Princess of Württemberg, at the time I am speaking of, was about nineteen or twenty years of age; she was handsome; the turn of her head gave her an expression of dignified pride which became her noble brow, and which would have been still more graceful had her neck, and indeed her whole figure, been something less short. She was not pretty in the general acceptation of the word, though all her features were good, for she seldom smiled, and the expression of her countenance wanted urbanity; it was, if not disagreeable, at least exceedingly haughty, and was dignified and serious, rather than pleasing and gracious; her head was too much sunk between her shoulders, though she held it as high as possible to lose nothing of her stature, which was low. At the moment I first saw her this characteristic haughtiness was more than usually conspicuous.

At first this expression struck me as very disagreeable, notwithstanding her extreme politeness to myself; but in a few minutes I understood her feelings, and, far from blaming them, felt myself much interested in her situation. It was really a very painful one, and it was not for me, *a woman,* to be insensible to it. Two days previously the Princess had been separated from all her German attendants. The Emperor, though he did not like Louis XIV, chose him for a model in matters of etiquette; and as he had isolated the foreign Princesses who came into France, whether from the North, as in the case of the wife of his brother, or from the South, as the Duchess of Burgundy, so the Princess of Württemberg was separated from her German Household, notwithstanding a reluctance very natural to one in her situation. This situation was not similar to that of all Princesses quitting their own country to share a foreign throne; she was obliged at the same time to surmount the national prejudice so strongly rooted amongst the Germans against unequal alliances (and if the Emperor, surrounded by the halo of his glory, that dominating spell which commands admiration, might be excepted from the ban, it was not so with his brothers); and the bitter consideration that she was about to give her hand to a man who had already contracted a marriage, which gave to another woman still living the rights of wife and mother.

This knowledge, sufficiently distressing to anyone, must have been doubly so to a Princess condemned to silence, constraint, and dissimulation, and to the concealment of her tears from new servants, whose presence thus made the hours of retirement more heavy than those of public ceremonial. The Princess of Württemberg, then, was received on her entrance into the French territory by the Court of Honour which the Emperor had sent to meet her, and which was wholly taken from that of the Empress, and Marshal Bessières had espoused the Princess as proxy for the Prince.

On the arrival of the Princess at Raincy she was offered a bath in the elegant bath-room, but refused it, and seemed desirous to have an early breakfast. As I did not know what she might like, I had prepared two breakfast services, that she might take hers in her own apartment if she preferred it; but she declined, and even expressed a wish that all my inmates should breakfast with her, desiring me to invite them in her name.

She seemed uneasy, as far as the impassibility of her countenance allowed me to judge, at the delay of her father's Minister, M. de Winzingerode, who did not arrive until ten o'clock: he was a young man, tall, fair, without the smallest degree of expression in his eye, smile, or attitude; his wife, who was also expected, did not come, for some reason which I do not now recollect. The countenance of the Princess, upon seeing the Ambassador, immediately changed, which further convinced me that my former observation of the constraint she had imposed upon herself was correct: it was clear she was in a state of great suffering; the unexpected removal of her German suite had depressed her, even to the injury of her health, which was manifestly affected.

Breakfast was over by half-past eleven o'clock; I asked the Princess whether she would like to witness a stag-hunt in the park, and whether she would ride on horseback or in an open carriage. She chose the carriage, and having ordered two of those sort of basket sociables which are used by the ladies who follow the chase at Fontainebleau and Rambouillet, we set out to make the round of the forest of Bondy; then re-entering the park by the gate of Chelles, we were met by the huntsmen and hounds, and a young buck was turned out, which was almost immediately taken and very much maltreated by the dogs. The Princess, who at first was serious, if not melancholy, became more cheerful as we rode, and at length seemed very well pleased. The heat being excessive, we returned to the house as the clock struck three, leaving, indeed, not more than time enough for the party to dress for dinner.

When the Princess came into the drawing-room half an hour before dinner-time I felt some regret that no one had had the courage to recommend her a different style of dress. She was about to have a first interview with a man on whom was to depend the happiness of her future life, and whose youthful imagination, poetical as is natural to the natives of the South, could adorn an absent object with additional charms, while Madame Jerome Bonaparte, without the aid of imagination, was really a charming woman.

As the Princess Catherine had made up her mind to give her hand to Prince Jerome, it was the more desirable that she should please him, as, notwithstanding his too ready submission to the will of Napoleon, it was certain he regretted his divorced wife, for Miss Patterson really was his wife, and it would have been politic to appear before him with all the advantages dress could bestow, while, on the contrary, hers was in inconceivably bad taste for the year 1807.

The gown was of white moiré, but of a bluish white, which was out of fashion at the time, and trimmed in front with a very badly-worked silver embroidery, in a style which had also been forgotten: then the cut of the dress itself corresponded exactly with its trimming in point of novelty; it was a very tight frock, with a little train exactly resembling the round tail of the beaver, and tight flat sleeves, compressing the arm above the elbow like a bandage after blood-letting. Her shoes were so pointed that they seemed to belong to the era of King John. The hair was dressed in a similarly old-fashioned style, and was particularly unbecoming to a countenance of which not only the features were good, but the expression very striking.

Her complexion was very fair and fresh, her hair light, her eyes blue, her teeth very white; all which, with a turn of the head at once gracious and dignified, gave her personal advantages which she seemed to despise by the total indifference with which she permitted those about her to take the entire management of her dress. She wore round her neck two rows of very fine pearls, to which was suspended the portrait of the Prince set in diamonds; the size of the medallion having probably been left to the taste of the jeweller, he had made it of dimensions capable of carrying the greatest possible number of jewels, but certainly much too large to be ornamental, as it dangled from the neck of the Princess, and inflicted heavy blows at every movement.

Rank, however, goes for much in all cases, for her Royal Highness, in this tasteless attire, entered the drawing-room of Raincy with the same majestic air which distinguished her at Saint Cloud two months after, when she walked the gallery in a full Court suit, embroidered by

Lenormand, and made by Leroy, her hair dressed by Frederic or Charbonnier, and her neck ornamented by a magnificent necklace admirably set by Foncier or Nitot. Then her apparent indifference to such trifles proved what widely different subjects occupied her really superior mind in this, perhaps, the most important moment of her life.

By her own desire, the ladies only were to dine with her, and in consequence I ordered the dinner in the library, a large rotunda in the left wing of the mansion looking upon the park. We were six, including the Princess and her three ladies, for her Royal Highness was good enough to permit my friend Madame Lallemand to join our party, though she had not yet been presented.

A few moments before the dinner was announced I remarked that the Princess was much agitated. I concluded that she had some wish which she felt unwilling to express to the strangers who surrounded her, and who, in a moment when above all others she stood in need of sympathy, would probably answer her only by a respectful smile or with perfect indifference. I therefore approached her, and, without abruptly putting the question, I led her on to speak to me with more confidence than she had yet done to any of the persons in her service. "Would it be possible," said she, "for me to have some minutes' notice previous to the Prince's arrival?" She coloured highly as she finished these words.

This emotion, which was certainly not the effect of love, must have been very painful; I appeared not to remark it, and congratulated myself on the facility with which I could gratify her Royal Highness's wishes. Raincy is perhaps the only country-seat in the neighbourhood of Paris which would afford this convenience. Its avenue of poplars leading from the highroad nearly to the grand entrance of the mansion is almost three furlongs in length.

I mentioned the Princess's wish to Junot, who thought with me that she was desirous of preparing her mind for an interview of which she had probably a painful anticipation. He immediately gave orders to M. de Grandsaigne to take his station at the end of the avenue nearest to the house, and the moment the Prince's carriages should appear to bring me word. I informed the Princess that her wishes should be attended to, and we sat down to table, while Junot entertained Marshal Bessières and the rest of her Royal Highness's suite in the dining-room.

The dinner was dull. I watched the movements of the Princess, which were more restless than in the morning; her cheeks were highly flushed, and her absent manner betrayed an inward agitation, disguised by the dignity which she had been taught. We remained but a short time at table; when I had twice asked whether her Royal Highness would like to take her coffee and ice in the park or in the great salon, she looked at me with the air of a person who hears without understanding, and said: "Eh? Whichever you please."

At half-past six we retired to the salon, and the Princess having asked me whether I had thought of her wishes, I went to inquire if Junot had taken care that his *vedette* was at his post. But finding that Junot, Bessières, and the rest of the gentlemen, relieved from their attendance by the wish of the Princess, thought only of lengthening out the pleasures of a good dinner, and that the dining-room was sending out loud evidences of their joviality, I went myself to the Russian cottage, where poor M. de Grandsaigne was dining all alone, and pointing his opera-glass down the avenue.

I also looked down the avenue and saw nothing.

But at the moment I was about to return into the house a cloud of dust arose on the road to Paris, and presently several carriages entered the avenue. I then immediately went to give notice to the Princess, who thanked me with a half-smile which was painful to witness. Her face assumed a deep scarlet hue, and her agitation for a moment was alarming; but it subsided, at least outwardly, and she quickly regained her self-command.

She called Madame de Luçay to her, and probably gave her orders that her departure should immediately follow the interview; she then took her station in the salon where it was to take place. This salon, as previously described, is divided into three parts, the music-room being at one extremity, the billiard-room at the other, and the reception or drawing-room in the middle. In this centre division the Princess seated herself beside the chimney, having an arm-chair near her which was intended for the Prince. We were all in the billiard-room, from whence we could see all that passed in the drawing-room, being separated from it only by a range of pillars with statues in the inter-columniations. The Prince was to enter by the music-room.

Already the rolling of the carriage-wheels in the avenue was heard, when Madame Lallemand, catching hold of my dress, exclaimed: "Do you know it has just crossed my mind that the sight of me at this moment may make an awkward impression upon the Prince. I had better retire." "Why?" "Because the last time he saw me was at Baltimore with Miss Patterson,* with whom I was very intimate. Do you not think that seeing me again, on such an occasion as the present, might recall a great deal that has passed?" "Indeed I do!" I exclaimed, thrusting her into the adjoining room, for at this moment a noise in the hall announced the Prince's arrival, and in a few seconds the door was opened and Marshal Bessières introduced him.

Prince Jerome was accompanied by the officers of his Household, among whom were Cardinal Maury, the Chief Almoner, and M. Alexandre le Camus, who already possessed great influence over him, and who felt it advisable not to lose sight of him on an occasion to which his advice had given rise, and which might prove important to his future career. I do not believe that Jerome would ever have abandoned Miss Patterson if he had not been urged to it by counsels which he had not strength of mind enough to resist.

The salon of Raincy seemed to be made expressly for the interview which was now to take place. The Princess was seated near the chimney, though there was no fire. The Prince's attendants remained in the music-room during the interview. On the Prince's entrance she rose, advanced two steps towards him, and greeted him with equal grace and dignity. Jerome bowed neither well nor ill, but somewhat mechanically, and he seemed to be there because he had been told "You must go there." He approached the Princess, who seemed at this moment to have recovered all her presence of mind, and all the calm dignity of the woman and the Princess. After the exchange of a few words she offered to the Prince the arm-chair, which had been placed near her, and a conversation was opened upon the subject of her journey. It was short, and closed by Jerome's rising and saying, "My brother is waiting for us; I will not longer deprive him of the pleasure of making acquaintance with the new sister I am about to give him."

The Princess smiled, and accompanied the Prince as far as the en-

* Jerome, while in Baltimore, had married Miss Patterson; the Emperor eventually forced a divorce on him.

trance of the music-room, whence he retired with his attendants. As soon as she had lost sight of him, the colour in her cheeks increased so violently that I feared the bursting of a blood-vessel. She admitted indisposition; we gave her air and eau-de-Cologne; in a few minutes she recovered her self-possession. This fainting-fit, though laid to the account of heat and fatigue, was certainly occasioned by the violent restraint the Princess had for some hours put upon herself.

I have heard the devotedness of the Queen of Westphalia* very highly eulogized, and in fact it was truly noble in her peculiar situation. She was ready to set out when Junot came to inform her that her carriages were drawn up. I stayed at Raincy, for the day had been so fatiguing that I was unable to undergo another Court ceremonial. The Princess at the moment of her departure approached me, and said with a gracious smile: "Madame Junot, I shall never forget Raincy and the hospitality I have experienced here. This place will always recall some of the most pleasing moments of my life." Here was a speech worthy of the King, her father, an adept in diplomacy; for, honestly, the moments which had preceded its utterance were certainly sufficiently bitter.

She set out accompanied by Junot and Bessières. I afterwards learned that on her arrival at the Tuileries the Emperor went to the top of the great staircase to meet her. On approaching him she made an effort to kneel and kiss his hand, but the Emperor, stooping immediately, constrained her to rise, and conducted her to the Throne-room, where all the Imperial Family were assembled, and where he presented her to them as a daughter and sister. She was surrounded, caressed, and received with every mark of satisfaction into the family circle.

The *fêtes* in celebration of the King of Westphalia's marriage still continued, and the Court of Fontainebleau was more brilliant than during the reign of Louis XIV, each successive day exceeding the past in magnificence. I was patiently awaiting my confinement at Raincy when I received an invitation, or rather an order, to repair to Fontainebleau for a few days. I obeyed; but not choosing to be an inmate of the *château,* I hired a small house close adjoining, and went every day to the Palace in a sedan-chair; although Duroc had told me in confidence

* Jerome became King of Westphalia in 1809.

that the Emperor, whom I certainly feared the most, was about to set out on a journey.

No language can convey a clear idea of the magnificence, the magical luxury, which now surrounded the Emperor; the diamonds, jewels, and flowers that gave splendour to his *fêtes;* the loves and joys that spread enchantment around, and the intrigues which the actors in them fancied quite impenetrable, whereas they were perhaps even more easily discernible than at the Tuileries. When the mornings were fine, and in October and November of that year the weather was superb, we went out hunting and breakfasted in the forest. The ladies wore a uniform of chamois cashmere, with collars and trimmings of green cloth embroidered with silver, and a hat of black velvet, with a large plume of white feathers.

Nothing could be more exhilarating than the sight of seven or eight open carriages whirling rapidly through the alleys of that magnificent forest, filled with ladies in this elegant costume, their waving plumes blending harmoniously with the autumnal foliage; the Emperor and his numerous suite darting like a flight of arrows past them in pursuit of a stag which, exhibiting at one moment its proud antlers from the summit of a mossy rock, in the next was flying with the fleetness of the wind to escape from its persecutors. The gentlemen's hunting uniform was of green cloth, turned up with amaranth velvet, and laced *à la* Brandenbourg on the breast and pockets with gold and silver; it was gay, but I preferred the more unpretending shooting-uniform.

Much gossip was at this time passing at Fontainebleau respecting both the present and the future, but all in whispers. The present was the very important subject of the Emperor's new amours. The beautiful Genoese, then at the acme of favour, had demanded to be presented at Court, which no other favourite had ever dared to think of; and the Emperor, though usually very little susceptible of influence from such connections, had on this occasion the weakness to accede.

But the future presented a far more serious consideration in the Imperial divorce, which occupied all minds, and was the subject of our conversation in the retirement of our own apartments. The designated Heir of the Empire was no more; and, though he had left a brother, Napoleon's hopes did not rest equally on him. He became thoughtful and abstracted, and would often ride into the forest in the morning, attended only by Jardin (his favourite equerry, who was much devoted to him), probably that he might meditate undisturbed upon the course he should adopt.

"How can you suffer the Emperor to ride almost alone in that forest?" said I one day to Duroc; "once in the way it would be immaterial, but if it is known to be habitual he may be watched for, and how easily may a mischance occur!" "I cannot hinder his going out unaccompanied," replied Duroc. "I have several times remonstrated, but he will not listen. I am, however, informed the moment he leaves the Palace, and do my best to watch over his safety. But the forest is large, and there is no ascertaining what direction he may choose, so that these solitary rides often cause me uneasiness."

This may serve as an answer to the assertions in some biographies as to the extreme vigilance with which it was the Emperor's pleasure to be uniformly guarded. He had always the greatest repugnance to attendance; even in seasons of real danger I have seen him going out continually accompanied by Bourrienne, Junot, or Rapp, never more than one at a time. If such was his antipathy to attendance in France, how great must have been his annoyance when at Saint Helena English sentinels were instructed to escort him wherever he went!

The Princess Pauline and the Grand Duchess of Berg were preeminent in the numerous train of young and pretty women who that year adorned the Imperial Court at Fontainebleau. Notwithstanding Napoleon's recent attachment to Madame G—— he had also a great fancy for Madame B——, who, as a lady-in-waiting on one of the Princesses, attended all the hunting-parties, and frequently breakfasted at the rendezvous. I know the whole of that affair, and can assert, in opposition to the reports of scandal, that the Emperor never succeeded; though so powerful was the impression made upon him that he committed it to writing, a circumstance very rare with him in his transient entanglements, for such this would have been, had not Madame B—— had the good sense to withstand the infatuation of that halo of glory, that cloud of dazzling light which surrounded Napoleon.

The Empress, in spite of all her efforts to appear gay and happy, was overpowered with melancholy. The rumours of a divorce seemed to acquire more and more consistency, and were all repeated to her; the frequent exchange of couriers between Paris and Petersburg inspired a fear that the consummation of the peace of Tilsit might be sought in a family alliance between the new friends; and, to complete her uneasiness upon the subject, she dared not mention it to the Emperor.

Once when I had been paying my respects to her, she did me the honour to say to me: "Madame Junot, they will never be satisfied till they have driven me from the throne of France—they are inveterate against me." She meant the Emperor's family. And in fact her two sisters-in-law, Jerome, and all to whom, as they said, the glory of the Empire was dear, desired a separation. The Emperor himself said nothing, but his silence was perhaps more alarming to his unfortunate consort than words would have been. The death of the young Prince of Holland had evidently overthrown all his projects.

The Empress burst into tears as she contemplated a lock of the child's beautiful yellow hair, which she had put under a glass on a ground of black velvet. The poor mother's despair no language can express: that Queen Hortense survived is satisfactory evidence that grief does not kill. But the sufferings of the Empress were scarcely less severe; her maternal affliction was enhanced by incessantly renewed anxieties about the divorce.

T H E death of Louis and Hortense's young son did, indeed, come as a shock to Napoleon; but, far from transforming his views on the succession, it merely served to intensify feelings he had been slowly developing. The Emperor, after all, had no lack of nephews; but as the Empire grew in size and power, he also came to believe that only his own son could be the right heir to the throne.

That was bad news for Josephine. Well past the childbearing age, she had never been able to provide her husband with the children he ardently desired. Until 1807, however, Napoleon believed that he was himself sterile: Josephine, after all, did have two children by her first husband. Then a young woman named Eléonore Denuelle, who was the Emperor's mistress, and whose absolute fidelity was vouched for by the secret police, became pregnant. In due course, she was delivered of a son: clearly Napoleon was capable of fathering an heir after all.

From then on, the marriage with Josephine was doomed. None of the tricks by which she had in the past controlled Napoleon worked this time: tears, faints, seduction, all was in vain. In 1809, the divorce was pronounced and the former Empress, who was given a very large income, retired to Malmaison. As for Napoleon, the question of a wife was now pressing. His first choice, a Russian Grand Duchess, was denied him, a strong indication that Tsar Alexander was not the faithful ally he seemed; that was when Metternich assured him that he would meet no such rebuff in Vienna. The proposal was sent off post-haste. To the horror of his family, the Emperor Francis accepted it while the Viennese commented that a fine heifer was being sacrificed to the Minotaur. The marriage took place in 1810; and Marie Louise promptly discharged her duty by providing Napoleon with a male heir.

When Junot left France for Portugal I was staying at Raincy. My condition afforded me a sufficient excuse for not paying my respects to Madame,* and I am bound to say that in this, as in all other circumstances, she behaved with great consideration and kindness towards me. I passed two months at Raincy, and only returned to Paris a few days previous to my *accouchement.*

I had already given birth to five daughters, and Junot anxiously wished to have a son. The day therefore on which I wrote to him, *"You are the father of a boy!"* was one of the happiest of my life. The intelligence reached him shortly after his arrival at Lisbon. He was in a transport of joy.

"I thank you," he wrote me in reply, "for having presented me with a son; I can now leave the Emperor another Junot, whose blood, like his father's, may flow for his Sovereign and his country."

Junot wished the Emperor to be godfather to his son, though he had already stood godfather to our eldest daughter, but he disliked being

---

* Madame, plain and simple, was the style borne by Napoleon's mother.

sponsor for two in the same family. However, as Junot urged me to prefer the request, I did so. The Emperor granted it with the best possible grace, observing: "I will do as Junot wishes; but who is to be godmother?"

This question was rather embarrassing. The divorce was at this time publicly talked of—at least, as publicly as people dared to talk, under Napoleon's government, of his domestic affairs. However, my embarrassment was not of long duration, and I replied:

"If agreeable to your Majesty, I should wish her Majesty the Empress to stand godmother."

The Emperor fixed upon me for a few moments his keen and penetrating glance, and rejoined:

"Would you not like Signòra Letizia to be godmother?"

"Your Majesty never did me the honour to speak of Madame Mère."

"Well, should you like her to stand?"

"I am," answered I, "ready to obey your Majesty's wishes."

"But this is no reply to my question. Who, I ask again, do you wish to stand godmother to your son?"

"Does your Majesty deign to allow me the choice?"

"I told you so," he replied, "an hour ago."

"Then," said I, "I request her Majesty the Empress to stand godmother to my son."

"Ah!" he responded, and gazed on me steadily for some time; at length he said:

"You wish the Empress to stand? Well, be it so."

The divorce took place in the following year. I have dwelt on the above circumstance because it has reference to a fact which gave a humorous turn to my child's christening, as already described.

The numerous Memoirs which detail the magnificence of Marly and Versailles convey no idea of the splendour which surrounded Napoleon's Court during the winter of 1808. One of its greatest attractions, and that which no other Court in Europe could equal, was the collection of beautiful women by whom it was graced. This may easily be accounted for when it is recollected that almost all the French Generals and the superior officers of the Imperial Guard had married for love, either in France or in other countries during their campaigns.

I have already spoken of the elegance which embellished the Consular Court; but we have now arrived at the period of the Empire when that elegance was doubled, nay, tripled, in refinement and magnificence. The Emperor's desire was that his Court should be brilliant; and this wish, being agreeable to everyone's taste, was implicitly fulfilled. The revolutionary law which prohibited embroidered coats was now forgotten, and the gentlemen rivalled the ladies in the richness of their dress and the splendour of their jewels.

I well recollect the truly fairy-like or magical appearance of the *Salle des Maréchaux* on the night of a grand concert, when it was lined on either side by three rows of ladies, radiant in youth and beauty, and all covered with flowers, jewels, and waving plumes. Behind the ladies were ranged the officers of the Imperial Household, and lastly the Generals, the Senators, the Councillors of State, and the Foreign Ministers, clothed in rich costumes and wearing on their breasts the decorations and orders which Europe offered to us on bended knee. At the upper end of the Hall sat the Emperor with the Empress, his brothers, sisters, and sisters-in-law. From that point he, with his keen glance, surveyed the plumed and glittering circle.

Paris was unusually brilliant this winter. The various Princes of the Confederation of the Rhine; Germany, Russia, Austria, Poland, Italy, Denmark, and Spain—in a word, all Europe, with the single exception of England, had sent to Paris the *élite* of their Courts to pay their respects to the Emperor, and to fill up the magnificent retinue which followed him on a grand presentation-day from the Salle du Trône to the play in the Tuileries.

The Grand Duchess of Berg was the youngest and prettiest of the Princesses of the Imperial Family. The Princess Borghèse, languishing and seemingly feeble, never produced so great an effect as her sister in a ball-room. Besides, the Grand Duchess danced, while the Princess Borghèse remained fixed to her sofa like an idol, of which, to say the truth, she loved to act the part. The Princess Caroline was the planet around which all the youth of the Court used to be grouped, without, however, encroaching upon the gentle and gracious empire of Queen Hortense, who, beloved by all, and adored by those more immediately connected with her, seemed to have formed the subject of M. de la Maisonfort's lively couplet:

"À chacun elle voulait plaire,
    Elle plaisait,
    Chacun l'aimait," etc.

The affairs of Spain now began to assume a troubled aspect. The thunder which roared over the beauteous plains of Aranjuez resounded even to the courtyards of the Tuileries. The Emperor despatched the Grand Duke of Berg to take the command of the troops assembled on the frontiers of Spain.

This departure was by no means agreeable to the Grand Duke. He had contracted habits of gallantry which he was foolish enough to believe were those of a man of fashion, while his connections were really of the lowest and most vulgar kind. He, moreover, made himself an object of ridicule by his affected manners and dress, his curls, his feathers, his furs, and all the wardrobe of a strolling player. The Grand Duke and the Princess Caroline then occupied the Palais de l'Élysée. At the time of the marriage of the King of Westphalia the Princess Caroline had been in the habit of giving entertainments on a most magnificent scale. The winter which succeeded the marriage was distinguished by less brilliant, though equally agreeable festivities.

The Princesses received orders from the Emperor that each severally should give a ball once every week, not that Napoleon was himself fond of dancing, but he liked to see others take part in the amusement. These assemblies were usually composed of from a hundred and fifty to two hundred visitors; and the ladies, who generally numbered above fifty, were almost all young and handsome, and attired with elegance and magnificence.

The Princess Caroline gave her balls on Fridays, Queen Hortense on Mondays, and the Princess Pauline on Wednesdays. The eternal indisposition of Pauline, whether real or pretended, formed no excuse for evading the Emperor's command. These balls were truly delightful! What excitement they occasioned! what business for the toilette!

We also admitted our children to a share of the pleasure we ourselves enjoyed. I set this example, being the mother of the eldest of the Emperor's goddaughters. My daughter's birthday was the 6th of January (Twelfth Day), and I invited in her name the children of Junot's brother officers, the families of the public authorities, and of my own private friends. On this occasion from 120 to 140 children were brought together, and we engaged for their entertainment General Jacquot, the learned ape, the performing canary-birds who fired off a pistol, Fitz-James the ventriloquist, Oliver the juggler, etc. How shall I describe the joy which pervaded this young assembly? What exclamations of delight! what ecstasy! Then we gave them a supper, or, rather, a collation of ices, pastry, and the most exquisite *sucreries* which could be procured. It was a scene of fairy enchantment!

Sometimes these little parties assembled in masks. One of the most conspicuous figures in the juvenile groups was the young Prince Achille Murat. He was a very fine boy, but a most mischievous little imp, whose boisterous romping manners formed a striking contrast to those of his cousins, the Princes Louis and Napoleon, who were exceedingly sedate. The second, who survived his elder brother, died even in a more distressing manner, at the age of seven-and-twenty. He was a remarkably fine boy. His younger brother,* who is now in Switzerland with his mother, was likewise a very lovely child. We used to call him the Princesse Louis, on account of his profusion of fine light hair, which gave him a strong resemblance to his beautiful and amiable mother.

One of the most remarkable entertainments in Paris that year was a masquerade given by the Grand Duchess of Berg. In the course of the evening a quadrille was danced: this was really the first one which deserved the name; for those introduced at the marriage of the Princess of Baden had none of the characteristics of a quadrille, except that of being danced by four couples, dressed in red, green, and blue.

The costume which the Grand Duchess of Berg selected was that of the Tyrolese peasantry, and her Highness had arranged that the quadrille should be exclusively danced by females. We made a party of sixteen Tyrolean peasant-girls, and we were headed by our *bailli*. This venerable personage was represented by Mademoiselle Adelaide de Lagrange. The Grand Duchess, for some reason or other, did not wish

* Afterwards Napoleon III.

the quadrille dancers to assemble at her residence in the Élysée Napo-léon.* She requested that they might meet at my house, and proceed altogether to the Élysée. Her Highness gave orders to this effect to Despreaux, the director of the Court ballets. About nine o'clock I had a rehearsal of the quadrille in the grand gallery of my house. Several of my friends who were not included in the Grand Duchess's invitation came to see the dance, and we were unexpectedly enlivened by an incident which I will here relate.

It was half-past ten o'clock: the moment for our departure to the Palace was fast approaching. I counted my masks. There were fourteen, the right number. There were the Comtesse du Châtel, the Comtesse Regnault de Saint Jean d'Angely, the Princess of Wagram (who was not then married), Madame de Colbert, Mademoiselle de la Vauguyon, and her sister, the Princesse de Beauffremont. Then there was the Baronne de Montmorency, and some others whose names I forget. I believe the Duchesse de Rovigo was one of them. We were engaged in adjusting our masks, when M. Cavagnari** entered and whispered me that a lady who was included in the quadrille was waiting in the next room; but as she had come too late she wished me to go and conduct her in.

I cast my eyes over the list sent me by the Grand Duchess. I found my number was complete; but as the Princesse de Ponte-Corvo, one of the masks, was not in my list, I concluded that she must be the lady who had just arrived. I therefore proceeded to the salon, which formed a sort of anteroom to the gallery. There I perceived, in the further corner of the apartment, a lady, whose short and bulky person was so ludicrous that at first I could not help starting back with astonishment. Imagine a figure about five feet some inches in height, but incredibly stout, and dressed in the Tyrolean costume. I approached this singular apparition; as I advanced, I became more and more amazed at the grotesque figure before me. *"Mon Dieu!* what an extraordinary person!" thought I to myself. "To whom have I the honour to address myself?" inquired I.

The mask answered only by a deep sigh. I now found it impossible

* Now the residence of the President of the Republic.
** M. Cavagnari was a confidential domestic of the Duc d'Abrantès.

to contain my laughter. A second sigh succeeded, much more profound than the first, and it was breathed with such force as to blow up the lace trimming of the mask. Being anxious to terminate this embarrassing sort of conversation, I extended my hand to the lady, and proposed to conduct her to the gallery; when she suddenly seized me by the waist, and, raising her mask, attempted to kiss me. I screamed, and, disengaging myself, flew to the bell, and pulled it with all my might. Truly, my precipitation might well be excused, for I felt a rough beard in contact with my chin. M. Cavagnari entered, and immediately burst into a fit of laughter. The stout lady laughed with him; and, to say the truth, I laughed too, though half inclined to be angry; for I now saw before me the unmasked face of his Royal Highness the Prince Camille Borghèse.

At length I proposed to conduct his Highness to the gallery, where the ladies were not a little astonished and amused by the extraordinary *travestie.* It would be difficult to convey an idea of the burlesque figure he presented, especially when, having removed his mask, he exhibited his bluish beard, black whiskers, and bushy hair, some stubborn locks of which escaped from beneath the Indian muslin veil. The whimsical effect of all this was heightened by the contrast of the young and elegant females who were grouped around him, and whose costume he had closely imitated. It was alternately amusing and provoking to find our Sosio reflecting us so admirably in caricature.

It was now time to proceed to the Palace, and it was agreed that the Prince should go with us. We found the Grand Duchess of Berg waiting to receive us in her private apartment, attended by the Princesse de Ponte-Corvo, both dressed exactly in the same style as ourselves. Great merriment was excited by the introduction of our newly recruited Tyrolese peasant-girl. We entered the ball-room headed by our venerable *bailli,* holding in her hand her little white staff, and wearing her wig most magisterially. As we were proceeding from the inner apartment to the gallery, a little mask in blue ran against me on his way to the closet, where the dominoes were changed. I was pushed aside with so much force that I almost felt inclined to be angry. But the little blue mask was no other than the Emperor!

Napoleon liked to divert himself, as he used to say, in these saturnalia. He loved to disguise himself completely, and allow some individual to assume his character. On the evening in question Isabey was to personate him. The humour of that celebrated artist was admirably calculated to enliven a masked ball, while the Emperor made but a poor figure in such an entertainment. In personating Napoleon, Isabey found it most difficult to disguise his hands, which were exceedingly large, while the Emperor's were small and beautifully formed. With the exception, however, of his hands, Isabey personated the Emperor to perfection.

The masquerade was kept up with great spirit; the costumes were elegant, and the entertainment was altogether one of the most delightful that had been given during that winter. In the course of the evening a little incident occurred which had well-nigh interrupted the general good-humour that prevailed. Suddenly the cheerful strains of the orchestra and the gay buzz of conversation were interrupted by the tones of a loud female voice, which exclaimed in an imperious tone: "I desire that she shall instantly quit my house!" This was the voice of the Grand Duchess herself.

Those who were connected with the Imperial Court at the time will recollect that a very pretty girl named Mademoiselle Gu——t had been in the service of the Empress before the appointment of Madame Gazani. Mademoiselle Gu——t was a most beautiful creature, and Queen Hortense, who to every other proof of good taste joined that of loving to see agreeable faces about her, had been very kind to Mademoiselle Gu——t. She took the young lady to the Grand Duchess's ball, where she was to be one of the characters in a quadrille. Whether the Grand Duchess was really ignorant of the presence of Mademoiselle Gu——t until the moment of the exclamation above cited, or whether she maliciously wished to place the young lady in a painful situation, I pretend not to decide; but certain it is that she seemed to evince great astonishment at learning that Mademoiselle Gu——t was in the room, and instantly gave vent to her indignation in the words I have recorded.

Poor Mademoiselle Gu——t, in tears, declared that the conduct of the Grand Duchess was most unjust and cruel, and could not be excused, even by the jealousy of an offended wife. The truth is, it was the love of the Grand Duchess for the Grand Duke which had given rise to this angry scene. Mademoiselle Gu——t had attracted the notice of his

Highness, and that was sin enough to be thus visited by a public censure.

Queen Hortense, however, warmly espoused the cause of the young lady, and with some success. But it may easily be conceived that the whole scene had a very ludicrous effect. I might myself have quarrelled with Mademoiselle Gu——t on the same grounds, but I restrained my feelings. I consoled myself with the idea that the Grand Duchess, from the recollection of our early friendship, had taken up my cause along with her own.

Be this as it may, Mademoiselle Gu——t was amply indemnified for the painful situation in which she had been placed. The Empress took her into her service. However, it is but just to all parties to mention that very shortly after the Empress's arrival at Bayonne it was found necessary to furnish Mademoiselle Gu——t with a passport to return to Paris to her mother.

I have not yet spoken of a most important circumstance in the political life of the Emperor, viz., the creation of his new Nobility. The institution of the Order of the Legion of Honour had already paved the way for this, but the work was not consummated until the creation of hereditary titles, with endowments. It was indeed expected that the Emperor would earlier have directed his attention to this matter, for the creation of the Duchy of Dantzic on the 28th of May, 1807, sufficiently revealed his intention.

I was on duty with Madame at the Tuileries, and used to accompany her to the family dinners which took place every Sunday. On one of these occasions, while I was waiting in the *salon de service* in the Pavilion of Flora, I perceived Savary approaching me. "Embrace me!" cried he; "I have good news." "Tell me the news first," said I, "and then I shall see whether it be worth the reward." "Well, then, I am a Duke." "That is news indeed," said I; "but why should I embrace you for that?" "My title is the Duke of Rovigo," continued he, marching up and down the room in an ecstasy of joy. "And what do I care for your ridiculous title?" said I in a tone of impatience.

"Had he told you that you are a Duchess," said Rapp, stepping up to me and taking both my hands in his, "I am sure you would have embraced him, as you will embrace me for bringing you the intelligence." "That I will," said I, presenting my cheek to my old friend

Rapp, whose frank and cordial manner quite delighted me. "And another for Junot," said he, smiling. "Well, be it so," answered I, "and I promise you I will inform him that you were the first to tell me this good news." "And, moreover," said Rapp, "you have the best title of the whole batch of Duchesses. You are the DUCHESSE D'ABRANTÈS." I perceived that the Emperor had given Junot the title of the Duc d'Abrantès as a particular compliment to him. I therefore was doubly gratified, and Junot was deeply impressed with the Emperor's kindness.

We descended to the salon at the foot of the staircase of the Pavilion of Flora for dinner. At the head of our table usually sat the Empress's Lady of Honour (then the Comtesse de La Rochefoucauld) or the Dame d'atours. Sometimes, in the absence of both these ladies, the lady-in-waiting at the Palace would preside. On the day I allude to Madame de La Rochefoucauld was at her post—an honour, by-the-bye, which she seldom conferred upon us. I found myself quite solitary in the midst of the company. The party was composed of individuals whose manners and conversation did not suit my taste.

Thus I was very glad when I saw Madame Lannes enter the salon. Her company was always welcome to me, but now it was especially so. We immediately drew near each other, and sat down together at the table. "Well," said I, "here are great changes, but I am sure they will work none in you." I was right. She might subsequently have conceived a taste for these pomps and vanities, but at that time she was a simple, kind, and perfectly natural creature. "You may indeed be sure that I care but little for them," replied Madame Lannes; "and I am sure Lannes will not feel himself elevated by them. You know his turn of mind; he is still unchanged; but there are many who surround the Emperor who entertain diametrically opposite opinions. Look around you."

I looked up, and beheld opposite to me the Duc de Rovigo, whose countenance was radiant with self-complacency. The Duchesse de Rovigo sat at some distance from us. "I'll wager," said I to Madame Lannes, "that she is not so vain of her elevation. She is an amiable woman, and not likely to assume any of these ridiculous airs." Madame Lannes smiled.

"And what title have you got?" said I, after some further conversation. "Oh, a charming one!" replied she: "Duchesse de Montebello!

Mine and yours are the prettiest titles on the list." Here she drew from her girdle a small card, on which were inscribed the names of all the Dukes the Emperor had created, as also the majorats* appertaining to the titles. The Palace of the Tuileries had never been the scene of more ambitious agitation. From the Marshal to the lowest *employé,* all were eager to obtain at least a feather of the nobiliary plume.

Our Sunday evenings at the Tuileries were not like others; for on that day we were not permitted to enter the Emperor's salon to wait for the Princess. Sometimes, when the Emperor was in a good humour, he would invite the *Dames de Palais,* or other ladies who accompanied Madame, to enter. It happened so on the day I here allude to.

"Well, *Madame la Duchesse Gouvernante,*" said the Emperor to me as soon as I entered, "are you satisfied with your title of Abrantès? Junot, too, ought to be pleased with it, for I intend it as a proof of my satisfaction with his conduct.** And what do they say of it in your salons of the Faubourg Saint Germain? They must be a little mortified at the reinforcement I have sent them."

Then, turning to the Arch-Chancellor, he said: "Well, monsieur, after all, nothing that I have done is more in unison with the true spirit of the French Revolution than the re-establishment of high dignities. The French people fought for only one thing: equality in the eye of the law, and the power of controlling the acts of their Government. Now, my Nobility, as they style it, is in reality no nobility at all, because it is without prerogatives or hereditary succession. The only prerogative it enjoys, if prerogative it can be called, is the fortune conferred by way of recompense for civil or military services; while its hereditary succession depends on the will of the Sovereign in confirming the title on the son or nephew of the deceased holder. My Nobility is, after all, one of my finest creations."

W H E N , in 1808, Napoleon and Tsar Alexander met at Erfurt, in what is today East Germany, the Emperor seemed both all-powerful and irresistible. All the European major powers—

* The pecuniary allowance attached to the title.
** I have already mentioned that the Emperor had directed Junot to enter Lisbon at all hazards; and it was Junot's bold entrance into Abrantès which decided the success of the expedition.

always with the exception of Great Britain—had been vanquished. Napoleon disposed of foreign states as if they had been his personal possessions, changing borders, transferring provinces, occasionally taking territory for himself—hence the creation of the wholly artificial Kingdom of Westphalia so that Jerome Bonaparte could become a sovereign. Just as important, there seemed to be no reason why this should not last for a very long time. At Erfurt, Napoleon was surrounded by a bevy of kings, all busily fawning so as to win his favor.

This prodigious success had its drawbacks, though, some visible, some still hidden. Chief among the first was Napoleon's growing megalomania. In France itself, he was becoming a tyrant, imprisoning people at will, suppressing all liberties, including that of the press. Nothing ever seemed to be enough: in 1808, the Emperor sent an army into Spain and replaced the Bourbon King by his own brother Joseph, a move made in arrogance and regretted at leisure. By 1810, in fact, France proper (so to speak) stretched from Hamburg to today's Yougoslavia and included most of Italy, while Spain, Naples, Holland, Westphalia were subject kingdoms. Not even Napoleon's genious for organisation could control so vast an empire especially since its several parts often had widely diverging interests.

The hidden drawbacks were just as important. Not only did the subservient monarchs resent their new master, the peoples themselves began to develop an anti-French national consciousness which came into its own during the "wars of liberation" in 1813 and 1814. Admittedly, the French defeats of these years might not have been possible without the catastrophic failure of the Russian campaign; but that, too, was bound to come. Even as Alexander hugged Napoleon at Erfurt, he secretly consulted Talleyrand as to the means of ending the intolerable French domination: under the treaty just concluded, the Russian Empire had been forced to join the anti-British System when, in fact, it desperately needed to trade with England. The result was massive smuggling which the Russian government chose to ignore; and that, in turn, led to the war of 1812.

The star of Napoleon Bonaparte was at this time shining in the zenith of its splendour. Alas! its radiance blinded him. The interview at Erfurth, in which the Emperor of Russia gave him so many proofs of fraternal friendship, was a snare of destiny to lure him to his ruin. One anecdote of this meeting is well known, but is too apposite to this subject to be omitted here. When Talma, in the part of Philoctetes, pronounced the line,

"The friendship of a great man is a gift of the gods!"

the Emperor Alexander, rising from his seat, threw himself into the arms of Napoleon with an emotion so manifest and sincere that no one could doubt the sentiment which excited it. I can guarantee the truth of another, and there are Memoirs in existence which will perhaps one day appear, and will confirm it.

When Count Nicholas Romanzoff came about this time to Paris, he was assailed on the way, both by Austria and Prussia, with arguments and inducements to join the famous alliance, to which Sweden was already pledged; but the Russians, M. de Romanzoff, and before him M. de Tolstoi, were inviolable in their fidelity, and turned a deaf ear to all such remonstrances.

Another fact, apparently indifferent, perhaps eventually decided the destiny of Napoleon. Being one day in company with the Emperor Alexander at Erfurth, and conversing confidentially with him as with a brother, Napoleon mentioned Ferdinand VII, spoke of the uneasiness he occasioned him, of the trouble of detaining him in captivity, and of his intrigues with dairymaids (such kinds of amours being always odious to Napoleon, he alluded to them in disgust). The Russian Emperor looked significantly at him for some moments, then, smiling, turned away his head in a very eloquent silence.

"Do you, then, possess a talisman for mastering this evil genius?" said Napoleon, laughing, observing that Alexander shrugged his shoulders with contemptuous impatience. "Why, really," replied the other, "when the captivity of an enemy is as inconvenient to the conqueror as it must be annoying and wearisome to the conquered, the best thing that can be done for both is to put an end to it." Napoleon stood for a moment motionless, but made no reply.*

It is certain that he did not adopt the counsel; and that, when in 1815 he had to choose an asylum, this sentence of Alexander's recurred to his memory; and probably he likewise reverted to it when in 1814 I sent him a message through the Duc de Rovigo, in consequence of a long conversation that I had held with the Emperor of Russia at my hotel in the Champs Élysées, which at that time I still occupied. Unfortunately, in 1808 and 1809, Napoleon was too much the dupe of Alexander's friendship, and afterwards he had not sufficient confidence in it. But such was the constitution of his mind, that neither his sentiments nor actions could ever accord with those of other men.

After several weeks passed at Erfurth in discussing the destinies and most serious interests of Europe, amidst the gayest and most brilliant *fêtes,* Napoleon crossed France, only to march upon Spain, and the Empress returned to Paris to celebrate the commencement of the new year. The Arch-Chancellor gave her a ball in his gloomy mansion of the Carousel, formerly the Hôtel d'Elboeuf. I never knew a *fête* given by Cambacérès to be gay, not even a fancy ball; but the present surpassed all its predecessors in dullness, although D'Aigrefeuille, who acted as Grand Chamberlain and principal Master of Ceremonies, was in himself, with his little sparkling eyes, short, round, and singularly attired figure, a sufficient provocation to laughter to all who beheld him.

The Arch-Chancellor's coronation robes had been made with a train much longer than the Emperor chose to permit, and it was consequently shortened. Cambacérès, who, as every one knows, loved economy, and had no objection to distribute the gifts required by his accession to the title of Grand Dignitary without paying too dearly, made D'Aigrefeuille a present of the velvet and ermine clippings from the curtailed mantle. D'Aigrefeuille was enchanted, but as the parings of violet velvet would have required too much seaming for a coat, he laid the fur, which unfortunately, coming from the extremity of the

* This entrancing little story cannot be true: the meeting at Erfurt took place in 1807; Ferdinand VII did not become a prisoner until 1808.

garment, afforded no ermine tails, in numerous bands upon an old Court dress of sky-blue velvet which had belonged to his grandmother.

This grotesque habiliment, with its uniform whiteness, resembled that of a cat or a rabbit, and, with the round, red, and jovial face of the fat little man peering above it, was altogether irresistibly ludicrous. The amusements were sombre, the Empress was serious, there was a scarcity of ladies; war with Austria was talked of, and Count Metternich, lately returned from Vienna, notwithstanding his habitual courtesy, wore an air of constraint which his perfect politeness could not entirely subdue.

Count Metternich* had made a journey to Vienna towards the end of November, under pretence (though in reality on affairs of the utmost importance, announced previously to leaving Paris) that he should not be more than two or three weeks absent. The Duc de Cadore, forgetting that M. de Metternich was no way accountable to him for his proceedings, thought fit, at this assembly, to rally him in a half-angry tone on his long procrastinated return. "Do you know, sir," said he, "that we may reasonably take exception at this delay; and, indeed, though you still protest that your intentions are pacific, we may justly construe it as a confirmation of the rumours promulgated by the English journals."

"I can only repeat to your Excellency," replied M. de Metternich, "what I have frequently told you on that head, that the Emperor, my master, desires to continue at peace with France. As for the delay of my return, I assure you it had no other cause than the obstacle which the entrance of General Oudinot's corps into Germany presents to free egress by the way of Bavaria."

The acuteness and fine tact of this reply bears the stamp of the school of the Prince de Ligne. I afterwards asked M. de Metternich if he had really made it; he laughed, but gave me no answer. "Did you say so?" I again asked. "Should I have done amiss if I had?" said he, still laughing. "Certainly not." "Then probably I said so, but I do not remember it." The words, however, were actually his; and the Duc de Cadore had not capacity to contend with this model of all that the high aristocracy can

* Then Austrian Ambassador to France.

furnish of elegance and exquisite polish, combined with the most perfect and unembarrassed assurance.

M. de Metternich must have stood high in the estimation of the Comte de Stadion, then at the head of the Austrian counsels, to be selected as Ambassador to Napoleon in the critical circumstances of Austria; and already did the fair-haired Ambassador display symptoms of that talent which gave him his after-supremacy amongst the steersmen of the European state vessel. The Emperor Napoleon's opinion of him, at first erroneous, was corrected; but it was then too late, the mischief was irreparably done. He had been treated at Court with a coldness that showed no friendly intentions. As an instance, amongst others, of the disrespect he experienced, his Countess was once, on a grand Court Day, neither invited to sup with the Empress nor with either of the Princesses; to complete this insult, an article was inserted in the *Moniteur,* under diplomatic auspices, detailing an imaginary conversation between the Ambassador and the Duc de Cadore, which certainly never occurred, in which the former, in demanding the cause of the slight offered to his lady, was made to appear in a most ridiculous light.

M. de Metternich, thus publicly humiliated, annoyed in his domestic privacy, attacked in his most valuable privileges, deceived in all he had a right to expect from the justice of a Sovereign whom he approached under a title sacred even amongst savages, wounded in his dearest affections when his wife and children were detained as hostages in Paris, his very life menaced, constrained to fly like a criminal in a carriage with closed blinds, must have been more or less than man could he have excluded resentment from his bosom.

He became the irreconcilable enemy of France; whereas, dazzled by Napoleon's genius, he might have been irresistibly influenced by the same charm which enthralled the Emperor Alexander. Austria declared war against us at that sinister moment when our political horizon was darkening on the side of Italy, and the Emperor was seeking victory in the mountains of the Asturias. Napoleon's parting words to the Legislative Body, when joining his army in eager pursuit of the English, were: *"They have at length invaded the Continent."*

His anticipations of victory were justified by the event; he saw the leopards of England fly before him the moment he appeared: Moore and his troops were driven out of Spain by his all-conquering legions. Why, then, did he not stay to complete the conquest?

I went to Court in my diamonds on the following day in compliment to Madame de Remusat, and was dressed in a white tulle mantle embroidered in silver llama, the petticoat and train bordered with wreaths of rosebuds, a few similar buds being placed between my diamond wreath and comb.

The Marshals' hall was filled, and supper was laid in the Gallery of Diana. I was amongst the last arrivals in the Throne Room, and very inconveniently seated—a circumstance, however, to which I was indebted for the choice of a seat in the Concert Room. Madame de Remusat smiled as she recognized me, and the direction of her eye led me to observe that the Empress was giving an order to M. de Beaumont, who, a few moments before the concert concluded, announced to me her Imperial Majesty's invitation to supper.

Scarcely had I paid my respects, on approaching the Empress, when her Majesty motioned me to sit down beside her, and fixed her eyes with an inquisitorial expression upon the rose of yellow diamonds in the centre of my wreath. I have since learned that this was at the instigation of the Emperor, who was very curious to know the truth respecting this wonderful rose, *formed of a single brilliant*. A smile of intelligence showed that she detected, at the second glance, both the absurdity and malignity of the reports that had reached the Emperor.

The Empress was sometimes thoughtless, but her nature was kind, and in this instance she showed it. Leaning towards me, she whispered:

"Do you know you have been ridiculously misrepresented to the Emperor? and Junot must needs give colour to the rumours by talking nonsense! He knows very well diamonds cannot be hollowed; then, why should he have said anything so absurd? The consequence is, that your courtyard is reported to be paved with gold, that your diamonds are too heavy to be worn, and that you have a Court dress embroidered with brilliants."

Here I could not suppress an exclamation, but the Empress, by a sign, imposed silence, and whispered to me:

"Come and breakfast with me to-morrow; you can then explain all."

The next morning I breakfasted at the Tuileries, and the Empress told me all the absurdities she had heard, amongst others that Junot had carried off the famous Portugal diamond, that my jewels were much finer than her own, and that my unfortunate rose of yellow brilliants was formed from a single stone, which, if it had been, the Regent, the Czarina, the Portugal, the Sancy and Great Mogul diamonds must have hidden their diminished heads before the superior splendour of this newly discovered rival.

The principal—or, at least, the most valuable—part of the Prince Regent's baggage, when he quitted Lisbon for Brazil, was composed of all the jewels and other treasures of the Crown. He was desirous also to have taken away the church plate and jewels; this, however, M. d'Araujo, though his influence was declining, found means to prevent; but all the treasure the Prince could obtain possession of, he transported with himself, including the Brazilian ingots of gold.

But the Cabinet of Natural History at Lisbon was furnished with a facsimile of the famous Portugal diamond, as large as an apricot, cut in white wood, and inscribed with the exact weight of the original stone. This Junot brought away; and considering the general renown of the diamond, I thought it might be amusing to the learned of Paris to examine its portrait, or more properly its statue, which I accordingly showed to Millin, and afterwards to Devois, my jeweller; not that I made any secret of it, but it never occurred to me as an object of curiosity, except as connected with science. One night, however, I exhibited it openly in my drawing-room, and not a fortnight had elapsed before all Paris, and even the provinces, rang with the news that the Portugal diamond was in my possession; and that the fact was incontrovertible, as I had myself exhibited it.

T H E   marriage of Napoleon to the Archduchess Marie Louise, on April 2, 1810, was celebrated with the utmost splendor; but acute observers realised that all was not well. For one thing, many of the French cardinals, affronted by the Emperor's imprisonment of the Pope, failed to attend the ceremony; for another, there were some doubts about the validity, in canon law, of the divorce from Josephine. What everyone noted, though, was that the new Empress wholly lacked the charm, the tact, the friendliness of her predecessor. Stiff, proud, uncommunicative, she was disliked almost immediately.

As a result rumors were rife. Marrying an Austrian, people said, was bad luck: look at what happened to Louis XVI. Again, it was Josephine who had carried the Emperor's famous luck. With her gone, it would be gone as well. These were all superstitions, of course, but they indicate a widespread state of mind. More important, having a Habsburg wife turned Napoleon into a reactionary. Before then, he had remained, even among the splendors of the court, the Emperor of the Revolution; now he began to behave like a monarch of the ancien régime, thus causing great resentment, not just in his entourage, but among the people as well.

As for Marie Louise herself, who had sobbed bitterly when she was told she was to marry the Corsican ogre, she found Napoleon an almost ideal husband: he was devoted to her, allowed her to indulge in almost every whim (as long as it did not break the now sacrosanct etiquette) and, best of all, introduced her to what eventually became her favorite pastime, sex. Her one complaint, in fact, was that he went away far too often.

While this was no doubt flattering, especially considering the difference in ages (she was nineteen, he was forty-one), Marie Louise, in the end, proved no bargain. As already noted, Austria pursued its anti-French policies quite regardless of the fact that a Habsburg was Empress of the French; and during the campaign of 1814, when Napoleon was constantly battling the allies and a strong, responsible ruler was desperately needed in Paris, Marie Louise proved to be passive and inadequate.

I was at Burgos when I received the first intelligence of Napoleon's intended marriage with Marie Louise. A friend who wrote to me from Paris spoke of the disastrous influence which a marriage with an Austrian Princess was likely to exercise on the destiny of Napoleon. He was, it is true, Emperor of the French, but he was likewise *General Bonaparte,* who had gained more than twenty pitched battles over Austria, and who had twice forced the Imperial Family to fly from their palace. These were injuries which could not but leave indelible stains behind them.

The sacrifice which the Emperor Francis was now about to make bore an odious stamp of selfishness. It appeared by no means improbable that at some future time the voice of his daughter, when appealing to him on behalf of her son and her husband, would be no more listened to than when she remonstrated for herself. It was evident that Austria, humbled and mutilated as she was, greeted this marriage only as a temporary balm to her wounds. Napoleon's object was to consolidate his Northern alliances, already well secured on the part of Russia, and to prosecute still further his fatal operations in the Peninsula.

Paris was enlivened by *fêtes* in honour of the Imperial nuptials. The letters which I received from my friends were like the descriptions in romances and fairy tales. As I was not in Paris at that time, I will not enter into a detail of matters which I did not witness; but I cannot forbear relating the following anecdote connected with Napoleon's marriage:

Berthier, Prince de Neufchâtel, was sent to Vienna to conduct the Empress to Paris. After she had been married by proxy [to her uncle, Prince Charles], and all the forms and ceremonies were gone through (which in Vienna is a work of no little time), the day of departure was fixed. The young Archduchess often shed tears of regret at her approaching separation from her family. In the Imperial Family of Austria the bonds of relationship are sacredly revered; and even in the reign of Maria Theresa, and under the cold and artful policy of Kaunitz, family ties were held dear. Marie Louise had been educated in these feelings: she wept to leave her sisters, her father, and her stepmother, and perhaps also she wept at the thought of being united to a man who must have been to her almost an object of terror.

At length the day of departure arrived. The young Empress bade farewell to all the members of her family, and then retired to her apartment, where etiquette required that she should wait till Berthier came to conduct her to her carriage. When Berthier entered the cabinet he found her bathed in tears. With a voice choked by sobs she apologized for appearing so childish. "But," said she, "my grief is excusable. See how I am surrounded here by a thousand things that are dear to me. These are my sister's drawings, that tapestry was wrought by my mother, those paintings are by my uncle Charles." In this manner she went through the inventory of her cabinet, and there was scarcely a thing, down to the carpet on the floor, which was not the work of some beloved hand. There were her singing birds, her parrot, and, above all, the object which she seemed to value most, and most to regret—a little dog.

It was, of course, known at the Court of Vienna how greatly the Emperor used to be annoyed by Josephine's favourite pet dogs, with *Fortuné* at their head. Therefore Francis II, like a prudent father, took care that his daughter should leave her pet dog at Vienna. Yet it was a cruel separation, and the Princess and her favourite parted with a tender *duo* of complaint.

But these regrets, childish as they may appear, Berthier regarded as proofs of a kind and affectionate heart, and when he beheld the tears of the young Archduchess, whom he had expected to find all radiant with smiles, a scheme entered his mind which he tacitly resolved to carry into execution. "I have merely come to acquaint your Majesty," said he, "that you need not depart for two hours to come. I will therefore withdraw until that time." He went immediately to the Emperor and acquainted him with his plan. Francis II, who was the most indulgent of fathers, readily assented to the proposition. Berthier gave his orders, and in less than two hours all was ready.

The Empress left Vienna and soon entered France; she found herself surrounded by festivals and rejoicings, and almost forgot the parrot and the dog. She arrived at Compiègne, and was there met by the Emperor, who stopped her carriage, stepped into it, and seated himself by her side; they proceeded to Saint Cloud, and thence to Paris. There Fortune bestowed one of her last smiles on her favourite son, when, leading into the balcony of the Tuileries his young bride, whom he regarded as the pledge of lasting peace and alliance, he presented her to the multitude who were assembled beneath the windows of the Palace.

On returning from the balcony, he said to her: "Well, Louise, I must give you some little reward for the happiness you have conferred on me;" and leading her into one of the narrow corridors of the Palace, lighted only by one lamp, he hurried on with his beloved Empress, who exclaimed: "Where are we going?" "Come, Louise, come, are you afraid to follow me?" replied the Emperor, who now pressed to his bosom, with much affectionate tenderness, his young bride.

Suddenly they stopped at a closed door, within which they heard a dog that was endeavouring to escape from the apparent prison. The Emperor opened this private door, and desired Louise to enter. She found herself in a room magnificently lighted; the glare of the lamps prevented her for some moments from distinguishing any object; imagine her surprise when she found her favourite dog from Vienna was there to greet her; the apartment was furnished with the same chairs, carpet, the paintings of her sisters, her birds—in short, every object was there, and placed in the room in the same manner as she had left them on quitting her paternal roof.

The Empress, in joy and in gratitude, threw herself in Napoleon's arms, and the moment of a great victory would not have been to the conqueror of the world so sweet as this instant of ecstasy was to the infatuated heart of the adoring bridegroom. After a few minutes had been spent in examining the apartment, the Emperor opened a small door; he beckoned to Berthier, who entered. Napoleon then said: "Louise, it is to him you are indebted for this unexpected joy: I desire you will embrace him, as a just recompense." Berthier took the hand of the Empress, but the Emperor added: "No, no; you must kiss my old and faithful friend."

Some weeks after his marriage the Emperor took the Empress with him into Belgium. Marie Louise received the homage that was paid to her with a certain air of indifference, and there then seemed little reason to expect that she would do the honours of the Court with the grace and amiability which she subsequently displayed.

The letters which I received from my friends in Paris after my departure for Spain naturally made mention of the new Empress. The most various opinions were pronounced upon her. Cardinal Maury sent me a letter in which he said: "I will not attempt to describe how much the Emperor is attached to our charming Empress. This time he may be said to be really in love; more truly in love than he ever was with Josephine, for, after all, he never saw her while she was very young. She was upwards of thirty when they were married. But Marie Louise is as young and as blooming as spring. You will be enchanted with her when you see her."

Marie Louise's brilliant complexion particularly charmed the Cardinal. For my own part, I did not see her till after her *accouchement,* and even then, though I was told that she had grown pale, I thought she had too much colour, especially when in the least heated. The Cardinal was a great admirer of Marie Louise, though he had wished the Emperor to marry one of the Russian Grand Duchesses. "The Empress," added he in the letter above mentioned, "is gay, gracious, and I may even say *familiar,* with those persons whom the Emperor permits her to receive in her intimate circle; her manners are charming to those who are admitted to the *petites soirées* at the Tuileries. Their Majesties join the company at reversis or billiards. I really wish that you and the Duke could see how happy the Emperor is."

I was informed by other friends that one of the amusements of the Imperial *soirées,* before the Emperor entered the salon, was to see the Empress turn her ear round, for, by a movement of the muscles of the jaw, she possessed the singular power of making her ear turn round of itself, almost in a circle. I never heard of anyone except Marie Louise who could do this.

The Emperor wished to remove, as far as was consistent with etiquette, a frequent cause of dissension between him and the Empress Josephine, namely, the numerous visitors received by the latter. Marie Louise was young, and ignorant of the world, and though accustomed to a great deal of Court etiquette, yet her private circle had been limited to the members of her own family. Thus the rules prescribed by the Emperor neither surprised nor displeased her. One of these rules was that she should receive no male visitors. Paër was the only exception, because he was her music-master, and it was ordered that one of the Empress's ladies should be present while she received her lesson.

One day, while the Court was at Saint Cloud, the Emperor unexpectedly presented himself in the Empress's apartments. He perceived a man whose countenance he did not at first recognize. This violation of his rule displeased him, and he expressed himself rather angrily to the *dame de service,* who, I think, was Madame Brignole. She replied that the gentleman was Bennais,* who had come himself to explain the secret spring of a *serre-papier* which he had been making for her Majesty. "No matter," said the Emperor, "he is a man. My orders on this subject must not be departed from, or we shall soon have no rules."

On my return to France in 1811 I found the Emperor much altered in appearance. His expression had acquired a paternal character. What a beautiful child was the young King of Rome!** How lovely he appeared as he rode through the gardens of the Tuileries in his shell-shaped *calèche,* drawn by two young deer, which had been trained by Franconi, and which were given him by his aunt, the Queen of Naples. He resembled one of those figures of Cupid which have been discovered in the ruins of Herculaneum. One day I had been visiting the young King; the Emperor was also there, and he was playing with the child—as he always played with those he loved—that is to say, he was tormenting him. The Emperor had been riding, and held in his hand a whip, which attracted the child's notice. He stretched out his little hand, and when he seized the whip, burst into a fit of laughter, at the same time embracing his father.

"Is he not a fine boy, Madame Junot?" said the Emperor; "you must confess that he is." I could say so without flattery, for he was certainly a lovely boy. "You were not at Paris," continued the Emperor, "when my son was born. It was on that day I learned how much the Parisians love me; it is a cruel time for you ladies. I remember well the day that Junot left his home when you were going to be confined; I can understand now why he quitted you. What did the army say on the birth of the child?" I told him that the soldiers were enthusiastic during many days; he had already heard so, but was happy to receive a confirmation of their joy. He then pinched his son's cheek and his nose; the child cried.

"Come, come, sir," said the Emperor, "do you suppose you are never to be thwarted; and do Kings cry?" He then asked if the accounts in the English newspapers relative to my *accouchement* at Ciudad-Rodrigo were true. I replied that they were too silly to be so.

As soon as the King of Rome was born, the event was announced by

* Bennais was goldsmith to the Emperor.
** Napoleon's son was given the title of King of Rome.

telegraph* to all the principal towns in the Empire. At four o'clock the same afternoon, the marks of rejoicing in the provinces equalled those in Paris. The Emperor's couriers, pages, and officers were despatched to the different Foreign Courts with intelligence of the happy event. The Senate of Italy, and the municipal bodies of Rome and Milan, had immediate notice of it. The different fortresses received orders to fire salutes; the seaports were enlivened by the display of colours from the vessels; and everywhere the people voluntarily illuminated their houses.

Those who regard these popular demonstrations as expressions of the secret sentiments of a people might have remarked that in all the faubourgs, as well as in the lowest and poorest quarters in Paris, the houses were illuminated to the very uppermost stories. A *fête* was got up on the occasion by the watermen of the Seine, which was prolonged until a late hour of the night. Much of all this was not ordered: it came spontaneously from the hearts of the people. That same people, who for thirty-five years previously had experienced so many emotions, had wept over so many reverses, and had rejoiced for so many victories, still showed by their enthusiasm on this occasion that they retained affections as warm and vivid as in the morning of their greatness.

The King of Rome was baptized on the very day of his birth—the 20th of March, 1811. The ceremony was performed at nine in the evening, in the chapel of the Tuileries. The whole of the Imperial Family attended, and the Emperor witnessed the ceremony with the deepest emotion. Napoleon proceeded to the chapel, followed by the members of the Household, those of the Empress, of Madame Mère, of the Princesses his sisters, and of the Kings his brothers. He took his station under a canopy in the centre of the chapel, having before him a stool to kneel on.

A socle of granite had been placed on a carpet of white velvet embroidered with gold bees, and on this pedestal stood a gold vase destined for the baptismal font. When the Emperor approached the font bearing the King of Rome in his arms, the most profound silence prevailed. It was a religious silence, unaccompanied by the parade

* The semaphore telegraph was invented in 1792 by Claude Chappe. It was first brought into use for military purposes in the summer of 1794.

358

which might have been expected on such an occasion. This stillness formed a striking contrast with the joyous acclamations of the people outside.

Marie Louise suffered a difficult and protracted *accouchement.* She was for some time in considerable danger. Baron Dubois went to acquaint the Emperor with this circumstance. Napoleon was in a bath, which had been ordered to calm the feverish excitement under which he was suffering. On hearing that the Empress was in danger, he threw on his *robe-de-chambre,* and ran downstairs, exclaiming to Dubois: "Save the mother! think only of the mother!" As soon as she was delivered, the Emperor, who was himself indisposed, entered the chamber and ran to embrace her, without at first bestowing a single look upon his son, who indeed might have passed for dead. Nearly ten minutes elapsed before he evinced any signs of life. Every method to produce animation was resorted to. Warm napkins were wrapped round him, and his body was rubbed with the hand; a few drops of brandy were then blown into his mouth, and the royal infant at length uttered a feeble cry.

When the first gun announced that Marie Louise was a mother, the most important affairs, as well as the ordinary occupations and duties, were one and all suspended; the people flocked to the Tuileries, hats were thrown up in the air, persons were seen kissing each other, tears were shed, but they were tears of joy. At eleven o'clock Madame Blanchard ascended in a balloon from the square of the École Militaire to announce to the people in the environs of Paris the birth of the son of the Emperor.

A multitude besieged the doors of the Palace for many days to read bulletins of the infant and of the Empress. The Emperor, on learning this, directed that a Chamberlain should be constantly in one of the rooms to publish the accounts of the Empress's health as soon as they were delivered by the physicians.

I have already mentioned the Emperor's fondness for his son. He used to take the King of Rome in his arms and toss him up in the air. The child would then laugh until the tears stood in his eyes; sometimes the Emperor would take him before a looking-glass, and work his face into all sorts of grimaces; and if the child was frightened and shed tears,

Napoleon would say: "What, Sire, do you cry? A King, and cry? Shame, shame!"

The hours at which the young King was taken to the Emperor were not precisely fixed, nor could they be; but his visits were most frequently at the time of *déjeuner*. On these occasions the Emperor would give the child a little claret by dipping his finger in the glass and making him suck it. Sometimes he would daub the young Prince's face with gravy. The child would laugh heartily at seeing his father as much a child as he was himself, and only loved him the more for it. Children invariably love those who play with them. I recollect that once when Napoleon had daubed the young King's face the child was highly amused, and asked the Emperor to do the same to "Maman Quiou," for so he called his governess, Madame de Montesquiou.

The Emperor's selection of that lady for his son's governess was a proof of his excellent judgment. It was the best choice which could have been made. Madame de Montesquiou was young enough to render herself agreeable to a child, whilst she had sufficient maturity of years to fit her for the high duty which the confidence of her Sovereign had appointed her to fulfil. She was noble in heart as well as in name; and she possessed what the world frequently bestows only on fortune and favour—the esteem of all. She was indeed universally beloved and respected.

The attentions she bestowed on the King of Rome during the period of his father's misfortunes would in itself be sufficient to inspire love and respect. Not only had she, from the hour of his birth, lavished on him all the cares of a mother, and a tender mother, but from the day when the unfortunate child was cut off from all his family, and deprived at once of his father and mother, Madame de Montesquiou devoted herself to him, for she alone was left to protect him. To accompany him she deserted country, friends, and family.

Madame de Montesquiou was not liked by the Empress, and the cause has never been satisfactorily ascertained. It has been said, by way of compliment to Marie Louise, that she never did anyone an injury; yet she possessed an apathy of soul, from the influence of which the governess of her child was not exempt. And what sort of love did she show for her own child? I have seen Marie Louise, when she was mounting or alighting from her horse, nod her plumed head to him, which never failed to set him crying; for he was frightened by the undulation of her feathers. At other times, when she did not go out, she would repair at four o'clock to his apartment. On these occasions she would take with her a piece of tapestry, with which she would sit down and make a show of working, looking now and then at the little King, and saying, as she nodded her head: "Bonjour, bonjour."

Perhaps, after the lapse of a quarter of an hour, the *august mother* would be informed that Isabey or Paër was in attendance in her apartments; the one to give her lessons in drawing, the other in music. It would have been as well had she remained longer every day with her child to take a lesson in maternal feeling from the woman who so admirably supplied her place. But it would have been of little use— feeling is not to be taught.

Every morning at nine o'clock the young King was taken to the Empress. She would sometimes hold him on her lap, caress him, and then commit him to the care of the nurse. And how did she employ herself afterwards? She read the papers. When the child grew peevish because he was not amused as his father used to amuse him, and cried at finding himself surrounded by serious and formal faces, his mother ordered him out of the room.

The public christening of the King of Rome took place on the return to Paris of the Emperor and Empress from a tour in the North of France. There have already been so many descriptions of this ceremony that it would be superfluous to enter into a fresh one. I will merely mention that the young Prince received names which show that the alliances formed by Sovereigns, the vows made at the baptismal font, the adoption by every religious formality and the ties of blood, are mere fallacies.

He was christened Napoleon François Charles Joseph! these are the names of his godfathers; they stand upon the register of his baptism, and they also appear on the tomb which closed over him at the early age of twenty-one. Who is there among us who does not recollect those days when he was still gracious and beautiful? There is a print of him which is now very scarce; he is kneeling, his hands joined, and below are the words: "I pray God for my father and for France." To the copy I have, the following are added: "I pray God for France and for my father;" lower down: "We now pray for Thee!"

One of the Ushers of the Chamber with whom I was lately conversing wept like a child at his recollections of the young Prince. This man told me that the King of Rome one morning ran to the State Apartments, and reached the door of the Emperor's cabinet alone, for Madame de Montesquiou was unable to keep pace with him. The child raised his eager face to the Usher, and said: "Open the door for me; I wish to see papa."

"Sire," replied the man, "I cannot let your Majesty in." "Why not? I am the little King." "But your Majesty is alone!"

The Emperor had given orders that his son should not be allowed to enter his cabinet unless accompanied by his governess. This order was issued for the purpose of giving the young Prince, whose disposition was somewhat inclined to waywardness, a high idea of his governess's authority.

On receiving this denial from the Usher, the little Prince's eyes became suffused with tears, but he said not a word. He waited till Madame de Montesquiou came up, which was in less than a minute afterwards. Then he seized her hand, and, looking proudly at the Usher, he said: "Open the door; the little King desires it." The Usher then opened the door of the cabinet and announced: "His Majesty the King of Rome."

A great deal has been said of the young King's violent temper. It is true he was self-willed, and was easily excited to passion; but this was one of the distinctive characteristics of his cousins: they almost all partook of similar hastiness of temper. I have known Achille Murat so violently overcome by strong passion as to be thrown into convulsions; and this when he was of the same age as the King of Rome. Madame de Montesquiou once corrected the young King for these fits of passion. On another occasion, when he was very violent, she had all the shutters of the windows closed, though it was broad daylight.

The child, astonished to find the light of day excluded and the candles lighted up, inquired of his governess why the shutters were closed. "In order that no one may hear you, Sire," replied she. "The French would never have you for their King if they knew you to be so naughty." "Have I," said he, "cried very loud?" "You have." "But did they hear me?" "I fear they did." Then he fell to weeping, but these were tears of repentance. He threw his little arms around his governess's neck, and said: "I will never do so again, Mamma Quiou! pray forgive me."

It happened one day that the King of Rome entered the Emperor's cabinet just as the Council had finished their deliberations. He ran up to his father without taking any notice of anyone in the room. Napoleon, though happy to observe these marks of affection, so natural, and coming so directly from the heart, stopped him, and said: "You have not made your bow, Sire! Come, make your obedience to these gentlemen." The child turned, and, bowing his head gently, kissed his little hand to the Ministers. The Emperor then raised him in his arms, and addressing them, said: "I hope, gentlemen, it will not be said that I neglect my son's education; he begins to understand infantine civility."

On Saint Louis's Day the Empress held a grand Court at Trianon. The Empress was very partial to Trianon, and the Emperor, always desirous to please her, ordered that the day of the *fête* should be celebrated there. Consequently, without regarding the inconvenience to which the ladies must be subjected in driving such a distance in full dress, the cards of invitation were issued for Trianon.

Madame Ney, the Duchesse de Ragusa, and myself were together when we heard of the intended *fête,* and the conversation immediately turned upon the difficulty of travelling four leagues and a half in our Court dresses.

"Well!" said Madame Ney, "I propose that we go to Versailles in our morning dresses, and take our Court dresses and our *femmes-de-chambre* with us. We can set out from Paris time enough to take a drive in the park, and as my husband and General Junot are here, they can escort us to Raimbaud's to dinner, and there we can dress, and afterwards go to Trianon without ruffling our dresses or fatiguing ourselves."

This plan was too agreeable not to be approved of. The Duchesse de Ragusa, however, proposed an amendment, which was also agreed to unanimously. She had an old friend named Ricbourg, who was formerly *maître d'hôtel* to the King, as well as I recollect, and who was now living at Versailles. He was the friend of the elder M. Perregaux, and had known Madame Marmont from her infancy. The Duchess proposed that we should dine at the house of this old gentleman, there dress, and proceed at once to Trianon. On M. Ricbourg being informed of our intentions he was delighted, for he was acquainted with us all.

Marshal and Madame Ney, Junot and I, the Duchesse de Ragusa, Lavalette, and the Baroness Lallemand all assembled in M. Ricbourg's dining-room on the 25th of August, 1811. We were all in high spirits, and sat down to an excellent dinner.

When we retired from table, Madame Ney told us that she had never been able to prevail on Ney to wear a full dress coat; but hoping that in our joyous party he might be a little less obstinate than usual, she had ordered the dress-coat to be brought from Paris, together with the point ruffles and all the other accessories of a full Court costume. However, the difficulty was, not to bring the coat from Paris to Versailles, but to prevail on the Marshal to wear it from Versailles to Trianon.

"My dear," said Madame Ney, in her soft tone of voice, and stepping up to her husband timidly, as if she expected to be repulsed in the attack, "you know we have no time to lose. We ladies are almost ready. Does your dress-coat require anything to be done to it?"

"My dress-coat!" exclaimed the Marshal, with evident consternation.

"Yes, you know it is the Emperor's wish that you should all appear in Court dresses, and you must——"

"Nonsense!" said Ney; "do not talk to me of that masquerade foolery. I will never put it on to get laughed at, as I laugh at others who wear it."

"But, my dear Ney, it is impossible to go without it. The Emperor——"

"Well, if the Emperor wishes to encourage velvet weaving and embroidery, I am very willing to buy dresscoats; but as to wearing them, that is another matter."

Madame Ney, hoping that ocular might be more effectual than oral persuasion, desired her *femme-de-chambre* to bring in the coat. But when the Marshal saw it, he was more resolutely set against it than before, and appealed to us all for our opinions. I must needs confess that the coat was not likely to be very becoming to Marshal Ney. It was of a light colour and was profusely embroidered with flowers; and though in very good taste for a coat of the kind, yet it was perfectly natural that Ney should prefer his General's uniform. In vain did Madame Ney eulogize the coat; her husband was inflexible. At length, tormented by our importunities, for we supported the lady, as was our duty, Ney took the coat from the *femme-de-chambre,* and, taking hold of her arms, thrust them into the sleeves before the girl knew what he was doing. There stood the poor *femme-de-chambre,* for all the world like one of those wooden horses on which coats and cloaks are hung in the tailors' shops of the Palais Royal. Ney burst into a fit of laughter, and asked us whether we could seriously advise him to dress himself up like a buffoon on *Mardi-Gras.* At this moment, Junot, who had finished dressing, entered in an extremely rich Court costume. On seeing him, Ney angrily exclaimed:

"How! Is it possible that you submit to wear this harness? . . . Oh, Junot!"

Junot, like all present, was much diverted at this little scene. He told Ney that since 1808 he had frequently worn a Court dress. But nothing could induce Ney to make any concession. He was determined to go in his uniform, and the embroidered coat was folded up and deposited in a portmanteau, to the great satisfaction of the Marshal and the great discomfiture of his lady.

We arrived at Trianon, and shortly after we entered the gallery we were joined by the Comtesse du Chatel. We walked through the beautiful alleys of the gardens, the refreshing coolness of which was delicious, after leaving the crowded gallery. The Empress was making her round of the company, which prevented us from leaving our places. At length she approached our little coterie, and addressed a few words to each of us; to me she put her usual question:

"Is it as warm as this in Spain?"

When I had made my reply, and her Majesty had passed us, we withdrew to the fragrant alleys of the gardens, remarking among ourselves the difference between Marie Louise and Josephine, who always had in readiness some pleasing observation, appropriate to the person to whom it was addressed. Marie Louise seemed merely to ring the changes of one subject in different keys.

Soon after my return to France, I resumed my attendance on Madame Mère. She received me with the utmost kindness and affability. Her Household was more numerous than it had been when I left her, and the additions made to it were all excellent. The post of *Dame pour accompagner Madame Mère* was a most enviable one. She made us all happy.

One day a curious mistake occurred at the residence of Madame Mère, which made us all laugh very heartily at the hero of the adventure.

Madame was engaged to dine with the Queen of Spain.* M. de Beaumont, her equerry, had gone to order her carriage, and Madame was sitting in one of the drawing-rooms with Madame de Fleurieu, who was that day lady-in-waiting. It was evening, and the room was but faintly lighted by the embers of the fire, when the two folding-doors opened, and the *valet-de-chambre* ushered in a gentleman dressed in a richly embroidered coat, silk stockings, shoe-buckles, having a sword at his side and a *chapeau bras* in his hand. The gentleman advanced into the apartment, bowed slightly to the two ladies, of whom he caught a glimpse in the twilight, then walked up to the fireplace, warmed his feet, hummed a tune, pulled out his watch, compared notes between it and the timepiece, and then said in a voice loud enough to be heard:

"What the devil is the old fool about? . . . Surely, his watch must have stopped."

Madame de Fleurieu knew not what to make of this; she was unable to guess what could have brought a Prefect (for she had descried the prefectorial embroidery on the gentleman's coat) to the residence of Madame Mère at that time of day, and especially when she was going out. The lady-in-waiting was about to ask him what he wanted, when he deliberately advanced to the sofa, and, addressing Madame, asked her whether his Serene Highness would be long making his appearance.

Madame, though generally very affable, was not always able to command herself. She had been surprised and annoyed at the intrusion,

---

* Joseph Bonaparte's wife, that is. Napoleon had made him King of Spain; his wife, however, declined to leave Paris.

and, finding herself addressed in this unceremonious way, she lost all patience.

"Monsieur," said she, "I must tell you . . . that——"

"Don't you understand me, madame? I ask you whether you can tell me when the Arch-Chancellor will make his appearance."

The mystery was now more inexplicable than before. Madame de Fleurieu was struck dumb, and gazed in silent amazement at the gentleman. The latter shrugged his shoulders, and returned to his post in front of the fire, put his feet on the fender to warm them, and by turns whistled a tune, and muttered words which sounded very much like the imprecations of a hungry man.

Madame de Fleurieu, who thought it high time to put an end to this singular scene, rose from her seat, and advanced towards the gentleman with that air of courtly dignity which she so well knew how to assume when she placed herself in the first position preparatory to a courtesy.

"Monsieur," said she, "will you be kind enough to inform me where you think you are?"

The gentleman turned round with a careless air, still holding his foot on the fender.

"Where I think I am, madame? . . . I think I am in the house of his Serene Highness the Arch-Chancellor of the Empire, who has done me the honour to invite me to dinner. I am much astonished at not seeing him, for half-past five was the hour appointed."

"Monsieur," gravely replied Madame de Fleurieu, "you are not in the Arch-Chancellor's house. This is the residence of Madame——"

"Madame! . . . Madame who, pray?"

"Madame Mère, the mother of his Majesty the Emperor and King."

On hearing this, the gentleman, without being at all disconcerted, stepped up to Madame, and said:

"How happy I am! how can I express my gratification at thus having the opportunity of becoming acquainted with the mother of the man to whom I owe so many obligations." He then informed her Imperial Highness that his name was Desmousseaux, and that he was Prefect of Toulouse.

Madame, with her usual affability, received him with the respect due to a public functionary; but the clock struck six, and she said:

"Sir, I would advise you to lose no time. Half-past five is the Arch-

Chancellor's dinner-hour. I cannot compensate you for the loss of your dinner, for I am myself engaged to dine with my daughter-in-law."

The Prefect took his leave. The mistake was no laughing matter to him. When he descended to the street, he found that the driver of his *voiture de remise,* after having set him down at Madame's door, which he thought was the Arch-Chancellor's, had taken his departure without concerning himself about the fate of the Prefect. It rained, the wind blew violently, and the streets were covered with mud. Now, though the Arch-Chancellor lived in the same street with Madame, yet the two houses were tolerably distant. The poor Prefect arrived, wet and splashed, and, worse than all, almost famished; for it was now half-past six o'clock. The Arch-Chancellor had sat down to dinner, for he made it a rule never to wait, except for ladies or men of very high rank.

PART IV

The Fall of
Napoleon

I T became increasingly clear, between 1810 and 1812, that there were many subjects of disagreements between France and Russia. The Tsar deliberately closed his eyes to what was, in effect, an end of the blockade; he resented the possession by France of the Grand Duchy of Warsaw, which he felt ought to be in Russian hands. Even so, it was not Alexander who started the war, but Napoleon.

The Emperor had, apparently every reason to feel the conflict would be brief and, for him, wholly successful. His Grand Army numbered over half a million men, and was vastly superior to the Russian forces. The Tsar's generals had, one and all, been beaten by Napoleon and were therefore not likely to prove menacing enemies. It was all very simple: the French would head straight for the capital, probably crushing the Russians on the way; there, as usual, Napoleon would dictate the peace; and that would be that.

Only this time, Napoleon made some very serious miscalculations. In the first place, the Russian capital was now Saint Petersburg: Alexander could lose Moscow and not be forced to sue for peace. Then, the Grand Army was an ill-assorted hodge-podge of nationalities, all ready to defect at the first reverse; and finally, there were the Russian people and the Russian winter.

It never occurred to Napoleon, that heir to the Age of Reason, that the Russian people, rather than gracefully admit defeat, would fight a ferocious guerrilla war and destroy its own houses and provisions rather than letting the French have them. He did not understand that Alexander would have lost his throne if he had acknowledged himself defeated when Napoleon reached Moscow. Finally, he did not take into account the terrifying Russian winter.

As a result, the Grand Army was already severely depleted when, after fighting the ferocious battle of Borodino, it reached Moscow in September. All along the way, horses had starved and men fallen by the wayside. Now, Napoleon, installing himself in the Kremlin, waited for what he felt sure must come; but instead of peace overtures, there was nothing but an ominous silence, eventually broken by the crackling of flames as the inhabitants of Moscow set their own city on fire.

By the time the French began their retreat, the cold had already begun. What might have been an orderly retreat turned into a debacle, helped along, to be sure, by the constant attacks of the Cossacks, but due mostly to the appalling weather. By the time the army had made its way back into Poland, almost ninety per cent of it was gone or dead. It was Napoleon's first great defeat; and it proved so severe that he never recovered from it.

The news which reached us from the Army of Russia was as scarce as it was discouraging. No letters passed; we were deprived even of that consolation which is so soothing to absent friends. Such was our painful situation in the years 1812 and 1813. At that time the first rumours reached Paris of the burning of Moscow—that horrible catastrophe which the blind rage of Napoleon's enemies led them to characterize as an heroic deed, and which would have been furiously anathematized had the deed been perpetrated by his order. When the deadly cold succeeded the flames of Moscow—those flames whose devouring tongues spread through the Holy City with her forty times forty cupolas; when the greater part of that army, surprised in the midst of security, saw that a return home was almost impracticable, then a fatal discouragement took possession of those brave men who had so often faced the most formidable dangers. Too soon our reverses began to assume a more decided aspect. In vain did the Emperor endeavour to conceal the real state of affairs by pretended confidence, and by issuing decrees respecting the theatres, dated from Moscow. Nothing could prevent the truth reaching the army; and nothing could prevent its coming to us, notwithstanding our distance from the scene of the terrible drama.

Meanwhile the clouds gathered more and more thickly, and the storm seemed ready to break. At this critical moment how was Marie Louise employed—she who, of all others, might be supposed to tremble when the Austrian cannon were about to roar on the heights of Montmartre? The Empress occupied herself in working embroidery and playing on the piano. She visited her son, or had him brought to her at certain hours of the day; and the child, who knew his nurse better than his mother, could sometimes with difficulty be prevailed on to hold up his little rosy face to let the Empress kiss him.

Marie Louise was not a general favourite with the frequenters of the Court. This may be easily accounted for. She associated solely with her own little interior circle, and the Duchesse de Montebello was almost the only individual admitted to any familiarity. This choice was doubtless a good one; but still she might have made herself more agreeable at those little *soirées* to which only about forty or fifty ladies were admitted. These ladies were alternately invited, so that about ten or twelve were present every evening. They were the *dames du palais,* and the Ladies of Honour to the Imperial Princesses.

I F 1813 turned out to be a bad year for France, it was worse still for the duchesse d'Abrantès. Junot had always been violent and rather stupid, a devoted, brave and reliable subordinate, but no leader. It was hardly fair, therefore, to give him the command in Portugal; and indeed it proved disastrous. From 1809 on, the new duc went from error to error, greatly to the annoyance of the unforgiving Emperor. Then, in the middle of the Spanish campaign, his usual bouts of temper turned into something very much worse: as his subordinates realized, and Napoleon soon learned, Junot was going mad. By the time, in early 1813, he returned to his father's house in Burgundy, the poor man had lost all reason; and, in an a moment of dementia, he committed suicide.

Junot's death may not have upset his wife quite as much as she pretends: the marriage was long since dead; Laure had every reason to resent the terrible beating her husband inflicted on her when he found out about her liaison with Metternich; and she certainly minded feeling ostracized at court because of him. Still, his death entailed a significant diminution of income at a time when she had young children to raise. That situation was compounded by the fall of the Empire the following year, and the consequent loss of all pensions from the Treasury. After having been an idle and elegant young woman, Mme Junot found herself having to face a frequently hostile world. She did so with courage and a spirit of enterprise.

The severe shock I had sustained by the death of my two valued friends, Bessières and Duroc, had produced a serious effect upon my health; but, alas! a still more dreadful blow awaited me. One day, as I was reclining on my sofa after a sleepless night and much suffering, I was startled by the voice of my brother, who was speaking loudly in the adjoining room. In his interlocutor I fancied I recognized the voice of the Duke of Rovigo. In a moment the door was opened, and the Duke, though kept back by my brother, pushed his way into the room.

"I come by command of the Emperor," cried the Duke, "and in his name I must have free access everywhere." At these words Albert ceased to dispute his entrance, and he advanced into the room. Albert stepped up to me, and, taking both my hands in his, said in a voice faltering with agitation: "My beloved sister—summon all your resolution, I implore you. The Duke brings you sad tidings—Junot has been attacked with a serious illness."*

These words pierced me to the heart; I uttered a stifled scream, but could not articulate a single word. Albert, perceiving the thought that crossed my mind, embraced me, and said: "No, on my honour, nothing has happened worse than what I tell you. My dear sister, compose yourself; for the sake of your children, for the sake of Junot, I entreat you."

He threw on my knee a letter which he had brought with him, and which enclosed another one from my husband. It was one which Junot had written in the first moments of his madness, and he had sent it off by a special courier to the Emperor, who now forwarded it to me, accompanied by a few words in his own handwriting:

> "MADAME JUNOT,—Look at the enclosed letter which your husband has written to me. I have been greatly distressed in reading it. It will give you a terrible insight as to his condition, and you should take immediate measures to remedy it. Leave without losing an instant. Junot must now be on the French frontier, according to the news given to me by the Viceroy.
>
> "N."

* Immediately on receiving the intelligence mentioned above, I, though in a delicate condition of health, set out for the frontier, and proceeded as far as Chamouni, where I awaited with impatience the arrival of Junot. The General, however, had been brought to Lyons, and thence was conveyed to my father-in-law's residence at Montbard.

When the news of Junot's death reached the Emperor, he was at the Marcolini Palace at Dresden. He had there an apartment where he transacted business, a very favourite one of his, as it opened immediately upon the garden, and also had a private exit, so that he was not obliged to run the gauntlet of the Chamberlains and Court officials.

When my brother's letter was given to him he hastily tore it open, holding it in his left hand. After he had read the first few lines he violently hit the letter with his right hand, striking it out of his grasp, and then, recovering his hold with the rapidity of a flash of lightning, exclaimed: "Junot! . . . Junot! . . . Great God! . . ." clasping his hands together so tightly that the letter was completely crushed.

I let the letter of the Emperor fall to the ground, and gazed half stupefied at my brother and at the Duke of Rovigo. Indeed, I was myself almost bereft of reason at that moment.

The suddenness of the intelligence completely overpowered me. I had received, only four days previously, a long letter from Junot, which bore not the slightest trace of the terrible mental illness that was now so unexpectedly disclosed to me. The Emperor would not allow Junot to be brought to Paris for medical aid, but directed that he should be taken to his family at Montbard. Alas! my most dreadful anticipations were realized. The most unfortunate scene had ensued on the arrival of my husband in his paternal home.

Junot's father, who was naturally of a melancholy temperament, sank into a state of helpless stupor on witnessing the afflicting malady of his son. Junot's sisters could do nothing but weep and lament, and his nephew, Charles Maldan, was a perfect nullity. Junot was, however, surrounded by the affection of the inhabitants of his native town, who seemed to vie with each other in showing him the most considerate attention.

There are events which the mind cannot endure to dwell on, in spite of any effort to summon resolution. I can scarcely ever bring myself to think or speak of the melancholy scenes which ensued at Montbard after the arrival of Junot, who breathed his last on the 29th of July, at four in the afternoon.

One morning a post-chaise entered the court of Secheron, and, to my surprise, my brother-in-law, M. Geouffre, got out of it. "My children, my children! What has happened to them?" I cried. "Nothing at all," he said. "I have come to bring you a letter from the Minister of State, in which he has officially demanded all the private correspondence of the Emperor with Junot." Junot possessed more than 500 letters in Napoleon's own handwriting, and these were kept in a secret drawer. Albert sprang up from his chair, and exclaimed in a voice of thunder: "It is false! The Emperor cannot have commanded such an insult!" The Duke of Rovigo had presented himself at my hotel, and had requested the presence of one of the guardians of my husband's property in order that he might obtain possession of the Emperor's letters. My brother-in-law attended, and informed him that the usual official seals after death had been placed on all the drawers in the absence of the owner. General Savary only laughed at this reply, and said: "Bah! I have my orders. You must give me the letters of the Emperor, and I must take them." My brother told him of an obstacle in the way—namely, a golden word-lock placed upon the secret coffer. "The Duchess is the only person who knows the word now my poor brother no longer exists; and the key which the Duke always carried about with him was lost during his illness." "I beg your pardon," said the Duke of Rovigo, holding out his hand, "here is your brother's gold key."

This was a circumstance I could never understand. Albert had seen the key recently at Montbard. How, then, could Savary have got possession of it?

The coffer was opened, for the Duke had also discovered the pass-word (which was my own name misspelt— "LORE"), and he took out all the letters of the Emperor, and also those of another member of his family, my brother-in-law protesting at the same time against the violation of the seals which had been placed upon my property by the Juge de la Paix.

T H E year 1814 saw the final collapse of the Empire. After the debacle in Russia, Napoleon went on winning victories, most notably at Lützen and Bautzen in 1813; but the enemy forces now vastly outnumbered an ill-trained and ill-equipped French army. Napoleon found himself forced to retreat through an increasingly hostile Germany. Early in 1814, the borders of France, for the first time since 1792, were breached. Once again, in the campaign of France, Napoleon showed himself a great general: indeed, some military historians consider he was never more brilliant.

That, however, availed him nothing. With enemy forces at least ten times greater than his own, a won battle meant nothing: even if one corps of the invading army was stopped, the others continued to progress. Then, too, the French people had come to resent the Emperor. After so many years of war, and so many dead, the only result was that increasingly large areas of France were occupied by the enemy. On their side, the Allied Powers—

England, Russia, Prussia and Austria—kept proclaiming that it was not France, but Napoleon alone they fought. The result was that, in Paris especially, people began to yearn for the end of the Empire, and that such resistance to the invasion as there was became less than halfhearted.

By the end of March, it was all over. The Allies entered Paris to the cheers of its citizens. Napoleon, who had retreated to Fontainebleau, tried to galvanize his remaining troops, but his exhausted marshals refused to fight. From Paris came the Allied offer of a toy kingdom, the island of Elba, and a substantial income: there was nothing left for the Emperor to do but give up.

At least, he tried to make his abdication conditional on the succession of his son, but the Allies would have none of it; so he tried to commit suicide. The poison he took failed to do its work, and it was a ravaged-looking man who, after bidding adieu to his Guard, left on the road to exile.

In Paris, the nature of the new regime was hotly debated among the Allies. After Napoleon II had been rejected, Talleyrand suggested restoring the Bourbons: they would be the guaranty that France would not repeat Napoleon's mistake, he said, and the argument convinced the Sovereigns. The rump of the Senate was induced to approve a Declaration recalling Louis XVIII, the brother of Louis XVI, to the throne of his ancestors, and the Restoration was under way.

Although it was greeted with a satisfaction mixed with surprise, the Restoration in no way evolved out of a wish of the people. The few noblemen who rode through Paris waving the white flag of the Bourbons did not represent a majority of the French; but once the new regime was installed, it struck most people as the least harmful of solutions, especially because with it came a Constitution guarantying the standard liberties and setting up a parliamentary regime.

On the 1st day of January, 1814, Napoleon for the last time received the New Year's homage of his Court. There was a pretty numerous attendance at the Tuileries. When all the company had arrived, the Emperor entered from the inner apartments. His manner was calm and grave, but on his brow there sat a cloud which denoted an approaching storm. Napoleon had appointed two Committees to draw up a report on the state of France. These Committees were formed from members of the Senate and the Corps législatif.

M. Raynouard was the orator of the Legislative Body, and he spoke with a degree of candour and energy which was calculated to produce a fatal impression on the rest of France. The Emperor immediately felt this. The report of M. Raynouard likewise contained expressions disrespectful to the Emperor, the effect of which could not fail to be like a tocsin summoning the people to revolt.

The Emperor said nothing the first day on learning what had passed in the Legislative Body; but on the 1st of January, when all the authorities of the Empire were assembled in the *Salle du Trône,* he delivered a speech, the violence of which filled the offenders with dismay:

"I have suppressed the printing of your address," said he; "it was of an incendiary nature. Eleven-twelfths of the Legislative Body are, I know, composed of good citizens, and I attach no blame to them; but the other twelfth is a factious party, and your Committee was selected from that number. That man named Lainé is in correspondence with the Prince Regent through the medium of the Advocate de Sèze. I have proofs of this fact. The report of the Committee has hurt me exceedingly. I would rather have lost two battles. What does it tend to? To strengthen the pretensions of the enemy. If I were to be guided by it I should concede more than the enemy demands. Because he asks me for the province of Champagne would you have me surrender that of Brie? Would you make remonstrances in the presence of the enemy? Your object was to humiliate me! My life may be sacrificed, but never my honour. I was not born in the rank of Kings; I do not depend on the Throne. What is a throne? A few deal boards covered with velvet. Four months hence, and I will publish the odious report of your Committee. The vengeance of the enemy is directed against my person, more than against the French people. But, for that reason, should I be justified in dismembering the State? Must I sacrifice my pride to obtain peace? I am proud, because I am brave. I am proud, because I have done great things for France. In a word, France has more need of me than I have need of her. In three months we shall have peace, or I shall be dead. Go to your homes;—it was not thus you should have rebuked me."

The Legislative Body, though mute that day, was nevertheless the organ of the nation. The Committee had been maladroit in speaking as it did; but Napoleon was no less so in his reply, which, though it did not appear in the *Moniteur* as it was delivered, was nevertheless known throughout Europe eight days afterwards. It was like issuing a manifesto against France, whilst he ought to have held out to her a friendly hand in the hour of her distress, when both mutually required support.

Nothing is more curious than to observe the sudden coldness of feeling which some persons betrayed towards Napoleon the moment his happy star began to grow dim. In one day I heard ten different versions of the manner in which he took leave of the National Guard, and confided his wife and child to their protection. Many, who had witnessed the scene, returned from it with tears in their eyes; whilst others regarded as affectation the burst of sensibility which he had evinced when he presented his son to the National Guard.

If I had seen him I could have guessed whether his feelings were genuine or not, for I knew him too well to be deceived. But from all that I heard, I should be inclined to say that he was really animated by the sentiments he manifested. He was a father, and he doted on his child. His heart must have been moved when he gazed on the lovely boy who had been destined at his birth to wear twenty crowns, but who had been dispossessed of his inheritance by those who were his natural protectors. Whatever may now be said of Napoleon's farewell to the National Guard, there can be no doubt that the enthusiasm of the Parisians was that day at its height.

No person who was then in the capital can forget the prolonged shouts of *Vive l'Empereur! Vive le Roi de Rome!* The Place du Carrousel resounded with the oaths of fidelity taken by the officers of the National Guard; and yet, before a few weeks elapsed, these oaths, so solemnly pledged, were betrayed and forgotten.

Even so, within four months, the Allies had actually entered Paris. The Duke of Ragusa had retired to Essonne, together with Generals Souham, Compans, and several others.

At two o'clock on the morning of the 31st of March, 1814, that day so important in the history of France, the capitulation of Paris was signed. The Bourbons would consequently have been proclaimed at daybreak by their party, had the assent of the Allied Powers been positive and unreserved; but even at eleven o'clock in the forenoon nothing betokened the intended restoration. It was not until twelve o'clock that some white cockades and flags became visible in the Place Louis XV.* These demonstrations of Royalty were paraded along the Place by about forty persons on horseback, who waved the flags and shouted *"Vive le Roi! Vivent les Bourbons!"* But the people were mournful and silent, and did not join in these cries. This is an unquestionable fact.

The Archbishop of Malines himself declared that however desirous he was to see the fall of Bonaparte, he neither heard nor saw anything on the 31st of March that could lead him to expect the return of the old Dynasty. The Duke Dalberg, who was at a window in the hotel of M. de Talleyrand, exclaimed: "They are mounting the white cockade!" Then some of the party assembled at M. de Talleyrand's went out merely *to see,* as one of them expressed it, what had caused the uproar. Ten men on horseback, with white flags, proceeded in the direction of the Boulevard de la Madeleine. As they passed through the Rue Royale the shouts became louder. Windows were opened, white cockades were thrown out, and ladies waved white handkerchiefs.

The group of persons described above were on the Boulevard de la Madeleine when they met M. Tourton, a General Officer of the National Guard. He was on horseback, and was accompanied by an aide-de-camp of the Emperor of Russia. Both were stopped by the group, who continued to shout *"Vive le Roi! Vivent les Bourbons!"*

M. Tourton said he could not grant them the protection they re-

* Now Place de la Concorde.

381

quired until he had orders from the Government; and the Emperor of Russia's aide-de-camp seemed very much embarrassed. These two gentlemen proceeded to the Barrière de Belleville, leaving the group on the Boulevard. The fact is that all this movement was only partial, and that if a squadron of the Imperial Guard had galloped through Paris the little party of Bourbonites would speedily have been dispersed.

On the 31st of March the Allied Sovereigns entered Paris. As they advanced into the capital the demonstrations in favour of the Bourbons became more positive, either because the fear of Napoleon had hitherto repressed the real sentiments of the populace, or because that populace merely followed the inclination natural to mankind, to salute the rising and to turn from the setting sun.

A circumstance, trivial in itself, had a singular influence at this crisis; it was observed that the Allied troops had all white scarfs tied round their arms: they were worn as the sign of victory, and not as the badge of French Royalism. Most people, however, regarded them in the latter point of view, and the Royalists, artfully profiting by the mistake, reported that Louis XVIII was acknowledged by the Emperor of Russia, and even by the Emperor of Austria, that Prince Schwartzenberg wore the white scarf, and that the King's arrival might be looked for next day.

On the 4th of April the Emperor reviewed at Fontainebleau his Guard and the troops who still remained faithful to him. Marshal Ney, Marshal Lefebvre, and Marshal Oudinot were present at this review. The Emperor had very properly forbidden any of the journals from being circulated among the military. He still cherished hope. The review passed off very quietly. When it was ended, Marshal Lefebvre entered the cabinet. "Sire," said he, in a voice faltering with emotion, "you would not listen to your faithful servants! You are lost! The Senate has declared the abdication!" Marshal Lefebvre had advised Napoleon to defend himself in Paris.

The Guard still continued faithful, but the troops of the Line had been tampered with. The Duke of Bassano was still at Fontainebleau. He would not leave the Emperor, and spared no effort to sustain his fortitude. The Duke of Reggio was likewise at Fontainebleau. After the parade on the 5th, the Emperor sent for him, and asked whether he thought the troops would follow him to Italy. "No, Sire," replied the

Marshal; "your Majesty has abdicated!" "Yes, but on certain conditions!" "Soldiers cannot discern these nice distinctions," observed the Marshal. The Emperor made no reply.

At one in the morning Marshals Ney and Macdonald returned from Paris. Marshal Ney, who entered first, said: "Sire, we have succeeded only in part." And he related how the defection of the 5th corps had prevented them from settling the question of the abdication by securing the succession of his son. Napoleon was deeply wounded by the conduct of the troops confided to the command of Marmont Duke of Ragusa. Marmont certainly was not a traitor; and yet no traitor could have done greater mischief.

"To what place am I to retire with my family?" inquired Napoleon. "Wherever your Majesty may please. To the Isle of Elba, for example, with a revenue of six millions." "Six millions! that is a large allowance, considering that I am only a soldier." At that moment Napoleon had with him at Fontainebleau the troops of Macdonald, Mortier, Lefebvre, and Marmont. These different corps amounted altogether to 45,000 men. Deducting 12,000 as the amount of Marmont's corps, there remained 33,000, with which Napoleon might have commenced civil war. Before the expiration of a fortnight he would have doubled his forces. His forbearance in this particular has never been fully acknowledged. It has even been pronounced want of firmness! His abdication was prompted by a noble impulse of his generous nature. He abdicated to save France from the horrors of civil war.

Let us pause awhile on the recollection of so many great actions—so many brilliant achievements. Even yet we may bow before a destiny unlike any other. Napoleon was to France, from 1795 to 1814, a tutelary Providence—a light which will shine during ages to come. Under gilded ceilings or roofs of thatch this truth will always be proclaimed and recognized; and I am happy that my name should be attached to this relation of events designed to perpetuate the memory of that epoch.

A s it turned out, Napoleon's abdication was only the beginning of an amazing series of events. With much of France occupied by the Allied armies, Napoleon, as provided by the treaty ratifying his abdication, was sent off to rule the island of Elba; and such was his unpopularity that he was very nearly lynched as he passed through Provence. This had always been a royalist area, more so recently because the blockade had virtually destroyed the economy of Marseille and its hinterland. The former Emperor, well aware that he was in grave danger, disguised himself as a postillion, and thus was able to avoid the people's anger. It was an amazing reverse for the man who had once ruled Europe.

Once he arrived in Elba, that little Mediterranean island half-way between Genoa and Corsica, the former Emperor seemed resigned to his fate. Characteristically, he reorganized the government, drilled the regiment which constituted his entire army, and read the classics. Pauline soon joined him, and served as his first lady. There was even the embryo of a court: the treaty granting him Elba had allowed him to retain the title of Imperial Majesty.

In Paris, the chief feeling was relief at the end of the war; the restoration of the Bourbons seemed a small price to pay for peace. Indeed, at first, the royal family provoked mostly curiosity. No one knew quite who was who anymore, but they soom learned that the duchesse d'Angoulême, the wife of Louis XVIII's nephew and eventual heir, was the daughter of Louis XVI and Marie Antoinette. They could hardly be unaware of this: the unfortunate woman fainted when she entered the Tuileries Palace, which she had last seen when the revolutionary mob stormed it on August 10, 1792. As for the new King, he was immensely fat, and not glamorous at all, but that did not matter. The French had had their fill of dash and dazzle, and Louis XVIII promptly granted a Constitution which made France into a constitutional monarchy, complete with regular elections and all the usual freedoms; so, with a great sigh of relief, the French settled down to an era of quiet prosperity. Of course, there was also a good deal they needed to learn: for the first time since the stormy early years of the Revolution, there was a free press and a representative government. Political debate was not only allowed, but actually necessary, while, at the same time, the country had to accept the fact that it no longer ruled Europe.

It was a little trickier for Mme Junot. She was, after all, very nearly ruined, and she had no reason to count on any special favors. That was not enough to stop her, though. She promptly attended the new court, as was her right; Louis XVIII confirmed the titles given by Napoleon, so she was still a duchess, and, as she is prompt to admit in her Memoirs, she did her best to ingratiate herself with the royal family. We may, however, suppose that it was her sharp tongue rather than her newfound devotion which pleased the king: there was nothing Louis XVIII liked better than a little spicy gossip. Even so, the duchesse d'Abrantès was aware that the King's favor would not go very far; and she also knew where the real power lay. In no time, she managed to meet Tsar Alexander, and he found her excellent company; through him, and through Metternich, her former lover, she was able to invite the chief Allied statesmen and generals, so that, in the winter of 1814–1815, her salon was more brilliant than ever. Of course, her creditors remained a considerable annoyance; but she felt quite sure that, one way or another, she would be able to rescue her fortunes with a little help from her new friends.

Having thus cleverly made the transition to the post-imperial world, Mme Junot greeted the news which reached Paris in March, 1815 with considerable annoyance. Napoleon, it seemed, had not been satisfied with Elba after all. Avoiding the English fleet, he had sailed to the French mainland, made for Grenoble, a notoriously anti-royalist city, and was marching on Paris. Worse, the troops who were supposed to stop him rallied to his flag instead. Within ten days, the King was forced to flee Paris—he stopped at Ghent, in Belgium—and the Emperor was installed, once more at the Tuileries.

It was unquestionably a dazzling achievement; only no one was really pleased except Napoleon himself, and the regiments who joined him on his way to Paris. It was all too obvious, after all, that the Allies would not allow him to remain on the throne, and that France was in no condition to fight the rest of Europe. As a result, prudent people, Mme Junot among them, decided this was a good time to be very quiet, while Fouché, the Emperor's own minister of police, secretly negotiated with the Allies in order to prepare for the re-Restoration of Louis XVIII.

The end of this particular episode is well known. Gathering an army, Napoleon moved north to meet the expected attack from the Russian, Prussian, Austrian, and British forces commanded by Blücher and Wellington. The battle took place on June 18, at Waterloo, just outside Brussels; and the Allies prevailed. Within ten days, Napoleon, rejected by the French Parliament and the country alike, abdicated once more, and embarked on a British ship. He was to spend his remaining years on the island of Saint Helena in the south Atlantic Ocean.

The Hundred Days turned out to have been an expensive mistake. The treaty which followed cost France a large chunk of territory and a vast sum in war indemnities. The works of art taken by Napoleon from the rest of Europe, which had been allowed to stay at the Louvre in 1814, were now repossessed; and the country settled down to several years of military occupation. The imperial epic was not just over, it had become a lingering nightmare.

As a result, the Bourbons, who had been returned to Paris by the Allies, now took a very bleak view of anyone connected to Napoleon. Mme Junot herself was in no particular danger, but it was all too clear she could no longer hope for the favor of the court. As her debts became more pressing, she was forced to sell her house, but even so, she struggled to keep her salon open. This time, however, having glamorous friends did not help. Her financial crisis became ever more acute; her salon was closed.

Her life now seemed over: too old for lovers, too poor for the brilliant social life to which she was accustomed, she had nothing left to do; and that was when Balzac encouraged her to write her

Memoirs. Always ready to meet a challenge, Laure took up her pen; and although writing did not make up for the loss of her former glamour, she found, to her delight, that she had acquired a vast and admiring public. Perhaps, after all, it was not such a bad trade-off, either for her or for posterity.